Connecticut

AN EXPLORER'S GUIDE

BARNETT D. LASCHEVER & ANDI MARIE FUSCO

PRINCIPAL PHOTOGRAPHY BY KIMBERLY GRANT

Third Edition

The Countryman Press
Woodstock, Vermont

Dedication
To Adam Laschever: Traveler, Soldier,
Beloved Son — B.D.L.
To V.J. Fusco — A.M.F.

Copyright © 1994, 1997 by Barnett D. Laschever and Barbara J. Beeching
Copyright © 1999 by Barnett D. Laschever and Andi Marie Fusco
Third Edition

No entries or reviews in this book have been solicited or paid for.

Library of Congress Cataloging-in-Publication Data
Laschever, Barnett D.
Connecticut : An explorer's guide / Barnett D. Laschever & Andi Marie Fusco.
—3rd ed.
p.   cm.
Includes index
ISBN 0-88150-415-7 (alk. paper)
1. Connecticut—Guidebooks. I. Fusco, Andi Marie. II. Title.
F92.3.L37 1999
917.4604'43—dc21
98-13751
CIP

Maps by Mapping Specialists,
© 1999 The Countryman Press
Text and cover design by Glenn Suokko
Cover photograph of Mystic Seaport by
Kimberly Grant

Published by The Countryman Press
PO Box 748, Woodstock, Vermont 05091
Distributed by W.W. Norton & Company, Inc.
500 Fifth Avenue, New York, NY 10110
Printed in the United States of America
10 9 8 7 6 5 4 3 2

Explore With Us!

Welcome to the third edition of *Connecticut: An Explorer's Guide*. We have been fine-tuning the *Explorer's Guide* series for more than 14 years. Our state-by-state guides to northern New England were the first on the market, and they stand out as the most personable, conscientiously researched, and knowledgeable guides available. As with every book in this series, all attractions, inns, and restaurants are chosen on the basis of personal experience, not paid advertising. Recommendations are given by the authors, both lifelong residents of the state and experienced writers about Connecticut.

WHAT'S WHERE

In the beginning of the book you'll find an alphabetical listing of special highlights, with important information and advice on everything from agricultural fairs to youth hostels.

LODGING

When making reservations, especially at B&Bs, we suggest you inquire about policies regarding smoking, children, pets, and the use of credit cards for payment. If it is important that you have a private telephone, air-conditioning, and/or television, by all means ask, as they are not standard in country inns and B&Bs.

Prices: Please don't hold us or the respective innkeepers responsible for the rates listed as of press time. Some changes are inevitable. In popular vacation areas, rates are often adjusted to the season. There is a 12 percent state room tax in Connecticut; prices given in the book do not include tax or gratuity. Campgrounds are not subject to tax.

RESTAURANTS

In most sections, please note a distinction between *Dining Out* and *Eating Out*. In the *Dining Out* listings, prices of entrées (not the cost of a full meal) are given to indicate the general price range of the restaurant. Prix fixe is specified. Remember that prices are likely to change.

By their nature, restaurants in the *Eating Out* group are generally inexpensive, with most entrées available for less than $10.

KEY TO SYMBOLS

☞ The special value symbol appears next to lodging and restaurants that combine quality and moderate prices.

✐ The kids alert symbol appears next to lodging, restaurants, activities, and shops of special appeal to youngsters.

♿ The wheelchair symbol appears next to lodging, restaurants, and attractions that are handicapped-accessible.

We appreciate your comments and corrections about the places you visit. Address your correspondence to *Explorer's Guide* Editor, The Countryman Press, PO Box 748, Woodstock, VT 05091. You can email us at countrymanpress@wwnorton.com, and for the most up-to-date information, visit our web site at www.countrymanpress.com.

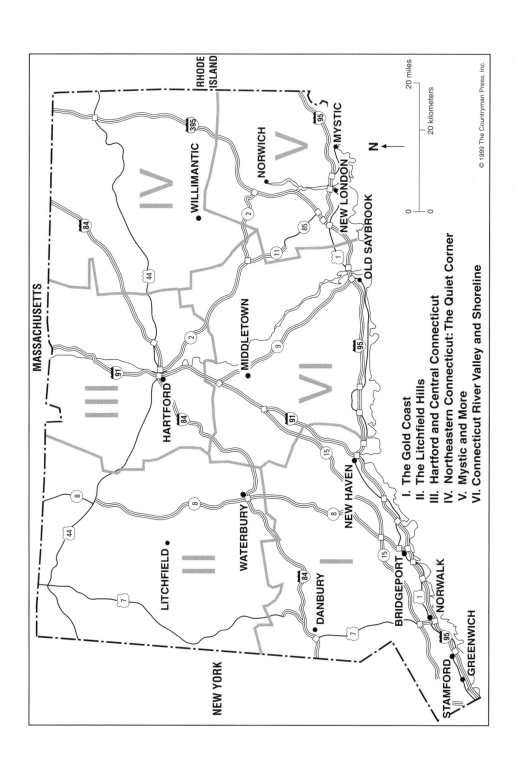

MASSACHUSETTS

NEW YORK

RHODE ISLAND

IV

WILLIMANTIC

NORWICH

V

MYSTIC

NEW LONDON

OLD SAYBROOK

III

HARTFORD

MIDDLETOWN

VI

LITCHFIELD

II

WATERBURY

NEW HAVEN

DANBURY

BRIDGEPORT

NORWALK

STAMFORD

GREENWICH

I

84

395

2

85

11

11

95

95

44

2

9

91

91

15

15

8

8

8

84

7

7

1

95

44

91

N

0   20 miles

0   20 kilometers

I.   The Gold Coast
II.   The Litchfield Hills
III. Hartford and Central Connecticut
IV.   Northeastern Connecticut: The Quiet Corner
V.   Mystic and More
VI.   Connecticut River Valley and Shoreline

© 1999 The Countryman Press, Inc.

Contents

where dark-suited, briefcase-toting men and women wait on Metro-North platforms each morning and return each evening to their trim homes and well-clipped lawns. Along the shoreline are grand estates and marinas crowded with yachts and sailboats. Still, this is an area of cities—Bridgeport, Norwalk, Stamford, New Haven—each with its own background and special qualities. Stamford has attracted so many corporate headquarters that it's a commuter destination in its own right, with a striking skyline against Long Island Sound. New Haven, at the eastern edge of the region, is enriched by the presence of Yale University and its many museums and theaters.

The northwestern corner of Connecticut, the Litchfield Hills, provides dramatic contrast to the Gold Coast, with wooded hills, clear streams, carefully preserved village greens, and white-steepled churches. The only signs of "progress" are antiques dealers, artisans' studios, and exquisite gift shops. Outdoor centers and state parks invite hikers and nature lovers to stretch their legs, while the picturesque villages offer Colonial and Victorian homes and visible history, from a collection of handmade tools to the nation's first law school—a neat little building about the size of your grandfather's one-car garage.

The central portion of the state, Hartford and its neighbors, is split by the Connecticut River, a smooth-flowing example of the possibility of recovery. A polluted embarrassment 25 years or so ago, the river today is clean enough to swim in and has become "people-friendly" once again with the completion of its Riverfront Recapture project. Hartford, once the nation's insurance capital, is crowned with a splendid state capitol—a wedding cake of grand proportions, with a golden dome, Gothic arches, brackets, crockets, niches, and stained glass. It surely must have appealed to Mark Twain, who lived some 20 years in his own elaborate mansion in Hartford, now open to visitors along with the neighboring home of Harriet Beecher Stowe. Hartford's Civic Center presents concerts, trade shows of every description, and sports events—notably the home games of hockey and both professional and men and women's college basketball. The excellent Hartford Stage Company, the Wadsworth Atheneum, and the original Old State House are among the downtown attractions.

Only a few miles away, in the historic district of Wethersfield, plain clapboard homes bear plaques declaring their 18th-century origins. George Washington, true to form, slept in at least one. The towns of Rocky Hill and Glastonbury are linked by the nation's oldest ferry service (started in 1655), which handles half a dozen autos at a time. To the west, the lively Farmington Valley combines history, art, and scenery, and to the north, the small towns where tobacco was once a major crop now harbor museums devoted to trolleys, fire-fighting equipment, and aircraft.

The Quiet Corner is the northeastern section of the state. With no large cities, it has retained an unhurried atmosphere that suits its rural character. In early times, the combination of hills and streams fostered mills of all sorts, and in the 19th century this part of the state became a major textile manufacturing area. The mills are gone now, but as you drive the tree-lined roads, you'll occasionally see an old mill complex beside a river or a cluster of former worker homes. You'll also discover Colonial houses virtually untouched by time, and miles of stone walls that undulate over the hills and into the woods, marking boundaries of long-abandoned homesteads. The area remains bucolic. It provides an ideal setting for the University of Connecticut in Storrs, which, fittingly, started as an agricultural land grant college and has blossomed into a full-fledged university. The many B&Bs in this part of the state offer a chance to get acquainted with old-fashioned Yankee hospitality.

Mystic Seaport, the re-created 19th-century maritime community on Long Island Sound, is the state's best-known single attraction, dedicated to the traditions of shipbuilding and whaling. The seaport has been joined by the Mystic Marinelife Aquarium and a number of lodgings, restaurants, and shops, with the result that the southeastern corner is the state's number one tourist area. The opening of two world-class Native American–operated gaming casinos nearby, Foxwoods and the Mohegan Sun, have further increased the region's popularity.

Our final division, the lower valley of the Connecticut River and the central shoreline, offers another approach to serenity. Middletown, home of Wesleyan University, was once the state's largest city and busiest trading port. Barges and pleasure boats still ripple the waters here, and Harbor Park on the riverbank affords a vantage point for watching the traffic. If you like, you can board an excursion boat for a ride. South of Middletown, Haddam, Chester, Deep River, and Essex are a series of small gems strung along the river. Gillette Castle looms on a high bluff above the water, and directly below, an ancient ferry operation offers a 3- to 5-minute crossing between Chester and Hadlyme. The Valley Railroad chugs its steam-driven way north along the river from Essex, and as the river enters the sound, Old Saybrook and Old Lyme stand on opposite banks, the one offering shoreline history, the other continuing its tradition as an artists colony. The other shoreline towns of Westbrook, Clinton, Madison, Guilford, and Branford are best known as summer havens for the beach crowd, where concerts and crafts shows enliven greens laid out in the 17th century.

Although we've been speaking of summertime visits, bear in mind that Connecticut is definitely open year-round. Skiers have five choices for downhill skiing and virtually all the great outdoors for cross-country, with trails open in most of the state's 52 state parks and nine state forests. Those same trails are perfect avenues for hiking into the splendor of autumn foliage displays or the miracle of wildflowers in spring. State parks, in fact, are a largely undiscovered treasure in what's thought of as a highly industrial state. The parks are well marked and well maintained, with picnic spots, toilet facilities, and activities that may include swimming, boating, and camping. Some have special or unexpected attractions, from the dramatic Kent Falls in Kent to the mansion at Harkness in Waterford, from the implausible Gillette Castle in its own state park, to a tower fit for Rapunzel on Talcott Mountain, to the ghostly cellar holes of Gay City.

Along with abundant outdoor life, you find artistic stimuli as well. There are a dozen museums scattered around the state, featuring modern artists in Ridgefield, American artists in New Britain, British artists in New Haven, and an inclusive collection, virtually all periods and all media, in Hartford. Visiting performers and local talent present music—classical, bluegrass, rock, experimental, and jazz—and dance programs of equal variety.

Connecticut theaters have earned so many drama awards in the past dozen years that critics speak of the state as a challenge to New York and London in introducing successful new plays and landmark productions. Such recognition is based on the work of Yale Repertory and Long Wharf theaters in New Haven, the Hartford Stage Company, and the Goodspeed Opera House in East Haddam. New London was the boyhood home of Eugene O'Neill, America's only Nobel laureate in drama. In his memory, each summer in Waterford the National Playwrights Conference brings together promising new playwrights to try out and polish their creations, many of which subsequently appear on stages in the state and in New York.

Connecticut's many craftspeople are known for innovation and quality. The state's major centers are in Guilford, New Canaan, Avon, New Haven, Middletown, and Brookfield. Each has its own exhibit space. Outdoor summer crafts shows are numerous and enormously popular.

If you travel with children, you'll be glad to know that Connecticut has museums designed specifically for them in New Haven, New Britain, Manchester, Bridgeport, Stamford, and West Hartford. Other ideas for youngsters: Dinosaur State Park in Rocky Hill; the Peabody Museum of Natural History in New Haven (with the world's largest dinosaur skeleton); Valley Railroad, a working steam train in Essex; trolley museums and rides in both Warehouse Point and East Haven; the *Nautilus*, the first nuclear submarine, in Groton; and the creaking planks and claustrophobic below-decks of the *Charles W. Morgan*, the last of the wooden whaling ships, in Mystic.

A word about the people of Connecticut: They're as varied as the landscape. You may run into a wry, laconic Yankee whose family has been here since 1636, but don't count on it. Connecticut's brand of Yankee ingenuity led to early industrialization, creating jobs that brought people from all over western Europe, the Balkans, Russia, Canada, and the American South. Connecticut's population today is made up of many ethnic and racial groups, drawn here by the prospect of work to be done. More recent settlers have been attracted by the state's advantageous location between Boston and New York, by its natural beauty, and by that nebulous quality called lifestyle. Among those who have chosen to live in Connecticut is a long list of notables from the worlds of books, theater, art, broadcasting, music, and politics, past and present. Examples range from Mark Twain to Henry Kissinger and include Paul Robeson, Paul Newman, William Styron, Marian Anderson, Katharine Hepburn, Tom Brokaw, Arthur Miller, Maurice Sendak, George Bush, and Martha Stewart. The list of historic figures *born* in Connecticut could serve as a crib sheet on US history: Nathan Hale, Noah Webster, Benedict Arnold, Harriet Beecher Stowe, Samuel Colt, P.T. Barnum, Eli Whitney, and J.P. Morgan, for example.

The authors of this book claim less fame but equal enthusiasm for the state. Andi is a true-blue Yankee, having been born in Litchfield County and spent every childhood summer on the Connecticut shore. A degree in journalism from Boston University began her career in writing for a variety of publications, from a community newspaper in Boston to an entertainment magazine in London. She returned to Connecticut to write for several newspapers. A stint as an education reporter led to a second career as an elementary school teacher. Andi now lives in the rural Litchfield Hills, where she enjoys mountain biking, backpacking, kayaking, and hiking in the woods with her basset hound, Cecil.

Barney, also a legitimate Yankee, was born and raised in Hartford and now lives in an 1810 Garrison Colonial in Goshen. He has left the state on occasion—to earn his degree at the University of Michigan, to participate in World War II, to serve for 10 years as the travel editor of the *New York Herald Tribune*. Back in God's country, as his father instructed him to think of Connecticut, Barney resumed travel writing as an editor for Eugene Fodor, pioneer of the modern travel guidebook. Author of five children's books, he put in time as a reporter and Sunday editor of the *Hartford Times* and, for 17 years, served as director of tourism for the State of Connecticut. Since his retirement, he, too, has found his affection for the state unabated. His special interests include gardening—he writes a garden column and hosts a radio show—sailing, short hikes, and long naps.

Both authors owe thanks to many helpful friends in the state's tourism industry who supplied information, advice, and opinions on manuscripts in preparation. We owe deep thanks to Jean Hebert of the state tourism office, to Carole Keogh McLemore, to Susan Cramer, to the courageous editor Dolores Laschever, and to Paul Beeching for significant contributions. We are grateful to all those at The Countryman Press who have been simultaneously supportive and exacting: Helen Whybrow, Emily Webb, Ann Kraybill, Cristen Brooks, Hugh Coyle, and Fred Lee.

As Connecticut partisans, our intention has been to open up new vistas for visitors who may not be aware of the range of possibilities here. We hope our book will help make your explorations of the Nutmeg State enjoyable from start to finish.

What's Where in Connecticut

AGRICULTURAL FAIRS

Though Connecticut holds no state fair, some 57 local fairs between July and October contain all the necessary elements: ox pulls, baking contests, livestock judging, ribbons for eggplants and string beans and for quilts and peach preserves. The largest is the **Durham Fair,** held in Durham in late September. The **Four Town Fair** in Somers, one of the state's oldest, has been

held in mid-September every year since 1838. Two of the largest fairs, in two of the smallest towns and in opposite corners of the state, attract thousands: the **Goshen Fair** in the Litchfield Hills and the **Woodstock Fair** in the Quiet Corner. A complete directory can be obtained by writing to: Association of Connecticut Fairs, Box 753, Somers 06071; or contact the Connecticut Department of Agriculture (860-566-4845), 165 Capitol Avenue, Hartford 06106.

AIRPORTS AND AIRLINES

Bradley International Airport at Windsor Locks is New England's second largest airport, with national flights on a daily basis. Major airlines into Bradley are American, Continental, Carnival, Delta, Midway, Northwest, TWA, United, and USAir. Commuter service is handled by American Eagle, Business Express, Continental Express, Downeast Express, TWA Express, USAir Express, United Express, and Air Ontario. **Groton/New London Airport** in Groton, on the state's southeastern coast, is served by Action Airline and USAir Express. **Igor Sikorsky Memorial Airport** in Stratford, on the state's southwestern coast, is served by USAir Express. **Tweed–New Haven Airport,** New Haven, is served by Continental Express and USAir Express commuter lines. Be advised that since deregulation, airlines add or abandon routes with frustrating frequency. Best to check first.

AMUSEMENT PARKS

In Middlebury, on CT 64, **Quassy Amusement Park** offers 30 rides and games, swimming, and a petting zoo. **Lake Compounce** in the center of the state, the oldest amusement park in the country, has exciting new water rides and other thrills. In southeastern Connecticut **Ocean Beach Park** in

EVENTS

This guidebook lists *major* annual events at the end of each chapter. The **Connecticut State Tourism Office** (1-800-CT-BOUND) publishes comprehensive, statewide, biannual calendars, each listing as many as 500 events. Each of the regional tourism districts (see *Information* in this section) produces a comprehensive calendar, generally seasonal, and the major daily and weekly newspapers print weekly events listings on Thursday, Friday, and/or Sunday.

FALL FOLIAGE

Peak season for autumn touring in Connecticut falls around **Columbus Day weekend.** All parts of the state offer excellent viewing, but the woods are especially colorful in the northeast and northwest sections. The legendary brilliance of fall in New England comes from the presence of abundant and varied hardwoods. Swamp and sugar maples, ash, birch, willow, oak, hickory—even the undistinguished sumac—all take part in the festival of color. Beginning in late September, you can phone 1-800-CT-BOUND for foliage progress reports.

FERRIES

Two ferries across the Connecticut River are the oldest in the country still in operation: The **Glastonbury/Rocky Hill Ferry** (860-566-9758) carries six cars and passengers from May through November, and the **Chester/Hadlyme Ferry** (860-526-2743) carries eight to nine cars April to mid-December. Both numbers are for messages listing ferry hours; for more information, call 860-443-3856. To cross Long Island Sound to New York, there are four ferry services. The **Bridgeport/Port Jefferson Steamboat Co.** (1-888-443-3779; 516-473-0286) carries both cars and people and operates year-round. **Cross Sound Ferry Services** (860-443-5281) takes cars and passengers

from New London to Orient Point, Long Island, New York, year-round. **Fishers Island Ferry District** (860-443-6851; 203-442-0165) travels from New London to Fishers Island, New York, year-round. Two ferries carry foot passengers and bicycles Friday and Saturday, Memorial Day through Labor Day, from **New London to Montauk** off the tip of Long Island. **Nelseco Navigation Co.** (860-442-9553; 203-442-7891) sails from New London to Block Island, Rhode Island, mid-June to mid-September.

FISHING

Freshwater fish abound in Connecticut's lakes and streams, stocked by the State Department of Environmental Protection; salt-

KIMBERLY GRANT

water species are found in Long Island Sound and beyond. A fishing license, obtainable from any town clerk, is required for anyone 16 or older fishing in the Inland District. Licenses are issued on a calendar-year basis, expiring on December 31. For non-residents, the fee is $25 for the season; a 3-day license is $8. Special access and free licensing are available to handicapped individuals. Many areas are open all year to fishing; in restricted waterways, the season opens at 6 AM on the third Saturday in April. Complete information on the above and on fishing sites, restrictions, season length, and species limitations is available from the **Fisheries Division** (860-424-FISH [3474]),

State Department of Environmental Protection, 79 Elm Street, Hartford 06106. Ask for the *Connecticut Angler's Guide.* Other sources for additional information: **Inland Fisheries** (860-424-3475), **Marine Fisheries** (860-424-6043), **Conservation Law Enforcement** (860-424-2012), and **Parks and Recreation** (860-424-3200). Special fishing areas for children have been set aside and are so posted. These include both trout streams and ponds in various parts of the state. (See also *Fishing, Saltwater.*)

FISHING, SALTWATER

Connecticut's recommended charter and party fishing boats are operated by US Coast Guard–licensed captains. Charter fishing boats cater to private groups that book the vessels for their own use. Party fishing boats are open to the public on a first-come, first-served basis, sailing from January through mid-November. For fishing- and charter-boat captains, see the *Fishing* sections throughout this book.

FLOWER FESTIVALS

You can get an early start on spring and follow the blooming flowers right through into summer. The preview comes in late February with the annual **Hartford Flower Show** (860-529-2123). In April, watch for the **Golden-bells Festival** (forsythia) in Hamden (203-248-3077) and the **Daffodil Festival,** Meriden (203-630-4259). In May, the **Dogwood Festival** (203-259-5596) takes over Greenfield Hill in Fairfield. June brings the **Laurel Festival** in Winsted (860-379-2713), the **Rose Arts Festival** in Norwich (860-885-0160), and **Rose Sunday** at Elizabeth Park, Hartford (860-523-4276). (See also *Gardens.*)

FORTS

Connecticut is rich in history, including the Revolution and the Civil War. In Groton,

Fort Griswold Battlefield State Park (860-424-3200), overlooking the mouth of the Thames River, is the site of a famous 1781 battle between the Continentals and the British. In New Haven, **Black Rock Fort,** from the Revolutionary era, and **Fort Nathan Hale** (203-946-8790), dating to the Civil War, have both been reconstructed; the site affords a spectacular view of New Haven Harbor. **Fort Saybrook Monument Park** (860-395-3123) in Old Saybrook is an 18-acre park with an exhibit on the history of the original settlement in the Connecticut colony (circa 1635) and a view of the mouth of the Connecticut River.

GARDENS

In addition to the annual flower festivals (see *Flower Festivals*), the state offers many opportunities to enjoy flowers, herbs, and other growing things. Gardens open to the public include the following (telephone numbers, addresses, and descriptions can be found within the appropriate chapters of this book): In the Gold Coast region are **Ansonia Nature & Recreation Center,** Ansonia; **Putnam Cottage,** Greenwich; **Bartlett Arboretum,** Stamford; and **Pardee Rose Gardens,** New Haven. In the Litchfield Hills are **White Flower Farm,** Litchfield-Morris line; **Catnip Acres Herb Nursery,** Oxford; **Northeast Audubon Center,** Sharon; **Cricket Hill,** Thomaston; **Hillside Gardens,** Norfolk; and the **Gertrude Jekyll Garden** at the Glebe House, Woodbury. In the greater Hartford region are **Elizabeth Park,** Hartford–West Hartford; plantings at the **Hill-Stead Museum,** Farmington; period gardens at the **Welles Shipman Ward House,** Glastonbury; **Wickham Park,** Manchester; and **Hatheway House,** Suffield. In the Quiet Corner are **Greystone Gardens,** Chaplin; **Caprilands Herb Farm,** Coventry; **Logee's Greenhouses,** Danielson; **Buell's**

Greenhouses, Eastford; **Martha's Herbary,** Hampton; **Sandra Lee's Herbs and Everlastings,** Pomfret; the **University of Connecticut Greenhouses,** Storrs; gardens at **Roseland Cottage,** Woodstock; the **Laurel Sanctuary,** Union; and the rhododendron sanctuary in **Pachaug State Forest,** Voluntown. In the Southeast are **Mohegan Park** and **Memorial Rose Garden,** Norwich; and **Harkness Memorial State Park,** Waterford. In the Lower Connecticut River Valley and Shoreline are the herb gardens at the **Harrison House** in Branford and **Sundial Herb Garden** in Higganum; and period gardens at the **General William Hart House** in Old Saybrook, the **Thomas Griswold House** in Guilford, and the **Thankful Arnold House** in Higganum.

GENEALOGY

As one of the nation's original 13 colonies, Connecticut is the ancestral home of many families across the country. It's no wonder that so many who are researching their family trees wind up here. Family, church, town, and other records of the **Connecticut State Library** (860-566-3692), 231 Capitol Avenue, Hartford 06106, make an excellent place to start. Researchers headed for the Litchfield Hills area should check the **Litchfield Historical Society** for its listing of additional collections in northwestern Connecticut (see below). Additional ancestral information can be found in the following record collections: **Connecticut Historical Society,** Hartford; **Bates-Scofield Homestead,** Darien; **Fairfield Historical Society,** Fairfield; **Salmon Brook Settlement,** Granby; **Thankful Arnold House,** Haddam; **Mansfield Historical Society Museum,** Mansfield; **General Mansfield House,** Middletown; **New Haven Colony Historical Society Museum and Library,** New Haven; **In-**dian and **Colonial Research Center,** Old Mystic; **Barnes Museum,** Southington; **Stamford Historical Society Museum,** Stamford; the **French-Canadian Genealogical Library,** Tolland; **Wethersfield Historical Society,** Wethersfield; and **Windsor Historical Society,** Windsor.

GEOGRAPHY

Although Connecticut is the third smallest state, it has a surprising variety of terrain—rocky heights, wooded hills, fertile valleys, and plentiful streams, brooks, rivers, and lakes, as well as 253 miles of shoreline. Its highest point is at 2,380 feet on Mount Frissel in Salisbury. The state is divided into 169 towns, the capital being Hartford. There are 91 state parks with a total of 30,043 acres and 30 state forests consisting of 138,377 acres. Amazingly, two-thirds of Connecticut is green—open land, woods, farms.

GOLF

Connecticut's golf courses add many acres of green to the state total. For a listing of 90 percent of Connecticut's golf courses, call the PGA at (860-257-4653). On request, the **Connecticut State Golf Association** (860-257-4171) will send you a list of its 150 members. In this guide we describe only those courses we know are open to the public.

HANDICAPPED ACCESS

Throughout this book, the wheelchair symbol ふ indicates restaurants, lodgings, and attractions that are handicapped accessible.

HIKING

Whether your preference is tough terrain or easygoing trails, Connecticut state parks have outstanding trails for hiking. For instance, **Talcott Mountain State Park** in Simsbury takes you on a rigorous 1-mile hike to a spectacular overlook with views of four states on a clear day and a picnic area and tower to enjoy while you're up there. **Macedonia Brook State Park** in Kent and **Sleeping Giant State Park** in Hamden are also known for particularly scenic trails. For information, contact the **Connecticut Bureau of Outdoor Recreation, Parks Division** (860-424-3200). There are also the **Appalachian Trail** (for information call the Appalachian Mountain Club headquarters in Boston at 617-523-0636) and the Connecticut **Blue Trails** (860-346-TREE), which total 700 miles throughout the state. The latter are maintained by the Connecticut Forest and Park Association, the major source of hiking information in the state.

HISTORIC HOMES

As one of the original colonies, Connecticut has a number of historic structures. Many have been carefully preserved and are open to the public. The towns of Wethersfield, Litchfield, Essex, and Norwich are especially known for their historic districts. The Henry Whitfield State Museum in Guilford (see "Central Shoreline") is believed to be the oldest stone house in New England. There are also notable Victorian homes in Norwalk (the Lockwood-Mathews Mansion); Hartford (the Mark Twain and Harriet Beecher Stowe houses); and Middletown, on the Wesleyan University campus. The **Antiquarian and Landmarks Society, Inc.** (860-247-8996), 66 Forest Street, Hartford 06105, provides excellent information on its

11 historic properties that are open to the public. (See also *Museums*.)

HORSEBACK RIDING

High Lonesome (203-758-9094) in Middlebury offers scenic trail rides through rolling hills. **Lee's Riding Stable** (860-567-0785), Litchfield, has trail rides through open and wooded land. In Falls Village, **Rustling Wind Stables** (860-824-7634; 860-824-7084) offers both Western and English trails. There's also **Cherry Ledge Farm,** Putnam (860-928-1016); **Meadowbrook Farms,** Newtown (203-270-0906); **Coventry Meadows,** Coventry (860-742-5540); **Coventry Riding Stables,** Coventry (860-742-7576); **Diamond A. Ranch,** Dayville (860-779-3000); **Hawthorne Farm,** Willington (860-684-5487); **Trapalanda Stables,** Woodstock (860-974-1064); **Woodcock Hill Riding Academy,** Willington (860-487-1686); and **Woodstock Acres Riding Stable,** Woodstock (860-974-1224).

HOTELS/MOTELS

In this guide we have rarely listed chain hotels and motels, since they're easy to locate and contact. (See *Lodging* in this section for information on a reservation service.) We have included a few chains, though, either because lodging choices are scarce in the particular area or because of a desirable location (such as at the airport terminal). Clearly, the major cities—Hartford and New Haven—have a full complement of Holiday Inns, Marriotts, and Motel 6s. For the purposes of this book we have concentrated on the establishments, inns, and B&Bs that are one-of-a-kind and especially identified with New England.

HUNTING

Connecticut offers opportunities for hunting deer and turkey. A wide variety of small game is found in abundance throughout the state's fields and forests. Pheasant are stocked in state and private lands open to hunting. Waterfowl abound in freshwater ponds and marshes, along rivers, and in the coastal estuaries and bays of Long Island Sound. For Connecticut residents a hunting license costs $10, and for nonresidents, $42; both need to be renewed annually. Hunting licenses are obtained through the **State Department of Environmental Protection, Wildlife Division** (860-424-3011), or from **Licensing and Revenue** (860-424-3105).

INFORMATION

The **Connecticut State Tourism Office** (860-270-8080;1-800-CT-BOUND; Web site: www.state.ct.us/tourism/), 505 Hudson Street, Hartford 06106, publishes an annual *Connecticut Vacation Guide* and a variety of other publications geared to special interests. There are also 11 tourism districts throughout the state that produce guide/event brochures for their areas: **Coastal Fairfield County Tourism District** (1-888-289-3353); **Greater New Haven Convention & Visitors District** (1-800-332-7829); **Connecticut River Valley Shoreline Visitors Council** (1-800-486-3346); **Connecticut's Mystic & More** (860-444-2206); **Waterbury Region Convention & Visitors Bureau** (203-597-9527); **Housatonic Valley Tourism District** (203-743-0546); **Litchfield Hills Travel Council** (860-567-4506); **Greater Hartford Tourism District** (860-244-8181); **Connecticut's North Central Tourism Bureau** (1-800-248-8283); **Central Connecticut Tourism District** (860-225-3901); and **Northeast Connecticut Tourism District** (860-928-1228).

INFORMATION CENTERS

Connecticut has 13 welcome centers located on its major roadways and at its largest airport, **Bradley International Airport** in Windsor Locks, where booths can be found in both terminals. The others are located as follows: on **I-95** in North Stonington (southbound) and Westbrook (northbound); on **I-84** in Danbury (eastbound), Southington (eastbound), and Willington (east- and westbound); on **I-91** in Middletown (northbound), Wallingford (southbound), and Windsor Locks (southbound); on **I-395** in Plainfield (southbound); and on the **Merritt Parkway** in Greenwich (northbound). Those in North Stonington, Danbury, Darien, and Willington are open year-round; the others are seasonal. In **Litchfield** an information booth is operated seasonally on the green. Another assists tourists at the bus depot in **Southbury** off I-84. The **Old State House** in Hartford dispenses tourist literature. A number of other towns and private tourism interests also staff small visitors centers. Some tourism literature is available at the service areas on the interstates.

INNS

Connecticut is dotted with more than 40 country inns—and as many as 200 bed & breakfasts—covering every style from Colonial to Victorian and modern. The guest rooms of country inns—lodgings that serve dinner as well as breakfast—are typically furnished with antiques (often four-poster beds), and many feature working fireplaces. (See also *Bed & Breakfasts.*)

INTERSTATES

Connecticut is served by **I-95** along the shoreline. **I-91** from New Haven runs through the center of the state and intersects in Hartford with **I-84,** which crosses the state from Danbury to Union. **I-91** continues northward through New England to Canada. **I-395** runs north and south in the eastern part of the state, and the **Merritt Parkway (CT 15),** an extension of the Hutchinson River Parkway in New York, roughly parallels the shoreline from Greenwich to Milford. From here to Meriden it becomes the **Wilbur Cross Parkway,** which then merges with **I-91.** Major limited-access superhighway **CT 8,** in the western part of the state, links Bridgeport with Winsted.

ISLANDS

Sheffield Island off Norwalk, with its now inactive lighthouse, is open to the public by ferry from Norwalk Harbor. On the island is a US Fish & Wildlife Sanctuary. Also in Norwalk Harbor, **Chimon Island** is a natural wildlife preserve, accessible to the public only by boat. Near Guilford, **Faulkner's Island** is a wildlife preserve open to the public. Off Stony Creek in Branford, the **Thimble Islands** are privately owned and not accessible to the public, but three skippers offer short cruises around the harbor and the islands on launches that primarily serve island residents. The mini-cruises are enlivened by legends—some of them true—of pirates and early settlers.

JAI ALAI/DOG TRACKS

There's only one jai alai fronton left in Connecticut: **Milford Jai Alai** (203-877-4211). The former Hartford Jai Alai is now an off-track betting center, and the center at Bridgeport is now the **Shoreline Star Dog Track and Simulcast Entertainment Center.** The state's first dog track is still racing the hounds in **Plainfield.**

LAKES

There are hundreds of lakes and ponds here. Many are in state parks and forests and are available for fishing, swimming, boating, ice skating, iceboating, and ice fishing. The state's largest is **Candlewood Lake,** a man-made waterway in New Milford, Sherman, and New Fairfield. Many lakes have boat-launch facilities, and some post restrictions regarding powerboats, speed limits, and times of operation. **Bantam** is the state's largest natural lake. Contact the **Connecti-**

KIMBERLY GRANT

cut Bureau of Outdoor Recreation, State Parks Division (860-424-3200) for locations and regulations.

LIGHTHOUSES

Connecticut has 13 lighthouses, most of them off-limits to the public but close enough for photographers with long lenses. **Sheffield Island Lighthouse** was originally built in 1826 and is accessible by boat. **Penfield Reef Lighthouse** in Fairfield was built in 1874 and is not open to the public. In Stratford, the **Stratford Point Lighthouse** is the most powerful lighthouse along the sound, originally built in 1821 and not open to the public. Two lighthouses are in Bridgeport—**Tongue Point Lighthouse** (built in 1891) and **Black Rock Harbor Lighthouse** (built in 1808)—but neither is open to visitors. Built in 1804, the **New Haven Harbor Lighthouse** was retired in 1877 and replaced by **Southwest Ledge Lighthouse** at Lighthouse Point Park; this one is available to the public. A 4½-acre bird sanctuary is located near the active **Faulkner's Island Lighthouse,** south of Guilford Harbor. There are two lighthouses in Old Saybrook: **Lynde Point Lighthouse** was built in 1803 (not open); and **Saybrook Breakwater Lighthouse,** built in 1886, is presently active but not open. **Avery Point Lighthouse** in Groton was built in 1942 by the US Coast Guard but never illuminated. It's

picnic pavilions. Connecticut Audubon Society's **Fairfield Nature Center** (203-259-6305) is adjacent to **Larsen Sanctuary,** a 160-acre park with 6 miles of trails, ponds, and a walk for the blind, disabled, and elderly. **Connecticut Audubon Society at Glastonbury** (860-633-8402) connects with **Earle Park** and its trail system. **Denison Pequotsepos Nature Center** (860-536-1216), in Mystic, has self-guiding trails, including one for the blind, in a 125-acre sanctuary. In Woodbury, **Flanders Nature Center** (203-263-3711) has a trail system, geologic sites, woodlands, wildlife, and a bog. **H. C. Barnes Memorial Nature Center** (860-585-8886) in Bristol contains 70 acres with trails. In Westport, there's a 62-acre wildlife sanctuary at the **Nature Center for Environmental Activities** (203-227-7253). Along with 40 acres of diverse habitats with walking trails, **New Canaan Nature Center** (203-966-9577) has a Discovery Center with hands-on natural science exhibits and live animals. **Roaring Brook Nature Center** (860-693-0263) in Canton has self-guiding trails, a Native American longhouse, and live animals. In Stamford, the **Stamford Museum & Nature Center,** on 118 acres, has a 19th-century working farm, a country store, woodland trails, a wildlife and picnic area, galleries, and planetarium shows on Sundays. The **West Rock Nature Center** (203-946-8016) in New Haven has native birds, reptiles, and mammals. The 146-acre **Woodcock Nature Center** (203-762-7280) in Wilton has 2 miles of hiking trails and a swamp boardwalk trail.

NATURE PRESERVES, COASTAL

Bluff Point Coastal Reserve State Park in Groton is a paradise for hikers and birders. Cars are not allowed in the 800-acre park; all exploring is done on foot. **Milford Point,** a 10-acre barrier beach, is a feeding area for great blue herons and snowy egrets, which nest on nearby **Chimon Island,** a 70-acre nature reserve in Norwalk Harbor. **Sheffield Island,** also in Norwalk Harbor, is a 60-acre nature refuge. Near Guilford, **Faulkner's Island** is a 4½-acre refuge owned by the US Coast Guard.

NATURE PRESERVES, INLAND

The **Katherine Ordway Preserve** spans 62 acres in Weston with self-guiding woodland trails and an arboretum. For information on the preserve and on the much larger (1,770-acre) nearby Devil's Den area, write to Box 1162, Weston 06883. **McLean Game Refuge** in Granby off CT 10 offers 3,400 acres with hiking trails over varied terrain and an abundance of small animals and birds. **White Memorial Foundation** in Litchfield, the state's largest nature center with 4,000 acres, offers bird-watching with observation platforms, hiking, swimming, camping, horseback riding, and many self-guiding trails including one for the blind. One of the East's finest natural preserves is **Connecticut Arboretum** in New London. Half of its 200 acres is preserved for nature itself and for hikers; the other half is maintained as an arboretum with a small stand of virgin pine, trees almost as high as California's famed redwoods. **Nipmuck State Forest** in Union is a cloud of pink and white flowers in late June and early July when the state flower, the mountain laurel, is in bloom. On the other side of the state, the profusion of mountain laurel in **Platt Hill State Park** in Winchester (Winsted) kicks off a week of celebration culminating in the crowning of a Laurel Queen.

PARKS AND FORESTS, STATE

The state parks and forests of Connecticut, 121 in all, account for some 180,000 acres of green. Much of the traprock ridge that runs roughly down the center of the state has been judged unsuitable (or impossible) for development, and as a consequence some choice hiking areas remain pristine woodlands. The state has purchased a number of parcels for preservation, and in addition, generous citizens have donated lands to the system of parks and forests that so successfully interrupt the crush of megalopolis. Boating, fishing, camping, picnicking, swimming, cross-country skiing, snowmobiling, rock climbing, hunting, scuba diving, and, of course, hiking are among the activities available in various developed parks and forests. Many have toilets, telephones, sports fields, bike paths, and rental boats. For detailed information on developed and undeveloped but accessible parks and forests, contact the **Connecticut Bureau of Outdoor Recreation, State Parks Division** (860-424-3200).

PICK YOUR OWN

Connecticut farms invite you to help with the harvest. You can pick strawberries, blueberries, apples, peaches, pumpkins, and, later in the year, cut your own Christmas trees. Signs along the roads point the way to pick-your-own farms, or get a complete listing from the **Connecticut Department of Agriculture** (860-566-4845).

POPULATION

Connecticut's population, according to a 1995 state estimate, is 3,274,238.

RESORTS

Connecticut has eight family resorts that offer swimming, either on ocean beaches or on lakeshores, and organized activities, as well as golf, tennis, fishing, boating, pools, health club facilities, and more. In Moodus are **Cave Hill Resort** (860-873-8347), **Klar Crest Resort & Inn** (860-873-8649), and

Sunrise Resort (860-873-8681). Others are **Heritage Inn** (203-264-8200) in Southbury; **Tamarack Lodge** (860-376-0224) in Voluntown; **Water's Edge Inn & Resort** (860-399-5901), Westbrook; and **Interlaken Inn** (860-435-9878; 1-800-222-2909) in Salisbury. **Club Getaway** (860-927-3664) in Kent is a sports resort for both adults and families. And then there's the **Foxwoods Resort Casino** in Ledyard.

SAFETY

As is the case elsewhere, Connecticut cities call for commonsense precautions. Stay out of depressed areas. Pay attention to your surroundings, and do your walking in the daytime; at night stick to the brightly lit areas where you find other tourists, diners, and theatergoers.

SCENIC ROUTES

In 1940 the nation's second median-divided, limited-access parkway (passenger cars only) was opened to traffic: The **Merritt Parkway,** a 38-mile roadway across Fairfield County from Greenwich to Stratford, has now been designated a Scenic Highway. Described by one historian as "one of the most beautiful and best-engineered highways of the time," it is neatly landscaped and treats the driver to a succession of 35 ornamental bridges, each of them different. Other stretches of road selected by the Department of Transportation and designated scenic are: **CT 234,** the Pequot Trail, from

Stonington to Westerly, 3.16 miles; **CT 146,** Branford to Guilford for 12.2 miles and then **CT 77** north to Durham for 11.56 miles; **CT 4** in Sharon, 3.9 miles; **US 7** in Sharon at the Cornwall Bridge and north for 4.29 miles, and also from New Milford north to Cornwall, 10.5 miles; **CT 41** in Sharon, 8.4 miles; **CT 160** in Glastonbury, 1.06 miles, ending at the Ferry Landing; **CT 169,** Lisbon to Woodstock, 32.1 miles; **CT 202,** Canton to New Hartford, 5.1 miles; **CT 53** in Redding, 2.03 miles; **CT 49** in the Quiet Corner, 18.8 miles; and **US 44** in Salisbury, 3.1 miles.

SKIING, CROSS-COUNTRY

Blackberry River Ski Touring Center (860-542-5100) in Norfolk has a little more than 15 miles of trails. **Cedar Brook Cross Country Ski Area** (860-668-5026) in West Suffield offers 6 miles of trails and a ski shop. In East Hartland, **Pine Mountain Cross-Country, Inc.** (860-653-4279) has 15 miles of trails and a ski shop. **White Memorial Foundation** (860-567-0857) in Litchfield offers 35 miles of trails. **Winding Trails Cross Country Ski Center** (860-678-9582), in Farmington, has 12 miles of trails. In Cornwall you'll find **Mohawk Mountain Ski Area** (860-672-6100), with 5 miles of cross-country trails. And in Woodbury, **Woodbury Ski & Racquet Area** (203-263-2203; 203-263-2213) maintains 20 miles of cross-country trails with lights and snow-making. Many state parks and forests permit cross-country skiing on hiking trails; contact the **Connecticut State Bureau of Parks and Recreation** (860-424-3200) for a complete listing.

SKIING, DOWNHILL

Connecticut has five major ski areas, all with snowmaking capability, ski shops, night skiing, snowboarding, and food service. None of these offers lodging on the property. In Cornwall **Mohawk Mountain** (860-672-6100) is where snowmaking was invented. This area has 22 downhill trails and 5 miles of cross-country trails. **Mount Southington** (860-628-0954) in Southington has 14 trails. **Powder Ridge Ski Area** (860-349-3454; 1-800-622-3321) in Middlefield maintains 14 trails. **Ski Sundown** (860-379-9851) in New Hartford offers 15 trails. **Woodbury Ski & Racquet Area** (203-263-2203; 203-263-2213) has 14 downhill trails and 20 miles of cross-country trails. Call 1-800-CT-BOUND for downhill ski area conditions.

SNOWMOBILING

On designated areas in some Connecticut state forests, the use of snowmobiles is authorized on established trails and forest roads. There are more than 95 miles of trails on state lands, including seasonal hiking trails, unplowed logging roads, abandoned railroad rights-of-way, and fire access lanes. For locations of trails, policies, procedures, and regulations, contact the **Connecticut State Bureau of Parks and Recreation** (860-424-3200).

SPAS

The **Spa at Grand Lake** (860-642-4306) is a weight-loss health spa with daily massages, aerobics, swimnastics, and yoga. It's in Lebanon in a scenic and rural setting overlooking Lake Williams. In Norwich the **Norwich Inn & Spa** (860-886-2401; 1-800-ASK-4SPA outside Connecticut) is a turn-of-the-century luxury inn with modern resort atmosphere and a full-service health spa. **Saybrook Point Inn & Spa** (860-395-2000; 1-800-243-0212) in Old Saybrook is a European-style luxury inn with spa facilities. Another resort with spa facilities is **Water's Edge Inn & Resort** (860-399-5901) in Westbrook, on 15 acres along Long Island Sound.

THEATER, SUMMER

First-rate summer theater is available in the state where it all really began. Before air-conditioning, New York thespians abandoned the city, but not their calling, during the summer months, traveling up to the cool "country"—Connecticut. Here they did comedy, tragedy, high drama, and slapstick in makeshift theaters, often barns, and—*voilà!*—strawhat was born. Summer stock offered work to established artists and apprenticeship opportunities to would-be actors. Now the tradition continues nationwide. In the greater Hartford area the **Centennial Theater Festival** (860-651-7295) in Simsbury schedules performances June through August. The **Levitt Pavilion for the Performing Arts** (203-226-2330) in Westport presents a full schedule of entertainers in the summer months. Also in Westport, the **Westport Country Playhouse** (203-227-4177) and the **White Barn Theater** (203-227-3768) offer summer-stock professional theater. At the University of Fairfield in Fairfield, the **Regina A. Quick Center for the Arts** (203-254-4010) presents children's programs in July and August. On Pleasure Beach in Bridgeport, the **Polka Dot Playhouse** (203-333-3666) holds performances June through October. The **Oakdale Theater** (203-265-1501) in Wallingford books family and children's shows and touring stars throughout the summer months. The **Sharon Playhouse** (860-364-1500) in Sharon is reopening with a schedule of musicals. (It regularly goes in and out of business, so check first.) The **Opera Theater of Connecticut** (860-669-8999) in Clinton "operates" in the summer. The **Eugene O'Neill Theater Center** (860-443-5378; 860-443-1238) in Waterford was founded in 1964 in honor of America's only Nobel Prize–winning playwright, Eugene

O'Neill. In June the center offers the International Student Exchange Program and the National Puppetry Conference. During July and August it presents the works of the National Playwrights Conference and National Music Theater Conference and Cabaret Symposium.

THEATER, YEAR-ROUND

Connecticut's award-winning professional theaters are recognized worldwide. The **Hartford Stage Company** (860-527-5151) received the 1989 Tony Award for Outstanding Achievement in Resident Theater. New Haven's twin theater giants, **Yale Repertory Theatre** and **Long Wharf Theatre,** have between them garnered dozens of Obie, Golden Globe, and other awards. All three have initiated runs of innumerable new plays that went on to Broadway and national stages. The **Goodspeed Opera House** in East Haddam has become famous as the birthplace and nurturer of American musical theater. Other professional-quality theater is found throughout the state. In Hartford the **Bushnell Memorial** (860-246-6807) is the state's premier performing arts center, presenting more than 300 events annually. In New Britain the **Hole in the Wall Theater** (860-229-3049) presents plays throughout the year. Top repertory and the best of Broadway's plays are mounted in the **Stamford Center for the Arts/Rich Forum & Palace Theatre** (203-325-9696). The **Warner Theatre** (860-489-7180), Torrington's elegant venue, is listed on the National Register of Historic Places. In Bridgeport the **Downtown Cabaret Theatre** (203-576-1636) is a year-round professional musical theater in a cabaret format, where you bring your own refreshments. Known as the "birthplace of the nation's greatest hits," the **Shubert Performing Arts Center** (203-562-5666;

1-800-228-6622) in New Haven offers the best of Broadway. In Ivoryton the **Ivoryton Playhouse** (860-767-8348) offers many types of performances year-round, including the nation's only magic-lantern shows of the 1890s. Located in Middletown, **Oddfellows Playhouse Youth Theater** (860-347-6143) is the state's oldest and largest theater for children. In Watertown the **Children's Dance Theater** (860-274-0004) also has year-round performances. The **Puppet House Theater** (203-931-6326; 203-488-5752) enhances Stony Creek. Wesleyan University's **Center for the Arts** (860-347-9411) offers year-round dance and theater performances. Similarly, **Connecticut Repertory Theatre** at the University of Connecticut, Storrs (860-486-4226) offers theater with a combination of professional and student actors. The **Garde Arts Center** (860-444-7373; 1-800-286-7900) in New London is a historic vaudeville/movie theater that presents national and international touring companies. The **Theater of Northeastern Connecticut** (860-928-7887) is located in Putnam. A year-round venue, **Beckley Dinner Theater** (860-828-7630), is in Berlin.

TRAILS

Several special "trails" have been designed to guide visitors to collections or sites with common themes. See the index for individual listings of the properties.

Connecticut's crafts centers, all with galleries and shops, make up one trail. They are: Brookfield Craft Center, Brookfield; Farmington Valley Arts Center, Avon; Wesleyan Potters, Middletown; Guilford Handcrafts, Guilford; Creative Arts Workshop, New Haven.

The **Connecticut Impressionist Art Trail** includes 11 museums and galleries, as well as one corporate office, devoted to the works by American impressionist artists,

many of whom worked or lived in the state. The trail includes: Bruce Museum and the Bush-Holley House, both in Greenwich; Yale University Art Gallery, New Haven; Florence Griswold Museum, Old Lyme; Lyman Allyn Art Museum, New London; William Benton Museum of Art, Storrs; Hartford Steam Boiler Inspection & Insurance Company, Hartford; Wadsworth Atheneum, Hartford; New Britain Museum of American Art, New Britain; and the Hill-Stead Museum, Farmington. For a descriptive brochure, write to Connecticut Impressionist Art Trail, PO Box 793, Old Lyme 06371.

Connecticut Hiking Trails, 700 miles in all, cleared and blazed with blue by the Connecticut Forest and Park Association (CFPA) and its members, are featured, in early June each year, on Connecticut Trails Day. More than 70 hikes are offered, with knowledgeable leaders. You can, of course, hike the trails on your own any day. For information, write to the Connecticut Forest and Park Association, 16 Meriden Road, Middlefield, 06481-2945.

The **Connecticut Wine Trail** invites you to tour state vineyards that are open to the public on a regular basis. Wineries on the trail are: Di Grazia Vineyard and Winery, Brookfield Center; Hopkins Vineyard, New Preston; Haight Vineyard, Litchfield; Haight Vineyard & Wine Education Center, Mystic; and Stonington Vineyards, Stonington. For a brochure, write to The Connecticut Wine Trail, 29 Chestnut Hill Road, Litchfield 06759.

The **Freedom Trail** traces the largely unknown history of African Americans in Connecticut. Homes, churches, and sites are listed, many of them connected with the Underground Railroad and with the *Amistad* incident, which involved Mende tribesmen who seized control of the ship carrying them into slavery and came ashore in Connecticut. Sites along the trail, not all open to the public, include the homes or sites of such notables as John Brown in Torrington, Marian Anderson in Danbury, Paul Robeson in Enfield, and other citizens, black and white, who have contributed to the heritage of African Americans. For a brochure, write to or call the Connecticut Tourism Office (860-258-4355; 1-800-CT-BOUND), 505 Hudson Street, Hartford 06106-7106.

TRAIN SERVICES

AMTRAK (1-800-USA-RAIL; 1-800-872-7245) links New York and Boston, with Connecticut stops at Stamford, Bridgeport, New Haven, Old Saybrook, New London, and Mystic. A connecting line at New London gives access to Willimantic (Storrs). Service to Springfield, Massachusetts, connects with New Haven, with the following stops in Connecticut: Wallingford, Meriden, Berlin, Hartford, Windsor, and Windsor Locks. **Metro-North** (1-800-638-7646) commuter line runs from New York City (Grand Central Station) to New Haven, scheduling stops at Greenwich, Cos Cob, Riverside, Old Greenwich, Stamford, Norton Heights, Darien, Rowayton, South and East Norwalk, Westport, Green's Farms, Southport, Fairfield, Bridgeport, Stratford, and Milford. A spur line to New Canaan serves Glenbrook, Springdale, and Talmadge Hill; one to Danbury stops at Merritt 7, Wilton, Cannondale, Branchville, Redding, and Bethel; the line to Waterbury also serves Derby/Shelton, Ansonia, Seymour, Beacon Falls, and Naugatuck.

US SERVICE ACADEMY

In New London, the **US Coast Guard Academy** (860-444-8444) is open to the public daily May through November. Visitors can take a close-up look at a military academy at work. Cadets pass in review in season on Friday afternoons. The Visitors Pavilion provides an overview of the Coast Guard's history and mission, and you're welcome to take a walking tour of the grounds. When the tall ship *Eagle,* a training vessel for the academy, is in port, visitors are invited to go aboard.

WATERFALLS

Some of Connecticut's largest falls are in state parks and forests. The most spectacular is **Kent Falls,** a series of cascades in Kent Falls State Park in the town of Kent on US 7. In East Haddam, Devil's Hopyard State Park on CT 156 has **Chapman Falls,** plunging some 60 feet down a rocky cliff. **Wadsworth Falls State Park** is on CT 157 in Middlefield. **Southford Falls,** located on CT 188 in Southbury-Oxford, is a series of several easily accessible falls, with the added attraction of a covered bridge at the bottom. **Spruce Brook Ravine** in Naugatuck State Forest hides a pretty stream in a setting of evergreens and a steep-walled gorge. **Pine Swamp Brook** is on US 7 in West Cornwall in a miniature canyon you can climb into. A helpful source is the *Connecticut Walk Book,*

KIMBERLY GRANT

distributed by the Connecticut Forest and Park Association (860-346-2372); for a copy, send $17 to the association at 16 Meriden Road, Middlefield 06481-2945.

WHITE-WATER CANOEING/ RAFTING

Champaign Canoeing Ltd. (914-762-5121) offers white-water canoeing instruction and trips on the Farmington, Housatonic, and Shepaug Rivers, as well as 2-day camping trips with food and equipment provided. For trips by canoe, kayak, or raft, **Clarke Outdoors** (860-672-6365) gives tours along the Housatonic River and guided white-water rafting during spring's high water. **Main Stream Canoe** (860-693-6791) offers white-water canoe trips on the Farmington River. **The Mountain Workshop** (203-438-3640) offers canoeing for all abilities on rivers, lakes, and the Long Island Sound. For white-water rafting on the Housatonic River at Bulls Bridge Gorge, try **North American Whitewater Expeditions** (1-800-RAPIDS-9) for Class IV–V technical drops and spectacular waterfalls; it also offers medium white-water scenic and historic floats from Falls Village to Housatonic Meadows. **White Creek Expeditions** (203-966-0040), New Canaan, has canoeing and kayaking adventures for flat water, quick water, and white water. (See *Canoeing.*)

WINDJAMMERS

The *Argia* (860-536-0416), a replica of a 19th-century, gaff-rigged schooner with 20th-century appointments, sails out of Mystic down the Mystic River to Fishers Island on half-day trips. Also available are full-day sailing adventures or sunset cruises. Aboard the *Brilliant* (860-572-5315), a 61-foot, classic brass and teak schooner, passengers can take turns steering, handling sails, and cooking. The classic schooner *Mystic Whaler* (1-800-697-8420) has modern berths and sails for 1-, 2-, 3-, and 5-day getaways along the New England coast. The *Sylvina W. Beal* (860-536-8422; 1-800-333-MYSTIC), an 84-foot knockabout schooner, sails from Mystic on 2- or 3-day excursions to bays and sounds of New England.

YOUTH HOSTELS

There are only two **American Youth Hostels** in Connecticut: one in Hartford, the other in Windsor. For information contact the AYH Yankee Council (860-236-2027).

I. THE GOLD COAST

Greenwich and Stamford
Westport and Norwalk
The Bridgeport Area
The New Haven Area
The Housatonic Valley

KIMBERLY GRANT

A gateway at Yale leads into courtyards surrounded by the classrooms, laboratories, and dormitories of one of the Ivy League's premier schools.

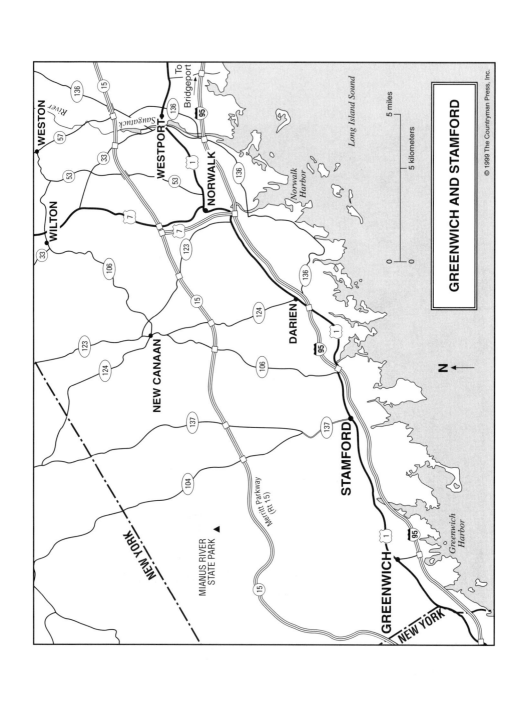

GREENWICH AND STAMFORD

© 1999 The Countryman Press, Inc.

5 miles

5 kilometers

N

Long Island Sound

Norwalk Harbor

Greenwich Harbor

WESTON

WILTON

WESTPORT

NORWALK

NEW CANAAN

DARIEN

STAMFORD

GREENWICH

NEW YORK

NEW YORK

Saugatuck River

Saugatuck

To Bridgeport

MIANUS RIVER STATE PARK

Merritt Parkway (Rt 15)

Greenwich and Stamford

Travelers entering Connecticut's southwestern corner take their first steps into New England, although Yankee customs, architecture, culture, even people, are not readily apparent. This is what has been dubbed the Gold Coast, a densely populated coastal plain more suburban New York City than New England. Here, bustling cities and gentrified towns are strung together along Long Island Sound by two major arteries, I-95 and US 1.

You must ply farther north to find New England's true flavor, its colonial greens and picturesque fishing coves. But by no means should you rush through the Gold Coast. It has its own charms, and much to offer in the way of history, the arts, and culture. The people who lend the area this distinction are an interesting mélange: CEOs from some of the world's greatest international corporations; top professionals in law, science, literature, and even sports; and a grand host of celebrities who earn their bread on Broadway and/or in Hollywood. Even such a politico as New York's infamous Boss Tweed once had a Greenwich estate where he entertained his cronies. Naturally, much of the Gold Coast is off-limits to the public. The amount of shoreline devoted to marinas and private beaches in Greenwich alone is greater than the entire amount of shoreline open to the general public along the remainder of Connecticut's 200-mile-long coast.

Greenwich is the quintessential commuter's town, even though in its earliest days as a foundling agricultural community the commuters it sent to New York were potatoes, shipped daily on sailing packets. Because Greenwich is so attractive and so accessible to New York (Times Square is less than 30 miles away!), in recent years it has attracted several large corporations. Indeed, some of the wealthiest people in the world live on great estates in this monied enclave.

Stamford, once a sleepy little residential town, has undergone a drastic transformation in the last decade and now sports a core center of Manhattan-style skyscrapers, in which dozens of major companies are headquartered. Modest homes that were probably built for $40,000 three decades ago now command high-six-figure prices. The tony communities of New Canaan and Darien are dotted with antiques, boutiques, and restaurants ranging from eclectic to haute-cuisine trendy.

Many of its residents reside behind stone walls and gates, in carefully restored clapboard farmhouses, stately Georgian mansions, and massive contemporaries of steel and glass.

Withal, there's still a pleasing amount of open space, numerous nature sanctuaries, arboretums, gardens, museums, historic homes, and much more of interest to the visitor.

Entries in this section are arranged in roughly geographic order.

AREA CODE
203

GUIDANCE

Coastal Fairfield County Tourism District (203-840-0770; 1-800-866-7925), Web site: http://visitfairfieldco.org, MerrittView, 383 Main Avenue, Norwalk 06851.

Greater New Haven Convention & Visitors District (203-777-8550; 1-800-332-7829), Web site: www.newhavencvb.org, 59 Elm Street, New Haven 06510.

GETTING THERE

By car: Three major east–west arteries link the Long Island Sound shore-line cities and towns of Connecticut with Boston and New York. Because I-95 runs in a southerly direction from New York almost all the way down the Atlantic Coast, the Connecticut Department of Transportation, in its ongoing campaign to confuse motorists, inscribes north and south direc-tions on its I-95 signs, despite the indisputable fact that I-95 runs east and west while it is in Connecticut.

I-95 hugs the coast and carries the most traffic. A few miles to the north, and proceeding to New Haven, where it veers off northward to-ward Hartford, the beautiful Merritt Parkway (CT 15), third oldest su-perhighway in the world, also serves the Gold Coast, with a pronounced bonus for motorists: Big trucks are excluded. This Depression-era road was landscaped as if it were a park, and includes a series of bridges, each unique in design. Then there's the venerable granddaddy of all American highways, historic US 1, named the Post Road in colonial days. Starting in Maine and ending in Key West, Florida, it snakes through all the met-ropolitan areas, a minefield of stoplights and shopping malls. At the same time, it's the most interesting of the southern arteries.

By air: **Westchester County Airport** (914-285-4860), just north of Greenwich, serves the area with daily flights by American, Business Ex-press, Northwest, United, United Express, USAir, USAir Express, and Continental. USAir Express runs scheduled service out of **Igor Sikorsky Memorial Airport** (203-576-7498), in Bridgeport. **Tweed–New Haven** (203-946-8283), in East Haven, is the airport of greater New Haven, which is also served by USAir Express. International arrivals access the Gold Coast through New York's **JFK airport** or **Bradley International** in Windsor Locks, both about 1½ hours away.

KIMBERLY GRANT

The Whitney Museum of American Art at Champion in Stamford

By bus or limo: **Bonanza** (1-888-751-8800), **Greyhound** (1-800-231-2222), and **Peter Pan Trailways** (1-800-343-9999), along with airport limousines, provide ground transportation.

By rail: There are two railroads: **AMTRAK** (1-800-872-7245), the main line along the entire Atlantic Coast, and **Metro-North** (1-800-638-7646), the busy New York commuter line. Metro-North connects with feeder lines at Stamford from New Canaan, at South Norwalk from

Danbury, and at Bridgeport from Waterbury. Originating out of Grand Central Station, it runs express and local trains to its final terminal at New Haven. Check schedules for the towns and times you plan to visit.

GETTING AROUND

Taxi service in Stamford: **Stamford Taxi** (203-325-2611) and **Stamford Yellow Cab** (203-967-3633). **Greenwich Taxi** (203-869-6000) and **Hoyt Taxi Service** (203-972-0677) in New Canaan also serve the area.

Day Trippers (203-656-2426), PO Box 36, Darien 06820. Escorted cultural and historic motorcoach trips depart from various Fairfield and New Haven County locations.

MEDICAL EMERGENCY

The statewide emergency number is **911.**

Greenwich Hospital (203-863-3000), Five Perryridge Road. The emergency number is 203-863-3637.

St. Joseph Medical Center (203-353-2000), 128 Strawberry Hill Avenue, Stamford. The emergency number is 203-353-2222.

The Stamford Hospital (203-325-7000), Shelburne Road at West Broad Street. The emergency number is 203-325-7777.

TO SEE

First Presbyterian Church (203-324-9522), 1101 Bedford Street, Stamford. Open year-round, Monday through Friday 9–5; July and August, weekdays 9–3. Donation suggested. You'll find here the largest mechanical-action pipe organ in Connecticut. The church, designed by Wallace K. Harrison, is shaped like a fish. The stained-glass windows are from France.

MUSEUMS

Bruce Museum (203-869-0376), One Museum Drive, Greenwich. Open Tuesday through Saturday 10–5, Sunday 1–5. Adults $3.50; seniors and children 5–12, $2.50. No charge on Tuesday. A private home was the nucleus for what is now a major museum with a variety of art galleries and educational workshops. A Science and Environment wing features a mine shaft, woodland habitat, minerals exhibit, wigwam, and marine touch tank. The museum sponsors an annual outdoor crafts festival in mid-May and an outdoor arts festival on Columbus Day weekend (see *Special Events*). Among the museum's latest acquisitions is a full-size bronze copy of Rodin's famous statue *The Kiss*, an anonymous gift. Call for schedules of other programs.

Putnam Cottage (203-869-9697), 243 East Putnam Avenue, Greenwich. Open year-round, Wednesday, Friday, and Sunday 1–3:30, and by appointment. Adults $4; children under 12 free. Popular lore has it that Connecticut hero Gen. Israel Putnam (see "The Villages of Northeastern Connecticut") caught a glimpse of a British patrol here while looking in his shaving mirror. Separated from his troops, he rushed to his

The working farm at the 118-acre Stamford Museum and Nature Center

horse and escaped by riding down a steep set of steps in a cliff in the Horseneck section of Greenwich. The doughty, paunchy old warrior—he was in his mid-60s—did escape the British by riding down the cliff; however, the steps (which you may see) were not cut into the cliff until after the Revolution! Antique furnishings, a huge fieldstone fireplace, an herb garden, and a restored barn are on the grounds.

Stamford Historical Society Museum (203-329-1183), 1508 High Ridge Road, Stamford. Open Tuesday through Saturday noon–4. Closed major holidays. Adults $2; children $1. Permanent and changing exhibits, mostly local history. Research library on the premises. The society also operates **Hoyt-Barnum House,** a restored blacksmith's home built in 1699 and located at 713 Bedford Street.

Stamford Museum & Nature Center (203-322-1646), 39 Scofieldtown Road, Stamford. Open year-round, Monday through Saturday 9–5, Sunday 1–5. Closed Thanksgiving, Christmas, and New Year's. Adults $5; seniors and children 5–13, $4. A pleasant relief in one of the state's most densely populated cities: 118 acres of forests, fields, and farms. The center holds one of the few planetariums in the state, with special shows on Sunday. There is also considerable culture here; the center contains seven galleries devoted to everything from fine art to farm tools and customs of Native Americans. There's a country store, picnic area, and woodland trails—but of special interest to children is the 19th-century working farm, with an area for petting domestic animals.

The Champion Greenhouse (203-358-6533), One Champion Plaza, corner of Atlantic and Tresser Boulevards, Stamford. Open year-round, Tuesday through Saturday 11–5. Free admission. Located on an upper

downstairs rooms serve as intimate dining areas where you can enjoy well-prepared Swiss specialties. The tender sirloin steaks and filet mignon can be cut with a fork. Entrées $19–32; prix fixe (Saturday only) $45.

    Sole (203-972-8887), 105 Elm Street. Open daily for lunch and dinner. A chic establishment with pastel walls, columns, an intricately tiled floor, and a sophisticated menu that matches its clientele. Northern Italian dishes such as Tuscan bread salad with fresh mozzarella and prosciutto, grilled chicken and fennel on focaccia, and house-made potato gnocchi with sausage, mushrooms, and basil. Among the exquisite desserts is torta di formaggio, white chocolate cheesecake with almond brittle and fruit compote. Entrées $7–25.

    Gates (203-966-8666), 10 Forest Street. Lunch and dinner daily, 11:30–3:30 and 5:30–10; Friday and Saturday 5:30–11. Sunday dinner 4:30–9:30. Enter through an antique wrought-iron Austrian gate, whence the name, where you'll be greeted with an eclectic menu that ranges from Cuban black bean soup, innovative shrimp, and tuna steaks to pasta. Fresh salads (no iceberg lettuce, thank you) with dressings of your choice. For dessert, Key lime pie that will bring back memories of the sunset at Mallory Dock over the waters of Key West. Frank the bartender plays jazz on weekends. $10.95–16.95. Children's menu.

    Blue Water Café (203-972-1799), 15 Elm Street. Open daily. Lunch 11:30–2:30; dinner 6–9:30; brunch on Sunday. A small eatery, a favorite with the locals. A variety of pasta dishes: Try the rigatoni with sweet Italian sausage and peas in a light Parmesan cream sauce. Fresh seafood. For dessert, guests rave about that old stalwart of the Great Depression, bread pudding! Call for reservations. $17–22.

In Darien

    The Black Goose Grille (203-655-7107), 972 Post Road (US 1). Open daily for lunch and dinner. This lovely old brick house with gleaming black shutters offers some of the best fine dining in town. Well-prepared, classic American dishes, from Black Angus sirloin to old-fashioned beef stew and roasted pork chops can be enjoyed in the rustic bar with its massive fireplace, on the terrace, or in the elegant dining room. The menu also offers combinations, such as grilled chicken and filet mignon, or crab cakes and grilled swordfish. Entrées $16.50–28.

    Giovanni's II (203-325-9979), 2748 Post Road (US 1). Lunch and dinner Monday through Friday. Dinner Saturday 3–10:30, Sunday 1–9. An inviting, locally liked restaurant serving Italian fare with an emphasis on seafood and steak. $14–25. Another location at 1297 Long Ridge Road, Stamford.

EATING OUT

In Greenwich

    Abis (203-862-9100), 381 Greenwich Avenue, Greenwich. Traditional Japanese cuisine in an airy space full of blond wood, mirrors, and greenery. Watch chefs in the open kitchen prepare tempura, donburi, and teriyaki dishes, as well as sushi and sashimi. For dessert, try cream mitsumame, an unusual combination of vanilla ice cream atop beans, peaches, mandarin oranges, and Jell-O. $11–20.

   Manero's (203-869-0049), 559 Steamboat Road, Greenwich. Open daily for lunch and dinner. For the steak-and-potatoes members of your family—nothing fancy, but everything substantial and well cooked. Fabulous prime ribs. $12.95–20.95 for a complete dinner.

Centro (203-531-5514), 328 Pemberwick Road, Greenwich. Lunch Monday through Saturday 10:30–3; pizza and salad 3–5:30; dinner Monday through Thursday 5:30–10, Friday and Saturday to 11, Sunday 5–9:30. An appealing restaurant in a former felt mill overlooking a 30-foot waterfall on the Byram River. Serves homemade pasta, thin-crusted European pizza, wonderful Caesar salad, grilled fish and meat. Children's menu. Outdoor dining in season. Reservations suggested. $7.95–17.95.

Elsewhere

Bank Street Brewing Co. (203-325-2739), 65 Bank Street, Stamford. Lunch and dinner daily. The city's first brewpub is housed in the former Citizens Savings Bank, a stately building with a lofty ceiling, stained-glass dome, Palladian windows, and a 40-foot marble bar that was once the tellers' counter. Fish-and-chips, pot roast, and blackened chicken are some of the house specialties. The bar is often packed with a lively happy-hour crowd; take it all in from an upstairs rail-side table. Entrées $11.95–22.95.

   Tequila Mockingbird (203-966-2222), 6 Forest Street (next to Gates), New Canaan. Open for dinner daily, specializing in the regional dishes of Mexico. Sip on a colossal margarita while the chef prepares chiles rellenos that melt in your mouth. A more hearty dish: grilled steak, Mexican-style (it's listed as Arrachera al Carbon on the menu). Colorful decorative tiles recall the rosy glow of a New Mexico sunset. Reservations suggested on weekends. $13.

Post Corner Pizza (203-655-7721), 847 Post Road (US 1), Darien. Open daily for lunch and dinner. Clean and friendly, often full of families. The Sofronas family has been serving Greek specialties and satisfying pizza house fare here since 1971. The souvlaki and moussaka are authentic and delicious. Locally liked, moderately priced. $4–10.

SNACKS

   Aux Delices (203-698-1066), Greenwich. Open daily from 8:30 AM, to eat in or take out. Debra Ponzek's innovative hand has won her many accolades; samplings from her gourmet deli prove they are highly deserved. In the morning, order fresh-baked scones and coffee and seat yourself at a shiny copper café table. Lunch and dinner are a changing selection of Provence-inspired dishes, such as three-bean salad with truffle vinaigrette, medallions of filet mignon with wild mushrooms, and smoked duck and arugula in a mustard vinaigrette on a baguette. French specialty food products. Sandwiches around $7; entrées $8–18.

  ♿ **Ole Mole** (203-461-9962), 1030 High Ridge Road (CT 137), Stamford. Open Tuesday through Saturday for lunch and dinner; dinner only on Sunday; closed Monday. A tiny, bustling take-out spot, with four self-seating tables in a Mexican-tiled store. Generous portions of tasty Mexican food with rice, beans, tortilla chips, and guacamole on the side. Delicious moles and salsas. $8.50–12.

  ♿ **Main Street Deli** (203-972-8889), 136 Main Street, New Canaan. Open daily. A casual, inviting place, with dark wood floors, pressed-tin ceiling, and interesting artwork on the walls. Breakfast means strong aromatic coffee and pastries; for lunch, a variety of salads and sandwiches, including many vegetarian and low-fat options. A good lunch or snack stop while shopping in town. $3–6.

Uncle's Deli (203-655-9701), 1041 Post Road (US 1), Darien. Breakfast and lunch daily. A snug deli in a tiny green and white shack dressed up with checked curtains. Primarily take-out, except in summer, when you can bring your picnic fixings to a table outside. Locals love the roll-ups; the Thanksgiving version (crammed with turkey, stuffing, and cranberry sauce) is especially popular. Sandwiches $3–7.

ENTERTAINMENT

MUSIC AND THEATER

Stamford Center for the Arts (203-325-4466) operates two first-rate performance venues: the **Palace Theatre** at 61 Atlantic Street, designed by noted theater architect Thomas Lamb; and the **Rich Forum** at 307 Atlantic Street. They offer varied fare: Broadway musicals, comedies, plays, dance, and music.

  ✎ **Stamford Theatre Works** (203-359-4414), 200 Strawberry Hill Avenue, Stamford. Year-round professional theater presenting new and experimental plays for adults and children; call for schedule. School for the performing arts also on-site.

Maxwell Anderson Playwrights Series (203-938-2770), 299 Greenwich Avenue, Greenwich. Staged readings by professional actors at the **Greenwich Arts Center,** weekends October through June. Call for schedule.

SELECTIVE SHOPPING

ANTIQUES

Church Street Antiques (203-661-6309), 77 Church Street, Greenwich. Fine antiques and decorative pieces.

Stamford Antiques Center (1-888-329-3546), 735 Canal Street, Stamford. More than 125 dealers offering everything from fine antiques and paintings to funky costume jewelry.

Antiques of Darien (203-655-5133), 1101 Post Road (US 1), Darien. Eight dealers, each with a specialty—fine art, Oriental carpets, country furniture, lamps, mirrors. Many unique finds.

ART GALLERIES

Silvermine Guild Arts Center (203-966-5617), 1037 Silvermine Road, New Canaan. Open year-round, except Monday and major holidays. One of the most beautiful and prestigious galleries in New England; there are rotating exhibits of works by top professionals for sale and for viewing. Crafts and jewelry are on sale in the shop.

BOOKSTORES

Just Books (203-869-5023), 19 East Putnam Avenue, Greenwich. The name says it all.

Diane's Books (203-869-1515), 8A Grigg Street, Greenwich. A full-service bookstore.

New Canaan Bookshop (203-966-1684), 59 Elm Street, New Canaan. A beautiful shop with a comprehensive selection of topics. Many best-selling authors sign their latest works here; call for schedule.

SPECIAL SHOPS

Orvis (203-662-0844), 432 Post Road (US 1), Darien. The Orvis name is synonymous with the sport (and art) of fly-fishing. Fly-fishing and -tying equipment, clothing, and advice. Call for a schedule of workshops and seminars.

Smith & Hawken (203-972-0820), 30 East Avenue, New Canaan. Like the legendary gardening catalog, this shop has every conceivable gadget to make your garden grow, while making it (and the gardener) look snazzy. Decorative spigots, galvanized plant markers, imported hand tools, rubber rain shoes, and the like.

☞ **United House Wrecking Company** (203-348-5371), 535 Hope Street, Stamford. Open Monday through Saturday 9:30–5:30 and Sunday noon–5. Billing itself as "The Junkyard with a Heart," this vast emporium, whose owners were in attendance when great estates and other buildings were being demolished, has amassed an astounding collection of "wreckables." Most of it is high quality. Wander through rooms filled with stained and beveled glass, old mantels, butcher blocks, fireplace accessories, unusual furniture, Victorian gingerbread, weather vanes, and cupolas. The list is endless.

Stamford Town Center (203-356-9700), 100 Greyrock Place. Clustered in a huge covered mall in the center of downtown Stamford are the cream of New York City's stores and boutiques such as Macy's and Saks Fifth Avenue. New Yorkers make the short train trip to Stamford because they argue that in New York they may be able to visit one or two stores on a good shopping day, but in Stamford, the stores are all together and easily accessible under one roof. Underground parking garage.

SPECIAL EVENTS

May: **Crafts Festival** (203-869-0376), Bruce Museum, One Museum Drive, Greenwich.

May–September: **Silvermine Chamber Music Series** (203-966-5617), Silvermine Guild Arts Center, 1037 Silvermine Road, New Canaan. Theatrical performances and chamber music concerts.

June: **Ox Ridge Charity Horse Show** (203-655-2559), Darien.

July: **Greenwich Polo Club** (203-661-5687), Greenwich. Players from around the world.

October: **Stamford Classic Half-Marathon** (203-854-7825), through rural, coastline, and downtown areas. **Arts Festival,** Bruce Museum, Greenwich. Juried show attracting artists from around the country.

November: **Holiday parade** (203-854-7825), Stamford.

Westport and Norwalk

Though sitting cheek by jowl on the western shores of Long Island Sound, Westport and Norwalk couldn't be more different in geography, topography, character, purpose, and population. Norwalk was a premier industrial town that also drew its sustenance from the water with a once thriving oyster-fishing industry. While the bulk of the factories have skipped town, the largest oystering operation on the East Coast is still in business here. South Norwalk (south of US 1 and the main-line railroad tracks) was particularly hard hit. But enterprising city officials and private civic leaders launched a remarkable restoration project in the early 1980s, transforming a decaying waterfront area and its shabby 1800s storefronts and factory buildings—even an old movie house— into an attractive row of outstanding restaurants (see *Dining Out*), galleries, funky boutiques, and cafés. Naturally, the area has attracted a hip, bohemian crowd and a vibrant artistic community, and offers unparalleled people-watching. Around the corner is a unique maritime center, complete with aquarium, nautical museum, marinas, and charter-boat docks. South Norwalk, known lovingly as SoNo, lives again!

Neighboring Westport has been home to the affluent New York commuter almost from the day it was connected to "the city" by rail. In the 1920s, it was the summer playground of Scott and Zelda Fitzgerald. Numerous theatrical celebrities enjoy their privacy, and one another's company, at lavish parties on their palatial estates. One of the customs in "the Land of Steady Habits" is to respect your neighbors' privacy no matter what their fame. So follow the lead of the locals and don't bother longtime residents Paul Newman and his wife, Joanne Woodward, if you bump into them in the aisle of a supermarket. Though Westport can't point to many conventional tourist attractions, its upscale restaurants and shops along the streets in the core of the village, radiating off US 1, annually draw thousands of visitors. The Westport Country Playhouse is one of the oldest in the nation. Its board of directors sounds like the roster of winners from an Oscar night. The surrounding towns of Wilton, Weston, Easton, and Monroe are for the most part wealthy residential areas. Of interest to tourists are their inns, elegant restaurants, and historical societies.

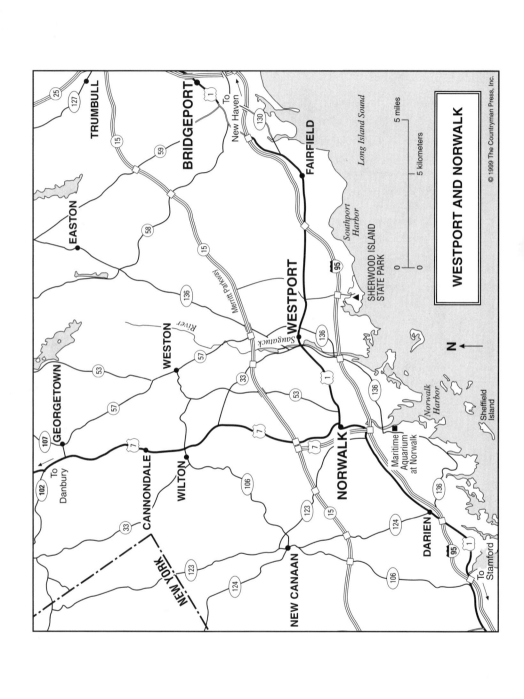

WESTPORT AND NORWALK

© 1999 The Countryman Press, Inc.

5 miles
5 kilometers
0
0

Entries in this section are arranged in roughly geographic order.

AREA CODE
   203

GUIDANCE
   Coastal Fairfield County Tourism District (1-800-866-7925), MerrittView, 383 Main Avenue, Norwalk 06851, Web site: http://visitfairfieldco.org.

GETTING THERE
   By car: Westport and Norwalk, and adjoining towns and villages, are accessible by car from I-95, the Merritt Parkway, and US 1, the Post Road.
   By rail: **New York–New Haven Metro-North** (1-800-638-7646) commuter trains make frequent stops from early morning to late at night.
   By bus or limo: **Connecticut Limousine** (1-800-472-LIMO) serves the three major metro New York airports. **Greyhound** (1-800-231-2222), **Trailways** (1-800-343-9999), and **Bonanza** (1-888-751-8800) bus lines serve this area.

GETTING AROUND
   Westport Star Taxi (203-227-5157), **Norwalk Taxi** (203-855-1764), and **Norwalk Yellow Cab** (203-853-1267) serve the area.

MEDICAL EMERGENCY
   The statewide emergency number is **911.**
   Norwalk Hospital (203-852-2000), 34 Maple Street, Norwalk. The emergency number is 203-852-2160.
   Greenwich Hospital (203-863-3000), Five Perryridge Road, Greenwich. The emergency number is 203-863-3637.
   St. Joseph Medical Center (203-353-2000), 128 Strawberry Hill Avenue, Stamford. The emergency number is 203-353-2222.
   The Stamford Hospital (203-325-7000), Shelburne Road at West Broad Street, Stamford. The emergency number is 203-325-7777.

TO SEE

National Hall Historic District, on the west bank of the Saugatuck River, Westport. Wharves, factories, and warehouses have been restored on 3 scenic acres, once a bustling seaport where Captain Kidd put in with his treasure-laden ships. Local lore has it that the dashing pirate buried his ill-gotten gains on nearby Sherwood Island, now a state park. Take a walk along the shoreline boardwalk. Photograph a replica of the original 1894 horse-watering trough. The cornerstone of the restoration is The Inn at National Hall (see *Lodging* and *Dining Out*).

MUSEUMS
   The Maritime Aquarium at Norwalk (203-852-0700), 10 North Water Street, South Norwalk. Open daily 10–5; closed Thanksgiving, Christmas, and New Year's Day. Additional IMAX hours Friday and Saturday evenings. Adults $7.75; seniors and children $6.50; IMAX extra. Unlike

The Maritime Aquarium at Norwalk has a small boat exhibit.

Mystic Seaport, which is spread over 17 acres, this maritime museum, one of Connecticut's newest attractions, is contained in a former iron factory. Exhibits devoted to the maritime history and ecological life of Long Island Sound are combined with demonstrations of boatbuilding, an aquarium with seals and sharks, and one of the few IMAX theaters in the country. Watching a film on the eight-story-high IMAX screen is like no other experience. Presentations are not limited to maritime subjects: One month you may be in the mountains of Rwanda mingling with a family of mountain gorillas; the next, watching around-the-clock flashes of lightning bolts in the clouds above the earth from an orbiting spaceship. Hands-on exhibits (including a touch tank) for children; lectures and workshops by scientists, divers, fishermen, and sailors.

The Norwalk Museum (203-866-0202), 41 North Main Street, Norwalk. Open year-round, Tuesday through Sunday 1–5. Donation. Housed in the imposing former City Hall, displays of local manufacturing, retail, and artistic history showcase period furnishings, paintings, and decorative art. A merchants courtyard depicts shops selling Dobbs hats and 19th-century Norwalk pottery. The gift shop carries Norwalk Pottery reproductions and Raggedy Ann and Andy dolls (creator Johnny Gruelle lived in Norwalk); a perpetual tag sale offers a little of everything.

Sheffield Island Lighthouse (203-838-9444), accessible by seasonal ferry from Hope Dock, adjacent to the Maritime Aquarium at Norwalk, or by private boat. Tours daily in summer; weekends May through September. Admission $10. Two-hour guided tours of a 10-room stone lighthouse and tower built in 1868 in Norwalk Harbor on a 3-acre island. Picnicking and swimming.

WPA Murals (203-866-0202), Norwalk City Hall, 125 East Avenue, Norwalk. Open Monday through Friday 9–5. During the Great Depression of the 1930s, President Franklin Roosevelt's Works Project Administration (WPA) created federal jobs in every endeavor from constructing schools and municipal buildings to promoting arts and culture. Hundreds of impoverished artists throughout the country were employed to paint murals in the new public buildings. Most murals have been destroyed, but Connecticut, recognizing their historic value, has restored and now displays 33 murals of life in the Norwalk area, the largest collection in the country of this unique art form. One shows Norwalk oystermen, remembered to this day at the annual Norwalk Oyster Festival (see *Special Events*). Other examples of the huge murals can be seen in other Norwalk public buildings: Two in the Maritime Museum depict oystering; two children's scenes are in the public library on Belden Avenue (203-899-2780), and two more are hung in Norwalk Community Technical College on Richards Avenue (203-857-7000).

Norwalk Seaport Association (203-838-9444), 132 Water Street, South Norwalk. Open Monday through Friday 9–5. Long Island Sound maritime exhibits, artifacts, and literature in the 1906-style Oyster House, with a huge pile of oyster shells at the entrance.

Raymond Fitch House/Wilton Heritage Museum (203-762-7257), 249 Danbury Road, Wilton. Open Monday through Thursday 9:30–4:30; some Sunday hours. Adults $2; seniors $1; children free. Period rooms in a classic 18th-century farmhouse with a central chimney. Dolls, dollhouses, and toys; special events and changing exhibits. Gift shop.

HISTORIC HOMES

Lockwood-Mathews Mansion (203-838-1434), 295 West Avenue, Norwalk. Guided tours Tuesday through Friday 11–3, Sunday 1–4. Adults $5; seniors and students $3; children under 12 free. In 1864, long before the coal barons and railroad tycoons built their "summer cottages" in Newport, industrialist LeGrand Lockwood built a magnificent 50-room mansion in Norwalk that for years was a showcase of American wealth and opulence. Under meticulous restoration for the past 20 years, the mansion, now a National Historic landmark, is a wondrous display of the art of interior decoration, from parquet floors to frescoed walls, with ornate trim and a 42-foot-high octagonal rotunda. Extensive collection of music boxes. Changing exhibits and special events; gift shop.

Wheeler House (203-222-1424), 25 Avery Place, Westport. Open year-round, Tuesday through Saturday 10–3. Donation requested. This Victorian Italianate villa, home of the Westport Historical Society, features a parlor, kitchen, and bedroom as they appeared in the elegant Victorian era. In the cobblestone barn—the only barn in the state with an octagonal roof—exhibits trace the history of Westport from the days of the Native Americans to the present.

Murals in South Norwalk depicting city life in earlier centuries.

TO DO

BICYCLING

The Sound Cyclists Bicycle Club (203-847-5541), 12 Camelot Drive, Unit D, Norwalk. Year-round rides along scenic back roads and the coastline in Fairfield County. Call for schedules and locations of that day's routes.

BOATING

Norwalk Cove Marina (203-838-2326), Calf Pasture Beach Road, Norwalk. Open year-round. Dry dock, full supply and repair services, 400 slips.

Rex Marine Center (203-831-5234), 144 Water Street, South Norwalk. Open year-round. Dry dock, full services, 676 slips.

White Bridge Marina (203-838-9038), 169 Rowayton Avenue, Norwalk. Open year-round. Full service, dry dock, 30 slips.

BOAT EXCURSIONS

Island Cruise Lines (203-838-9444), 144 Water Street, South Norwalk. Memorial Day through Labor Day. The 60-passenger *Island Girl* departs on 30-minute narrated cruises to **Sheffield Island,** a 3-acre oasis in the outer harbor, where guided tours of the historic lighthouse are offered. Bring a picnic and stroll along the beach. Private charters available April through October.

Belle Island Harbor Cruises (203-855-9326), Beach Road, East Norwalk. Charters April through December.

Norwalk Yacht Charter (203-852-7092), Norwalk. Open Memorial Day through September. Charter broker for crewed yachts; half-day, day, and overnight trips available. Reservations required.

FISHING
Fishing boats may be chartered in Norwalk Harbor from: **Miss Nora** (203-866-9671), Ischoda Dock, South Norwalk, Capt. Don Kovacs; **My Bonnie Charters** (203-866-6313), Village Creek, Norwalk, Capt. Sal Tardella.

Norwalk Recreation and Parks Department (203-854-7806). Call for locations of 18 offshore islands where you can fish, swim, picnic, or bird-watch.

GOLF
Oak Hills Country Club (203-838-0303), 165 Fillow Street, Norwalk. Par 71, 18 holes, 6,382 yards.

HIKING/RUNNING
Sierra Club (203-847-7869), Norwalk. A wide variety of organized hikes year-round, from walks along Norwalk Harbor to more rigorous treks on the Appalachian Trail. Special trips for singles, seniors, families, and students; call for schedules.

Lightfoot Running Club (203-854-7806), South Norwalk. Year-round events. Races in summer.

See also *Green Space.*

SAILING
Longshore Sailing School (203-226-4646), 260 South Compo Road, Westport. Sailing lessons for all skill levels; reservations required. Sailboat, canoe, rowboat, and windsurfer rentals available.

Norwalk Sailing School (203-852-1857), Calf Pasture Beach, Norwalk. Private and group lessons for all skill levels; sailboat and sea kayak rentals available. Call for reservations.

Women's Sailing Adventures (203-227-7413), Saugatuck Harbor, Westport. Open June through Labor Day. Day courses for all levels; longer courses and weekend sails available. Reservations required.

Sound Sailing Center (203-838-1110), 160 Water Street, Norwalk. Certified instruction in Norwalk Harbor. Sailboat rentals and charters.

See also *Boat Excursions.*

SEA KAYAKING
Norwalk Islands Sea Kayaking Tours (203-866-6771), 160 Water Street, South Norwalk. Day and overnight paddling trips for all skill levels; winter seal trips on Long Island Sound available for experienced paddlers. Call for reservations.

The Small Boat Shop (203-854-5223), 144 Water Street, South Norwalk. Day trips for beginning kayakers and experienced paddlers around the Norwalk Islands, a string of islands stretching from Stamford to Westport along the coastline. Instruction and equipment provided; bring lunch and water. Call for information and reservations. May through October, weekends only.

The Lockwood-Mathews Mansion in Norwalk has been meticulously restored.

SWIMMING

Sherwood Island State Park (203-226-6983), Westport, exit 18 off I-95. Of the state's three major Long Island Sound beach parks, this one is the closest to New York City. The gentle surf along the 2-mile strand is ideal for children. Indulge in their food service or bring a picnic basket. Tables and grills are set, perhaps a bit too closely, in groves of beachside trees. Fishing, hiking. Parking fee. On sizzling weekends in July, arrive early. After 11 AM, you're likely to find the parking lots filled and the gates shut.

Calf Pasture Beach (203-854-7806), Norwalk. The beach is open Memorial Day through Labor Day for swimming, sailing, windsurfing. Fishing pier. $15 per car for all-day parking.

TENNIS

Norwalk Recreation and Parks Department (203-854-7806). Forty-eight tennis courts in town parks, along with ice-skating ponds, sledding hills, cross-country skiing. Call for locations.

WINDSURFING

Gone With the Wind, Inc. (203-852-1857), Calf Pasture Beach, Norwalk. Windsurfer lessons at Weed Beach in Darien during the summer months; call for schedule. If you're agile and swift enough, you may be invited to join one of the weekly races held throughout the summer.

GREEN SPACE

NATURE CENTERS

The Nature Center for Environmental Activities (203-227-7253), 10 Woodside Lane, Westport. Open Monday through Saturday 9–5, Sunday 1–4; closed major holidays. Grounds open daily, dawn to dusk. Donation suggested: adults $1; children 50 cents. A 62-acre wooded retreat in the suburbs. Hiking, cross-country skiing, canoeing. Hands-on exhibits for children. Nature programs; call for schedule.

Lucius Pond Ordway, Devil's Den Preserve, Pent Road, Weston. Open daily, sunrise to sunset. One of 52 preserves in Connecticut owned by The Nature Conservancy, this is the largest nature preserve in southwestern Connecticut—1,600 acres of woods, valleys, and rock ledges laced with streams and swamps. Conscientious birders can spot 145 species along 21 miles of marked trails. There are 23 species of mammals, too, including the red fox, the bobcat, and the now ubiquitous coyote, not to mention reptiles and salamanders. Gardeners delight in identifying myriad trees and wildflowers. Archaeologists have uncovered the site of prehistoric Native American encampments.

Devil's Den Nature Conservancy (203-223-4991), Weston. A 1,746-acre wooded oasis offering 21 miles of well-marked trails for hiking, birding, cross-country skiing. Hikers on the Ambler Trail are rewarded with a spectacular vista; it's worth the effort. Call for a schedule of guided hikes.

Woodcock Nature Center (203-762-7280), 56 Deer Run Road, Wilton. Grounds open daily, sunrise to sunset; call for nature center hours. A 146-acre nature preserve invites visitors to hike along 2.5 miles of trails and on a swamp board across rich wetlands forested with maple, oak, and hickory. An Interpretive Center, with exhibits and a small store overlooking scenic Woodcock Pond, offers birding, lectures, and year-round outdoor recreation programs, such as cross-country-skiing clinics.

PARKS

The Norwalk green on East Avenue is a classic, 2-acre colonial village green in the midst of what has become a major bustling urban area on US 1, the Post Road. Bring a lawn chair or blanket in summer for the free concerts and other special events organized by First District Water Department, Norwalk (203-847-7387).

Cranbury Park (203-854-7806), Grumman Avenue, Norwalk. The parks department maintains 130 acres of preserve with walking and hiking trails, picnic groves, and even cross-country skiing when nature cooperates.

LODGING

INNS

The Inn at National Hall (203-221-1351; 1-800-NAT-HALL), 2 Post Road West, Westport 06880. In the historic district. Go for the history, treat yourself to one of the state's remarkable culinary experiences, and stay for the night. The stately brick Italianate building dating back to 1873 was, in succession, a bank, plumbing business, newspaper office, high school, and state police headquarters. The Hall was rescued from the wrecking ball by Arthur Tauck, of the pioneering, Westport-based Tauck Tours company, and converted at a cost of $15 million into what is being hailed as a European manor house on the banks of the Saugatuck River. The 15 lavishly designed and furnished rooms and suites boast 18-foot-high ceilings. Exceptional restaurant (see *Dining Out*). Continental breakfast. $225–625.

Silvermine Tavern (203-847-4558), 194 Perry Avenue, Norwalk 06850, exit 40-A off the Merritt Parkway or exit 15 off I-95. This 1785 hostel at the edge of a rushing waterfall is what you probably had in mind when you conjured up an image of a Connecticut country inn. Antiques in each of the 11 cozy rooms (one suite); all have private bath. Two of the rooms have porches overlooking the river, and there are working fireplaces in the parlor and dining room. Continental breakfast for house guests. Highly acclaimed restaurant (see *Dining Out*). $95–115.

The Inn at Longshore (203-226-3316), 260 Compo Road South, Westport 06880. A clapboard Victorian on Long Island Sound, built in the 1890s as a summer estate. Today it offers 12 guest rooms with three suites; all have private bath. Outdoor pool and privileges at the town beach for nonresident guests. Tennis, golf, and access to boating. Continental breakfast. $125–195.

♿ **Westport Inn** (203-259-5236), 1595 Post Road East, Westport 06880. Fitness center with sauna, whirlpool, and indoor swimming pool; 116 rooms (two suites). $103–159; special senior discounts.

Norwalk Inn & Conference Center (203-838-5531), 99 East Avenue, Norwalk 06851. Offers 71 rooms, three suites. Outdoor pool and barbecue pits. Restaurant and coffee shop. $50–94.

MOTEL

Garden Park Motel (203-847-7303), 351 Westport Avenue, Norwalk 06851. Offers 21 rooms, picnic area. $55–75.

WHERE TO EAT

DINING OUT

In Westport

♿ **Da Pietro's** (203-454-1213), 36 Riverside Avenue, Westport. Dinner Monday through Saturday 5–10; lunch on request. Closed Sunday. Step through the door of this tiny storefront into a romantic, elegant trattoria adorned with simple wall tapestries. Chef-owner Pietro Scotti has made an art of the cuisine of northern Italy and southern France, with an award-winning menu that includes a variety of veal dishes, game in season, and duck. His roast rack of lamb ranks with the best in the Gold Coast. Reservations recommended. Prix fixe $38.95; à la carte $15–25.95.

♿ **Café Christina** (203-221-7950), One Main Street, Westport. Open for lunch Wednesday through Sunday; dinner Tuesday through Sunday. Closed Monday. French and Italian bistro. Start with roasted red beets on shaved fennel, orange, and arugula, or baked polenta with a rosemary

Gorgonzola sauce. For entrées, the sesame-seared yellowfin tuna with vegetable–basmati rice and the grilled Black Angus sirloin *au poivre* are especially well prepared. An elegant café with a changing menu. $16–25; prix fixe menu $29.

Sakura (203-222-0802), 680 Post Road, Westport. Watch the chef deftly cook your dinner on the hibachi, or you can relax in tatami rooms nibbling on sushi. One of the best traditional Japanese restaurants in the state. Reservations suggested. $12–20.

&. **The Restaurant at National Hall** (203-221-7572), Two Post Road West, Westport. Open daily for lunch and dinner; Sunday brunch. Start your meal in the elegant dining rooms with truffle-scented white bean and vegetable soup followed by grilled wild striped bass on soft herb polenta or roasted chicken with eggplant and kasha with spiced chicken crépinette. Hot espresso soufflé and dark chocolate and banana brûlée are among the works of art that grace the dessert menu. This is only a sampling of the lavish cuisine that has won the praise of local celebrities and visiting gourmets. $17.50–26.50.

&. **Bridge Cafe** (203-226-4800), Five Riverside Avenue, Westport. Lunch and dinner daily; Sunday brunch. An airy, sophisticated space on the west bank of the Saugatuck River, with plush Oriental rugs on tile floors, handcrafted wooden tables, and adobe hues reminicent of Santa Fe. The cuisine is a visual match for the surroundings—artful and elegant. The appetizers might include Belgian endive with Roquefort and roasted walnuts; among the entrées may be grilled tuna with mango salsa and saffron risotto or herb-crusted lamb alongside roasted root vegetables. From the outdoor patio, diners have a view of its namesake bridge. $16–28.

Clemente's (203-222-8955), 256 Post Road East, Westport. Open daily for lunch and dinner. Enjoy northern Italian cuisine in elegant surroundings. Pasta, chicken, veal, and seafood complement the pride of the chef: zuppa di pesce, an enticing combination of a variety of fresh fish in red or white sauce. $9.95–15.95.

&. **Beach House** (203-226-7005), 233 Hillspoint Road, Westport. Open daily; closed Tuesday in winter. The view through the windows of this old house may be Long Island Sound, but the all-shellfish bouillabaisse will conjure up images of the Mediterranean and the jambalaya will certainly carry you back to lazy days in Montego Bay. Other specialties: lobster and scallop étouffée, soft-shell crabs, grouper with mango papaya salsa. $16.50–25.

&. **Sole e Luna Ristorante Toscana** (203-222-3837), 25 Powers Court, Westport (next to the Westport Country Playhouse; see *Entertainment*). Lunch and dinner Monday through Friday; dinner Saturday. Closed Sunday. The name tells it all—northern Italian cuisine served in the style of Tuscany. The osso buco ranks with the famed dish of Carbone's in Hartford. The wood-burning brick oven is used for roasting red snapper, pompano, and sea bass. Polenta and couscous might replace pasta as a bed for entrée specials. $15–26.

Tavern on Main (203-221-7222), 146 Main Street, Westport. Open daily for lunch and dinner. Innovative takes on traditonal Yankee fare in an elegant 1810 sea captain's home with low-beamed ceilings, dark wood floors, and double-sided fireplace. Start with the tavern's award-winning New England clam chowder, then try the Maine scallops with grilled leeks dressed in a pepper vinaigrette, or the Parmesan-herb-crusted lamb chops with vegetable ratatouille. Leave room for desserts like chocolate soufflé cake and house-made ice cream. Reservations suggested. Entrées $15–24.

&   **Three Bears Restaurant** (203-227-7219), 333 Wilton Road, Westport. Open Tuesday through Sunday for lunch and dinner; closed Monday. Tiffany lamps and a priceless collection of antique glass set a Victorian mood in the six dining rooms of this popular eatery. Chef Steve Vazzano's award-winning contemporary cuisine garners rave reviews from locals and critics. The innovative seasonal menu includes many seafood, pasta, and game choices. You might start with a beggar's purse stuffed with Maine lobster, sweet corn, and asparagus with a wild leek and cheddar sauce; and continue to grilled pork tenderloin in a ginger-mustard sauce, or pan-roasted rabbit with polenta, seared spinach, and shallots. Desserts come highly recommended. $14–25.

In Norwalk

Pasta Nostra Trattoria & Pasta Store (203-854-9700), 116 Washington Street, South Norwalk. Open for dinner only, Wednesday through Saturday. An intimate trattoria with a weekly menu emphasizing traditional food: *baccala al forna, pasta con sarde*, but also many original dishes. Reservations suggested. $16–29.

Silvermine Tavern (203-847-4558), 194 Perry Avenue, Norwalk. Open for lunch and dinner; Sunday brunch. Closed Tuesday. Classic New England tavern with creaky wide floorboards. A great place for chicken potpie or seafood capellini, roast boned half duckling, crab-stuffed fillet of sole with shrimp risotto or filet mignon with onion-garlic potato cakes. Innkeeper Frank Whitman Jr. is proud of his Sunday brunches. Dine on the terrace overlooking the waterfall and duck pond in warm weather. Take care—don't fill up on the honey buns. The tavern runs a country store across the street selling New England foods and gifts; a collection of antique tools and Currier & Ives prints are on display. (The tavern also features 11 rooms; see *Lodging*.) $14.50–24.95.

&   **Cote d'Azur** (203-855-8900), 86 Washington Street, Norwalk. Open for lunch and dinner. Country French Provençal cuisine, which translates into lavish use of olive oil, garlic, and fresh tomatoes, as well as dishes sauced with heavy cream. Some favorites with loyal guests: confit of duck, bouillabaisse, pan-seared lamb, rabbit in red wine sauce. Reservations suggested. $25 prix fixe dinner; $11–18 à la carte.

&   **Ganga Haute Cuisine of India** (203-838-0660), 41 Wall Street, Norwalk. Lunch and dinner daily. Proud of its "royal" dishes such as Chicken Mougli, tender chicken in a curry cream sauce, fit for a Mogul prince.

Tandoori lamb as well as the more traditional tandoori chicken. Another house specialty is the *dosa*—a lentil pancake stuffed with potatoes, chicken, or lamb. Reservations suggested. $9.95 for vegetarian dishes to $14.95 for the lamb.

In Weston

Cobb's Mill Inn (203-227-7221), CT 57, Old Mill Road, Weston. Lunch and dinner Tuesday through Friday; dinner only on Saturday; brunch and dinner Sunday. Nine dining rooms in a rambling, 200-year-old mill building overlooking the Saugatuck River waterfall. If you've just come in from riding to the hounds, try the game specialties. The house specialty, however, is Chicken Williamsburg, which bears no relation to the famous Brunswick chicken stew served in Colonial Williamsburg. Here chicken breasts are deftly stuffed with apples, nuts, and raisins. Other favorites are grilled swordfish and grilled salmon. $16–26.50.

EATING OUT

In Westport

&✐**Onion Alley** (203-226-0794), 42 Main Street, Westport. Open daily for lunch and dinner; Sunday brunch. In the midst of Westport's Main Street shops, tucked down a quiet brick alley behind wrought-iron gates, is a friendly place that is ideal for families—the menu has something to please everyone. One person can nosh on a burger with crisp onion rings, another can dine on medallions of filet mignon topped with Gorgonzola and sauced with green pepper bordelaise. Sandwiches around $6; entrées $12–18.

&☞**Panda Pavilion**. Four locations: 1300 Post Road East, Westport (203-255-3988); 370 Main Avenue, Norwalk (203-846-4253); 923 Post Road, Fairfield (203-259-9777); 137 West Putnam Avenue, Greenwich (203-869-1111). Open daily. Pat the stone pandas on the head at the entrance to these roomy and airy Chinese food emporiums. Szechuan and Hunan specialties, which translates into spicy hot. General Tso's chicken is a good choice. If you've shied away from eggplant, you're in for a nice surprise. The dish called Dragon and Phoenix, a combination of lobster meat and chicken in a Hunan sauce, is also very popular. Entrées $7–16.

☞ **Pal Joey's Restaurant** (203-223-9979), 383 Post Road East (US 1), Westport. Open Monday through Saturday for breakfast and lunch. A friendly, no-frills luncheonette offering homemade rice pudding, cakes, and daily specials. Come on Monday for the *avgolemono*, a traditional Greek soup of chicken broth, beaten egg yolks, lemon juice, and rice. Breakfast special $2.75; lunch around $5.

In Norwalk

☞&**Siam Rialto** (203-855-7855), 128 Washington Street, South Norwalk. A turn-of-the-century movie house (theater balcony and brass railings intact) is now a popular Thai eatery. Open for lunch and dinner Monday through Saturday; dinner only on Sunday. Try the wild boar flavored with garlic and curry. (It's really pork tenderloin, not "wild" at all.) Special sauces from Thailand and specialties like coconut soup distinguish the dishes from Chinese. All meals are prepared hot, medium, or, for wimps, mild. $6–16.

   ᕕ **SoNo's Little Kitchen** (203-855-8515), 49 South Main Street, South
Norwalk. Authentic Jamaican fare—try the codfish fritters, oxtails, or
curried goat. Traditional spicy patties (beef, vegetable, or chicken) will
sauté the lining of your stomach. $6–10.

   ᕕ **The Brewhouse Restaurant** (203-853-9110), at the New England Brewing Co., 13 Marshall Street, South Norwalk. Lunch and dinner served
daily in a 1920s factory-turned-brewery. If you have always hankered to
watch beer brewed, the tables in this fun place are grouped around the
kettles where the fermentation takes place before your very eyes. All the
while you can fill your tummy with brewpub fare: sandwiches, grilled
meats, German specialties. Tours of the brewery are available. $7–16.

   ᕕ **Amberjacks** (203-853-4332), 99 Washington Street, South Norwalk. Lunch
and dinner daily. No, the bar is not setting sail for distant waters—it's just
shaped like the prow of a ship. In keeping with this nautical icon, the
menu highlights Pacific Northwest seafood stew, a variety of dishes
featuring mussels and scallops, and grilled yellowfin tuna with celery–
white bean salsa and a pepper-tomato-mango relish. Start your meal
with Maryland crab and noodle cakes or oysters in a shot glass topped
with gazpacho salsa. $8–20.

   ᕕ **Barcelona** (203-854-9699), 63 North Main Street, South Norwalk. Dinner
until midnight. Tapas are moving to center stage in Connecticut's
newest restaurants, and diners are raving over Barcelona's risotto cakes
stuffed with artichokes and fontina cheese, as well as the calamari salad
with baby tomatoes. Full entrées run the gamut from steaks to pasta to
fish, all with a Mediterranean touch, which translates into garlic and olive
oil. Beautiful outdoor patio. $13–19.

      Lighthouse (203-847-7500), 2 Wilton Avenue, Norwalk. Nautical atmo-
sphere in a converted hat factory. International cuisine, pasta, beef, and
chicken, with an emphasis on fresh seafood and authentic German specialties, such as Wiener schnitzel with rösti. Raw oyster and clam bar. Sip
your cocktails on the deck overlooking the Norwalk River. $13–16.

   ᕕ **Swanky Frank's** (203-838-8969), 182 Connecticut Avenue, Norwalk. Open
daily. Famous since the 1940s for its "swanky" hot dogs.

SNACKS

      Gold's Delicatessen (203-227-0101), 421 Post Road East (US 1), West-
port. This Jewish-style deli has been a neighborhood icon since 1959.
Knishes, chicken soup with matzo balls, pastrami, corned beef, New
York cheesecake. Seat yourself at the back of the store—you're likely to
rub elbows with some very loyal patrons.

   ᕕ **Hay Day** (203-254-5220), 1385 Post Road East, Westport. Gourmet store
and upscale country farm market with satellites in Greenwich, Fairfield,
Hamden, and Milford. Open daily 8–8; Sunday until 7. Full meals, soups
salads, and baked goods to take home, or seat yourself at a café table or
on the outdoor patio. The sweet potato and chile vichyssoise and grilled
vegetable gazpacho from the summer menu are particularly delicious.
(See also *Selective Shopping.*)

&☞**Deli-Land's Seaport** (203-838-6492), 88 Washington Street, South Norwalk. Lunch and dinner daily. Kosher pastrami, tongue, corned beef sandwiches, dill pickles, and other deli standards. Red-and-white-checked tablecloths for those eating in.

& **Uncommon Grounds** (203-855-0441), 124 Washington Street, South Norwalk. Open daily for breakfast, lunch, pastries, and, of course, coffee. A funky gathering spot for SoNo's hip set. For breakfast, try the country French toast with raspberry honey sauce. Lunch means generous sandwiches, soups, and salads, eaten at copper or black marble café tables. Sandwiches around $5.

&☞**L'Epicure** (203-544-6000), 991 Danbury Road (US 7), Wilton. Open daily. Gourmet deli/grocery/bakery serving a daily changing selection of healthful items with accents of France, Italy, and the Middle East. Grilled vegetables with house-made mozzarella, hummus on pita, or a baguette filled with pork, sliced apples, and melted Swiss might be on the menu. $4–7.

ENTERTAINMENT

The **Fairfield Orchestra** (203-255-1011) and the **Norwalk Symphony** (203-866-2455) are two outstanding orchestras that perform in the acoustically renowned auditorium attached to the **Norwalk City Hall** (203-854-7746). In addition to their own performances, they host visiting musical groups and guest soloists.

Levitt Pavilion for the Performing Arts (203-226-7600), off Jessup Road, behind the Westport Library in downtown Westport. About 60 free performances staged in an outdoor setting June through August. Special ticketed events; call for schedule.

White Barn Theatre (203-227-3768), Newtown Turnpike, Westport.

Westport Country Playhouse (203-227-4177), 25 Powers Court, Westport. A popular summer theater for nearly 70 years.

SELECTIVE SHOPPING

Hay Day (203-254-5220), 1385 Post Road East, Westport. Every gourmet grocery item imaginable, plus an impressive selection of fresh produce and herbs. A popular spot for take-out lunch and dinner. Other locations along the shoreline (See also *Snacks*.)

✍ **Stew Leonard's Dairy** (203-847-7213), 100 Westport Avenue (US 1), Norwalk. A dairy in a guidebook? A fair question. What started out as a small milk mart has evolved into a grocery amusement park. Foods of every variety from all over the world, including a fabulous hot bar, complete with animated cows, singing farm animals, and cartoon characters. The sign evident on entering proclaims that the customer is king. A squad of security guards is necessary to prevent traffic gridlock in the parking lots. A sister store, modeled after the original but with wider

South Norwalk's Washington Street—19th century factories turned upscale shopping and dining.

aisles, now operates in Danbury, just off I-84 and US 7, and is just as mobbed. The King of Chickens says Leonard's sells more Perdue birds than any other store in the world!

Cannondale Village (203-762-2233), 30 Cannon Road, Wilton, off US 7 north of the Merritt Parkway. Open Tuesday through Sunday 11–5. A small collection of restored pre–Civil War buildings offering antiques, collectibles, crafts, and gourmet food in an old New England schoolhouse.

ANTIQUES

Parc Monceau (203-319-0001), 1375 Post Road East (US 1), Westport. Country French antiques, furnishings, wallcoverings.

Aladdin of Westport (203-222-8770), Nine Post Road West, Westport. Antique Persian and Caucasian rugs.

Curran & Curran (203-762-9662), 444 Danbury Road (US 7), Wilton. American antiques, furnishings, paintings, and decorative arts of the 17th, 18th, and 19th centuries.

Sign of the Cat (203-838-1421), 75 Cedar Street, Norwalk. This shop features an eclectic selection of antiques, collectibles, glassware, toys, and memorabilia.

Eagle's Lair Antiques (203-846-1159), 565 Westport Avenue (US 1), Norwalk. American antiques, unique items.

BOOKSTORES

Klein's of Westport (203-226-4261), 44-50 Main Street, Westport. A wide stock of new books for adults and children.

Hannslik & Wegner (203-454-7750), 20 Railroad Place, Westport (across from the train station). Specializes in language studies, literature in foreign languages, and travel. Impressive selection of maps.

SPECIAL EVENTS

Throughout the year: **Antiques shows**—indoors, outdoors, and in armories but most often in local historical societies throughout the region (check local newspaper listings). **Gallery openings** are pandemic. **Concerts** on village greens in the summer months.

July: **Round Hill Highland Scottish Games** (203-324-1094), Cranbury Park, Norwalk. Tossing the caber, bagpipe competitions, parade of the clans in their distinctive tartans. Scottish food, oatmeal cookies, but definitely not haggis. Jackie Robinson Foundation's **Afternoon of Jazz** (203-624-0033), Cranbury Park, Norwalk.

July: **Fireworks and concert** (203-854-7806), Calf Pasture Beach Park, Norwalk. **Victorian Ice Cream Social** (203-838-1434), Lockwood-Mathews Mansion, Norwalk. For a quintessential New England summer experience, take the family to the **Norwalk Seaport Clambake** (203-838-9444) for games, entertainment, dancing, and the food.

August: **SoNo Arts Celebration Weekend.** The artisans and restaurateurs along Washington Street invite you to a juried arts and crafts show, a kinetic sculpture race, and, for the children, an art playground. The weekend winds up with an exuberant block party. The celebration starts on Washington Street and spills out onto North and South Main Streets. Call 203-866-7916 for information.

September: Enjoy crafts and top entertainers at **Norwalk Seaport's 4-Day Oyster Festival** in Veterans Memorial Park. Tour tall ships in port.

December: The halls, rooms, and rotunda of the Lockwood-Mathews Mansion are decorated for its **Victorian Christmas Celebration.** Boutique and entertainment. There are **First Night** celebrations in both South Norwalk (203-866-7925) and Westport (203-454-6699).

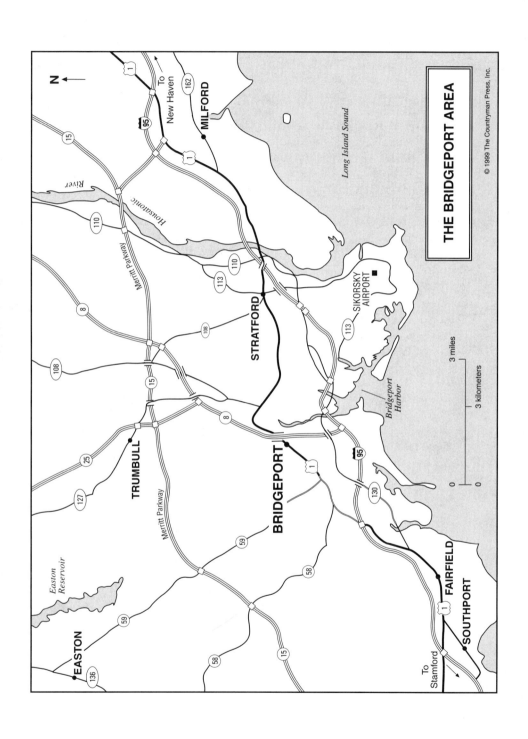

N

THE BRIDGEPORT AREA

© 1999 The Countryman Press, Inc.

Long Island Sound

Housatonic River

MILFORD

To New Haven

STRATFORD

SIKORSKY AIRPORT

Bridgeport Harbor

BRIDGEPORT

TRUMBULL

Merritt Parkway

Merritt Parkway

EASTON

Easton Reservoir

FAIRFIELD

SOUTHPORT

To Stamford

3 miles

3 kilometers

0

0

The Bridgeport Area

One of the oldest, and still the largest, city in Connecticut, Bridgeport was for years an industrial giant. Its bustling factories fed America's war machines since the Civil War. During its golden period, Phineas Taylor (P.T.) Barnum, the legendary circus impresario and creator of the Greatest Show on Earth, made Bridgeport his home and served as its mayor. He later contributed most of his estates to the city as parks, hence the nickname Park City. But even before the Cold War ended, industry slipped away to the South and to Asia.

Today working-class Bridgeport stands in stark contrast to its stylish neighbors. Much of this port city is now littered with empty, deteriorating factories and depressed neighborhoods. To prevent the University of Bridgeport from going under, it was taken over by an Asian religious community. However, an earnest revitalization is under way, and the city is dotted with unique attractions that lure thousands of visitors annually. The Barnum Museum and annual Barnum Festival honor the famous show-biz entrepreneur; the "please touch" Discovery Museum and the state's largest zoo appeal to the young and young-at-heart. Captain's Cove Seaport on Black Rock Harbor has a marina, restaurant, and boardwalk shops, a popular family destination. The city also supports a professional baseball team, as well as performances by an active thespian community and the acclaimed Bridgeport Symphony. Bridgeport is now a city rife with potential.

You can explore the affluent residental towns of Fairfield, Stratford, and Trumbull by visiting their nature centers and carefully preserved historic homes. Fairfield, founded in 1639, was one of the earliest settlements along the old Post Road linking Boston and Philadelphia. Today the presence of Fairfield University has fostered a respectable arts community. Its town green, with steepled churches and elegant white town hall, offers a glimpse of colonial history amid the Gold Coast's suburban sprawl.

Entries in this section are arranged in roughly geographic order.

AREA CODE
203

GUIDANCE
Coastal Fairfield County Tourism District (203-840-0770; 1-800-473-4868), MerrittView, 383 Main Avenue, Norwalk 06851 (Web site:

http://visitfairfieldco.org).
   Greater New Haven Convention & Visitors District (203-777-8550; 1-800-332-7829), 59 Elm Street, New Haven 06510 (Web site: www.newhavencvb.org).

GETTING THERE

By car: The Bridgeport area is accessible by car from I-95; the Merritt Parkway; US 1, the heavily trafficked historic Post Road that passes through the centers of towns and cities; and the superhighway CT 8 from the north.

By air: Visitors can fly USAir Express into **Igor Sikorsky Memorial Airport** (203-576-7498), Great Meadows Road, in nearby Stratford.

By train: **AMTRAK**'s (1-800-872-7245) mainline trains running from Boston to New York and Washington make scheduled stops at Bridgeport's main station. There is frequent service to New York City by **Metro-North** (1-800-638-7646), the busiest commuter line in the world. Four daily connecting trains make local stops up the Naugatuck Valley to Waterbury.

By ferry: The **Bridgeport & Port Jefferson Steamboat Co.** (1-888-44-FERRY) runs daily car and 1,000-passenger ferries between Bridgeport and Port Jefferson on the North Shore of Long Island.

GETTING AROUND

Taxi service in Bridgeport: **Ace Cab Co.** (203-334-6161) and **Bridgeport Taxi Service** (203-368-0529). **Fairfield Cab Co.** (203-255-5797) serves the greater Bridgeport and shoreline areas.

MEDICAL EMERGENCY

The statewide emergency number is **911.**

Bridgeport Hospital (203-384-3000), 267 Grant Street, Bridgeport. The emergency number is 203-384-3566.

St. Vincent's Medical Center (203-576-6000), 2800 Main Street, Bridgeport. The emergency number is 203-576-5171.

TO SEE

MUSEUMS

Barnum Museum (203-331-9881), 820 Main Street, Bridgeport. Open year-round, Tuesday through Saturday 10–4:30, Sunday noon–4:30; Monday during July and August 10–4:30. Closed major holidays. Adults $5; seniors and students $4; children $3. The Byzantine–Romanesque Revival building was a gift of Bridgeport's most famous citizen, the great circus entrepeneur. Inexplicably, the first two floors are devoted to the industrial history of the city; you have to make your way to the third level to view a complete scale model of Barnum's world-famous Three-Ring Circus. Other exhibits and memorabilia tell the story of General Tom Thumb and Jenny Lind, the opera singer Barnum brought to America and sent on wildly successful tours as the Swedish Nightingale. Changing art exhibits are displayed in a new wing. Gift shop. Be advised to park in a nearby garage.

Housatonic Museum of Art (203-332-5203), Housatonic Community-Technical College, 510 Barnum Avenue, Bridgeport. Open September through May, weekdays 8:30–5:30. Free admission. Interesting collection of Hispanic and modern Connecticut art; European and American art of the 19th and 20th centuries; Asian and African collections.

Captain's Cove (203-335-1433), One Bostwick Avenue, Bridgeport, on Black Rock Harbor, just west of Bridgeport Harbor. Open daily April through October. Restaurant, boardwalk shops, fishing charters, and boat rides. Climb aboard and tour a full-size sailing replica of the 22-gun frigate HMS *Rose,* a British man-of-war whose attacks on American ships and bombardments of New England shore towns forced Washington to order the building of a navy for the Continental armed forces. The *Rose* is the world's largest wooden square-rigger afloat. (Call ahead to see if she's in port.) Ask to see a replica in an adjacent shed of the airplane invented by Bridgeport native Gustave Whitehead, whom locals claim flew before the Wright brothers' historic flight at Kitty Hawk.

Discovery Museum (203-372-3521), 4450 Park Avenue, Bridgeport. Year-round, Tuesday through Saturday 10–5, Sunday noon–5; Monday in July and August. Closed major holidays. Adults $6; seniors, children, and students $4. Easily one of the most "child-friendly" museums in the country, with its 100 hands-on science exhibits. Youngsters can learn all about the stars in one of the state's few planetariums. The Challenger Learning Center is devoted to space travel and honors the memory of the *Challenger* crew. Make reservations for computer-simulated rocket ship space missions. Gift shop and food court.

Catherine B. Mitchell Museum (203-378-0630), 967 Academy Hill, Stratford. Open mid-May through October, Wednesday, Saturday, and Sunday 11–4. Adults $2.50; seniors $1.50. Native American artifacts, early African American history, baskets, story of the town's soldiers who fought with the British in the French and Indian War. Extensive genealogy library open Tuesday and Thursday 9–2.

HISTORIC HOMES

Captain David Judson House (203-378-0630), 967 Academy Hill, Stratford. Open mid-May through October, Wednesday, Saturday, and Sunday 11–4; other times by appointment. Captain Judson built this circa-1750 Georgian home on the site of his great-grandfather's 1639 stone house. Collection of farm and craft tools; home of the Stratford Historical Society.

Ogden House & Gardens (203-259-1598), 1520 Bronson Road, Fairfield. Open mid-May through mid-October, Saturday and Sunday 1–4:30. Adults $2; children $1. Kitchen and wildflower gardens at an 18th-century saltbox farmhouse.

The Barnum Museum in Bridgeport

HISTORIC SITES

P.T. Barnum Statue in Seaside Park, Bridgeport, depicts "the Greatest Showman on Earth," a Connecticut native, sitting atop a high block of marble and looking out to Long Island Sound in the park he gave to the citizens of Bridgeport. He served as mayor of the city and as a state legislator. Close by is a statue of Elias Howe, the inventor of the sewing machine. Three great Bridgeport showplace homes of Barnum, including Iranistan—a model of a Persian mosque—sadly were all destroyed.

Boothe Memorial Park & Museum (203-381-2046), Main Street Putney, Stratford. Park open June 1 through September, daily 9–5; museum open Tuesday, Thursday, and Friday 11–1; Saturday and Sunday 1–4. Free admission. Two wealthy, eccentric brothers left a 32-acre estate with a collection of 20 buildings and exhibits that can only be described as, well, eccentric. There's nothing quite like it in all of New England, where eccentricity is commonplace. The Blacksmith Shop has 44 corners and 44 sides and houses 2,000 ancient implements. The brothers loved lighthouses, so they built a model lighthouse. The outdoor basilica and organ house have attracted 4,000 people to Easter sunrise services. The Technocratic Cathedral defies description. The Clock Tower Museum houses hundreds of artifacts collected by the brothers during their world travels. The Boothe Homestead is listed on the National Register of Historic Places.

ZOO

Beardsley Zoological Gardens (203-394-6565), Noble Avenue, Beardsley Park, Bridgeport. Open year-round, daily 9–4. Closed Thanksgiving, Christmas, New Year's. Adults $5; children and seniors $3; children under 3 free. A 36-acre nature preserve just off CT 8, Beardsley is the largest zoo in Connecticut. But it is ideal for families, for it is relatively small compared to the big zoos in New York, and many New Yorkers find a day here less tiring for the children. Especially for the youngsters, the zoo has a rustic New England farmyard with goats and bunnies to feed and pet, friendly cows, pony rides, and a children's stage. Wildlife includes the timber wolf, mountain lion, and bison; boa constrictors and rain forest animals in the New World Tropics building; plus 120 other species of animals including the exotic Siberian tiger. New operating replica carousel and carousel horse exhibit; snack bar and gift shop. Special events.

TO DO

BALLOONING

Connecticut Yankee Balloons (203-255-1929), 120 Flax Road, Fairfield. Hot-air-balloon flights over the Litchfield Hills, central Connecticut, and the Housatonic and Naugatuck River valleys. Year-round, weather permitting. Call for reservations.

BOATING

Captain's Cove Marina (203-335-1433), Black Rock Harbor, Bridgeport. Open year-round. Full services, restaurant, and shops along a lively waterfront boardwalk.

Cedar Marina (203-335-6262), 86 Bostwick Avenue, in Black Rock Harbor, Bridgeport. Open May through October. Full services, snack bar.

Hitchcock Marina (203-334-2161), 40 California Street, Bridgeport. Open year-round. Full services, snack bar.

FISHING

Charter boats are available for hire for various fishing excursions. In the area are the following: **Somertime Sport Fishing** (203-438-5838), Captain's Cove Marina, Black Rock Harbor, Bridgeport, Capt. Bill Somers; **Reel Thing Charters** (203-375-8623), Captain's Cove Marina, Bridgeport, Capt. Jim Ring; **Outdoor Recreation Services** (203-336-9117), 244 Melody Lane, Fairfield, offers fishing and/or cruising trips from several Fairfield County ports, Capt. John Jensen; **Mako Charters** (203-261-8821), Birdseye Ramp, Stratford, Capt. Robert Leonard.

GOLF

D. Fairchild Wheeler Golf Course (203-373-5911), 2390 Easton Turnpike, Fairfield. Par 71, 36 holes, 6,559 yards.

H. Smith Richardson Golf Course (203-255-7300), 2425 Morehouse Highway, Fairfield. Par 72, 18 holes, 6,676 yards.

KIMBERLY GRANT

Boothe Memorial Park and Museum

Tashua Knolls Golf Club (203-261-5989), 40 Tashua Knolls Lane, Trumbull. Par 72, 18 holes, 6,540 yards.

SPECTATOR SPORTS

Bridgeport Bluefish (203-334-TIXX), The Ballpark at Harbor Yard, Bridgeport. Independent Atlantic League professional baseball team. Games April through September; call for schedule.

Shoreline Star Greyhound Park and Entertainment Complex (203-576-1976), 255 Kossuth Street, Bridgeport. Open year-round for matinee and evening events. Call for schedules. This dog track has been built next to the former jai alai fronton. Dogs race outside; patrons sit under shelter. Simulcast horse races are viewed on giant screens inside the fronton building. Terrace dining.

GREEN SPACE

Connecticut Audubon Society's Fairfield Nature Center (203-259-6305), 2325 Burr Street, Fairfield. Sanctuary open daily, dawn to dusk. Nature center, Tuesday through Saturday 9–4:30. Closed major holidays. Admission to the nature center: adults $2; children 50¢. Six miles of trails in 160-acre **Larsen Sanctuary** are free and open to the public.

LODGING

BED & BREAKFAST

Nathan Boothe House (203-378-6489), 6080 Main Street Putney, Stratford 06497. A circa-1843 Greek Revival farmhouse surrounded by large sugar maples, on the National Register of Historic Places. Inn-keepers Jean and Ken Smith offer four guest rooms with period fur-nishings and private baths. Full breakfast is served in the formal dining room or on the open veranda. Common rooms have fireplaces, wide-board chestnut floors, original hand-carved woodwork. $100.

HOTELS/MOTELS

 ♿ **Bridgeport Holiday Inn** (203-334-1234), 1070 Main Street, Bridgeport 06604. In the heart of the city, within walking distance of train and bus stations and the Barnum Museum (see *Museums*). Major hotel with 234 rooms (two suites), health club, indoor pool. Excellent hotel dining room; bountiful Sunday brunch. There's a carnival ambience in the PT (as in P.T. Barnum) Lounge. Free CNN, Showtime, and ESPN in rooms. $109–119.

 ♿ **Trumbull Marriott** (203-378-1400), 180 Hawley Lane, Trumbull 06611. Often the alternate hotel when the downtown Holiday Inn is full. Quiet country setting but close to parkways; 323 rooms, health club, sauna, indoor and outdoor pools. $110–164.

WHERE TO EAT

DINING OUT

In Bridgeport

 ♿ **King & I** (203-374-2081), 545 Broadbridge Road, Bridgeport. Open for lunch Tuesday through Friday 11:30–2; dinner Tuesday through Sunday 5–10. Closed Monday. If you need a crash course in the language of Thailand, Yale has a world-famous Asian language department. Otherwise, ask the friendly waiters to explain the exotic dishes on the menu. Start off with shrimp soup, followed by spiced fish or duck and a vegetable–fried rice combination, happily less oily than traditional Chinese-American fried rice. Or forgo the rice and try the authentic pad Thai noodles or the chicken satay. At your request, many items on the lavish menu can be prepared with spices from mild to hot. Lemongrass appears in most Thai dishes, adding its subtle but distinct flavor. $7.95–14.95.

 ♿ **Ralph 'n Rich's** (203-366-3597), 121 Wall Street, Bridgeport. Open Mon-day through Saturday for lunch and dinner; closed Sunday. Choose from a variety of pastas in a tasteful, high-ceilinged dining room. Start your meal with an excellent hot antipasto. $10–25.

In Stratford

 ♿ **Blue Goose** (203-375-9130), 326 Ferry Boulevard, Stratford. Lunch and dinner served daily. A favorite for years with patrons of the nearby Shakespeare Theatre (soon to be restored). Enjoy fresh, no-frills prime rib and steaks, and fresh seafood in a congenial atmosphere. $9.95–16.95.

 ♿ **Shell Station** (203-377-1648), Main Street at the railroad station, Stratford. Lunch and dinner daily. Acclaimed for its seafood—lobster, shrimp, and scallops—a sushi bar is the eatery's latest venture. Fresh pasta made daily. The name refers to the scalloped seashell, not the gas station. $9.75–16.95.

     Seascape (203-375-2149), 14 Beach Drive, Stratford. Lunch Monday through Friday, dinner daily, brunch on Sunday. A popular waterfront establishment offering a standard, dependable shore menu of seafood, veal, steak, pasta, and chicken with some eclectic deviations—ravioli stuffed with lobster, for example. $8.95–16.95.

In Fairfield

     Cinzano's Inc. (203-367-1199), 1920 Black Rock Turnpike, Fairfield. Daily lunch and dinner. The pink sponged walls set the style as Victorian; the large mural of peasants at harvest bent over in the fields north of Rome flags the cuisine as northern Italian. Sole is layered with eggplant, mushrooms, and mozzarella; veal is sautéed in a wine sauce with peas and sun-dried tomatoes and topped with fresh mozzarella; and chicken Portuguese is a tasty commingling of tomatoes, shrimp, and black olives. $5.95–23.

     Spazzi (203-256-1629), 1229 Post Road, in the Brick Walk Plaza, Fairfield. Lunch and dinner Monday through Saturday; brunch and dinner Sunday. The trompe l'oeil wall and columns give the illusion of stepping back in time to ancient Rome for a meal with Julius Caesar. Favorite northern Italian eatery for an exuberant clientele. Open-to-view wood-fired brick oven. Diners are treated to crusty bread with olive oil and roasted garlic while anticipating the generous portions of hearty yet imaginative pastas, pizzas, and seafood dishes to come. Entrées $13.95–19.95; pizzas around $12.

     Centro (203-255-1210), 1435 Post Road, Fairfield. Lunch Monday through Saturday; dinner daily. High ceilings, white columns, and walls sponged in yellow, pink, and peach create a sophisticated yet relaxing atmosphere that attracts a stylish crowd. An imaginative repertoire of Italian dishes such as portobello mushrooms stuffed with spinach, goat cheese, sun-dried tomatoes, and garlic; penne tossed with shrimp, beans, arugula, and onions and sauced with roasted garlic and olive oil. Hearty thin-crust pizzas. Outdoor seating. Entrées $8–17; pizza around $8.

EATING OUT

In Bridgeport

     Arizona Flats (203-334-8300), 3001 Fairfield Avenue, Bridgeport. Lunch Monday through Saturday; dinner daily. The menu is as close as you can get in Yankeeland to the unique cuisine that has evolved in New Mexico and Arizona. Chicken enchiladas, chiles rellenos, and pork mole poblano are good choices. Chef Dave Hamilton also offers wild-game specials featuring alligator, ostrich, wild boar, and buffalo. We always opt for that superb Mexican beer, Dos Equis. $11.95–16.95.

     Restaurant at Captain's Cove (203-335-7104; takeout: 203-368-3710), One Bostwick Avenue, Bridgeport. Two-level spacious dining rooms serve vast quantities of fish and seafood from the restaurant's own tanks, all accompanied by hearty fries and a bowl of coleslaw. A scale model of a tugboat dominates the center of the second-floor bar. (See also *Museums*.) $2.99–18.95.

In Fairfield

Hunan Pavilion (203-254-3444), 80 Post Road (US 1), Fairfield. Open daily for lunch and dinner. A pleasant, affordable, family-run restaurant on the busy Post Road that's easy to pass by—make the effort to find it. The chefs have mastered the art of concocting a variety of delicate sauces that enhance the beef, chicken, and seafood dishes. No heavy hand here, thankfully, with cornstarch! Buddha's Delight and chicken with pine nuts are especially tasty. A house specialty, Hawaii Five "O," combines lobster meat, jumbo shrimp, scallops, chicken, and beef sautéed with mushrooms, snow peas, water chestnuts, baby corn, and broccoli ($8.95).

 Luigi's (203-259-7816), 170 Post Road, Fairfield. Open daily for lunch and dinner. A family restaurant and pizzeria acclaimed by the locals for its seafood, chicken, and veal, and for its restraint with eggplant Parmesan—a minimum of oil and a sprinkling of cheese. Entrées $8–17.

Elsewhere

 Station House (203-375-6737), 2505 Main Street, in Stationhouse Square, Stratford. Open daily from 6 AM. A lively, no-frills diner that can get noisy when times are busy, but a good place to grab a quick bite before catching the train. Black-and-white train photos and memorabilia lining the walls appeal to railroad buffs, and kids love the red caboose parked outside. Breakfast around $4; sandwiches and entrées $4–10.

Old Towne Pizza (203-261-9436), 20 Quality Street, Town Hall Shopping Plaza, Trumbull. Open daily for three meals. Typically we avoid steering visitors to restaurants in shopping malls, but in this part of crowded Fairfield County, the mall eateries are convenient and they serve quality food. This fine pizza house starts breakfast at 7 AM and is still satisfying diners until 11 PM with steak, seafood, veal, chicken, and a variety of pasta dishes.

SNACKS

In Fairfield

 Along Came Carol (203-254-0200), 1779 Post Road (US 1), Fairfield. Open Tuesday through Saturday 11–8. Renowned caterer Carol Lentini Mojcher offers a daily sampling of her impressive roster of internationally inspired dishes for the public to enjoy. Try the chilled gazpacho, fragrant rosemary focaccia, and a heavenly slice of raspberry shortbread, and you'll understand why she has a loyal clientele along the Gold Coast. Sandwiches and entrées around $6.

 Firehouse Deli (203-255-5527), 22 Reef Road, Fairfield. Open daily. Don't despair at the long line—a cadre of workers busily assembles gargantuan Dagwood-style sandwiches and grinders with amazing speed. Check the blackboard for daily soup, sandwich, and quiche specials. Grab a sidewalk table for prime people-watching. Sandwiches around $5.

 Sprouts for Better Living (203-333-3571), 2250 Black Rock Turnpike, Fairfield. Open daily. An eclectic café with an earnestly healthy menu—the bacon is nitrate-free, the chicken is free-range, the tortilla chips are

Captain's Cove Marina in Bridgeport emphasizes local maritime history and fresh seafood.

organic. Sandwiches with world accents—try a tortilla stuffed with seared tempeh, lemon-curry rice, cashews, and vegetables dressed with coconut curry sauce. Wash it down with a Samurai, an elixir of carrot, spinach, celery, ginger, and garlic. If this overwhelms you, have a burger (organic, of course) and a coffee (ditto).

ENTERTAINMENT

MUSIC
Klein Memorial Auditorium (203-576-8115), 910 Fairfield Avenue, Bridgeport. The city's major auditorium holds concerts by the Greater Bridgeport Symphony (203-576-0263) and the Connecticut Grand Opera and Orchestra (203-327-2867).

Summer Concert Series (203-255-1011), at the Sherman Green Gazebo, Post Road at Reef Road, Fairfield. Free performances Memorial Day through August, Wednesday, Thursday, and Sunday 7 PM. Orchestras, country/western, big band, jazz, polkas, and oldies, under the stars. Call for schedule.

THEATER
Downtown Cabaret Theatre (203-576-1636), 263 Golden Hill Street, Bridgeport. A popular venue for Broadway favorites and original musicals starring professionals. Year-round schedule; children's shows October through May.

The Polka Dot Playhouse (203-333-3666), 167 State Street, Bridgeport. The area's oldest continually running theater. Weekend productions

June through August; call for schedule.

✐ **Quick Center for the Arts** (203-254-4010), North Benson Road, on the campus of Fairfield University, Fairfield. Music, dance, and drama at the Kelly and Wien Experimental Theaters during the school year; summer concerts and children's programs July and August.

SELECTIVE SHOPPING

ANTIQUES SHOPS

Stratford Antique Center (203-378-7754), 400 Honeyspot Road, Stratford. More than 200 dealers, offering a huge selection of antiques and collectibles.

Aaron Marcus Antiques (203-377-2231), 221 Honeyspot Road, Stratford. This shop carries a little of everything: furniture, silver, jewelry, decorative arts.

ART GALLERIES

The Finer Things Gallery (203-367-1533), 892 Wood Avenue, Bridgeport. Open Wednesday through Saturday and by appointment. Changing exhibits showcase textiles, jewelry, pottery, and glass art objects.

Silver Lining (203-334-3773), 181 State Street, on the McLevy green, Bridgeport. Open Tuesday through Saturday; call for hours. Many works by Connecticut artists and artisans. Paintings, photographs, jewelry, and small furniture.

BOOKSTORES

✐ **The Whistle Stop Bookshop** (203-375-4146), 2505 Main Street, Stratford. Comprehensive selection of new and used books in a browser-friendly shop. Many children's programs; call for schedule.

✐ **The Dinosaur Paw** (203-256-0797), 1275 Boston Post Road, in the Brick Walk Plaza, Fairfield. A sunny, cheerful bookstore devoted exclusively to young readers. An impressive stock of quality children's books. Masks of Clifford, Arthur, Max (of *Where the Wild Things Are* fame), and other heroes of children's literature line the walls.

The Fairfield Open Book Shop (203-259-1412), 27 Unquowa Road (near the train station), Fairfield. Claudette Giblin's pleasant shop has been a literary landmark in town since 1951.

SPECIAL EVENTS

Early May: **Dogwood Festival** (203-255-1011) in the Greenfield section of Fairfield, exit 20 off I-95 and just south of the Merritt Parkway. Some 30,000 dogwood trees burst into bloom on the village green and on the streets radiating from the center. Garden lovers make an annual pilgrimage to this breathtaking floral display. Lunch served at the Congregational church during the 5-day festival. The late Leonard Bernstein's Connecticut home is among the handsome dwellings in this affluent old residential community. Guided garden tours, historic walks, arts and crafts shows, free concerts.

May: **Garlicfest** (203-372-6521), Notre Dame High School, Fairfield. Area restaurants offer a variety of garlicky foods and (really!) desserts featuring the pungent bulb.

June: **Barnum Festival** (203-367-8495), Bridgeport. Various events honor the city's former mayor and "Greatest Showman on Earth" P.T. Barnum. Car shows, parades, a circus under the big top, and fireworks in Bridgeport Harbor.

September: **Giant Model Aircraft Fly** (203-467-0915), Connecticut Model Airplane Club, Stratford. The club hosts this annual event at various locations; call for schedule.

The New Haven Area

Just as the Colossus of antiquity bestrode the harbor at Rhodes, New Haven is flanked on both sides by two huge geological outcroppings—East Rock and West Rock. On a flat plain between and at the confluence of three rivers—the West, the Mill, and the Quinnipiac—New Haven and its satellite communities sprawl from the harbor northward like a great fan. Indeed, it was the deepwater harbor that attracted the first Pilgrims from Massachusetts to settle here in 1638. The village plan called for nine squares, one being the 16-acre New Haven green. In 1665 New Haven joined the more liberal Connecticut Colony, which included Hartford. After the Revolutionary War, a happening unique in the annals of American politics took place: For nearly 60 years the capital of the state alternated between Hartford and New Haven. The frugal burghers eventually realized the folly of their ways, and the state government settled permanently in Hartford.

A historical footnote: During those early days, three judges presided over the trial of King Charles I in England, and they sentenced him to death. When his supporters seized power again, the three judges were accused of regicide, and they were sentenced, in turn, to the chopping block. They escaped to the New World and for a while hid out in a cave high atop West Rock, now known as the Three Judges Cave. Their memory lives on in the names of three major New Haven streets: Whalley, Goffe, and Dixwell!

As the Industrial Revolution swept through New England, New Haven became an important industrial center and famous for many historic firsts. New Haven's Eli Whitney invented the cotton gin. The world's first telephone switchboard and exchange began operation in 1878 with 21 New Haven customers. The lollipop was invented in a local candy factory in 1892. And Louis' Lunch on Crown Street served the nation's first hamburger in 1895. But manufacturing soon was on the decline, and when the fledgling Yale College, founded in Old Saybrook, moved to New Haven, it became the city's saving grace. Thanks to Yale's overwhelming cultural influence, this blue-collar city boasts some of the state's finest museums, art galleries, concert halls, libraries, research centers, and topflight college sports. Downtown also

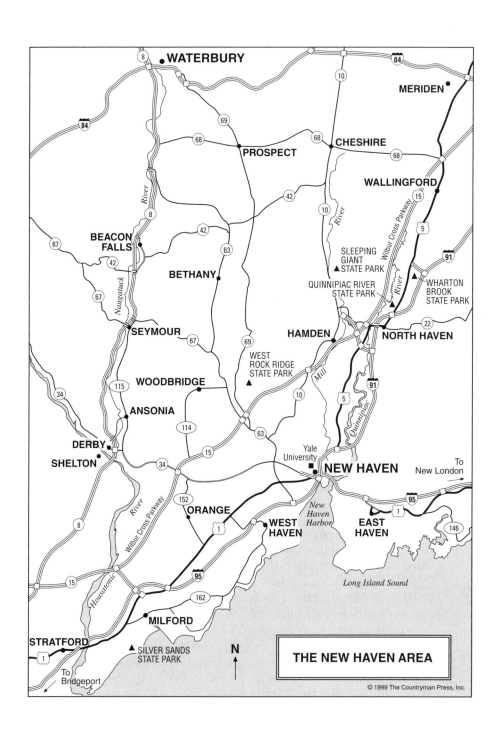

THE NEW HAVEN AREA

© 1999 The Countryman Press, Inc.

supports a palette of bistros, coffeehouses, bookstores, and ethnic restaurants offering authentic and reasonably priced international cuisine.

As you travel east out of the city, crossing the Quinnipiac River, the populous Gold Coast gives way to quieter shoreline towns that draw the bulk of the state's summer visitors. The towns surrounding New Haven offer a plethora of museums, historic homes, beaches, and restaurants.

Entries in this section are arranged in roughly geographic order.

AREA CODE
203

GUIDANCE
Greater New Haven Convention & Visitors Bureau (203-777-8550; 1-800-332-STAY), 59 Elm Street, New Haven 06510 (Web site: www.newhavencvb.org).

GETTING THERE
By car: New Haven is accessible by car from I-95, east- or westbound. From the north, I-91 joins I-95 at New Haven.

By air: **Tweed–New Haven Airport** (203-946-8283), in East Haven, is served by USAir Express. **Bradley International Airport** in Windsor Locks is 1½ hours up I-91.

By limo: **Connecticut Limousine** (1-800-472-LIMO) serves JFK, La Guardia, Newark, and Westchester airports.

By rail: **AMTRAK** (1-800-872-7245) links Boston and New York with stops at New Haven and Wallingford. **Metro-North** (1-800-638-7646) is the busy New Haven–New York commuter line.

By bus: **Greyhound** (1-800-231-2222), **Trailways/Peter Pan** (1-800-343-9999), and **Bonanza** (1-888-751-8800) offer frequent service.

GETTING AROUND
Metro Taxi (203-777-7777) and **Checker Cab Co.** (203-468-2678) serve Greater New Haven.

City bus service is reliable and runs day and night. **Connecticut Transit** (203-624-0151) operates an information booth on Chapel Street, at the New Haven green. It's open Monday through Friday 7:30–5:45.

MEDICAL EMERGENCY
The statewide emergency number is **911**.

Yale–New Haven Hospital (203-688-4242), 20 York Street, New Haven. The emergency number is 203-688-2222.

Hospital of St. Raphael (203-789-3000), 1450 Chapel Street, New Haven. The emergency number is 203-789-3464.

TO SEE

Yale Visitors Information Center (203-432-2300), 149 Elm Street, between College and Temple, New Haven. The campus of one of the world's greatest universities is home to a number of unique attractions, so many, indeed, that the organized campus tour office hosts thousands

Yale University's campus has many walkways like this one.

every year on daily tours conducted by student guides. View exhibits and videos about Yale and New Haven in the oldest surviving residence in the city. Go on a self-guided walking tour, or take a scheduled 1-hour guided tour. See the building, now a dormitory, where Connecticut hero Nathan Hale lived and studied before joining Washington's army. Behind these ivy-covered walls, President Bill Clinton and former presidents William Howard Taft, George Bush, and Gerald Ford studied, not to mention Noah Webster, Hillary Rodham Clinton, and a host of other American luminaries. Tours leave at 10:30 AM and 2 PM Monday through Friday; 1:30 Saturday and Sunday. No charge. After your overview tour, plan to spend more time at the other Yale attractions (see

Museums; Entertainment—Music; and *Entertainment—Theater*). Myriad fascinating events take place at Yale, too, from sporting to cultural. Call the new **Yale Events Hotline** at 203-432-9100.

MUSEUMS

Beinecke Rare Book and Manuscript Library at Yale (203-432-2977), 121 Wall Street, New Haven. Open year-round, Monday through Friday 8:30–5; Saturday 10–2; closed Sunday. Unique architecture with translucent marble wall panels. Among the treasured gifts from an affluent Yale alumnus is one of the world's few remaining Gutenberg Bibles, the first books printed with movable metal type in the 15th century. A few years back, a visiting German travel writer gazed at the precious book in its pressurized glass case and declaimed: "Those damn GIs, they stole everything!" There's also a large collection of original manuscripts of such authors as Dickens. The library overlooks a sunken sculpture garden.

Yale Collection of Musical Instruments (203-432-0822), 15 Hillhouse Avenue, New Haven. Open Tuesday through Thursday 1–4; closed July and August. More than 850 European and American instruments from the 16th to the 20th centuries, including a Stradivarius. Concerts on original instruments are held regularly. Call for schedules.

Peabody Museum of Natural History at Yale (info tape: 203-432-5050; events tape: 203-432-5799), 170 Whitney Avenue, New Haven. Open Monday through Saturday 10–5; Sunday noon–5; closed major holidays. Adults $5; children and seniors $3. Marvel at the huge skeleton of the brontosaurus and of other dinosaurs in the Great Hall, which houses the largest mural in the world depicting the age of the dinosaurs. Expeditions to the far corners of the world by Yale archaeologists fill other exhibit rooms with minerals, fossils, and rare birds in one of the top natural history museums in the country. Ongoing lecture series and special events. Weekend orientation video shows. Books, dinosaur models, paintings, and prints in a well-stocked gift shop.

Yale University Art Gallery (203-432-0600), 1111 Chapel Street, New Haven. Open Tuesday through Saturday 10–5; Sunday 1–6. Donation. Innovative, changing exhibits complement the more than 75,000 works— paintings, sculpture, and artistic artifacts ranging from ancient Egypt, the Middle East, and Europe through French and American Impressionists to the present. Oldest university art gallery in America. Gift shop.

Yale Center for British Art (203-432-2800), 1080 Chapel Street, New Haven, across the street from the Yale University Art Gallery. Open Tuesday through Saturday 10–5; Sunday noon–5. Free admission. Largest collection of British art outside the United Kingdom, a gift of philanthropist Paul Mellon. The last building designed by the late, famed American architect Louis Kahn. Paintings, drawings, rare books, prints. Changing exhibits.

New Haven Colony Historical Society (203-562-4183), 114 Whitney Avenue, New Haven. Open Saturday and Sunday 2–5. Adults $2; seniors

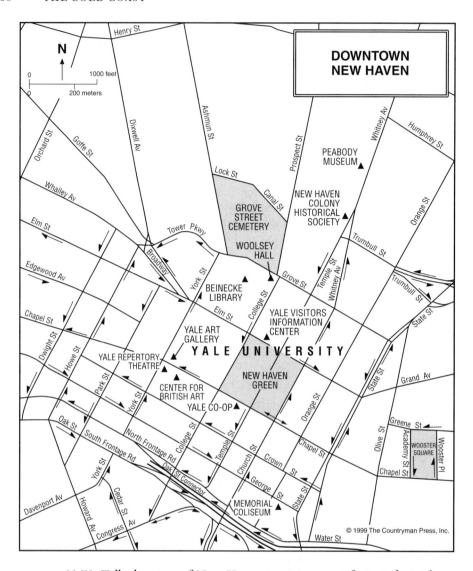

$1.50. Tells the story of New Haven in pictures, artifacts, industrial exhibits. Unique gallery of New Haven tableware.

- **102nd Infantry Regiment Museum** (203-784-8615), National Guard Armory, Goffe Street, New Haven. Open for tours by appointment. Traces the role of Connecticut in America's conflicts, with displays of weapons, maps, uniforms, and other military artifacts from the Civil War to World War II.

Jewish Historical Society of Greater New Haven (203-392-6125), Wintergreen Avenue, on the campus of Southern Connecticut State University, New Haven. Open year-round Monday through Friday 9–noon. Free admission. Tells the story of the thriving Jewish community of New Haven from the earliest days of the colony. Memorabilia and archives.

Knights of Columbus Headquarters Museum (203-772-2130), One Columbus Plaza, New Haven. Open Monday through Friday 8–4; tours on Saturday by appointment. Free admission. This worldwide Catholic fraternal order was founded in New Haven and maintains its world headquarters here. Changing and permanent exhibits.

Connecticut Children's Museum (203-562-KIDS), 22 Wall Street, New Haven. Call ahead for hours and schedule. Admission $3. Creative programs for parents and young children. Play hospital and neighborhood. Special projects.

Eli Whitney Museum (203-777-1833), 915 Whitney Avenue, Hamden. Open year-round Wednesday, Thursday, Friday, and Sunday noon–5; Saturday 10–3; daily 11–4 in summer. Explore buildings where one of Connecticut's, and America's, first inventive geniuses worked. While living in the South, Whitney invented the cotton gin; little did he know that his invention would lead to the agricultural slave economy that eventually tore the country apart. Back in Connecticut, he devised the method of interchanging parts in muskets, formerly made of individual handmade components. Interchangeability made the Industrial Revolution possible. Clearly, here was a man whose impact on the lives of millions of people after him was incalculable. The museum holds an annual Holiday Toy Train Exhibition during the Christmas season (see *Special Events*).

Shore Line Trolley Museum (203-467-6927), 17 River Street, East Haven. Open daily Memorial Day through Labor Day 10:30–4:30; weekends September through December and April through May; closed January through March. Adults $5; seniors $4; children under 12, $2. Take the children on a 3-mile round-trip ride along tracks of the country's oldest continuously operating suburban trolley line. Visit 100 vintage trolley cars collected from municipal transit systems all over the country. The museum is a registered National Historic Site. The trolley line has starred in several Hollywood movies.

HISTORIC HOMES

Pardee-Morris House (203-562-4183), 325 Lighthouse Road, New Haven. Open June through August, Saturday and Sunday 11–4. Adults $2; seniors and children under 12, $1.50. An elegantly furnished, circa-1750 home on Morris Cove near Lighthouse Point Park, the city's best-preserved 18th-century dwelling.

General David Humphreys House (203-735-1908), 37 Elm Street, Ansonia. Open year-round, Monday through Friday 1–4. Admission $2. The restored 1698 home of General Washington's aide-de-camp. After the war, the general imported merino lambs from Europe. Gift shop.

Osborne Homestead Museum (203-734-2513), 500 Hawthorne Avenue, Derby. Open May through December, Tuesday and Thursday 10–3; Saturday and Sunday 10–4. Donation. Outstanding collection of fine art in an elegant 1850 estate. Formal gardens.

Stone-Otis House (203-795-9466), Orange Center Road, Orange. Open April through October, Sunday 1–4. Restored 1830 farmhouse with colonial herb garden and blacksmith shop.

Thomas Darling House (203-387-2823), 1907 Litchfield Turnpike, Woodbridge. Open June through October, Sunday 2–4. The headquarters of the Amity and Woodbridge Historical Society are in this 18th-century home, which is on the National Register of Historic Places.

HISTORIC SITES

Fort Nathan Hale and Black Rock Fort (203-946-8005), Woodward Avenue, New Haven. Open daily Memorial Day through Labor Day. Free admission. Built on the shores of New Haven Harbor during the Revolution to repel British attackers, later rebuilt during the Civil War. Now the scene of reenactments of barracks life and maneuvers.

Grove Street Cemetery, 227 Grove Street, New Haven. Enter through an imposing 1845 Egyptian Revival gate and visit the last resting places of some of Connecticut's most inventive minds: Noah Webster, author of America's first dictionary; Charles Goodyear; Eli Whitney; Samuel F.B. Morse; an original member of the Plymouth colony; and early leaders of the New Haven colony.

Amistad **Memorial.** A majestic new 14-foot, three-sided bronze relief sculpture on the New Haven green in front of City Hall recalls a stirring story of an early fight against slavery. In 1839, 50 Africans were kidnapped for the slave market in Cuba. Under the leadership of Joseph Cinque, they seized their prison ship, *La Amistad,* and wound up in the New Haven Harbor. Former president John Quincy Adams came out of retirement to plead before the US Supreme Court and won their freedom. A replica of the *Amistad* is being built at Mystic Seaport and will be berthed in New Haven. Some years ago, the leader of the Symbionese Liberation Army, an African American activist group, took the name Field Marshal Cinque.

TO DO

AMUSEMENT PARK

The Only Game in Town (203-239-GOLF), 275 Valley Service Road, North Haven. Open daily in warm weather from 10:30 AM. A large entertainment complex that will keep every member of the family busy, with attractions ranging from a go-cart track—with banked curves, a bridge, and a tunnel—to eight batting cages for baseball and softball. There's a lighted driving range, 18 holes of miniature golf, and other amusements.

BOATING

Visiting yachters may rent slips at area marinas or put in for a short visit to take on supplies and fuel. Most of the New Haven marinas are in the waters off Milford. Call ahead for reservations and information.

New Haven Yacht Club (203-469-9608), 56 Cove Street, New Haven. Reciprocal hospitality for members of other clubs.

Oyster Point Marina Village (203-624-5895), South Water Street, New Haven.

West Cove Marina (203-933-3000), 13 Kimberly Avenue, West Haven. Full services, 120 slips, winter storage.

Flagship Marina (203-874-1783), 40 Bridgeport Avenue, Milford. Open year-round, full services, 80 slips.

Milford Harbor Marina (203-878-2900), Two High Street, Milford. Open year-round, 250 slips, dry dock, full services.

Milford Yacht Club (203-877-1261), 131 Trumbull Avenue, Milford. Dry dock, full services, 63 slips.

Port Milford (203-877-7802), 164 Rogers Avenue, Milford. Full services, dry dock, open year-round, 100 slips.

Spencer's Marina, Inc. (203-874-4173), 44 Rose Street, Milford. Open spring through fall, full services, dry dock.

BOAT EXCURSIONS

Liberty Belle **Cruises** (1-800-745-BOAT), Long Wharf Pier, New Haven. April through October. Step aboard a classic wooden motor vessel for a daysail into the waters of Long Island Sound and along the Connecticut coast. Live music and food service on weekend cruises. Full bar. Capacity 200. May be chartered by groups; call for schedules.

Schooner, Inc. (203-865-1737), 60 South Water Street, New Haven. Sails May through September. Half-day, all-day, and sunset cruises aboard New Haven's flagship the *Quinnipiac*, a gaff-rigged, 91-foot wooden schooner. Sailor-guides explain the ecology, culture, and history of the Sound.

GOLF

There's only one public golf course in New Haven; the others are scattered about in neighboring towns. Visitors who are members of clubs back home should check on visiting privileges at the following private clubs. Yale alumni have access to the Yale links. Call ahead for tee-times and reservations.

Alling Memorial Golf Course (203-946-8014), 35 Eastern Street, New Haven. Par 72, 18 holes, 6,241 yards.

Laurel View Country Club (203-281-0670; 203-287-2656), 310 West Shepard Avenue, Hamden. Par 72, 18 holes, 6,899 yards.

Meadowbrook Country Club (203-281-4847), 2761 Dixwell Avenue, Hamden. Par 35, nine holes, 2,758 yards.

Grassy Hill Country Club (203-795-3100), 441 Clark Lane, Orange. Par 70, 18 holes, 6,325 yards.

Orange Hills Country Club (203-795-4161), 489 Racebrook Road, Orange. Par 71, 18 holes, 6,451 yards.

Millstone Country Club (203-874-5900), 348 Herbert Street, Milford. Par 36, nine holes, 2,910 yards.

Woodhaven Country Club (203-393-3230), 275 Miller Road, Bethany. Par 36, nine holes, 3,387 yards.

HAYRIDES AND SLEIGH RIDES

Fieldview Farm (203-795-5415), 707 Derby Avenue, CT 34, Orange. Year-round by appointment. The oldest farm in the state, operated by the same family since 1639. Hayrides and sleigh rides; pony rides in summer. Farm store open year-round, offering produce, herbs, cheese, homemade ice cream; flour and cornmeal ground on the premises.

✐ **Maple View Farm** (203-799-6495), 603 Orange Center Road, Orange. Available year-round by appointment only. Pony rides plus horse-drawn sleigh rides or hayrides, depending on the season. Wedding coach. A party barn with petting zoo is available for groups, with prior arrangement.

HIKING

Sleeping Giant State Park (ranger station: 203-789-7498), CT 10, Hamden, exit 61 off the Merritt Parkway or exit 10 off I-91. The name of the 1,500-acre park comes from the crest, which resembles the head of a sleeping giant, arising from its center. Picnicking, hiking, and 33 miles of nature trails featuring cliffs, views, and spectacular rhododendron displays in spring. Pond fishing.

See also *Green Space.*

HORSEBACK RIDING

B&R Riding Stables (203-758-5031), 120 Roaring Brook Road, Prospect. Open daily, May through November, weather permitting. Guided trail rides on a 200-acre farm for children 10 years of age to adults. Reservations suggested.

See also *Hayrides and Sleigh Rides.*

SEA KAYAKING

The Sea Kayaking Co. (203-235-1507), Wallingford. Open May to October. Full- and half-day guided trips including moonlight paddles, shoreline picnics, and lake tours. Instruction and equipment provided. Call ahead for reservations.

SPECTATOR SPORTS

The Beast of New Haven Hockey Club (203-777-7878). An American Hockey League affiliate of the Carolina Hurricane and the Florida Panthers. Games October through mid-May at the New Haven Veterans Memorial Coliseum. Call for schedule.

New Haven Ravens (1-800-RAVENS-1). April through September. New Haven's first professional baseball team, the Ravens—an AA farm team of the Colorado Rockies—plays in a nicely renovated Yale baseball stadium. Call for schedules and ticket information.

Sports Haven (203-946-3201), 600 Long Wharf Drive, New Haven. Open daily. There are no thoroughbred racing tracks in Connecticut. Four giant screens broadcasting live thoroughbred, harness—and greyhound—racing are a nice substitute. Virtual reality games, a 17-foot-tall aquarium, and restaurants round out this unique entertainment complex.

Milford Jai Alai (203-877-4242), 311 Old Gate Lane, Milford. Open year-round; call for hours. Wager on world-class players in the world's fastest ball game.

CROSS-COUNTRY SKIING

This trendy aerobic sport is wholly dependent on the weather. There are no snowmaking machines on the area's trails. In a normal winter, the mercury is at least 15 degrees higher here than in Litchfield County, so this is an iffy

sport in greater New Haven. Play it safe—bring your own equipment.
That said, here's a list of the area's leading cross-country grounds:
Alling Memorial Golf Course (203-946-8014), Eastern Street, New Haven. **Edgerton Park** (203-946-8009), Cliff Street, New Haven. **Edgewood Park** (203-946-8028), Edgewood Avenue, New Haven. **East Rock Park** (203-946-6086), East Rock Road, New Haven. **East Shore Park** (203-946-8338), Woodward Avenue, New Haven. **Ansonia Nature Center** (203-736-9360), 10 Deerfield Lane, Ansonia. **Brooksvale Park** (203-287-2669), 524 Brooksvale Avenue, Hamden. **Osbornedale State Park** (203-734-2513), Hawthorne Avenue, Derby. **The Regional Water Authority Grounds** (203-624-6671) offer a wide variety of recreational activities, including cross-country skiing, on land in Branford, Orange, Woodbridge, and Bethany.

SWIMMING

In addition to freshwater swimming at inland state and municipal parks and nature centers, visitors are welcome at the Long Island Sound saltwater beaches of New Haven, West Haven, and Milford. Be advised that these beaches do not boast the pure white sands and crystal clear waters of the Caribbean, but on a hot day when the kids are cranky, as we say, any port in a sweaty storm. Special fees for nonresidents.

Lighthouse Point Park and Carousel (203-946-8005), Two Lighthouse Road, New Haven, exit 50 off I-95. Open Memorial Day through Labor Day. Daily fee $6; carousel 50¢. Swim, hike, and picnic on 82 acres on Long Island Sound. The antique carousel operates Tuesday through Sunday at varying hours. Bird-watching programs in March and April. Marine animal touch tank.

In Milford, swimmers can head to **Gulf Beach** (203-783-3280), Gulf Road, exit 39A off I-95; and **Walnut Beach,** on Viscount Drive, exit 34 off I-95. The daily fee at both beaches is $5.

The West Haven Recreation Department operates four beaches, all accessible from exit 42 off I-95: **Bradley Point, Morse, Oak Street,** and **Sandy Point Beaches** (203-937-3651). Daily fee, $10; $5 after 4 PM.

Silver Sands State Park, exit 35 off I-95, Milford, is the latest Long Island beach park acquired by the state parks system after 20 years of negotiation. Still under development.

Wharton Brook State Park (ranger station: 203-269-5308), US 5, Wallingford. Swimming, picnicking, a brook stocked with trout; food concessions.

TENNIS

Yale field. In summer, between tournaments, practice courts are open to the public on a limited schedule. Call the **Yale Athletic Department** (203-432-4747) for schedules and reservations.

ICE SKATING

State and local parks, some already listed, offer skating on outdoor ponds when the mercury dips below freezing and stays there long enough to create safe ice. Indoor rinks make their own ice. Rentals, a food concession, and

KIMBERLY GRANT

The Connecticut Audubon Coastal Center in Milford is a birder's paradise.

a fireplace are available at the **Ralph Walker Skating Pavilion** (203-946-6071), Blake Field at State Street, New Haven. Rentals also are available at the **Edward L. Bennett Ice Skating Rink** (203-937-3651), West Haven; the **Hamden Ice Skating Rink** (203-287-2579), Hamden; and the **Veterans Memorial Ice Rink** (203-468-3367), East Haven. Bring your own skates at the following: **Osbornedale State Park** (203-734-2513), Derby; **Old Tavern Recreational Area** (203-891-2188), Orange; and **Brooksvale Park** (203-287-2669), Hamden. Call town recreation departments for details.

GREEN SPACE

NATURE CENTER
Connecticut Audubon Coastal Center (203-878-7440), One Milford Point Road, Milford. Grounds open daily, dawn to dusk. Center open Tuesday through Saturday 10–4; Sunday noon–4. Closed Monday. Adults $2; seniors and children $1. Excuse the pun, but birders have a field day on this 840-acre spit of land, known as the Charles E. Wheeler Salt Marsh, that curls into the Housatonic River, splitting it off from Long Island Sound. In pleasant weather, plan on spending an hour or two. Bring binoculars, the bird books of Connecticut naturalist Roger Tory Peterson, and your own notepads. Call for schedule of nature programs.

PARKS

Unless otherwise noted, the parks are open all year from sunrise to sunset. Call for program schedules.

The New Haven green is the city's Central Park. Bordered on one side by buildings of Yale University, it is a grassy retreat in the heart of downtown. Three churches of Gothic, Federalist, and Georgian design dominate the center of the green. Concerts and other community events are held in warm weather. Legend has it that hundreds, perhaps thousands, of Continental soldiers are buried under the green. Although generally regarded as the property of the city, it actually is owned by five proprietors, dating back to colonial days, who have the final say on its uses.

Wooster Square, across the railroad tracks in New Haven, is a picture-perfect copy of a typical square in London—an oasis of grass and trees flanked by gracious homes. In Wooster Square, the Victorian homes, slated for demolition, were saved and from 1958 to 1963 were restored by community action and the government. They are now the town houses of fortunate New Haven residents who have but a short commute to work in the city. Behind the homes is a row of some of the best pizza restaurants in New England (see *Eating Out*).

East Rock Park (203-946-6086), East Rock Road, New Haven. Open April through October daily, sunrise to sunset. Closed November through April 1, except on Friday, Saturday, and Sunday when the roads are open, weather permitting. From atop the huge promontory, you get a panorama of New Haven, West Haven, and more, almost to Bridgeport, a spectacular view of the harbor (marred only by an oil tank firm) and Long Island Sound beyond. Hiking trails. Special nature programs; call for schedule.

Edgewood Park (203-946-8028), Edgewood Avenue, New Haven. There are nature trails, a children's fishing pond, and wildlife displays in this 140-acre park. Special programs.

Edgerton Park (greenhouses: 203-946-8009), Cliff Street, New Haven, exit 3 off I-91. Greenhouses with a variety of perennials set amid an 18th-century landscaped garden on 22 acres of woodsy tract.

New Haven Sea Walk, beyond the end of Howard Avenue. Open daily until 6. A pleasant path along the shore of New Haven Harbor, looking out toward the Sound.

West Rock Ridge State Park (for information, call Sleeping Giant State Park ranger station: 203-789-7498), Wintergreen Avenue, New Haven. New Haven is flanked by two huge outcroppings—East Rock and West Rock (see also East Rock Park). Scenic views of New Haven and the Sound can be found along the hiking trails on the park's 40 acres. A nature center is across the road. Small zoo with reptiles, mammals, and native birds.

Bradley Point Park & West Haven Promenade (203-937-3651), exit 42 off I-95, West Haven. Daily fee $10; $5 after 4 PM. Fly kites over Long Island Sound. Bicycle trails; swimming beach (but not highly recommended).

✎ **Ansonia Nature & Recreation Center** (203-736-9360), 10 Deerfield
    Road, Ansonia. Open year-round, daily 9–5. Two miles of wooded hiking
    trails; butterfly, hummingbird, native fern, and wildflower gardens;
    nature center shop. Special programs.

✎ **Brooksvale Park** (203-287-2669), 524 Brooksvale Avenue, Hamden. Do-
    mestic animal petting zoo, picnicking, and 195 acres covered with hiking
    trails.

Osbornedale State Park (203-735-4311), Chatfield Street, Derby. Pic-
    nicking, 415 acres of woods and ponds. Hiking trails.

LODGING

BED & BREAKFASTS

In addition to the listings below, a number of bed & breakfast reservation
    services offer access to rooms available in establishments throughout
    the state. For a list, see *What's Where—Bed & Breakfasts*.

& **The Three Chimneys Inn** (203-789-1201; 1-800-443-1554), 1201 Chapel
    Street, New Haven 06511. Close to the Yale campus. Open year-round.
    Visitors are welcomed in a luxurious 1870 Victorian mansion. Each of the
    10 guest rooms sports a different style of bed, from four-poster to canopy
    and French country; all have private bath. Room amenities include
    feather pillows, bathrobes, crystal glasses, and hair dryers. Full breakfast
    served in the morning room; in the evening, relax in Queen Anne chairs
    with tea and refreshments in the formal parlor. The front porch over-
    looks a landscaped courtyard. $160.

Betsy B&B in Bethany (203-393-1005), 12 Bethany Wood, Bethany 06524-
    3103. This stone English country manor, in a tranquil setting only 6 miles
    from New Haven, offers four guest rooms with bath, two with fireplace.
    Continental breakfast and afternoon tea. All rooms are $95.

HOTELS/MOTELS

At present there are very few small hotels or inns in the central business
    district. For a complete list of lodgings, call the Greater New Haven
    Convention & Visitors Bureau (203-777-8550).

& **Omni New Haven Hotel at Yale** (203-772-6664; 1-800-THE-OMNI), 155
    Temple Street, New Haven 06510. Housed in the former Park Plaza,
    near the New Haven green, Yale campus, and Chapel Street shops. An
    elegant four-star hotel with 306 rooms (seven suites), all with private
    bath. Health club and American restaurant. $139–290.

& **Colony Inn** (203-776-1234), 1157 Chapel Street, New Haven 06511. Quiet,
    elegant hotel overlooking the hustle and bustle of busy Chapel Street.
    Eighty rooms, six suites. Restaurant, health club privileges. $89–109.

☞ **Hotel Duncan** (203-787-1273), 1151 Chapel Street, New Haven 06511.
    The oldest hotel in New Haven, the Duncan rubs shoulders with the Yale
    campus and is within walking distance of the Shubert and Yale Rep
    theaters (see *Entertainment—Theater*). Ninety rooms (eight suites), all

with bath. There's a Thai restaurant on the lower level. $40 single, $60 double.

 ♿ **Residence Inn by Marriott** (203-777-5337), Three Long Wharf Drive, New Haven 06511. A new wrinkle in hotels: All 112 suites have kitchens, and some have fireplaces. Outdoor pool, Jacuzzi. Continental breakfast, unless you want to pick up a slab of bacon and a carton of eggs and cook up your own American breakfast! $130–179.

Milford, just west of New Haven, and Hamden, to the north of the city, have a plethora of budget accommodations on main thoroughfares, most of them medium-size motels of about 35 rooms.

WHERE TO EAT

DINING OUT

The choice eating places in downtown New Haven, if you're visiting the major museums of the university or attending performances at Yale Rep, are clustered along Chapel Street and its immediate side streets. Some of the finest Italian restaurants in the state have been serving satisfied gourmets—and gourmands—in the area for years. But because of the cosmopolitan mix of folks who eat out, in good part from the Yale student body, New Haven has an unusually varied mix of ethnic restaurants, from Mexican to Indian, from Chinese and African to Thai, Vietnamese, and Japanese. In the Ninth Square District, only a 5-minute walk from the New Haven green, nine eateries offer lunch for under $5.

☞ **Indochine Pavilion** (203-865-5033), 1180 Chapel Street, New Haven. Open daily for lunch and dinner. Americans have had a long love affair with Chinese cuisine—ever since Chinese laborers, building the western railroads, threw together an Americanized dish called chop suey. Now new Asian chefs have appeared on the scene, and in recent years we've been happily discovering the subtleties and exotic spices of Vietnamese, Thai, and Laotian cooking. Saigon City's lime chicken is a special treat, along with its superb shrimp dishes. And as with the Thai, egg rolls are really made of egg and delicately fried. This spot is our choice for dinner before attending the Yale Rep, just down the street (see *Entertainment*). $6.50–10.50.

☞ **Bangkok Gardens** (203-784-8684), 172 York Street, New Haven. Lunch and dinner daily. New combinations of spiced, diced, and sliced chunky vegetables added to classic Chinese fried rice make for a satisfying main course. Ask for a seat in the greenhouse sunporch and watch the passing parade of Yale students with their ubiquitous book bags. $7.50–12.95.

 ♿ **Scoozzi Trattoria and Wine Bar** (203-776-8268), 1104 Chapel Street, New Haven. Lunch Monday through Saturday; dinner daily. Reservations suggested. Spaghetti with meatballs, if you insist, but more adventurous palates may opt for the grilled chicken, arugula, sun-dried tomatoes, and toasted fennel seeds tossed with penne. Try the piccoli antipasto. $10–20.

&   **Union League Café** (203-562-4299), 1032 Chapel Street, New Haven. Lunch Monday through Friday; dinner daily. Reservations suggested. An elegant building that formerly was the home of the Union League has been converted into a French bistro. Steamed mussels, oysters, warm lobster salad, codfish cake with leek fondue, and smoked salmon top the list of appetizers. Duck leg confit, warm goat cheese salad, sautéed trout, vegetarian risotto, and spit-roasted chicken highlight the entrées. For dessert, don't pass up the *chocolat plaisir.* Prices range from $3 (for a sandwich) to $14–16.50 for entrées.

&☞**Pika Tapas Cafe** (203-865-1933), 39 High Street, New Haven. Open Monday through Saturday for lunch and dinner. Closed Sunday. Traditionally, tapas were snacks Spanish grandees ate while sipping their afternoon sherry in Seville. Since then these little nibbles have been raised to a fine culinary art in Spanish restaurants. At Pika Tapas, happy diners are filling their plates from a choice of two dozen different morsels ranging from grilled salmon punctuated by a sherry vinaigrette to medallions of pork loin, spicy chorizo, and white beans drenched in garlic. A selection of larger plates rounds out the menu. Average tapas $5.

&   **Café Adulis** (203-777-5081), 228 College Street, New Haven. In a city with a year-round international community, an Eritrean restaurant should come as no surprise. Traditional specialties include Tibsie, a medley of chicken, tomatoes, sun-dried peppers, and garlic; Alitcha, a vegetable stew with a curry base; and Gored Gored, filet mignon sautéed with curried vegetables. $6.95–18.95.

☞   **Tandoor** (203-776-6620), 1226 Chapel Street, New Haven. An unusual combination: Indian cuisine in a gleaming, chrome, art deco diner car. What was formerly the Elm City Diner was a New Haven institution; today the aroma of Asian spices greets you at the door. Inside, the exquisite cuisine of India and Pakistan is served in the diner's original booths, now covered in pink linen. Try the mughlai korma—chunks of chicken simmered in yogurt with spices and almonds; or skewered chicken, lamb, or seafood, barbecued in a clay tandoori oven. All dishes are accompanied by fragrant basmati rice. $7.95–12.95.

EATING OUT

☞   **Louis' Lunch** (203-562-5507), 263 Crown Street, New Haven. Open Tuesday and Wednesday 11–4; Thursday through Saturday noon–2 AM; closed Sunday and Monday. Birthplace of the hamburger in America. In this unprepossessing building, now crowded at noon with business types, Yalies, and knowing tourists, Louis Lassen declared that he cooked the first hamburger sandwich in the United States more than a half century ago. Who is to deny him? A threat of demolition by the city's redevelopment agency raised a hue and cry. The building, now on the National Register of Historic Places, mercifully was moved and saved. One wall was built with bricks brought from all over the world by loyal patrons; a second displays bricks donated by every business establishment in the redeveloped project. All 500 bricks carry the names of their donors. Burgers, all mixed fresh daily, are cooked in an old-fashioned, upright broiler and served between two slices of toast. After all, Louis predates even the hamburger roll. Tuna salad sandwiches are served on Friday. Smaller portions for children. Burgers around $5.

☞ **Pepe's Pizzeria** (203-865-5762), 157 Wooster Street, New Haven. Open for lunch and dinner daily; closed Tuesday. The pizza has come a long way since its humble beginnings in Naples as a disk of dough topped only with a bit of tomato sauce and a sprinkling of cheese. In America, we've thrown everything but the kitchen sink on our pizzas. But Pepe takes the cake (the dough?) for crowning his pizzas with white clam sauce. Local lore has it that folks all the way from Vermont make a pilgrimage to New Haven for Pepe's white clam pizzas. Always busy. Prepare to stand in line, even if you arrive at 5 PM. It's a no-nonsense food factory, and the line moves fast. If it's too crowded, go down the alley to **The Spot,** 163 Wooster Street (203-865-7602), owned by Pepe's.

☞ & **Sally's Pizza** (203-624-5271), 237 Wooster Street, New Haven. Open for dinner Tuesday through Sunday from 5; closed Monday. Guess who else serves clam pizza? Sally, that's who. Like Pepe, her menu is rounded out with standard Italian American pizzas, grinders, pasta dishes, and fresh salads. Sally's pizzas were a staple of Yale law students Bill Clinton and Dick Blumenthal, Connecticut's attorney general, when they were studying together in a drab Olive Street rooming house.

& **Claire's** (203-562-3888), 1000 Chapel Street, New Haven. Open daily. This gourmet vegetarian restaurant is a neighborhood landmark, offering home cooking to students and others with healthy appetites for nearly 25 years. The Mexican specialties should not be missed. Some people come just for the incredible desserts. $5–9.

Seoul Restaurant (203-497-9634), 343 Crown Street, New Haven. Open for lunch and dinner daily, 11 AM to 10 PM. Authentic Korean and Japanese dishes, hot pots, stews. Entrées accompanied by bean sprouts, cold potatoes, and warm smoked fish. Sushi bar. $7.95–19.95.

& **Amarante's Dinner Theatre** (203-467-2531), 62 Cove Street, New Haven. Performances Wednesday and Thursday: dinner at 6, show at 7:30 (and special Sunday matinees). Centrally located in New Haven overlooking the harbor. Start your evening with hors d'oeuvres on the deck, then indulge in a scrumptious all-you-can-eat buffet while enjoying the best of Broadway.

& **H. Lender & Sons,** (203-248-4564), 2400 Dixwell Avenue, Hamden. The bagel is of Eastern European Jewish origin—but it now rivals the Danish as an authentically American treat. It first popped up in Connecticut in 1927 in the H. Lender bakery in West Haven. Acquired by Kraft, the Lender bagel is now the largest-selling bagel in America. The Lender shop here serves bagels but is also a full-service restaurant featuring soups, salads, omelets, and hot sandwiches.

COFFEE

Daily Caffe (203-776-5063), 316 Elm Street. Open daily. Coffee—and all its variations—as it should be, aromatic, strong, hot. A friendly spot, popular with college students.

ICE CREAM

Ashley's (203-865-3661), 278 York Street, New Haven. Open Sunday through Thursday, noon–11 PM; open noon to midnight on Friday and Saturday. Scooping out homemade ice cream for more than 25 years. Bring all your friends and order the Banana Republic, a colossal mound of ice cream graced with every fixing imaginable.

Wentworth's (203-281-7429), 3697 Whitney Avenue (CT 10), Hamden. Open daily 10–10 Monday through Thursday; 10 AM–11 PM Friday through Sunday. Wentworth's is a local institution thanks to its rich, creamy homemade ice cream. Loyal patrons sing the praises of many flavors, but the peach ice cream is the kingpin. It's made only when the fruit crop is at its peak; well worth waiting for. A good stop after hiking at Sleeping Giant State Park (see *To Do—Hiking*).

ENTERTAINMENT

With the Yale drama and music schools as a catalyst, New Haven has become one of the major entertainment cultural centers in the country. At one time, nearly all major Broadway shows staged their pre-Broadway "tryouts" at the old Shubert Theater in New Haven. If it didn't make it in New Haven, it rarely made it to the Great White Way. The Shubert no longer is Broadway's principal tryout theater, but it has been renovated and, as a performing arts center, mounts road show performances of the best in American dramatic arts. But New Haven is now much more than just the Shubert. In addition to the theaters and performing groups listed below, every town in this culture-crazed area has an active arts council. Check for schedules of performances and exhibits.

MUSIC

New Haven Symphony Orchestra (1-800-292-NHSO), 33 Whitney Avenue, New Haven. Regular season September through May; summer events. Now entering its second century, the New Haven is the fourth oldest symphony in the United States. Its regular concert series is held in Yale's beautiful, spacious Woolsey Hall on College and Grove Streets. The New Haven also brings international symphonies and guest soloists to Woolsey. Check newspapers or call for schedules.

Orchestra New England (203-934-8863), a traveling orchestra based in New Haven, performs regularly at Yale's Battell Chapel, College and Elm Streets.

Yale School of Music (concert office: 203-432-4158). Chamber music, faculty and student recitals, and other performances throughout the school year in Sprague Memorial Hall, Sudler Hall, and Woolsey Hall. Check schedules for public concerts by the world-famous Yale choir, the Whiffenpoofs.

Veterans Memorial Coliseum (772-4200), 275 South Orange Street, New Haven. The town's covered stadium offers a year-round schedule of popular events: hockey, rock concerts, music superstars, horse shows, and the circus—when it comes to town.

Greater New Haven Acoustic Music Society (203-421-0021), 16 Sperry Road, Madison. Contemporary and traditional folk concerts for young and old are held at various venues; call for schedule.

THEATER

Long Wharf Theatre (203-787-4282), 222 Sargent Drive, New Haven. October through June. Located in a rather unlikely setting—one of several buildings in a row of wholesale food markets—Long Wharf has attracted top stars, top dramatic works, and appreciative New England, New York, and international audiences to prizewinning plays. Longtime Connecticut resident Arthur Miller's *The Crucible* premiered here. Early in 1994, Miller's latest work, *Broken Glass*, also premiered at Long Wharf. Along with Yale Rep, the theater is a consistent Tony winner.

Yale Repertory Theatre (203-432-1234), 1120 Chapel Street, New Haven. Open October through May. In this experimental theater, located in an old church, students of the Yale Drama School and other new playwrights have an opportunity to present their creations, professionally mounted, before live audiences. Numerous playwrights, particularly the emerging group of African American dramatists, get their start here. **Yale University Theatre,** on campus at 222 York Street, is an important adjunct of Yale Rep.

Shubert Performing Arts Center (1-800-228-6622), 247 College Street, New Haven. Broadway plays, dances, musicals, and music. During the 1998–1999 season, the Shubert offered such diverse entertainment as Ballet Hispanica, Wynton Marsalis, Harry Belafonte, Alvin Ailey's American Dance Theater, and a New York National Opera Company production of *Madame Butterfly*.

Summer Cabaret at Yale (203-432-1566), 217 Park Street, New Haven. Performances Tuesday through Saturday at 8 PM; after-hours shows Friday and Saturday at 10:30. Reservations recommended. Dinner available before the 8 PM performance. Comedies, one-act plays, original works by students from the Yale School of Drama.

You may also want to check the schedules of the **Lyman Center for the Performing Arts** at Southern Connecticut State University (203-392-6161), 501 Crescent Street, and the **New England Actors' Theatre Inc**. (203-458-7671), for drama and music in and around New Haven.

NIGHTLIFE

Pick up a free copy of the *New Haven Advocate* to see what's going on around the city.

Toad's Place (203-624-TOAD), 300 York Street, New Haven. This is the place! From all over America fans of the Rolling Stones, Bob Dylan, U2, Johnny Cash, and other modern-day pop legends fight to get the nod from the doorman of this entertainment mecca. Call for schedules.

Bar (203-495-1111), 254 Crown Street, New Haven. Open daily. Something for everyone—a bar crowded with Yalies and suits; pool tables; a dark, intimate space with overstuffed couches; and a dance floor in the back room. Delicious brick-oven pizzas served upstairs.

Richter's (203-777-0400), 990 Chapel Street, New Haven. Renowned for the large selection of beers on tap and in half-yard glasses. Old wood decor and a long bar. Good lunches.

Anna Liffey's (203-773-1776), 17 Whitney Avenue, New Haven. Lunch and dinner daily. An authentic Irish pub featuring Irish ballads and sing-alongs on Saturday afternoon, and traditional Irish music Sunday and Monday nights.

Rudy's, 372 Elm Street, New Haven. A fun pub close to Yale. Live blues, jazz, rock.

SELECTIVE SHOPPING

ANTIQUES SHOPS

In the New Haven area alone there are 34 antiques dealers. Milford also has a large colony of antiques shops. Here's only a sampling.

In New Haven you'll find **Antiques Market** (203-389-5440), 881 Whalley Avenue; **Antique Corner** (203-387-7200), 859 Whalley Avenue; and **Antiques Forever** (203-776-1753), Three Edwards Street. In Hamden there are **Gallery 4** (203-281-6043), 2985 Whitney Avenue; and **The Unbroken Circle Antiques** (203-248-3788), 2964 Dixwell Avenue.

BOOKSTORES

Atticus Bookstore Cafe (203-776-4040), 1082 Chapel Street, New Haven, just opposite the Yale Art Gallery. Fully stocked bookstore but perhaps best known as a gathering place for students and professors, who sit and kibitz over coffee and hot chocolate and pastry at its coffee bar.

Yale Co-op (203-772-2200), two locations: 924 Chapel Street (main store) and 44 York Street (medical branch), New Haven. The official bookstore of Yale, described by locals as the Yale Department Store. Though it caters primarily to the needs of the students, it is open to the public. Holds a wider variety of esoteric and intellectual books than the average bookstore. Full complement of Yale accessories and souvenirs: T-shirts, caps, banners, and so on.

Arethusa Bookshop (203-624-1848), 87 Audubon Street, New Haven. John Gearty's shop is crammed with out-of-print and used books, including special ones devoted to art, decorative arts, typography, ancient history, and languages.

Book Haven (203-787-2848), 290 York Street, New Haven. A small shop with a general selection of new books; some used titles.

Foundry Bookstore (203-624-8282), 33 Whitney Avenue, New Haven. New books for adults and children.

Bookstores, antique shops, boutiques, and a plethora of ethnic eateries front the campus of Yale University.

Barnett Books (203-265-2013), 20 North Plains Industrial Road, Wallingford. Walk into this warehouse and enter book heaven. Thousands of remainders, closeouts, and overstocked titles.

Whitlock Farm Booksellers (203-393-1240), 20 Sperry Road, off CT 69, Bethany. Open daily 9–5; closed Monday. Picnic tables, gardens, horses, goats, and two barns chock-full of old, out-of-the-ordinary books, maps, and prints.

SPECIAL EVENTS

May: **Kite Fly and Spring Festival** (203-230-5226), Radio Towers Park, 495 Benham Street, Hamden. Attracting hundreds of kite flyers each spring since 1966. Food, exhibits, children's activities, live entertainment.

July: **Celebrate New Haven Fourth** (203-946-7821), Long Wharf Park, New Haven. Festivities include one of the state's largest fireworks displays, strolling musicians, waterfront picnicking, live music. **Feast of Society Santa Maria Maddalena** (203-789-9280), Conte School, Chaplin and Franklin Streets, New Haven. Four nights of Italian entertainment and food; since 1898.

Midsummer: **Annual Pilot Pen International Tennis Tournament** (1-888-99-PILOT), at the Connecticut Tennis Center on the grounds of Yale's athletic fields. Main court and adjoining side courts attract the top-seeded male players in the world. **New Haven Summertime Street Festival** (203-946-7821), Chapel Street. Dancing, music, food, entertainment, games.

September: **North Haven Fair** (203-239-3700), North Haven Fairgrounds, CT 5. Agricultural fair featuring livestock and agricultural exhibits, pony rides, petting zoo, entertainment, vendors, rides, and food; since 1942. **Engine 260 Antique Fire Apparatus Show and Muster** (203-874-2605), Eisenhower Park, Milford. A great family event for nearly 30 years.

October: **Meet the Artists and Artisans** (203-874-5672), Milford green, Milford. Juried craft show with more than 200 exhibitors from around the nation.

Autumn: Yale hosts Ivy League gridiron contests in the Yale Bowl. Join the alumni in blue at the world's most lavish tailgate luncheons when the Crimson boys come to town.

December: **United Illuminating's Fantasy of Lights** (203-777-2000), Lighthouse Park, New Haven. Drive through an enchanting land of more than 200,000 twinkling lights and 38 spectacular displays, many animated. **Holiday Toy Train Exhibition** (203-777-1833), Eli Whitney Museum, 915 Whitney Avenue, Hamden.

Winter and spring: Intercollegiate basketball, hockey, and baseball on campus.

The Housatonic Valley

The western gateway to Connecticut, the Housatonic Valley is anchored by the city of Danbury, former "hat capital" of America, where the "hat that won the West"—the 10-gallon Stetson—was first fashioned. But in colonial days Danbury was known (take notice, Bostonians) as Beantown, because its major crop was beans, which were exported to Norwalk. Then came men's hats in 1780, and some 40 factories that produced fedoras, derbies, top hats, stovepipe hats, as well as the Stetson. Then in the 1960s, when President Kennedy went bareheaded in all his public appearances, hats trickled out of style in America, and Danbury went into a decline.

Today Danbury is a pleasant residential town with historical and cultural attractions. The Scott-Fanton Museum explores the city's glory days as America's hatmaker, as well as its colonial history and Revolutionary War ties. Nationally known musicians grace the stage at Ives Concert Park, a beautiful outdoor venue named for native son, Pulitzer Prize–winning composer, and "Father of American Music" Charles Ives.

By contrast, the other valley towns are charming colonial villages that could each serve as a model for Hollywood set designers working on scripts based in New England. Of these, Ridgefield is the most attractive, with tree-lined streets, restored Colonial and Victorian houses, a historic Revolutionary War tavern, and a world-class modern art museum. Redding also has a place in Revolutionary War history: Part of Washington's Northern Army set up quarters here during the harsh winter of 1779. Relics of this encampment, known as Little Valley Forge, remain at Putnam Memorial State Park. In Brookfield, a prestigious craft center housed in an 18th-century gristmill opens its exhibition gallery and retail shop to visitors. In Wilton, America's Giverny, similar to Monet's estate near Paris, is taking shape at the studio farm of J. Alden Weir, the leader of American Impressionism. Newtown is filled with beautifully restored 18th-century homes; a stroll along Main Street might end with ice cream at a 200-year-old general store. This is also the birthplace of tire manufacturer Charles Goodyear and the game of Scrabble. Quiet vineyards with acres of gnarled grapevines dot the countryside; visitors can tour the wineries and taste their highly regarded vintages.

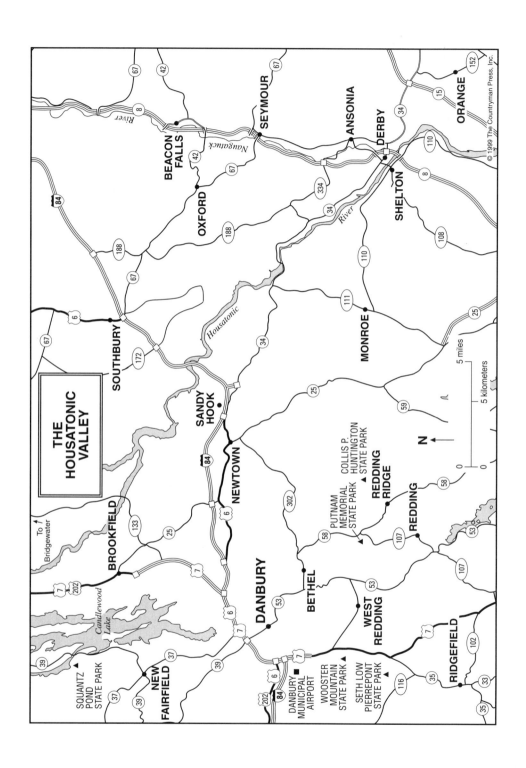

THE HOUSATONIC VALLEY

© 1999 The Countryman Press, Inc.

Although the main north–south artery, US 7, is fast becoming over-built and choked with traffic, much of the hills and countryside of the valley have been set aside as nature preserves and sanctuaries. Rivers and lakes dot the region. Some of Connecticut's best restaurants attract gourmets from the state as well as visitors. And as in most of Connecticut, it's hard to take a few steps without tripping over an antiques shop.

Entries in this section are arranged in roughly geographic order.

AREA CODE
203 and **860**

GUIDANCE
Housatonic Valley Tourism District (203-743-0546; 1-800-841-4488), 30 Main Street, Danbury 06810 (Web site: www.housatonic.org).

GETTING THERE
By car: The valley is accessible by car from I-84, east- and westbound, and from US 7, a heavily trafficked, two-lane road that runs from the shoreline arteries north all the way up into Vermont.

By air: **Danbury Municipal Airport,** (203-748-6375), adjacent to the Danbury Mall, is one of the busiest general aviation airports in New England, offering a full range of corporate and charter services.

By rail: A rail spur from **Metro-North** (1-800-638-7646) connects Danbury with the main line at South Norwalk. Frequent trains serving Grand Central Station also may be boarded just across the state line in nearby Brewster.

By bus: **Peter Pan** (1-800-343-9999) and **Bonanza** (1-800-751-8800) offer frequent service to the area.

Airport transport: **Connecticut Limousine** (1-800-472-5466) serves New York's JFK and La Guardia Airports and **Bradley International Airport** in Windsor Locks.

GETTING AROUND
JIN Transportation Inc. (203-792-TAXI; 203-790-6396) and **Washington Cab** (860-355-4859) provide taxi service to Danbury and other towns in the Housatonic Valley.

MEDICAL EMERGENCY
The statewide emergency number is **911**.
Danbury Hospital (203-797-7000), 24 Hospital Avenue, Danbury. The emergency number is 203-797-7100.

TO SEE

Walking Tour of Ridgefield. A picturesque New England town with most of its early buildings still intact and meticulously maintained and land-scaped, Ridgefield in recent years was surveyed by the local Preservation Trust. From the data collected on more than 700 buildings, a user-friendly brochure and map has been published that leads the visitor down beautiful Main Street and onto several of the side roads, with drawings and explanations of the buildings with architectural or historical significance.

The brochure is available from the Housatonic Valley Tourism District (see *Guidance*).

MUSEUMS

Aldrich Museum of Contemporary Art (203-438-4519), 258 Main Street, Ridgefield. Open year-round Thursday through Sunday noon–5; Friday noon–8. Adults $5; seniors and students $2; children under 12 free. This pioneer contemporary art museum in both an old and a modern building with a three-story atrium is a village center landmark. Paintings, photography, sculpture, and all forms of mixed media are displayed in nine galleries. Changing exhibits. Relax on the flagstone terrace and look out over the 2-acre sculpture garden. One of America's finest small museums, Aldrich has an international reputation. Gift shop.

✐ **Keeler Tavern Museum** (203-438-5485), 132 Main Street, Ridgefield. Open year-round Wednesday, Saturday, and Sunday 1–4. Adults $4; seniors $2; children under 12, $1. A tavern before the Revolutionary War, it became a rallying place for patriots during the conflict. While retreating to their ships through Ridgefield after torching Danbury, the British fired on the tavern. A cannonball is still embedded in a cornerpost. Famed American architect Cass Gilbert acquired the building as a summer home in 1907, added a large ell, and planted a formal garden for his wife. He also designed the fountain across the street, a gift to the town. Guides in colonial costume tell the story.

✐ **Danbury Railway Museum** (203-778-8337), 120 Water Street, Danbury. Open April through November, Tuesday through Sunday 10–4; call for winter hours. Adults $2; children $1; under 5 free. History of the rails in a restored 1903 train station. Dioramas, model trains from the 1920s to '60s. Railroad yard with vintage locomotives, a 1944 caboose, and five Reading Railroad coaches. The station was a location for Alfred Hitchcock's thriller *Stranger on a Train*. Museum shop.

Scott-Fanton Museum Complex (203-743-5200), 43 Main Street, Danbury. Wednesday through Sunday 2–5. Donation. Step back into the days when Danbury was America's "hat town." The 10-gallon Stetson was born here. Exhibits tracing the history of men's headwear are on view in the John Dodd Shop of this museum complex. Furnishings from the 18th and early 19th centuries are in the John and Mary Rider house. Excellent collection of early carpenter's tools. Gift shops and library.

✐ **Military Museum of Southern New England** (203-790-9277), 125 Park Avenue, Danbury. Open year-round, Tuesday through Saturday 10–5; Sunday noon–5. Adults $4; children, seniors, and active military $2. Local military enthusiasts have collected an impressive array of military vehicles, from tank destroyers to one of the first self-propelled howitzers—and even a 1941 Fiat staff car used by a German officer in the Afrika Corps. But the pride of the museum is the first tank made in the United States—a rare 1917 Renault.

KIMBERLY GRANT

The sculpture garden at the Aldrich Museum of Contemporary Art

WINERIES

Di Grazia Vineyard & Winery (203-775-1616), 131 Tower Road, Brookfield. Modern American techniques and traditional winemaking are combined to produce medal-winning wines from 50 acres of grapes. Neighbor Arthur Miller is a partner but has not been known to plant, pick, or crush a grape. Free pourings in the cozy, wood-paneled tasting room.

McLaughlin Vineyards (203-426-1533), Alberts Hill Road, Sandy Hook. Year-round tours of the vineyards and winery. After tasting a bit of the bubbly, you're invited to hike or bicycle on the trails in the 160-acre estate, which flows down the mountainside to the banks of the Housatonic River.

HISTORIC HOME

Charles Ives Birthplace (203-743-5200), Five Mountainville Avenue, Danbury. Open by appointment. Winner of the Pulitzer Prize in 1947, Charles Ives is considered the father of American music. His simple, gambrel-roofed birthplace is now part of the Scott-Fanton Museum Complex (see *Museums*). The piano he learned to play on is in the parlor, along with family furniture.

HISTORIC SITES

Weir Farm (203-834-1896), 735 Nod Hill Road, Ridgefield. Visitors Center open Wednesday through Sunday 8:30–5; grounds open daily from dawn until dusk. J. Alden Weir, one of the founders of the American school of Impressionism, paid $6 and a painting in 1882 for some 50 acres of pristine land in the woods of Ridgefield, where he then set up his studio. Not far from New York, it attracted other artists—Childe Hassam, John Twachtman, and John Singer Sargent among them—and Weir soon founded the famous "School of Ten." The property, studios, and home are now under restoration in Connecticut's only National Historic Site. Visitors can tour the grounds, hike the self-guided Painting Sites Trail, and view changing exhibits.

Putnam Memorial State Park (860-566-2304), CT 58, Bethel-Redding. In the bitter winter of 1779, Connecticut's Gen. Israel Putnam commanded a shivering army of Continental soldiers. A typical cabin thrown together by the men holds the meager utensils and implements they used in their struggle for survival. Nutmeggers call the encampment Little Valley Forge. Military reenactments by men (and women) garbed in Revolutionary War uniforms are staged in summer.

Meeker's Hardware (203-748-8017), White Street, Danbury. Quaff a 5¢ Coke at the only hardware store on the National Register of Historic Places. In business, and run by the Meeker family, since 1883.

Mark Twain Library (203-938-2545), Redding Road, Redding. Open daily, call for hours. Closed Sunday in summer. After his daughter died of meningitis in the Hartford mansion, Mark Twain, then 73, and his wife built a new home, Stormfield, in Redding. It burned but has been rebuilt. Twain founded the library, which annually holds a gigantic used-book sale, attracting readers and bookshop owners from all over New England (see *Special Events*).

TO DO

AIRPLANE RIDES
Capital Aviation (203-264-3727), 288 Christian Street, Oxford Airport, Oxford. Scenic plane rides offered year-round; create your own flight plan.

BALLOONING
Gone Ballooning (203-888-1322), 5 Larkey Road, Oxford. Year-round hot-air-balloon rides over scenic countryside. Flights leave early morning and late afternoon. Call for reservations.

BIRDING
Shepaug Bald Eagle Observation Area (1-800-368-8954) at the Shepaug Dam, River Road, Southbury. Open December to mid-March by reservation only. Free. Wintering bald eagles favor this site on the Housatonic River, thanks to a hydroelectric plant that keeps the water from freezing over, making it easy for them to find fish. Visitors watch behind observation blinds as these majestic birds perch, forage, and soar nearby. A unique and wonderful experience.

FISHING
Freshwater fishing opportunities are found in **Collis P. Huntington State Park,** Sunset Hill Road, Redding; **Pierrepont State Park,** off CT 116, Ridgefield; **Lake Lillinonah,** Danbury; **Squantz Pond State Park,** in New Fairfield; and **Putnam Memorial State Park,** Redding.

GOLF

Richter Park Golf Course (203-792-2550), 100 Aunt Hack Road, Danbury. Rated one of the top 10 public golf courses in America by *Golf Digest.* Par 72, 18 holes, 6,741 yards.

Ridgefield Golf Club (203-748-7008), Ridgebury Road, Ridgefield. Par 71, 18 holes, 6,005 yards.

HORSEBACK RIDING

Meadowbrook Farms (203-270-0906), 34 Meadowbrook Road, Newtown. Open March through November by appointment. Guided rides on wooded trails for adults and children 8 and older. The easy terrain and quiet horses are especially good for novice riders.

MOUNTAIN BIKING

Kettletown State Park (203-264-5169), 175 Quaker Farms Road, Southbury. Some of the area's first settlers obtained this large tract of land along Lake Zoar from the Pototuck Indians by trading a brass kettle. There are plenty of easy trails suitable for beginning riders; however, the routes are poorly marked.

Other nearby rides include the **Steep Rock Reservation** in Washington and Litchfield's **White Memorial Foundation** (See *To Do* in "Litchfield Hills").

Class Cycles (203-264-4708), 77 Main Street North, Southbury, doesn't rent bikes, but it has a repair shop and knowledgeable employees who can offer sound advice on local rides.

CROSS-COUNTRY SKIING

Collis P. Huntington State Park (860-424-3200), Sunset Hill Road, Redding. Cross-country skiing around several ponds.

OUTDOOR ADVENTURE

Mountain Workshop (203-438-3640), PO Box 625, Ridgefield 06877. Year-round. Canoeing on rivers, lakes, and Long Island Sound. White-water, flat-water, nature, architectural tours. Sea kayaking, rock climbing, caving, and more. Programs run 1 day to 2 weeks; instruction, equipment, and guides provided. Call for schedule of programs.

SWIMMING AND SAILING

Candlewood Lake. The dam built by a power company here created the largest constructed lake in Connecticut, the third largest in the world, and the largest east of the Mississippi. Extending through three towns—Danbury, Brookfield, and New Fairfield—it's a major recreation area. There are many summer cottages, inns, restaurants, and state boat-launching ramps.

Squantz Pond State Park (860-424-3200), at the southern end of Candlewood Lake, in New Fairfield, is open to the public for swimming, picnicking, and boating.

Danbury's **Lake Kenosia** (203-797-4632); **Lake Lillinonah** (203-270-2360), CT 133, Brookfield; **Lake Zoar** (203-270-4350), CT 34, Newtown; and some **Candlewood Lake** town beaches also offer swimming for a fee.

A pastoral scene in Southbury

GREEN SPACE

The Saugatuck Valley Hiking Trail System (203-938-2551), CT 53, Redding. More than 65 miles of trails, some marked, through dense woods and across fields. You get a view of a shimmering reservoir from atop a 200-foot-high cliff. Trails pass through three towns—Redding, Weston, and Easton. Birders, bring your glasses and Roger Tory Peterson bird guides; botanists, your notebooks.

Pierrepont State Park (203-438-9597), CT 116, Ridgefield. Picnicking, fishing, hiking, ice skating, cross-country skiing.

Bear Mountain State Park (203-743-0546), off CT 37, Danbury. Hiking and picnicking near Candlewood Lake.

Collis P. Huntington State Park (860-424-3200), Sunset Hill Road, Redding. Anna Huntington's wildlife sculptures grace the entrance to this secluded park, which is off the beaten path but worth finding. Picnicking, hiking, and cross-country skiing on an 878-acre open tract crisscrossed by scenic roads canopied with sugar maples. Five ponds for canoeing and fishing.

Highstead Arboretum (203-938-8809), Lonetown Road (CT 107), Redding. A former farm, now 36 acres of protected native woodlands. Several miles of hiking paths meander through forest and meadows before climbing to a rugged outcropping, from where hikers can see Long Island Sound on a clear day. A boardwalk winds through a swamp filled with native calla lily, marsh marigold, and cinnamon fern. Call for information about lectures, classes, and events.

LODGING

RESORT

 ♿ **The Heritage** (203-264-8200; 1-800-932-3466), Heritage Village off US 6, Southbury 06488. The rustic wood exterior belies the fact that this is a relatively new building, erected on the grounds of the former estate of Danish piano comedian Victor Borge. Recreation and sports facilities—including outdoor pools, golf, tennis, bicycles, and fishing—entertain guests staying in the 163 rooms. Relax weary muscles in a complete health club, with steam bath, Jacuzzi, exercise equipment, and an indoor pool. $139–149.

INNS

 ♿ **Stonehenge Inn** (203-438-6511), Stonehenge Road, US 7, Ridgefield 06877. Situated back off the road on a lovely duck pond, the garden setting of Stonehenge has few rivals in New England and is a magnet for visitors from all over the world looking for the perfect "weekend in Connecticut." Each of the 16 rooms (two suites) has its own ambience. Host Douglas Seville also presides over an exceptional kitchen (see *Dining Out*). Breakfast is included in the rates. $90–200.

West Lane Inn (203-438-7323), 22 West Lane, Ridgefield 06877. When you step into the hall of this luxurious country inn, you feel as if you've been invited for a stay at a grand 19th-century manor estate. Antiques are in each of the 18 cozy rooms, all with private bath, some with a fireplace—and some with a bidet. Ranked among the top 16 inns in the country, this luxurious inn offers a quiet retreat, yet is close to restaurants, museums, and antiques shops. Continental breakfast. $125 and up.

The Elms Inn (203-438-2541), 500 Main Street (across from Ballard Park), Ridgefield 06877. You'd be hard put to find a 200-year-old Colonial-style inn without an array of authentic antiques. The Elms is no exception. Your hosts will be happy to explain the history and origin of the antiques in each of the 15 comfortable rooms and five suites. Highly acclaimed restaurant (see *Dining Out*). Continental breakfast. $120 and up.

 ♿ **The Mary Hawley Inn** (203-270-1876), 19 Main Street, Newtown 06470. John and Jane Vouros have extensively renovated this colonial-era landmark in Newtown's historic district. The result is a stunning country inn—no small feat considering they are both veteran teachers in addition to being gracious and attentive innkeepers. Guest rooms are named after the town's historic one-room schoolhouses (in fact, one of these old schools has been converted into the Vouroses' home!). Three cozy rooms are simply furnished with country reproductions; all have private bath. Continental breakfast. An elegant dining room features traditional New England fare; the taproom has a warm, pubby feel. $125–150.

BED & BREAKFASTS

In addition to the listing below, a number of bed & breakfast reservation services offer access to rooms available in establishments throughout the state. For a list, see *What's Where—Bed & Breakfasts*.

Far View Manor (203-438-4753), 803 North Salem Drive, Ridgefield 06877. A private entrance leads into a high-ceilinged grand suite in this 1911 home, a former boys school and performing arts academy that was once considered as a site for the United Nations. The peaceful, 5-acre pastoral grounds are matched by the 30-mile view from the front door. Honeymooners can curl up in front of the blazing fireplace. Private bath and a continental breakfast. $110–135.

HOTELS/MOTELS

& **Ethan Allen Inn** (1-800-742-1776), 21 Lake Avenue, Danbury Extension (exit 4 off I-84), Danbury 06811. A modern, sprawling, 195-room inn with Ethan Allen interior home furnishings just off the interstate, convenient to the mall, Danbury, and the historic towns of Ridgefield and Bethel. Outdoor pool. $112-plus.

Ridgefield Motor Inn (203-438-3781), 296 Ethan Allen Highway, Ridgefield 06877. Nothing fancy but all the amenities—restaurant and lounge—are offered in this modern, 25-unit roadside motel. $65 and up.

Seagull Motel (203-743-3855), 21 Stony Hill Road, Bethel 06801. Thirty-three rooms, two efficiencies. $40–75.

Bethel Motor Lodge (203-743-5990), 18 Stony Hill Road, Bethel 06801. Forty-four units, some with Jacuzzi. $50–100.

& **Twin Tree Inn** (203-775-0220), 1030 Federal Road (US 7/US 202), Brookfield 06804. A comfortable, 47-unit hostelry located on a heavily trafficked stretch of US 7, but close to Candlewood Lake, the state's largest lake. A hearty continental breakfast is included. $65–90; lower off-season rates.

WHERE TO EAT

DINING OUT

& **Bangkok** (203-791-0640), 72 Newtown Road, Danbury. Open Tuesday through Sunday for lunch and dinner. Here's where it all started: the Thai revolution in Connecticut. The first restaurant to introduce the hottest cuisine in the world (Mexican pales by comparison), it's still one of the best. Lemongrass, Thai hot pepper, ginger, and other spices distinguish this Asian cuisine from the more ubiquitous Chinese. $7–16.

& **Kabuki Japanese Steak House** (203-744-6885), 39 Lake Avenue Extension, Danbury. Guests at this restaurant will enjoy sampling a varied cuisine that includes a sushi bar and hibachi-grilled delicacies. The owners defer to more conventional American tastes and serve steaks as tender as any laid on a plate in Omaha. $13.95–26.95 for a complete meal.

& **Bella Italia Ristorante e Osteria alla Villa** (203-743-3828), Two Padanaram Road, Danbury. Lunch and dinner daily. With a name this long, it has to be good. And happy diners have been returning for years for the Continental and seasonal specials, served in your choice of three dining rooms. $8–18.

   ♿ **Ondine** (203-746-4900), 69 Pembroke Road, Danbury. Dinner only, Tuesday through Saturday 5:30–9:30; Sunday 4–8. Closed Monday. A beautiful dining room serves contemporary French cuisine. Fresh foie gras with fig and rhubarb compote, braised monkfish with morels. Wild game is also a specialty. For dessert, the praline soufflé will melt in your mouth. Reservations suggested. $42 prix fixe, weekends.

   ♿ **Ernie's Road House** (203-790-0671), 30 Padanaram Road, Danbury. Open for lunch and dinner daily. American fare—barbecued ribs, steaks, prime rib, pasta, and seafood, served in a dining room overlooking a waterfall. $8–20.

     The Elms Restaurant and Tavern (203-438-9206), 500 Main Street (CT 35), Ridgefield. Chef-owner Brendan Walsh takes traditional New England dishes and applies an innovative twist, creating a menu lauded by locals and critics. Seafood stew in a fennel-leek broth with tomatoes and herbs and grilled venison with sweet potato spoon bread might be found on the winter menu. Dinner is served in several intimate rooms in this beautifully restored, 200-year-old building. Lighter fare served in the rustic wood-beamed taproom. Reservations suggested. $23–27.

   ♿ **Stonehenge Inn** (203-438-6511), US 7, Ridgefield. Open for dinner only on weekdays; brunch and dinner Sunday. Closed Monday. The Stonehenge has consistently served the finest in French country cuisine. The large dining room overlooks the swan and goose pond; a smaller dining room is in the rear. Beef, duck, and lamb are all beautifully executed with a variety of classic French sauces. Entrées $18–32; Sunday brunch $28.

   ♿ **The Inn at Ridgefield** (203-438-8282), 20 West Lane, Ridgefield. Open Monday through Saturday, lunch and dinner; Sunday brunch and dinner. A landmark restaurant founded in 1947. These three dining rooms in a restored clapboard inn are a happy marriage of classic European cuisine and Yankee hospitality. It's hard to single out one entrée—although the roast rack of lamb is special. Fresh seasonal fish is served daily. Entrées $18–32; five-course prix fixe $48.

   ♿ **Spinning Wheel Inn** (203-938-2511), CT 58, Redding Ridge. Open for dinner Tuesday through Sunday; exceptional Sunday brunch. Reservations suggested. Built as an inn in the saltbox style, the Spinning Wheel has been entertaining stage passengers and luminaries, such as former Redding resident Mark Twain, since 1742. The original saltbox now has big picture windows; a large addition on the northern side opens onto a terrace and a gazebo, popular with wedding couples. The lavish dinner menu runs the gamut from scallops Abrusca (sautéed sea scallops on a bed of pasta with julienne peppers and lemon, garlic, and white wine sauce), to Old New England Country Pot (a superb lamb stew), to steak-and-ale pie. $16–20.

   ♿ **Country Tavern** (203-264-6771), 418-D, Heritage Village, Southbury. Open daily for lunch and dinner. Five elegant dining rooms, all with fireplaces, in a former estate overlooking a golf course. Continental cuisine. There's dining on the terrace in good weather. The Sunday jazz brunch attracts a big crowd. Live entertainment on weekends. $14.95–21.95.

 ♿ **Tartufo** (203-262-8001), 900 Main Street South, Southbury. Open daily for lunch and dinner; brunch on Sunday. This quietly elegant place, named for the elusive truffle, is deemed by locals and critics to be one of the area's top romantic spots. Outstanding treatment of northern Italian dishes. Fresh mozzarella is wrapped with prosciutto, basil, and steamed romaine, then grilled and drizzled with a sun-dried tomato balsamic vinaigrette. Sautéed veal is scented with truffle oil and topped with wild mushrooms and black truffle shavings. Live entertainment Thursday through Saturday in the evening. Reservations suggested. Entrées $15–23.

 ♿ **Timbers on the Green** (203-264-8325), in The Heritage, Heritage Village, Southbury. Open daily for three meals. The dining room is large and rustic, with a massive stone fireplace and a nice view of the woods, fields, and golf greens. Contemporary New England fare. The popular Sunday brunch is noted for its myriad selections; reservations required. Entrées $14–20.

Christopher's (203-775-4409), CT 7, Brookfield. Lunch Monday through Friday; dinner daily; Sunday brunch. Roaring fireplaces and linen-covered tables enhance the romantic ambience in this quaint old restaurant, where fisherman's chowder is a signature dish and fresh seafood is a specialty. Steak, veal, and poultry round out the essentially American menu. Entrées $9–23.

EATING OUT

Ciao! Cafe and Wine Bar (203-791-0404), 2B Ives Street, Danbury. Visit this delightful place for innovative Italian cuisine and more than 35 wines available by the glass. Entrées $9–12.

♿☞**Cor's** (203-792-9999), 65 West Street, Danbury. Open daily for breakfast and lunch. A great place for breakfast—which is, intelligently, served all day. You can barely get your hands around the bulging deli sandwiches. Check out the impressive collection of celebrity photos filling the walls. Sandwiches around $4.

 ♿ **Deep's Trellis** (203-792-0494), 49 North Street, Danbury. Open Monday through Saturday for breakfast and lunch. A family-run eatery for nearly 20 years. Sandwiches, homemade muffins, soups, desserts. Under $7.

☞♿**Marcus Dairy Bar** (203-748-9427), Five Sugar Hollow Road, Danbury. Open daily for three meals. The name says it all: Marcus has every variety of ice cream devised. There's a '50s Cruise Night most Saturdays, and there are motorcycle rallies most Sundays. Sandwiches and light meals.

☞ **New Englander Diner** (203-744-1837), Railroad Place and Ives Street, Danbury. Breakfast and lunch daily. An old-style diner serving standard but satisfying diner fare, from corned beef hash to tuna melts, washed down with strong coffee. Top it all off with a large slice of apple pie à la mode. Breakfast $2–6; all lunch items under $7.

♿✎**Two Steps Downtown Grille** (203-794-0032), Five Ives Street, Danbury. Open daily. A historic firehouse-turned-restaurant. Kids will love the fire engine on the second floor, as well as the Wild West show. Sizzling fajitas and juicy ribs are favorites here. Don't miss the spicy Jamaican jerk chicken with sweet island relish. $5.95–16.95.

San Miguel (203-748-2396), Eight P.T. Barnum Square, Bethel. Dinner only. Closed Monday. Here in the heart of the birthplace of circus man Phineas T. Barnum (also see "The Bridgeport Area"), authentic Mexican cooking with real Spanish paella. All desserts are from family recipes—worth saving room for. The signature raspberry margaritas are concocted with homegrown fruit. Entrées $11–15.

Gail's Station House Restaurant & Bakery (203-438-9775), 378 Main Street, Ridgefield. Open daily for breakfast and lunch; dinner Thursday through Sunday. John and Gail Finnegan's cozy eatery is *the* place for Sunday breakfast; be prepared for a line that stretches out the door. Locals gladly wait for corn and cheddar pancakes, Gorgonzola omelets, and Station House skillet specials like the Texas Pink, a skillet of red-skinned hash potatoes, jalapeño peppers, and scrambled eggs topped with salsa and sour cream. For dinner, try their creative takes on ethnic dishes: The baked acorn squash with zucchini, tahini, and tofu mayonnaise comes highly recommended. Breakfast around $6; dinner $10–18.

SNACKS

    European Shoppe (203-262-1500), 109 Playhouse Corner (US 6), Southbury, exit 15 off I-84. Breakfast and lunch daily from 6:30 AM. In the morning, locals and commuters crowd in for some of Anik de Giverney's freshly baked, handmade bagels. Pair one with a strong cappuccino and you have a satisfying, inexpensive breakfast. If you're not eating on the run, get a café table at the back of the shop. Hearty sandwiches for lunch. Bagels 55¢; sandwiches $4.75.

Newtown General Store (203-426-9901), Main Street, Newtown. Open daily 5 AM to 11 PM. A 200-year-old general store nestled among preserved homesteads and historic churches on a Main Street that hasn't changed much since the 1700s. Breakfast sandwiches, lunch, snacks, homemade ice cream. A popular spot for coffee and the morning paper.

COFFEEHOUSES

    Dr. Java (203-791-8121), 114 Greenwood Avenue, in P.T. Barnum Square Plaza, Bethel. Open daily. Bills itself as a caffeine emporium, and delivers with a respectable selection of coffee featuring varying degrees of potency. Pastries and light meals.

Basset's (203-775-4957), 806 Federal Road (US 202/US 7), Brookfield. Open daily. Matt and Jamie Gillotti serve fine java and light meals in this popular local spot named for their hound, Mr. Stanley. Inside is decorated like home, with couches and a kitchen table. Live music, TV, puzzles, and games offer diversion.

ICE CREAM

    Dr. Mike's (203-792-4388), 158 Greenwood Avenue. Open daily. Since 1975, locals have been eagerly waiting in line for a scoop or two of pure decadence. Flavors like Chocolate Lace, an overwhelming favorite (maybe it's the locally produced chocolate), will make you swoon. In fact, Dr. Mike's is so revered that local schoolchildren come here on field trips!

ENTERTAINMENT

MUSIC

Ives Concert Park (203-837-9226), on the west campus of Western Connecticut State University, University Boulevard, Danbury, exit 2 or 4 off I-84. The stage is set on a small island in a pond. Guests with blankets or beach chairs listen to symphonies, jazz, folk music, and pop stars in a beautiful outdoor setting.

Richter Association for the Arts (203-798-2245), Richter Park, Aunt Hack Road, Danbury. Summer concerts—classical, opera, big band, jazz, folk—in an outdoor theater, which also hosts dance performances and art exhibits. Call for schedule.

THEATER

Ridgefield Workshop for the Performing Arts (203-431-9850), 37 Halpin Lane, Ridgefield. Musicals, plays, holiday performances, and original works staged from March through December. Call for information.

Brookfield Playhouse (203-775-0023), Whisconier Road (CT 25), Brookfield. A former school for boys, now home of the Country Players since 1958. Year-round schedule of performances; call for information.

Candlewood Playhouse (203-746-4441), CT 39, New Fairfield. Broadway and pre-Broadway performances.

Town Players of Newtown (203-270-9144), Little Theatre, Orchard Hill Road, Newtown.

SELECTIVE SHOPPING

Danbury Fair Mall (203-743-3247), Backus Avenue, Danbury, exit 3 off I-84. The largest regional shopping mall in New England, with 225 topflight stores, including five major department stores. There's a carousel (plastic horses) for the children, and a variety of food shops. It's on the site of what was for many years the second largest country fair in New England.

Stew Leonard's (203-790-8030), 99 Federal Road, Danbury. This unique dairy–grocery store, sister to the original in Norwalk (see "Westport and Norwalk"), is listed in the *Guinness Book of World Records* for the world's fastest-moving stock!

Hauser Chocolatier (203-794-1861), 137 Greenwood Avenue, Bethel. European techniques and imported Swiss and French chocolate are used to create butter-smooth truffles, chocolate dessert cups, and assorted other confections.

Mother Earth Gallery and Mining Company (203-775-6272), 806 Federal Road (US 7/202), Brookfield. Children can don headlamps and search for sparkling minerals and gemstones in an indoor cave. The gallery shop features handcrafted jewelry, minerals, fossils, shells, nature toys, games, and more.

ANTIQUES SHOPS

With 30 antiques shops, Woodbury is the acknowledged antiques capital of Connecticut, but Ridgefield comes in a close second with 20 antiques dealers, and many other shops are scattered around the Housatonic Valley. Pick up a copy of the *Newtown Bee* newspaper, the bible of Connecticut antiques dealers.

Antiquity (203-748-6244), 66 Sugar Hollow (US 7), Danbury. This eclectic shop has a little of everything. Victorian items and decorative accessories.

Red Petticoat, 113 West Lane, Ridgefield. A trove of collectibles, plus larger pieces, such as Early American blanket chests and 18th-century card tables.

Ridgefield Antiques Center (203-438-2777), 109 Danbury Road, Ridgefield. Country and formal furniture, paintings, folk art, silver, porcelain, jewelry.

Country Gallery Antiques (203-438-2535), 346 Ethan Allen Highway, Ridgefield. An 18th-century barn full of European country pine antiques and reproductions. Custom-crafted antique barnwood tables.

Heritage Antiques Center (203-262-8900), Heritage Road, Southbury. The area's largest consortium of dealers, offering a nice variety of antiques, fine art, collectibles, books.

ART GALLERIES

Ridgefield Guild of Artists (203-438-8863), Halpin Lane, Ridgefield. Open year-round, Thursday through Sunday 1–5. A former monastery is the site of 13 exhibitions a year featuring the work of regional and national artists. Galleries, workshops, classes. Call for schedule.

ARTISANS

Brookfield Craft Center (203-775-4526), 286 Whisconier Road (CT 25), Brookfield. Open Monday through Saturday 10–5; Sunday noon–5. Free admission. A sprawling crafts center in four Colonial buildings overlooking the Still River at Halfway Falls. Visitors can watch artisans at work, or participate in weekend workshops in ceramics, woodworking, weaving, and more. Gallery, gift shop, and bookstore. The center's annual holiday crafts sale features hundreds of artisans from around the country (see *Special Events*).

BOOKSTORES

Books on the Common (203-431-9100), 109 Danbury Road, Ridgefield. Unique titles, books on tape, classical CDs.

More Good Books (203-264-6464), Heritage Village Bazaar, Southbury.
Book Review (203-426-1711), Sand Hill Plaza, Newtown.
FARMS AND GARDENS

Blue Jay Orchards (203-748-0119), 125 Plumtrees Road, Bethel. Farm market open mid-July to mid-January, daily 10–5. Loyal patrons come for the homemade chunky applesauce and cider doughnuts; you can also get fresh pies, breads, and muffins baked in their ovens. Pick your own apples and pumpkins in season. Take your children on a hayride or to a storytelling session. Cider pressing in the fall.

Catnip Acres Herb Nursery (203-888-5649), 67 Christian Street, Oxford. Browse in the herb gardens, the greenhouse, and the herbal gift shop. The nursery grows 400 varieties of herbs and flowers and is noted for its scented geraniums. Year-round classes and workshops in growing, harvesting, preserving, and using herbs medicinally.

SPECIAL EVENTS

August: **Mark Twain Library Book Sale** (203-938-2545), Redding. Huge used-book sale, nearly 40 years old. Get there early before the stacks have been pawed over by the horde of owners of stores specializing in used books, who descend on the library from all over New England.

September: **Taste of Greater Danbury** (203-743-0546). Chefs from the area's best restaurants entice you to their booths to sample their specialties.

Mid-November through December: **Annual Brookfield Craft Center Holiday Craft Exhibition & Sale** (203-775-4526), 286 Whisconier Road (CT 25), Brookfield. More than 200 local and national artisans offer their works for sale in the valley's largest show of American handcrafts. The sale is held on three floors of a restored gristmill at the craft center.

December: **First Night Danbury**—New Year's Eve nonalcoholic, midtown entertainment-go-round. One ticket admits you to a wide variety of events in theaters, schools, galleries, and libraries. Modeled after Boston's First Night, the first in the country.

II. THE LITCHFIELD HILLS

Litchfield and Surrounding Towns

KIMBERLY GRANT

A remote gravel road in the verdant Litchfield Hills winds through a mixed landscape of forests and fields.

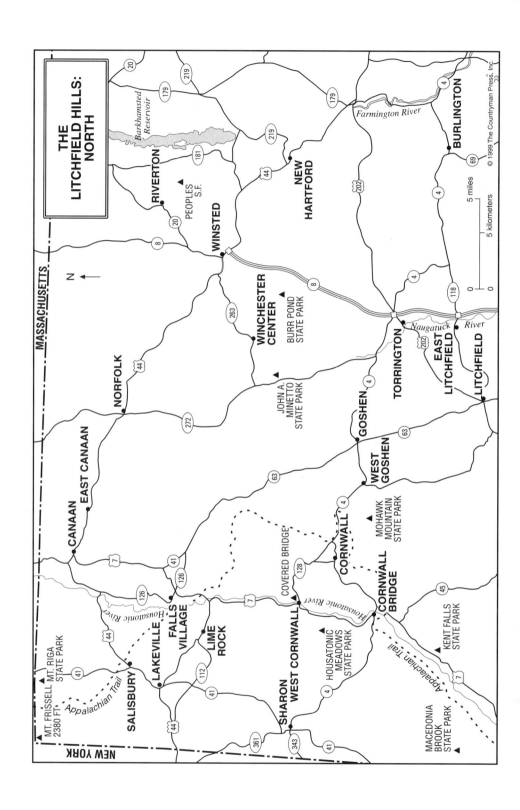

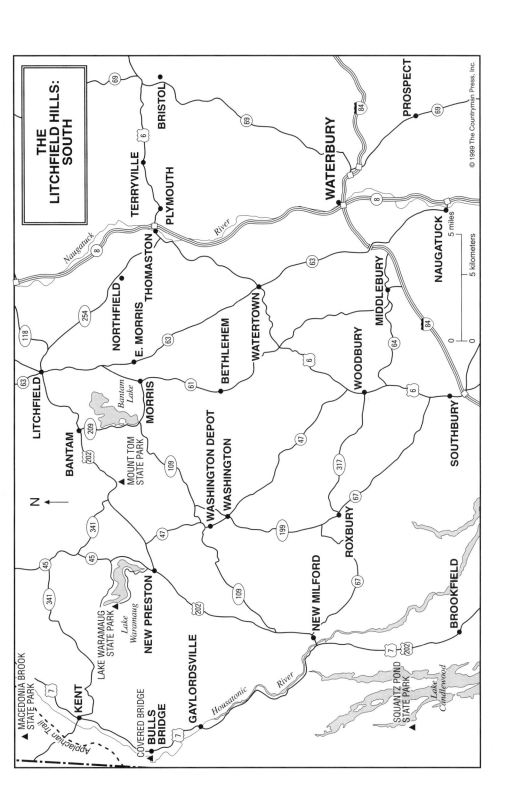

THE
LITCHFIELD HILLS:
SOUTH

N ←

5 miles

5 kilometers

BRISTOL

PROSPECT

WATERBURY

TERRYVILLE

PLYMOUTH

NAUGATUCK

River

Naugatuck

NORTHFIELD

THOMASTON

E. MORRIS

WATERTOWN

MIDDLEBURY

BETHLEHEM

WOODBURY

LITCHFIELD

MORRIS

Bantam
Lake

MOUNT TOM
STATE PARK

SOUTHBURY

BANTAM

WASHINGTON DEPOT

WASHINGTON

NEW PRESTON

Lake
Waramaug

LAKE WARAMAUG
STATE PARK

ROXBURY

NEW MILFORD

BROOKFIELD

KENT

MACEDONIA BROOK
STATE PARK

GAYLORDSVILLE

BULLS
BRIDGE

COVERED BRIDGE

Housatonic

River

Appalachian Trail

SQUANTZ POND
STATE PARK

Lake
Candlewood

69

6

69

84

69

8

8

84

8

254

118

63

63

63

61

6

47

317

67

67

199

109

109

202

202

202

209

341

45

45

341

47

341

7

7

7

7

64

6

Litchfield and Surrounding Towns

It comes as a surprise even to born-and-bred Nutmeggers how time has so dramatically passed by the northwestern corner of Connecticut, leaving the living image of quintessential colonial America almost intact in the verdant Litchfield Hills. Indeed, the village of Litchfield itself has been hailed as picture-postcard New England and attracts thousands of visitors annually who come to walk historic North and South Streets and admire the spectacular mansions. In July, many of the great homes are opened to the public for one day as a benefit for Litchfield's Connecticut Junior Republic, America's oldest boys town. In December the historic houses are decorated in holiday finery for a second tour. The Congregational church at the edge of one of the nation's largest greens (or commons, as they were first called) is arguably the most photographed Colonial-style church in New England. Litchfield's West Street runs along the southern border of the green and hosts an eclectic collection of restaurants, women's clothing stores, bookstores, art galleries, antiques shops, and a tawny-colored Methodist church. It closely resembles the better-known Main Street just up the road in Stockbridge, Massachusetts, recognized throughout the country from the famous painting by Norman Rockwell. West Street in Litchfield glows with myriad blossoms in window boxes on every store front.

Although the big homes are not museums, Litchfield does boast several other unique attractions worth visiting. On South Street, a New Jersey judge with the unlikely name of Tapping Reeve founded America's first law school, now a National Historic Site. The Litchfield Historical Society traces Connecticut history from the early settling of what was then Connecticut's western frontier to more recent days, when a vicious tornado unexpectedly savaged the western part of the state on a hot July day. The White Memorial Foundation will lure you to its 4,000 acres of forests, lakes, and ponds.

Other villages in the county would meet a movie-set designer's dreams. Washington, the first municipality in the country named after the Father of His Country, is a lovely collection of white-clapboard homes set around a green square dominated by the Congregational church. A short jaunt into the nearby woods brings you to the Institute for American Indian Studies, a museum and teaching facility that concentrates on the unique lifestyle of the forest-dwelling Native Americans, who did not live in tepees or hunt buffalo.

The beautiful Battell Stoeckel estate in Norfolk is the summer home of the Yale Music School, which stages a world-renowned annual festival of chamber music in an acoustically perfect redwood music shed. A host of artists have gravitated to Kent, on the banks of the Housatonic River, turning this once sleepy town known only for its prestigious Kent prep school into the art center of Connecticut. The hand tools that shaped the dwellings and furniture of colonial Americans are displayed in the Sloane-Stanley Museum. It's on the outskirts of Kent, just below Kent Falls State Park. Kent Falls is not exactly Niagara, but it is picturesque enough to attract hundreds of visitors daily.

The Litchfield Hills, which really are the foothills of the Berkshires just over the Massachusetts border to the north, contain Connecticut's highest mountains, in the Mount Riga area; its longest river (the Housatonic); and, at West Cornwall, its most beautiful covered bridge.

During the spring thaw, the white waters of the Housatonic challenge kayakers and canoeists. In summer, less intrepid boaters can venture out on calmer waters. In autumn, when the foliage catches fire, the drive from West Cornwall down US 7 along the river to Kent is a leaf-peeper's paradise. Campers vie for sites in the state park on the banks of the Housatonic, while backpackers and hikers slog, happily we can only assume, along the section of the Appalachian Trail that slices through the region.

At the time of the American Revolution, the village of Litchfield was a major manufacturing center, producing supplies for Washington's army. Iron was mined from the hills around Mount Riga and Kent for cannons and for the huge iron chain that the Continentals strung across the Hudson to block British ships. (It didn't work.) A leaden statue of King George III was pulled down in New York, cut up, and dragged to Litchfield, where the ladies melted it down and produced thousands of bullets for Washington's army. The soldiers dubbed them "Melted Majesty."

At war's end, towns such as Torrington and Winsted, sitting on the banks of the Naugatuck River almost at sea level, attracted the major industries, particularly brass and copper. Consequently, Litchfield went to sleep. Its little factories withered and died, and the hill country regained its trees.

Before World War II, a few train spurs penetrated the hills, bringing vacationers with steamer trunks who settled into lakeside country inns for the summer. After the war, fast and comfortable cars, new roads, and the dismemberment of the railroads led to new tourists: the day-

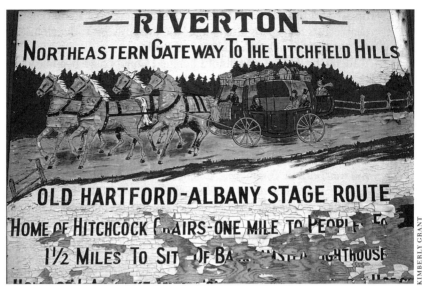

Riverton keeps its past visible with a colorful handpainted road sign.

Litchfield Hills Travel Council (860-567-4506; fax 860-567-5214; www.litchfieldhills.com), Box 968, US 202, Litchfield 06759. Mail or phone inquiries only. Pick up literature at the information booth on the green or in state highway information centers. The council publishes an annually updated, comprehensive folder, "Unwind in the Litchfield Hills," plus an Auto, Bike and Hiking Tours guide to seven selected loops. The eighth tour highlights the best photo sites. Folders of individual attractions and events also are available.

Northwest Connecticut Chamber of Commerce (203-482-6586), 333 Kennedy Drive, Suite R101, Box 59, Torrington 06790. Guides, local maps, town profiles. Brochure rack.

State of Connecticut Highway Information Center, Danbury, I-84 eastbound. One of a network of highway centers maintained by the state tourism office on superhighways, the center is open 24 hours a day, year-round. In addition to rest facilities, there are racks filled with folders and brochures mainly for the Litchfield County area. State guides and maps are a staple. Information on other parts of the state often is available. There's also an information center in Southbury, at exit 14 off I-84.

Waterbury Region Convention & Visitors Bureau (203-597-9527), 83 Bank Street, Waterbury 06721.

GETTING THERE

By bus: **Bonanza** and **Peter Pan** serve Waterbury, 20 miles south of Torrington.

By rail: A spur of the coastal commuter line, **Metro-North,** provides limited rail service from New York City, via Bridgeport, to the Waterbury station.

GETTING AROUND

Public transportation is practically nonexistent. Private car is the vehicle of choice. Otherwise, plan on renting a car.

MEDICAL EMERGENCY

The statewide emergency number is **911.**

Charlotte Hungerford Hospital (860-496-6666; emergency 860-496-6650), 540 Litchfield Street, Torrington.

Sharon Hospital (860-364-4141; emergency 860-364-4111), 50 Hospital Hill Road, Sharon.

St. Mary's Hospital (203-574-6000; emergency 203-574-6002), 56 Franklin Street, Waterbury.

Waterbury Hospital (203-573-6000; emergency 203-573-6290), 64 Robbins Street, Waterbury.

Winsted Medical Center (860-738-6600), 115 Spencer Street, Winsted. Emergency room services only.

New Milford Hospital (860-355-2611; emergency 860-350-7222), 21 Elm Street, New Milford.

VILLAGES

The Cities, Towns, and Villages of Litchfield County

Goshen. Bordering Litchfield to the north and suited mainly for dairy farming, Goshen early on became America's first center for cheese making. In 1792, Alexander Norton, using a wooden pineapple mold, started shipping out his famous "pineapple" cheese. After the Revolution, Goshen cheese makers shipped out, too, mainly to Wisconsin, which has four cheese-making towns named Goshen. At an altitude of 1,400 feet, Goshen shares with Norfolk—its immediate neighbor—the unenviable reputation as the "Ice Box of Connecticut." A long-standing aphorism proclaims: "In Goshen, we don't use our snow until it's two years old"! A variety of events are staged on the spacious fairgrounds, from dog shows, hot-air-balloon fairs, grange fairs, Indian powwows, and, of course, the statewide famous Goshen Fair over Labor Day weekend (see *Special Events*). And Goshen is now home to a new live animal farm (see *Amusement Parks*). The scenery is striking.

Norfolk. As in Goshen, only dairy farming is practical on this cold, rugged land. Because this has discouraged condo and development growth, Norfolk probably retains more restored and beautifully maintained homes dating back to colonial days than any other Connecticut town. Its quiet beauty and cool summers attracted prosperous businessmen from New York in the 1850s, who built large estates. Most notable among them is Whitehall, now Yale's Summer School of Music and home of the nationally known Norfolk Music Festival (see *Entertainment*). The village green is a gem. For such a small village, too, Norfolk has an unusually opulent library. Two wealthy families, competing with each other to do good for the town, did very well indeed, pouring money into the library—which now attracts visitors to lectures, poetry readings, and other cultural events.

Riverton. This town's claim to fame is the Hitchcock Factory, established in the 1800s and still producing the prize hand-stenciled furniture that graces so many New England homes. The factory store invites you to browse. Located on the banks of the Farmington River, Riverton is a visual feast in spring and fall. The old Riverton Inn fronts the banks of the river just across the bridge. Connecticut's smallest country fair winds up the fair season in October.

Separated by less than a mile, the twin towns of **Salisbury** and **Lakeville** boast some of New England's most authentic colonial buildings, which now serve as inns and bed & breakfasts. The **Falls Village** section is home of the Lime Rock Race Track, the most beautiful racetrack in America. Olympic hopefuls hone their skills on the downhill ski jump in Salisbury. Gourmet dining caters to the sophisticated tastes of its summer visitors—and of luminaries such as actors Meryl Streep and Michael J. Fox, among others. The famed Hotchkiss Prep School was favored by the Rockefellers.

Sharon was founded in 1738. Farming kept the early settlers of this border town busy, but Sharon is also famed for the invention of a notable mousetrap. A widely used rifle-cannon explosive shell was invented here, too, by two brothers, Andrew and Benjamin Hotchkiss. Quiet, semirural, and still nearly 50 percent forested, Sharon is now a haven for retirees, summer vacationers, and weekenders. An Audubon Center (see *Green Space*) and the Sharon Playhouse (see *Entertainment*) are its principal attractions.

The Cornwalls. Great Britain has one Cornwall, Connecticut has six: Cornwall, Cornwall Bridge, West Cornwall, Cornwall Hollow, East Cornwall, and North Cornwall. Secluded by high hills, the early settlers of Cornwall (1740) engaged mainly in logging. Today the villages are home to weekenders, summer residents, and teachers at the many private schools in the area. The state's largest ski area swoops down Mohawk State Forest; the once towering giants of the Cathedral Pines, battered by a recent tornado, lie tumbled one upon another. Visitors come from miles around to hike, fish, and boat on the beautiful Housatonic River and photograph the classic covered bridge at West Cornwall. Advisory to tourists: The covered bridge is in West Cornwall, *not* Cornwall Bridge.

Washington and **Washington Depot.** The first municipality in the country named after the Father of His Country, Washington is nestled in an upland area of hills and forests, high above the Shepaug River Valley. Because of the steep hills, agriculture was impractical. Instead, starting in 1872 the Shepaug Railroad brought in summer folk. Nowadays, theatrical and communications celebrities spend quiet weekends in opulent Colonial homes clustered around the classic green. Deep in the woods, the Institute for American Indian Studies maintains a unique museum that portrays 10,000 years of Native American life in Connecticut (see *Museums*). In late winter, nesting American bald eagles can be viewed from a nature preserve blind on the Shepaug River in nearby Southbury. Down in the valley, at Washington Depot, the Art Association is a beehive of cultural activity; and the famous and busy authors who call the Litchfield Hills home hold frequent book signings in the unusually well-stocked Hickory Stick bookstore.

Kent. US 7, the main north–south artery in this part of the Hills, is also the Main Street of what was once a sleepy town—first settled by Native Americans—on both sides of a flat alluvial plain of the Housatonic River. Catering for years mainly to the needs of the prestigious Kent School, it was "discovered" in the mid-1980s. New York designers, artists, and politicos converged on Kent. Main Street is now lined with trendy boutiques, art galleries, and exotic-clothing shops. When Henry Kissinger bought a big estate here, his security people advised him to uproot a grove of blueberry bushes on his property that had for years kept townspeople in pies and cobblers for the winter. There was an immediate outcry. Local folk and Kent School students descended upon the bushes and transplanted them to the campus, where their berries can still be picked by anyone with a basket or pail. Kent Falls and Bull's Covered Bridge are natural attractions. The *Boston Globe* ranks Kent as one of the prettiest villages in New England.

Waterbury. Once the center of huge brass and copper factories, which became world famous for buttons, watches, and then—during World War II—brass casings for artillery shells, Waterbury has now become a center of small business. Its statuary and well-preserved architecture are of prime interest as well. A statue of Father McGivney honors the native son who founded the international Catholic fraternal order Knights of Columbus. The Waterbury Republican building, formerly the town's main railroad station, is an architectural gem, modeled after the Palazzo Publico (City Hall) in Siena, Italy. Its soaring tower is a Waterbury landmark. The City Hall is widely regarded as one of the most attractive municipal buildings in New England. Along with five other midtown buildings, it forms the Cass Gilbert Historic District; all the buildings are listed on the National Register of Historic Places, and the district itself honors Gilbert, one of America's outstanding architects. Waterbury's green is a 2-acre oasis in the center of the city. And don't miss the Mattatuck Museum (see *Museums*).

TO SEE

Dudleytown, Dark Entry Road, Cornwall Bridge. A tangled, overgrown dirt lane leads up from the state road to the barely visible remains, mostly broken foundations, of what was once a thriving community. Started back in the mid-1700s, it became home to the Dudley family,

KIMBERLY GRANT

America's first law school was founded by a new Jersey lawyer, Judge Tapping Reeve. Two vice presidents and other legal dignitaries studied here.

whose forebears in England lived cursed lives. Although many of Dudleytown's progeny went on to success and fortune, most ended up mad, or worse. The wife of a New York doctor, the last family to live in Dudleytown, went mad nearly 80 years ago—another victim, say locals, of "the Dudleytown Curse." Drive east on CT 45, off US 7, for 0.5 mile to the Dark Entry Wildlife Preserve. Turn left on Dark Entry Road to the top of the mountain. Follow the trail to the ruins. Birders say the preserve is one of the best in the state.

Litchfield Historical Society (860-567-4501), corner of East and South Streets (CT 63 at the Litchfield Green), Litchfield. Open April 15 through October, Wednesday through Saturday 11–5, Sunday 1–5. The society has collected examples of Early American paintings and furniture, and a photographic history of the town. Changing exhibits are mounted in a large gallery where lectures by experts in colonial history and culture are held. Adults $3 (includes admission to the Tapping Reeve House); children free.

Tapping Reeve House and Law School, 82 South Street (CT 63), Litchfield. Open mid-May through November, Tuesday through Saturday 11–5, Sunday 1–5. An adjunct of the historical society, these two buildings comprise America's first law school. A permanent exhibit, "The Noblest Study," tells how the fundamentals of American jurisprudence, as it differs from British common law, evolved here, including the first moot court in law education. Judge Reeve came to Litchfield from the College of New Jersey—which changed its name in 1890 to Princeton—

and trained in the law two vice presidents, his brother-in-law, Aaron Burr, and John Calhoun; numerous Supreme Court justices; and 130 members of Congress—1,000 students in all. A new series of exhibits and interactive stations on the first floor of the home tell the story of the law school from the students' point of view with videos and state-of-the-art displays. One section tells the story of the girls of the nearby Pierce Academy, America's first private school for girls. (More than a few of the young ladies found husbands at Judge Reeve's.) The adjacent law school building displays early law books, journals, notebooks, and dissertations. It will also be used to discuss the learning of the law. Special lectures have been scheduled. On the National Register of Historic Places. Adults $6, includes admission to law school and historical society; children free.

Cobble Court, Litchfield. Behind Litchfield's first coffee shop on the green, in a cobblestone square resembling a British mews, you'll find a custom furniture shop, a nature lover's gift shop, and a stone bench for a moment of rest and meditation.

White Memorial Foundation and Conservation Center (860-567-0857), US 202, Litchfield. Spring through fall, Tuesday through Saturday 9–5; winter 8:30–4:30. This private, unique 4,000-acre tract of lakes, woods, bogs, and fields, established by conservationist and chess expert Alain White, is the largest nature preserve in Connecticut. Other tracts of land, totaling 11,000 acres, gifts of the foundation, formed the basis of the state park system. White Memorial features a nature museum; library; nature, hiking, and cross-country ski trails; horseback riding; camping; swimming; boating; fishing; and special lecture programs for adults and children. The museum charges adults $2; admission is $1 for children under 12.

Lourdes in Litchfield Shrine (860-567-1041), CT 118 just east of the Litchfield green. A noteworthy attempt to replicate the famous French grotto on a lovely tract of land. There is a rugged Stations of the Cross trail, and Masses daily in the grotto. Once a year the peace of the county is rent by the roar of the big bikes when the Montford Missionary priests perform the Blessing of the Motorcycles. Picnic grounds and gift shop.

Lime Rock Park (860-435-0896), CT 112 off US 7. April through October, Saturdays and holidays. When he was an active racer, this was the favorite track of actor Paul Newman. Now watch today's top stock-car superstars as they race around the pretzel oval at America's most beautiful racetrack. Regular events: vintage and historic automobile races and the NASCAR season finale. (Also see *Self-Improvement Vacations* and *Special Events.*)

MUSEUMS

The Institute for American Indian Studies (860-868-0518), 38 Curtis Road, off CT 199 in Washington. Year-round, Monday through Saturday 10–5, Sunday noon–5. A relatively modern museum building that houses a unique collection of artifacts of the northeastern Native Americans—

Pequots, Iroquois, Algonquians, Mohawks—who tended gardens, hunted for small game, fished, and in summer migrated to the shore, where they gorged themselves on lobsters and oysters. Changing exhibits. Weekly lectures and films, not limited to the Native American. An unexpected highlight: the almost complete skeleton of an extinct mastodon. Outside, wander through a reconstructed replica of an Algonquian village, an example of an archaeological dig. Adults $4; children 6–16, $2.

Sloane-Stanley Museum (860-927-3849), US 7, Kent. Open mid-May through October, Wednesday through Sunday 10–4. Americana artist and author Eric Sloane collected authentic hand tools when he was writing and illustrating his popular books on colonial life. The unique collection, along with a reproduction of Sloane's Connecticut studio, a replica of an early log cabin, and the remains of an early iron forge, comprise this unique museum. Adults $3; children and seniors $1.50.

Holley-Williams House and Cannon Museum (860-435-2878), US 44, Lakeville. Open July to September, Saturday and Sunday 1–4, or by appointment. Silver, glass, china, and portraits by early-colonial painters reflect the lifestyle of the Holley family, who lived in this Classical Revival house built in 1808. Clementi piano, exhibit of Holley knives. Adults $3; seniors $2; children 5–15, $1; free admission for children under 5. The Cannon section of the museum tells the story of the area blast furnaces that made cannons for Washington's army. A special exhibit traces the critical events of 1775 that ignited the American Revolution. Free admission.

Hitchcock Museum (860-738-4950), CT 20, Riverton. Open only by appointment. The walls of an 1829 Gothic church are festooned with original hand-stenciled Hitchcock chairs, crafted in the Hitchcock factory just down the road. Other antique furniture is also on display.

Kerosene Lamp Museum (860-379-2612), CT 263, in a private home on the green in Winchester Center. Open daily 9:30–4. Some people collect stamps, others baseball cards. The owner of this house invites you to see his collection of 500 hanging and standing lamps from 1856 to 1880. Free admission.

✑ **New England Carousel Museum** (860-585-5411), 95 Riverside Avenue, Bristol. Open year-round, Monday through Saturday 10–5, Sunday noon–5. (Closed Mondays from November 1 through March 31.) This museum traces the history of the once popular merry-go-round through displays of antique wooden carousel horses and carriages. There's a replica of an old carving shop and occasional demonstrations by visiting artisans. Adults $4; children 4–13, $2.50; seniors $3.50.

American Clock & Watch Museum (860-583-6070), 100 Maple Street, off US 6, Bristol. Open March through November, daily 10–5 (closed Thanksgiving). America once kept time by the clocks and watches invented and manufactured in Bristol and elsewhere in Connecticut. The first, and now invaluable, Mickey Mouse watches were made in nearby

KIMBERLY GRANT

The Hopkins Vineyard overlooks New Preston's beautiful Lake Waramaug.

Waterbury. The factories are gone, but the memories are timeless in the only museum in the country devoted entirely to clocks and watches. More than 3,000 instruments that keep time are on display in an 1801 house. Museum shop and sundial garden. Adults $3.50; seniors $3; children 8–15, $1.50.

Lock Museum of America (860-589-6359), 130 Main Street (US 6), Terryville. Open daily, May through October, 1:30–4:30; closed Monday. The invention and making of locks is another example of Yankee ingenuity. The industry has all but vanished in Connecticut, but here you can view the largest collection of locks, keys, and Victorian hardware in the country. Adults $3; seniors $2.50; children free.

Mattatuck Museum (203-753-0381), 144 West Main Street, Waterbury. Open year-round, Tuesday through Saturday 10–5, Sunday noon–5. Closed Sunday in July and August and on major holidays. The premier attraction in the former Brass City, this unique museum, now installed in spacious quarters in the old Masonic Temple building, has mounted impressive exhibits that chronicle the industrial history of this once thriving manufacturing city. Period rooms illustrate the social and cultural lives of both the vast numbers of industrial workers and their bosses. The principal art gallery is devoted to works of Connecticut artists and Connecticut scenes. Changing exhibits and special programs. Café; museum shop. Free admission; donation suggested.

WINERIES

Haight Vineyard and Winery (860-567-4045), Chestnut Hill Road, off CT 118, just east of the green, Litchfield. Open year-round. First of the modern wineries now dotting the state, the Haight Vineyard is open to guided tours. The winemaking process is explained inside the Swiss-style winery building. There's complimentary tasting of award-winning chardonnay and cabernet sauvignon blends. Gift shop. The annual Taste of Litchfield festival is held here (see *Special Events*).

Hopkins Vineyard (860-868-7954), Hopkins Road, New Preston. Open daily May through December; Friday through Sunday, January through April. Overlooking Lake Waramaug, this 30-acre vineyard welcomes visitors. The winery is in a weathered old red barn. There are tastings and a gift shop. Picnic area. Next to the Hopkins Inn (see *Lodging*). .

HISTORIC HOMES

Hotchkiss-Fyler House (860-482-8260), 192 Main Street, Torrington. Open April through December, Monday through Friday 9–4, Saturday 10–3. This is one of the most spectacular Victorian mansions in the state, built in 1900 by one of Torrington's leading industrialists. Original family furnishings, decorative art, superb woodwork. Rare paintings by American artists Ammi Phillips and Winfield S. Clime. An adjoining museum features changing exhibits. The entire town turns out in dark-est December when the mansion is dressed in its Christmas finery. This is also the home of the Torrington Historical Society. $2 adults; free for children under 12.

Bellamy-Ferriday House and Gardens (203-266-7596), Nine Main Street North (CT 61), Bethlehem. Open mid-May through October, Wednesday, Saturday, and Sunday 11–4. Group tours by appointment. This spectacular estate, built by the Rev. Joseph Bellamy (who also founded the first theological seminary in America), was opened to the public in mid-1994 following the death of the last member of the Bellamy family and after extensive restoration work. A 13-room white-clapboard house with Litchfield green shutters, it's a treasure trove of Oriental art, delftware, candlesticks, and furniture. Although the house and formal gardens sit on 9 acres, the nature trails of an adjoining 80 acres left to the Bethlehem Land Trust also may be visited. Lilacs, old roses, peonies, and topiary yews are the highlights of the gardens. Here is a unique opportunity to step back in time. Deeded to the Antiquarian and Landmarks Society, the estate is listed on the National Register of Historic Places. Adults $6; children $1.

Sheldon Tavern, North Street (CT 63), Litchfield. Now a private home, this beautiful colonial mansion was at first an inn. Washington records in his diary that he slept here while en route from West Point to Hart-ford or Wethersfield to confer with his ally, General Rochambeau, commander of the French expeditionary army based in Rhode Island. Together they plotted the Battle of Yorktown, the decisive and last major battle of the Revolutionary War

The Bull House, North Street (CT 63), Litchfield. An imposing mansion built by Ludlow Bull, the American explorer and Egyptologist who par-ticipated in the opening of one of history's most astonishing discoveries:

the tomb of Egyptian King Tutankhamen, completely intact with all its gold treasures. A private home, it occasionally is opened for the annual Litchfield House Tour (see *Special Events*).

Solomon Rockwell House (860-379-8433), 225 Prospect Street, Winsted. Open June through September, Thursday through Sunday 2–4. Original Hitchcock chairs and Thomas and Whiting clocks greet you upon entering this magnificent, antebellum-style home built by an early industrialist. There's memorabilia from both the American Revolution and the Civil War. Don't miss the collection of wedding gowns. On the National Register of Historic Places. Free admission.

Glebe House (203-263-2855), Hollow Road, Woodbury. Open April through November, Wednesday through Sunday 1–4. This 1740 farmhouse off US 6 is of special interest to gardeners and religious-history buffs. Here in 1783 the Episcopal Church in America selected Samuel Seabury as its first bishop. Surrounding the house, the only garden in America created by the legendary English artist and garden designer Gertrude Jekyll has been restored. Period furnishings and a gift shop. $3 donation.

HISTORIC SITES

McAuliffe Manor, on the Litchfield green, corner of CT 63 and US 202. A state prison since colonial days, the jail was converted in 1994 into a halfway house for drug-addicted women. Benjamin Franklin's illegitimate son, William, was incarcerated here during the American Revolution. A royal governor of New Jersey, he refused to join the American cause. Harassed in New Jersey prisons, his disconsolate father had him removed for his safety to Litchfield for the duration of the conflict. In confinement for more than three years, at the end of the war William settled in England. Father and son never again communicated with each other. The village's infamous "hanging tree" stood on the front lawn.

Obookiah Burial Site, CT 4, Cornwall. Hawaiian-born Henry Obookiah swam to a New Haven–bound seal-hunting ship after his family was killed in a tribal war in Hawaii. In New Haven, he became a convert to Christianity and spent many days preaching in the Litchfield Hills. He was buried in the Cornwall cemetery after he died at the age of 26 from typhus. His journal inspired the American Missionary Board of Boston to organize and send to Hawaii the now legendary first group of missionaries, led by the Rev. Hiram Bingham. The saga was fictionalized in James Michener's book *Hawaii*. Obookiah's grave was a goal for years for Hawaiian pilgrims. In 1993 the Hawaiians wanted Henry back. His bones were dug up and shipped back to the islands for final interment. The inscribed sarcophagus still attracts visitors.

Indian Missionary School Marker, Cornwall center, across from the church. After independence, the local Congregational church opened a missionary school for "Indians and heathens." Henry Obookiah studied here. It was closed and torn down when two local maidens fell in

The Congregational Church on the Green in Litchfield reputedly is one of the most photographed in New England.

love with and married two of the Native American converts.

Holy Land Cross. You may wonder as you drive through Waterbury on I-84 why a large rock outcropping is topped by a huge cross, lit and visible for miles at night. It marks the location of Holy Land, a miniature of Jerusalem that has deteriorated beyond repair and is no longer open to the public. The cross is all that remains.

SPECIAL CHURCHES

Congregational Church on the Green, US 202, Litchfield. A classic of its kind, pictures of this much photographed church appear on calendars, on postcards, and in photo files of countless visitors. In 1898 the congregants didn't think much of their architectural treasure, for they picked it up and moved it 300 yards down the road, where it served as an armory, recreation hall, and movie house. In 1929 the parishioners came to their senses and moved the building back to its present spot at the gateway to the village. It was only then that the pillars and the steeple were added. Acoustically perfect, it's often used as a concert hall.

Congregational church, CT 63 and CT 4, Goshen. Hiram Bingham was ordained and married in this church before setting out as head of the first group of US missionaries to Hawaii. A picture of Bingham and his bride and the route their little ship took to what were then called the Sandwich Islands can be seen in the vestry. The church is only one of two on the mainland that hang the Hawaiian flag year-round. Locals like to say the church steeple is "the highest in the state of Connecticut." It is—from sea level!

COVERED BRIDGES

West Cornwall Bridge. The bright-red-painted covered bridge spanning the Housatonic at West Cornwall links CT 128 with US 7. Built in 1837 by famous bridge architect Ithiel Town, it incorporated strut techniques that were copied by bridge designers around the country. Restored recently by the Connecticut Department of Transportation, it won a national prize for bridge restoration. The setting is spectacular and attracts thousands of photography fans annually. Experienced sports enthusiasts maneuver canoes and kayaks over the turbulent waters that flow under the bridge.

Bull's Bridge. The only other historic covered bridge in Connecticut open to vehicular traffic also spans the Housatonic near Gaylordsville, a short way south of Kent on US 7. Weather-beaten gray, it attracts more artists than photographers.

SCENIC DRIVES

Three state agencies—transportation, parks, and tourism—joined in driving the highways and byways of Connecticut and designating certain stretches as official scenic roads. Watch for the signs.

CT 4, from its intersection with US 7, is among the official scenic drives.

US 7 is an unofficial scenic drive. From West Cornwall south through Kent and onto New Milford, US 7 is as pretty a road as you can find anywhere in New England. Along the Housatonic, high cliffs remind you of Vermont. In fall they are ablaze with color.

CT 63. A pleasant, bucolic road as it meanders north out of Litchfield. From Goshen, just before it starts to descend to the North Canaan plain, you come upon a breathtaking mountain vista not dissimilar to those from atop the Great Smokies of North Carolina.

TO DO

AMUSEMENT PARKS

Quassy Amusement Park (1-800-FOR-PARK), CT 64, Middlebury. Open Memorial Day through Labor Day 10–10. More than 30 rides and a sandy beach on Lake Quassapaug will keep the family occupied all day. Boat rides, petting zoo, food concessions, but plenty of picnic tables if you want to bring your own vittles. The 20-acre playground is the state's largest amusement park. Free admission, but a $3 parking fee.

Lake Compounce (860-583-3300), 822 Lake Avenue, Bristol. Closed Tuesday. After several abortive starts, America's oldest amusement park in continuous operation is now America's newest park with the addition of 20 exciting rides, many of them high tech, that will more than satisfy families in search of fun, excitement, and relaxation. Located on a beautiful swimming pond, the park has one of the oldest roller coasters in the country, plus a new steel coaster, white-water raft ride, mountain skyride, a 12,000-square-foot Wave Pool, and a circus world kiddieland. The miniature railroad that originally ran around the estate of actor William Gillette, whose castle is now a state park on the Connecticut River (see "Lower Connecticut River Valley"—*Historic Homes and Sites*), is on exhibit. One of Gillette's two engines has been returned to the park in East Haddam, where it can now be seen. Call for hours and prices.

Animal Action Foundation (860-482-4464), Torrington Road, Goshen. Summer, 10–7 Tuesday through Friday, weekends 12:30–7. Closed Monday. The first major theme park up in the Litchfield Hills. A unique collection of mounted and live animals. The mounted animals, "harvested" by big-game hunter Jim Mazzarelli, are scheduled for display in a two-story building containing a miniature mountain with a waterfall. The live animals are on view in two series of outdoor pens; another section has been described as a *Jurassic Park* setting with a mixture of animals including bison and other rare species. The entire complex is set behind recently constructed New England–style stone walls that are so extensive they have been dubbed "The Great Walls of Goshen." Mazzarelli, founder of the park, plans educational programs on wild animal conservation throughout the year. Admission free.

BALLOONING/GLIDING

Watershed Balloons (860-274-2010), 179 Gilbert Road, Watertown. Float over the hills of Litchfield in a colorful hot-air balloon just for a family outing, or take a champagne flight for a special occasion. Balloons fly best during the early morning or late afternoon. Year-round, weather permitting. About $150 for a half-hour ride.

Mount Tobe Aviation (860-283-5819), Box 262, Plymouth 06782. Open May through October, Wednesday through Sunday 9–6. Here's a new thrill: soaring over the countryside in a glider, you and the pilot. Instruction is available. Gliders for rent.

BOATING

Dotted with lakes and crisscrossed by two major rivers—the Housatonic, longest in the state, and the Farmington—the Litchfield area is a natural for boating: canoeing, kayaking, sailing, rowing, rafting, tubing, even crew racing, and, in winter, iceboating. Launching ramps are maintained by the state on **Dog Pond** in Goshen, **Bantam Lake** in Morris, **Lake Waramaug** (the state park), and **Squantz Pond State Park** in New Fairfield.

Clarke Outdoors (860-672-6365), on the banks of the Housatonic, 163 US 7, West Cornwall. Canoe, kayak, and raft rentals, March 15 through December 2. Instruction and guided trips are available. During the spring thaw, white-water rafting in the Bull's Bridge Gorge.

O'Hara's Landing (860-824-7583), Twin Lakes Road, Salisbury. Launch your own or rent a rowboat, canoe, pontoon boat, or motorboat. Water skis are also available, with all safety accessories for children. There's a lakeside restaurant and a snack bar for a pick-me-up after a day on one of the state's prettiest small lakes. Anglers take notice: Connecticut's largest brown trout was hooked in these waters!

Farmington River Tubing (860-693-6465), US 44, New Hartford, in Satan's Kingdom State Recreation Area. Memorial Day through Labor Day 10–5. Individual river tubes, specially designed, take you on a thrilling 2½-hour ride through three churning rapids. For safety, you must be at least 10 years old and stand 4 feet, 5 inches tall.

FISHING

Housatonic Anglers and Cabins (860-672-4457), West Cornwall 06796, three miles north of the covered bridge on US 7. Rob and Nell Nicholas, veteran fisherfolk, fly-tiers, and guides, have set up a fly-fishing school, and will also take you on half-day tours to where the "big ones are biting." All equipment and flies provided, or bring your own favorite rod and flies. Enjoy a tasty lunch on the shores of the Hoosie, as the river is known to its fans. Two riverside cottages have been recently renovated for fishing guests. Continental breakfast. $125 for lodging; fishing for a full day with guide, $150 for one; $250 for three.

GOLF

Eastwood Country Club (860-489-2630), 1301 Torringford West Street, Torrington. Par 36, nine holes, 3,105 yards. A pleasant little course in a suburban neighborhood. Much favored by local business golfers.

East Mountain (203-753-1425), East Mountain Road, Waterbury. Par 68, 18 holes, 5,720 yards.

Western Hills (203-756-1211), Park Road, Waterbury. Par 72, 18 holes, 6,246 yards.

Crestwood Park (860-945-3054), Northfield Road, Watertown. Par 71, 18 holes, 6,376 yards.

Stonybrook Golf Club (860-567-9977), Milton Road, Litchfield. Par 35, nine holes, 2,902 yards. The exquisitely manicured grounds provide a unique challenge to the beginner as well as the more accomplished player.

HAYRIDES AND SLEIGH RIDES

Wood Acres (860-583-8670), Griffin Road, Terryville. Horse-drawn hayrides, carriage rides, and sleigh rides.

HORSEBACK RIDING

H.O.R.S.E. of CT (860-868-1960), 43 Wilbur Road (of US 202), Washington. Principally devoted to caring for neglected and abused horses, this unique facility also offers trail rides for beginners and advanced riders on Friday, Saturday, and Sunday. Helmets are supplied. Riders and horses get "acquainted" in a 15-minute riding session in the ring. Adults only. $50 for a 90-minute trail ride, $75 for a 2½-hour ride with picnic lunch on the trail.

Lee's Riding Stable, Inc. (860-567-0785), CT 63 just south of the Litchfield green. English and western saddles for the cowboy in you. Ponies for the kids. Walking trails only, mostly in the woods (wide open spaces are hard to come by in Connecticut). Indoor ring for rainy days. No bronco busting; these Yankee horses know their manners.

Loon Meadow Farms' Horse & Carriage Livery Service, (860-542-6085), Box 554, Norfolk 06058. Take a nostalgic sleigh or carriage ride through the historic village of Norfolk, past Revolutionary-era homes and the encampment where General Burgoyne's English army rested after its defeat at Saratoga. Enjoy a picnic along the trail or arrange for a stop at the Pub (see *Dining Out*) or the White Hart Inn (see *Lodging*) for a romantic dinner. $120-160.

KAYAKING

The Cycle Loft (860-567-1713) 25 Commons Drive, US 202, Litchfield, rents kayaks for flat-water sections of the Bantam and Shepaug Rivers; guides and instruction available. Call for specific trips, rates, and reservations.

MOUNTAIN BIKING

Off-road terrain in Litchfield County is generally rugged and hilly, but suitable trails can be found for riders of all abilities. **White Memorial Foundation** in Litchfield offers 35 miles of trail through pine forests laced with ponds, streams, and swamps (see *To See*). Trails can be reached from the several trailheads on US 63. The **Steep Rock Reservation** (860-868-9131), Washington Depot, can be accessed by two trailheads, one on CT 47, another on River Road. Riders are allowed on the dirt roads and trails—including a former railroad bed—that follow the Shepaug River. Call ahead in early spring. Trails are sometimes closed during the spring thaw. **The Cycle Loft** in the Litchfield commons (also see *Kayaking*) rents mountain bikes and offers advice on planning rides. It also carries a full line of cycling accessories and parts.

SWIMMING

Freshwater beaches abound on secluded ponds and lakes in many state parks, in addition to town beaches that are open to the public for a fee.

Sandy Beach, on the western end of Bantam Lake, is operated by the town of Litchfield. Lifeguard; concession. Daily fee for nonresidents.

Mount Tom State Park, US 202 southwest of town, Litchfield. The best swimming in the cleanest waters of the Litchfield Hills. The beach is sandy, the lifeguards alert. Dressing rooms, picnic tables, and a food stand. For the vigorous, a mile-long hike to the top of Mount Tom rewards you with a stone tower at the top and a great view of the hills. Parking fee.

Lake Waramaug State Park, CT 45 off US 202, New Preston. Recalls the high mountain lakes of Austria and Switzerland. Eighty-eight campsites (see *Campgrounds*). Fishing, scuba diving, and paddleboats for rent.

✐ **Burr Pond State Park,** 5 miles north of Torrington on old CT 8. This is a popular family swimming area. Lots of splashing kiddies shouting, nonstop, "Mommy, look at me." Rustic dressing facilities.

John A. Minetto State Park, 6 miles north of Torrington on CT 272. Less trafficked and in a lovely bucolic setting, this pond is the beach of choice if you're looking for peace and quiet.

Northfield Dam Recreation Area, CT 254, south of Litchfield. The federal government operates this nicely landscaped beach in a flood-control area—that is, on a pond behind a dam that protects Thomaston and Waterbury during spring-thaw floods. It's well equipped, with solid picnic tables and dressing rooms. No need to worry about floods during July and August, when the flow from the river is only a trickle.

Lake McDonough (860-379-3036), Beech Rock Road, CT 219, Barkhamsted. Open weekdays 1–8; weekends and holidays 8–8. A beautiful swimming beach on a lake created by overflow from the huge Barkhamsted Reservoir. Rowboats and paddleboats for rent. Picnic tables. Hiking trails. Fishing in season. Parking $5.

TRAIN RIDE

✐ **New England Railroad Museum** (203-597-9527), 83 Bank Street, Waterbury. A new tourist train, the Naugatuck Railroad (nicknamed "the Naugy"), and a rail museum have been established in the Waterville section of Waterbury, just north of the town center. The trains operate scheduled 1-hour rides on weekends May through October. There also are special excursions during the fall foliage season and on major holidays. The museum has 70 pieces of historic New England rolling stock for display. The train leaves Waterville and runs up alongside the Naugatuck River and onto the Thomaston Dam in Black Rock State Park, highlighting the history of this important industrial valley. Diesel engines will pull the cars until the line's steam locomotives are restored. A special excursion takes holidaygoers to Torrington on First Night (see *Special Events*). Round-trip, adults $8; children to 16, $6.

CROSS-COUNTRY SKIING

Equipment rental is usually available at areas that emphasize cross-country skiing. Bring your own skis to the trails in state parks and forests.

Blackberry River Ski Touring Center (860-542-5100), US 44, Norfolk. Fifteen miles of groomed trails.

Mohawk Mountain Ski Area (860-672-6464), Great Hollow Road, off CT 4, Cornwall. Five miles of cross-country trails (see also *Downhill Skiing*).

Pine Mountain Cross-Country, Inc. (860-653-4279), CT 179, East Hartland. Fifteen miles of trails.

White Memorial Foundation (860-567-0857), 71 Whitehall Road, US 202, Litchfield. Thirty-five miles of trails through pine forests and open fields, around frozen brooks, ponds, and lakes. One of the most beautiful and popular ski-touring areas in the state.

Woodbury Ski & Racquet Area (203-263-2203), CT 47 (north off US 6), Woodbury. Twenty miles of trails (see also *Downhill Skiing*).

(See also *Green Space* for the many state parks that allow cross-country skiing.)

DOWNHILL SKIING

Mohawk Mountain Ski Area (860-672-6464), Great Hollow Road, off CT 4 in Cornwall. The largest ski resort in the state and the birthplace of snowmaking, with 23 slopes and trails and five lifts. There's a Swiss-style base lodge with cafeteria, rental shop, and ski instructors. Near major metropolitan centers. No overnight facilities, but there are inns and B&Bs close by. Now open nights.

Ski Sundown (860-379-9851), Route 219, New Hartford. A 65-acre winter wonderland of 15 groomed downhill trails for novices and advanced skiers. Refreshments in the cozy base lodge. Rentals and lessons. Overnight facilities in the vicinity. This is the second largest ski resort in Connecticut. Night skiing. Snowmaking.

Woodbury Ski Area (203-263-2203), CT 47 (north off US 6), Woodbury. Downhill skiing on 14 trails, day and night, and a lot more. Groomed cross-country trails, tobogganing, sledding, ice-skating rink. If you're a fan of skateboarding, you'll take to snowboarding in the half pipe, a huge, U-shaped wall much like a toboggan run. In summer you'll find concerts, tennis courts, and a skateboard park. Rentals and lessons. New base lodge and ski shop.

OTHER WINTER RECREATION

Because of their higher elevation, the Litchfield Hills are colder than the rest of the state. When the deep freeze settles in, iceboaters whip around **Bantam Lake** in Morris and **Tyler Lake** in Goshen at break-neck speeds. Closer to shore, demented ice anglers set up their little huts, drill holes in the ice, and patiently shiver, waiting for a nibble. Limited winter camping is permitted in selected state parks. Check with the **Bureau of Parks and Forests** of the Connecticut Department of Environmental Protection (860-566-2305), 79 Elm Street, Box 5066, Hartford 06106-5066. Most state parks and forests in Connecticut also allow cross-country skiing. The very hardy can hike or snowshoe the many trails that crisscross the county.

Norfolk Curling Club (860-542-5579), Golf Drive, Norfolk. One of only two curling rinks in Connecticut. For more than 30 years, the locals have been whirling heavy round stones down an ice rink, then running backward in front of the stones and frantically sweeping the ice with little brooms to reduce friction. Occasionally, visiting teams from Scotland and Holland pop over for some friendly competition.

SELF-IMPROVEMENT VACATIONS

The Silo Cooking School (860-355-0300), Upland Road, off US 202, New Milford 06776. Noted conductor Skitch Henderson and his talented wife, Ruth, import world-famous chefs from New York along with cookbook authors and local professionals to guide you through the intricacies of the culinary arts in 100 classes held in an old barn from March through December. Attached kitchen store and art gallery with changing exhibits. **Sarah's Flowers** (860-355-2254), a full-service flower shop, is down the hill at the entrance to the farm on US 202.

Skip Barber Racing and Driving Schools (800-RACE-LRP), Lime Rock Park, CT 112, Lime Rock Village. If you have aspirations to become a stock-car racer, former champion Skip Barber and his team of veteran instructors are the men who will put you behind the wheel of a souped-up Stratus and teach you the ropes.

GREEN SPACE

Follow US 7 a mile north of Cornwall Bridge to **Housatonic Meadows.** Stretching 2 miles along the Housatonic River, this mainly wooded area is popular with campers, hikers, and picnickers. Chemical pollution from Massachusetts, now stopped, restricts anglers to catch-and-release fishing. Surprisingly, this restriction has increased the river's popularity because a fish, once caught, is thrown back for another day and another Izaak Walton. The Housatonic is also a magnet for canoes and kayaks.

Macedonia Brook was created by another major bequest of Alain White, father of Connecticut's state park system. This 2,300-acre tract, 4 miles north of Kent off CT 341, winds its way up to an elevation of 1,400 feet and attracts the more rugged outdoor enthusiasts. Campsites and stream fishing. In winter, there's challenging cross-country skiing (more like downhill skiing on cross-country slats).

Less demanding is **Topsmead,** located 1 mile east of Litchfield Center on Buell Road, off CT 118. This is the 511-acre former estate of a Waterbury bronze tycoon. The grounds are open only for picnicking, hiking on nature trails, and cross-country skiing. Tours of the estate's Tudor house and gardens are available.

The gurgling waters of the Farmington River lap the shores of **Peoples State Forest,** 1 mile north in Pleasant Valley on CT 181. To this rugged setting, bring a book (this one) or the Sunday *Times* and a picnic, and spend a meditative day under the branches of 200-year-old pines in Mathies Grove. Fish, hike, bird-watch.

Mohawk State Forest, CT 4 in Cornwall just over the Goshen town line. Park your car in the small lot at the entrance to the forest, which extends southward along a high ridge. Hike through the woods to the state police radio antenna tower for a magnificent view down the mountainside of the Mohawk Mountain Ski Area to Cornwall Village. In fall this spot becomes a ringside seat for some of the brightest foliage in all of New England.

Mount Riga State Park is located in the farthest northwestern corner of the Litchfield Hills just above Salisbury, off CT 41. The highest point in the state, at 2,380 feet, is **Mount Frissel.** Rustic hiking trails, including a section of the Appalachian Trail, snake upward through the woods. Rugged hiking boots, a stout heart, and sturdy legs are requisites, along with a small backpack with water and refreshments.

Hollenbeck Preserve, Page Road and US 7, Canaan. This 182-acre recent acquisition of The Nature Conservancy is open for hiking and other recreational activities. View rare plants and animals. Bordered by the Hollenbeck and Housatonic Rivers, this is one of 57 preserves in Connecticut owned and operated by the Conservancy.

NATURE CENTERS

Five nature centers complement the state parks in the Litchfield Hills. All feature interpretive buildings with a variety of nature displays, guided and/or self-guided tours, wildflowers, and gift shops.

Flanders Nature Center (203-263-3711), Church Hill and Flanders Road, Woodbury. Open year-round, daily, dawn to dusk. Offers programs for adults and children and invites you to explore its unique nut tree arboretum, bogs, and geologic sites. Maple syrup demonstrations in March (see *Special Events*).

Sharon Audubon Center (860-364-0520), CT 4, Sharon. The interpretive building is open year-round, Monday through Saturday 9–5, Sunday 1–5. Trails are open daily, dawn to dusk. Watch for beavers, muskrats, even the elusive otter—and, of course, the myriad birds. Nature trails, exhibits, programs, and classes are available at this 684-acre sanctuary of the National Audubon Society; also herb and wildflower gardens, the Children's Discover Room, and a gift shop. Adults $3; children and seniors $1.50.

White Flower Farm is a nationally known nursery (and a mail-order catalog) with extensive display gardens.

H. C. Barnes Nature Center (860-585-8886), 175 Shrub Road, Bristol. Trails open daily sunrise to sunset. Center hours: Saturday 9–4:30, Sunday 1–5. Call for weekday hours. Self-guiding trails wind through 70 acres of a variety of natural habitats. Nature library for children, special animal exhibits, games, educational programs. Gift shop.

Cathedral in the Pines, Cornwall. Pass through the village of Cornwall to a beautiful field at the eastern end of town. You might fancy that you've entered a hidden mountain pass and come upon Shangri-La. Turn left, and in moments you're on a 47-acre tract of what once were towering virgin pines, protected by The Nature Conservancy as a shaded "Cathedral in the Pines"—until a rogue tornado smashed most of these giants to the ground on an oppressively hot day in July in the late 1980s. The Conservancy has let them lie, a lesson in the enormity of the forces of nature. A decade later, a new growth of shrubs and seedlings is emerging; it soon will obscure the fallen logs.

Sessions Wildlife Management Area (860-675-8130), CT 69, Burlington. Kept open year-round, sunrise to sunset, by the state's wildlife management agency. Two self-guided hiking trails—one 0.6 mile long, the other 3 miles—take you alongside a beaver marsh and a small waterfall. From the observation tower you can glimpse other wildlife busy making a living. Youngsters will enjoy the backyard habitat demonstration. They may even learn something. Free admission.

Burlington Trout Hatchery (860-673-2340), Beldon Road (Off CT 4), Burlington. Open daily 8–3:30. Some 90,000 trout are raised here each year to stock state fishing streams.

NURSERIES/GARDENS

White Flower Farm (860-567-8789), CT 63, East Morris (the mailing address is Route 63, Litchfield 06759-0050). Open 9–6 daily. To visit this nationally known garden-cum-nursery, proceed south out of Litchfield on CT 63 and continue a few hundred yards past the Morris town line sign. Ten acres of perennial gardens are spread out on each side of the sales area. Plantings have been designed to greet you with dazzling color from early May through fall. Depending on the time of your visit, you'll see in bloom perennial borders of spring bulbs; tree peonies, Oriental poppies, herbaceous peonies, and tuberous begonias; or mums, asters, and fall foliage. White Flower is famed for its rare plants, many imported. It's the only nursery in the United States that propagates and sells the spectacular English Blackmore and Langdon tuberous begonias, on view in their own special greenhouse. Guided tours of the farm may be arranged four weeks in advance.

Walnut Hill Greenhouse (860-482-5832), 217 Wheeler Road, Litchfield. Open year-round. The outside garden is small, but for ardent gardeners, the long greenhouse is a visual feast. You're invited to meander through a veritable jungle of thousands of house- and garden plants from all over the world, in every stage of development—from tiny seedlings to mature specimens. Outstanding variety of cacti. At Christmas, the greenhouse is a red riot of poinsettias.

Hillside Gardens (860-542-5345), 515 Litchfield Road, CT 272, Norfolk. Open May through September, daily 9–5; closed holidays. Fred and Mary Ann McGourty have personally created a unique, 4-acre perennial garden that rises gently from the road into the woods. It's distinguished by its variety of borders, some freestanding, others against or on stone walls. Properly designed borders, the McGourtys feel, are the easiest way to maintain any well-designed garden. Gardeners from all over come to study the McGourty designs. Bring a large pad. Many of the uncommon plants have been brought back from Europe. Free admission.

Litchfield Hills Nurseries (860-567-9374), US 202, just east of the green, Litchfield. For the gardener in the family who can't resist bringing home another begonia or African violet to add to the collection. This popular nursery has an excellent variety of bedding plants in season, shrubs, perennials, trees, and, at the end of the year, dried floral and evergreen arrangements for Christmas. No outdoor gardens.

Litchfield Horticultural Center (860-567-3707), 258 Beach Street, Litchfield. A wide variety of annuals, perennials, and exotic and dwarf conifers set against a backdrop of 20,000 Christmas trees. Stroll in the spacious greenhouse for houseplants and tropicals that you can set outside for the summer.

Cricket Hill Garden (860-283-1042), 670 Walnut Hill Road, Thomaston. David Furman and his wife, Kasha, contend that they have "30 children and love them all equally." The "children" are 30 species of classical tree peonies, imported from China and descendants of plants developed more than 1,000 years ago in the Sui Dynasty. The Furmans are among the few gardeners in the United States to propagate these rare and beautiful plants.

LODGING

The Litchfield Hills Travel Council describes 58 places to put in for the night, the bulk of which are beautifully appointed bed & breakfasts. Some of the most famous country inns and resorts overlook the area's sparkling lakes; others are hidden in the woods or front colonial village greens. Hotels are located in the main in the larger cities; motels are scattered about. Don't look for the typical family cottages in the woods that you'll find in the more rural New England states. Summer vacation cottages for rent in Connecticut are, for the most part, in the wealthy shoreline towns. *Note:* Some "inns" are really hotels; others are more like resorts. And an occasional B&B even calls itself an inn. We've tried to sort them out for you.

RESORTS

  ♿ **Club Getaway** (860-927-3664; reservations: 212-935-0222; out-of-state: 1-800-6-GETAWAY; fax 860-927-1890), South Kent Road, South Kent 06757. Open May through October. Modeled after Club Med, this 300-acre resort provides a wide range of sporting activities, from tennis to water skiing on a private lake, windsurfing, volleyball, archery, swimming, mountain biking, in-line skating, sailing, technical rock climbing, and more. Instruction in all of the above. Evening entertainment. Eighty-four cabins. $250–300 includes three meals. Golf carts are available for the disabled to use to get around the resort.

The Birches Inn (860-865-0229), West Shore Road, New Preston 06777. This former Austrian-style inn overlooking Lake Waramaug has undergone a complete and extensive renovation and now ranks with the best upscale inns in the Litchfield Hills. Private beach; water and winter sports. In season, midweek $150–225, weekends $175–300; lower rates off season. Continental breakfast with one hot item. The restaurant has already won raves from top food critics (see *Dining Out*).

The Mayflower Inn (860-868-9466), 118 Woodbury Road (CT 47), Washington 06793. A century-old country inn was razed to the ground, a few timbers were saved, and a beautiful new inn has risen in its place on 28 tranquil acres of woods, ponds, and fields. Spectacular gardens have been carved into the hillside. Some of the 24 rooms and suites have not only fireplaces but also balconies overlooking the trees. Outdoor heated pool, tennis, health club with sauna. A deserved reputation as *the* place for a romantic getaway in Connecticut. Outstanding restaurant (see *Dining Out*). $225–355 double, $395–495 suites, per night. Two-night minimum on weekends.

The active pastoral: A working farm in Woodbury

INNS
Inns are listed in roughly geographic order.

In Litchfield

  ♿ **The Litchfield Inn** (860-567-4503; fax 860-567-4503), US 202, Litchfield 06759. A new building in the Colonial style, the Litchfield Inn is west of the borough green on the main state highway. Thirty-one nicely decorated rooms all have private bath. There are eight theme rooms and a formal parlor with baby grand piano and roaring fireplace. Continental breakfast. The new **Bistro East Restaurant** is winning raves (see *Dining Out*). Popular happy-hour bar; live entertainment on some weekends. $110–175 double; lower off-season.

  Tollgate Hill Inn (860-567-4545; 1-800-445-3903), US 202 on the eastern outskirts of Litchfield. This quiet old hostelry set back from the highway in a grove of white birch trees is just the place for romantic lovers, young and old, or for settled folk hoping to stir the embers of a marriage grown too familiar. The 18th-century paneling, floorboards, and fireplaces have been meticulously restored by suave innkeeper Fritz Zivic. Twenty exquisitely furnished rooms, many with canopy bed. Continental breakfast; gracious dining in two Colonial-style dining rooms, the Tavern and the Formal Room. Extensive wine cellar. $110 for double rooms to $175 for suites.

Elsewhere

  ✐ **Yankee Pedlar Inn** (1-800-777-1891), 93 Main Street, Torrington 06790. In the heart of downtown Torrington and a short drive to two major ski slopes, this 108-year-old inn is across from the Warner Theatre (see

Entertainment) and in the midst of antiques shops, a coffee shop, a library, and places of worship. Four-poster beds, Hitchcock furniture, private bath in each of the 60 rooms. Paneled dining room with an in-house, English-style tavern. Rates start at $89 per room and include a buffet breakfast. Senior discounts. Children under 12 free. No pets.

& **Old Riverton Inn** (860-379-8678; 1-800-EST-1796; fax 860-379-1006), CT 20 just north of Winsted, Riverton 06065. Open year-round. An inn since 1796 on what was then the Post Road between Hartford and Albany, the Old Riverton still welcomes the hungry, the thirsty, and the sleepy. Your hosts, Mark and Pauline Telford, invite you to climb into a canopy bed in one of the 12 comfortable guest rooms, all with private bath, and listen to the murmur of the Farmington River meandering past the front door. Hunker up to the Hobby Horse Bar and sip your cocktails while sitting on old saddles. On the National Register of Historic Places. Award-winning dining room. $80 double to $175 for a deluxe suite with canopy beds and fireplace. Full breakfast. Handicapped accessible first floor only.

& **Interlaken Inn** (860-435-9878; 1-800-222-2909; fax 860-435-2980), CT 112 off US 7, Lakeville 06039. In a country setting across the state road from the prestigious Hotchkiss prep school and on the banks of Connecticut's deepest lake—and also its most unpronounceable, Wononskopomuc. The Interlaken offers 80 rooms—including seven duplex suites with fireplaces and kitchens—a complete health center, and fine dining in a relatively modern building. Swimming, boating, and fishing in the lake are available, or you can bathe in the heated outdoor pool. Tennis, chip-and-pitch golf. Inn guests can also tee off on the challenging Hotchkiss course. The inn is close to Lime Rock Park (see *To See*) and the music festivals of the Litchfield Hills (see *Entertainment*) and Berkshires. $109 double, $272 suites. Two-night minimum in season. Winter rates. Two rooms in main building are handicapped accessible. Adjacent **Sunnyside B&B,** $189 (same phone number as the inn).

& **Iron Masters Motor Inne** (860-435-9844), 229 Main Street, Lakeville 06039. Recalls the days when iron forges belched forth flames in the woods and produced the cannons for Washington's army. Twenty-eight rooms with Ethan Allen furniture. Chat by the large fieldstone fireplace in the Hearth Room; dine in the Carriages Restaurant. English garden surrounds the outdoor pool. $75–135 includes continental breakfast. Limited handicapped accessibility.

& **White Hart Inn** (860-435-0030), CT 41 and US 44, Salisbury 06068. Recently restored, the 26 guest rooms of this landmark inn now have private baths, cable TV, air-conditioning. One room is equipped for the handicapped. Some suites. From the wide porch or from your canopy bed, you can look out on the village green. There's a historic tavern, the Garden Room. Another favorite for romantic getaways. $75–150 November through April; $90–180 May through October. Two-night minimum in season on weekends, 3-night minimum on holiday weekends.

Under Mountain Inn (860-435-0242), CT 41, Salisbury 06068. A thorned locust tree, said to be the oldest in Connecticut, shades this charming, circa-1700 white-clapboard farmhouse. The seven guest rooms, all with private bath, are uniquely decorated. Several intimate dining rooms (see *Dining Out*). English-style pub, for innkeeper-chef Peter Higginson hails from the mother country. His wife, American-born Marged, joins with her husband in asking, "When was the last time you had a 'proper' cup of tea, read the *Manchester Guardian,* and ate steak and kidney pie?" British library also has videos. $170–195 MAP, holiday packages.

Curtis House (203-263-2101), US 6, Woodbury 06798, is Connecticut's oldest inn—built before 1736. On the main street, it's in the heart of Woodbury's myriad antiques shops and near the Glebe House (see *Historic Homes*). Canopy beds add to the charm of the 18 guest rooms in the main house. Eight have private bath. Four additional rooms in the former carriage house are connected to the main grounds by a footbridge. Popular dining room (see *Dining Out*). $39 for shared bath; $61.60–123.20, all double.

Cornwall Inn (1-800-786-6884), US 7, Cornwall Bridge 06754. Playing host to travelers since 1871, this gracious inn has five rooms in the main building, three with private bath. An eight-room country motel is adjacent. Excellent restaurant. Country breakfast. Pets welcome. $50–125 in the inn, $50–100 in the motel, double occupancy.

Boulders Inn (860-868-0541; fax 860-868-1925), East Shore Road, New Preston 06777. A sprawling mansion overlooking Lake Waramaug serves as the centerpiece for this country retreat, which includes four rooms and two suites in the main house, eight guesthouses with fireplaces, and a carriage house with three rooms. All rooms are furnished with antiques or in traditional country style. Private beach and boat house; tennis, bicycling, and a hiking trail up Pinnacle Mountain. Superb dining room (see *Dining Out*). $225–265 double, MAP.

Hopkins Inn (860-868-7295; fax 860-868-7464), 22 Hopkins Road, New Preston 06777. Best known for its haute cuisine, this attractive, 19th-century Federal-style country inn high above Lake Waramaug opens its 11 guest rooms and two apartments from late March through December. Private beach. (See also *Dining Out.*) Myriad sports and cultural activities in nearby towns. $65–82 double. No pets.

The Homestead Inn (860-354-4080), Five Elm Street, New Milford 06776. Your hosts, innkeepers Rolf and Peggy Hammer, have furnished the eight rooms in the 140-year-old main house and six in the newer adjacent Treadwell House with country antiques and reproductions. All guest rooms have private bath, TV, and air-conditioning. An antique Steinway in the common room invites the talented to tinkle the keys. Relax on the front and back porches, or stroll in the perennial gardens. Two-night minimum stay on in-season weekends. $70–92.

Mountain View Inn (860-542-6991), CT 272, Norfolk 06058. This gracious 1875 Victorian house overlooks the picture-postcard village of Norfolk. Innkeeper Michele Sloane extends her hospitality. Guests can choose from among seven intimate rooms, most with private bath, some with four-poster bed, others opening onto an enclosed porch or an adjoining study. Tea and games in the parlor. On weekends and holidays, the public is invited to enjoy gourmet fireside dining. There's a full, hearty American breakfast for guests. $60–125 weekends; $20 less midweek. Holiday surcharge, $10.

BED & BREAKFASTS

Bed & breakfasts are listed in roughly geographic order. In addition to the listings below, a number of bed & breakfast reservation services offer access to rooms available in establishments throughout the state. For a list, see *What's Where—Bed & Breakfasts.*

The Country Goose (860-927-4746), 211 Kent Cornwall Road, Kent 06757. Closed March. Off the road just north of Kent, this restored Federal-style house is set on 5 acres on the lee side of towering St. Johns Ledges. Owner Phyllis Dietrich has decorated the four guest rooms (one a single) with antique furnishings, goose shade pulls, and watercolors by local artists. Relax in the library browsing through vintage magazines; there's also a formal parlor. The continental breakfasts—Phyllis's prizewinning homemade coffee cakes, muffins, quick breads, and jams—are served in the original kitchen, with its working beehive oven. There's great birding in the area. $90.

Constitution Oak Farm (860-354-6495), 36 Beardsley Road, Kent 06757. Four guest rooms, two with bath, in this 1830s house on 160 acres, all furnished in period pieces. Open year-round. A mile from Lake Waramaug State Park. Breakfast. $55–65.

The Gibbs House (860-927-1754), 87 North Main Street, Kent 06757. Two bright and sunny rooms with color TV and coffeemaker are within walking distance of Kent's prestigious art galleries and international boutiques. The suite has a private bath. Continental breakfast. Single $75, double $85.

Hillside Studio B&B (860-868-6607; e-mail: ann.vonhoorn@snet.net), 179 West Shore Road, New Preston 06777. A pair of working artists, Ann DeLorier and Richard vonHoorn, have opened the first and only B&B directly on the shores of Lake Waramaug. Enjoy the view from one large room with triple windows overlooking the water. Relax with wine and cheese by the homey fireplace. Swim off the dock. Bike, jog, or walk around the lake or up into the hills. Jacuzzi, coffeemaker, and microwave. The "studio" is where the couple works. $150 and worth it just for the spectacular view.

1890 Colonial (860-364-0436), 150 Gay Street, Sharon 06069. Open year-round. The three spacious guest rooms, with high ceilings, all have private bath. In summer, guests can rest on the screened-in porch after a hike around the property. A private furnished apartment is available at special weekly or monthly rates. Outdoor pool; flower gardens. Owner Carole "Kelly" Tangen is proud of the breads and muffins she bakes for the hearty breakfasts. $107 May through October; lower off-season rates.

Hilltop Haven (860-672-6871), 175 Dibble Hill Road, West Cornwall 06796. Open year-round. There are breathtaking views of the Housatonic Valley, Berkshire foothills, and Taconic Mountains from this hilltop, 64-acre scenic estate. Two rooms are furnished with antiques, each with a private bath and private phone. Full breakfasts before the stone library fireplace. Owner Everett Van Dorn proudly tells you how his father, a professor, built the fireplace by hand, stone by stone, on weekends. In season, break your morning fast on the flagstone terrace. $110 double; 2-night minimum.

Cathedral Pines Farm (860-672-6747), 10 Valley Road, Cornwall 06753. One big beautiful room in an 18th-century-style farmhouse overlooking some of the most beautiful scenery in the Litchfield Hills. Relax under the stars in the outdoor hot tub. Roam in the gardens and greet the llamas playing in the pastures. Convenient to fine dining, skiing, antiquing, and music festivals. The $125 stipend for a double includes a full breakfast.

Skinny Dog Farm (860-435-8155; fax 860-435-6257), 500 Lime Rock Road, Falls Village 06039. Easy access to the Lime Rock Race Track (see *To See*). Step inside this 1750 Colonial farmhouse onto a foyer floor lined with bricks salvaged from the ruins of old iron forges. A Shaker-style stairwell to your left curves up to the second floor. Straight ahead is the charming living room with a working fireplace. The TV set is in the former "keeping room"—ask owner Andrea Salvadore to explain what *that* means. One of the three bedrooms has a queen-size cannonball bed, another has twin brass beds; the king-size bed in the third is known as a pencil post. One room has a private bath. Guests can poke around in the greenhouse and help weed the vegetable and flower gardens. Full breakfast. Caters to special diets. $90–95 per room.

Alice's Bed & Breakfast (860-435-8808), 267 Main Street, Lakeville 06039. A full breakfast is served in the dining room of this early Victorian house, and then it's off for an easy walk to the village or lake for swimming, boating, fishing, or picnicking. Three affordable rooms are priced at $65 single, $85 double.

Cornerstone B&B (860-824-0475), 159 Belden Street, Falls Village 06031. Outdoor "activists" can drop their canoes, kayaks, or fishing lines in the Housatonic River near this renovated 18th-century Dutch Colonial farmhouse. The Appalachian Trail, Mohawk Mountain ski resort, and Lime Rock Race Track are nearby. Then relax in one of two comfortable rooms. Children and all manner of pets, including horses, are welcome. Full breakfast. $60–135 depending on season.

Greenwoods Gate (860-542-5439, fax 860-542-5897), 105 Greenwoods Road East, Norfolk 06058. A warm welcome awaits you in this elegantly restored 1797 Colonial home. Each of the four luxuriously decorated suites has a private bath; one has a Jacuzzi. A truly romantic setting. Full gourmet breakfast; afternoon tea and refreshments. No pets, no smoking. $175–245; off-season discounts.

Weaver's House (1-800-283-1551), 58 Greenwoods Road West, Norfolk 06058. The guest rooms in this modest home overlook the spacious estate where the Yale Music School mounts its prestigious summer music festival (see *Entertainment*). In winter, deep snows encourage cross-country skiing and horse-drawn sleigh rides. Downhill ski areas are within a 30- to 60-minute drive. Hikers can explore three state parks all within the borders of the town. Fruit breads highlight the hearty, simple breakfast. Four double bedrooms share two baths. $43–53 single, $48–58 double.

Loon Meadow Farm (860-542-6085), 41 Loon Meadow Drive, Box 554, Norfolk 06058. The uniquely decorated Carousel suite in this 19th-century farmhouse offers the comforts of a queen-size bed, wood-burning fireplace, and private bath with an extra-deep tub. Friendly animals—turkey, deer, fox, and even an elusive coyote—roam the farm's 20 acres. Hiking trails. Livery service. (See *Horseback Riding*.) Hearty breakfast. $120.

Angel Hill B&B (860-542-5920), 54 Greenwoods Road East, Norfolk 06058. Minutes from the village green and the Norfolk Music Festival (see *Entertainment*). Two adjoining rooms—a sitting room and a bedroom with a canopy bed—in this 1880 mansion's Victorian Cottage Suite make it a favorite of honeymooners. But all guests are pampered in the three other large rooms and suites, each with a distinctive theme, all offering bathrobes, stereo tape players, wine buckets, and picnic baskets to borrow. One suite has a Jacuzzi, the other a whirlpool. The Carriage House, for weekends or an extended stay, has a complete kitchen. Sumptuous breakfasts are served on the verandas. Eight acres to explore. $110–150 double.

Manor House (860-542-5690; fax 860-542-5690), 69 Maple Avenue, Norfolk 06058. Tiffany windows and a paneled cherry staircase are only some of the architectural delights of this elegant Victorian Tudor estate built in 1898 by the architect of London's subway system. Each of the nine guest rooms has its own distinctive touch, whether it be a four-poster or lace canopy bed, fireplace, or balcony. One guest room has a two-person Jacuzzi; another, a two-person soaking tub. The living room is truly baronial. Innkeepers Diane and Henry Tremblay invite you to enjoy their perennial gardens and stroll the 5-acre park. The tantalizing smells of the hearty full breakfast will lure you out of bed to a table decorated with homemade bread or muffins and a changing menu of waffles or scrambled eggs with chives; honey harvested from the Manor House's own hives is also served. No pets or smoking. A romantic setting in a quintessential New England village. $95–225.

B&B by the Lake (860-738-0230), 19 Dillon Beach Road, Winsted 06098. Open May 15 through October 15. Continental breakfast is served on a lattice-covered dock in a rustic lodge overlooking West Hill Lake, one of the cleanest lakes in Connecticut and a favorite with anglers (there's a public boat launch in Barkhamsted's town park). Private beach; canoe available for guests. There are three rooms, one with private bath. Inn-keeper Anastasio Rossi entertains at night on the piano; he loves to play Gershwin. $85 double.

The Rose & Thistle (860-379-4744), 24 Woodland Acres, Barkhamsted 06022. There are four rooms with private bath in this secluded English Tudor home, set on 10 acres that offer myriad outdoor activities. Swim or skate in season on the spring-fed pond; play badminton or croquet on the large open lawn; relax beside the huge stone fireplace in the living room under a beamed cathedral ceiling; hike into the adjoining woodlands to a wildlife bird sanctuary. *Warning:* Don't disturb the nests of the great blue herons! Game room; large fenced-in area for dogs. Full breakfast and afternoon tea. $80 double.

Abel Darling Bed & Breakfast (860-567-0384; fax 860-567-2638), 102 West Street, Litchfield 06759. Wide floorboards and exposed beams attest to the authenticity of this 1782 Colonial in Litchfield's borough section. Historic North and South Streets—with their impressive mansions and the spacious green rimmed with trendy restaurants, art galleries, and a mini–shopping center—are within easy walking distance of this charming old home. Continental breakfast. Two pleasant rooms, with private baths, are priced at $85 and $95, double.

Tir' na nóg Farm Bed & Breakfast (860-283-9612), 261 Newton Road, in Northfield. Two rooms and adjoining sitting room in a 1775 farmhouse with stunning views of the southern hills overlooking Litchfield. Hearty continental breakfast. Convenient to the area's outdoor sports activities. If by the wildest chance you are arriving by helicoper the farmstead has a private heliport. The Indian name means "Land of the Young." $95–135.

Chimney Crest Manor (860-582-4219; fax 860-584-5903), Five Founders Drive, Bristol 06010. A large cut above your typical B&B, the manor will take your breath away. Guests driving up to this 32-room Tudor mansion overlooking the Farmington hills fancy they've been invited to a weekend in an English castle. You walk to the cherry-paneled library through a beautiful 40-foot-long, glassed-in arcade. Each of the five guest suites has a private entrance. Two have working fireplaces. A canopy bed graces another. One has a Jacuzzi. The Rose Garden Suite, with a 40-foot salon, is ideal for family groups. Hosts Dante and Cynthia Cimadamore serve piping hot, full breakfasts on the grand patio off the salon. The ultimate bed & breakfast experience! $95–165 double occupancy; senior discount.

Tucker Hill Inn (203-758-8334; fax 203-598-0652), 96 Tucker Hill Road, Middlebury 06762. Ancient oaks and maples shade this gracious Colonial home. The four rooms—two with private bath—are bright and spacious. The public rooms feature an extensive library of books, videos, and CDs. Quassy, one of the state's major amusement parks, is nearby (see *To Do—Amusement Park*). A full breakfast is served in the dining room or, in season, on the patio. $70 single, $110 double.

Mill at Pomperaug (203-263-4566), 29 Pomperaug Road, Woodbury 06798. Relax with a good book and a glass of wine on the deck overlooking the waterfall. Hike in the woods or pick pumpkins at a nearby farm. At night enjoy the privacy of your modern suite, adjoining the old mill, built by your host, architect Andrew Peklo. Home-baked breads and muffins and Starbucks coffee for breakfast. In a quiet country setting, but close to town. Access to fax and copy machine for business travelers. Or writers on deadline. $100.

The Everview Inn (203-266-4262), 339 Hoophole Hill Road, Woodbury 06798. In a region where scenic views are commonplace, the views from this mountaintop aerie are nothing short of spectacular. As they enter this modernistic home with walls of glass built in 1987, Everview guests first step into the grandeur of a 1,000-square-foot Great Room. All the guest rooms offer views of the hills. Decks and patios wind around the 24-foot pool. Who says every B&B in the Litchfield Hills has to be a white-clapboard house on the National Historic Register? Continental breakfast. $125–210.

The Dutch Moccasin (203-266-7364), 51 Still Hill Road, Bethlehem 06751. Five rooms, three with bath, one with Jacuzzi, in a beautifully preserved early-18th-century gambrel Colonial in a scenic, secluded area. Three cozy sitting rooms. Your host, John Georgette, a former antiques dealer, is happy to proffer advice on antiques shopping in nearby Woodbury and share with you his wealth of local lore. Full country breakfast. No pets. $70–130.

Merryvale (203-266-0800), 1204 Main Street South, Woodbury 06798. Five rooms and suites, each with its own decor, welcome guests to this simple, rambling Colonial house. Large covered porch, wide oak floorboards, and fireplaces. Large, homemade country breakfast; complimentary tea, coffee, and biscuits available all day. Situated on 4 wooded acres on the Pomperaug River. $79–99.

CAMPGROUNDS

The Litchfield Hills are ideally suited to camping vacations. Campgrounds are nestled alongside the region's beautiful rivers, on lakeshores, and in scented pine forests. There's a mix of both private and public camps. By design, state facilities are minimal and best suited for return-to-nature tenting or very small RVs. Private campgrounds, on the other hand, have become almost complete resorts, with sports fields, food shops, recreation halls, and entertainment. They can accept and service the largest RVs. Without exception they also have electric hookups, and at some you can connect RVs with sewer lines. Rates run from $10 to $30 per night per site. Reservations are strongly suggested, particularly for holiday weekends. Otherwise, call around; usually you can find an opening. All the state park campgrounds in this region, except one, charge $10 per night per site and, unless otherwise noted, exclude pets.

Black Rock (860-283-8088), US 6 west out of Thomaston 06787, exit 38 off CT 8. Swimming at a pleasant pond, fishing, and hiking are the principal activities for campers on 96 wooded and open sites run by the state. Dumping station, flush toilets, and showers are available. Concession.

Branch Brook (860-283-8144), 435 Watertown Road, Thomaston 06787. Pool, laundry and game room, playground, fishing pond; 68 sites; also trailer sales. Bills itself as a quiet campground. Senior discounts on seasonal sites. Fully stocked store.

Burr Pond (860-379-0172), 385 Burr Mountain Road, Torrington 06790, just off old CT 8 north of the city. Swimming at a public beach is available to campers staying at the 40-site state campground, which is heavily wooded. Dumping station but no concession. Fishing. The foundation of Gail Borden's Condensary, where he invented condensed milk at the time of the Civil War, is at the entrance to the campground.

Housatonic Meadows (860-672-6772), River Road (US 7), Cornwall Bridge 06754. One of the prettiest state campgrounds in Connecticut. The 104 sites are strung along the banks of the beautiful Housatonic River, most in the woods but some in open fields. Dumping station, flush toilets, and showers. Alas, beneath the waters of the river lurk chemicals dumped into it years back from an industrial plant up in Pittsfield, Massachusetts. Swimming is thus out, and only catch-and-release fishing is allowed. But it's a great river for kayaking and canoeing, photographing, painting, contemplating. No concession.

Lake Waramaug (860-868-2592), 30 Lake Waramaug Road, New Preston 06777. Strung along the banks of a spectacular lake that reminds world travelers of Switzerland or Austria, this premier state campground offers 88 wooded and open sites. Swimming and fishing, and you can launch a light canoe or kayak into the water. Dumping station, flush toilets, showers, concession.

Macedonia Brook (860-927-4100), 159 Macedonia Brook Road, Kent 06757. Just west of the Kent School, this 84-site state area runs uphill into the woods along a stream ideal for fishing. No swimming, but bring your hiking boots. No concession. $9 per night.

Treetops Campresort (860-927-3555), Enico Road, off CT 341, Kent 06757. All facilities, 260 sites.

American Legion State Forest (860-379-0922), West River Road, Pleasant Valley 06063. Pine woods shelter 30 sites alongside the Farmington River. No swimming, but great fishing, steep hiking trail. Dumping, flush toilets, showers. No concession. Pets welcome.

Lone Oaks Campsites (1-800-422-CAMP), US 44, East Canaan 06024. Largest private area in the state, with 200 wooded sites and 300 open, grassy sites on 180 acres of rolling hills. Hookups, free cable TV, laundry, flush toilets, store, nightclub specializing in country western and '50s and '60s bands. Recreation hall and special events.

Valley in the Pines (1-800-228-2032), Lucas Road, Goshen 06756. There are 20 to 30 feet of trees between each of 33 sites. Pool, recreation hall, electric hookups, store. Really in the woods, but surprisingly close to Litchfield, historic sites, ski area, rivers and lakes.

Mohawk (860-491-2231), CT 4, Goshen 06756. Fifty sites with swimming pool on a main state road. Ideal for RVs. Easily accessible to other sightseeing and recreational attractions in the area.

✐ **Hemlock Hill** (860-567-2267), Hemlock Hill Road, Litchfield 06759. Child and adult pools, outdoor Jacuzzi, duck pond, 125 sites in the woods. Daily and seasonal camping.

Folly Point (860-567-0089), North Shore Road, Bantam Lake, Litchfield 06759. Operated by the White Memorial Foundation, this 68-site campground is on a peninsula jutting out into the state's largest natural lake. Swimming, fishing, and boating.

✐ **White Pines** (1-800-622-6614), 232 Old North Road, Winsted 06098. Complete family vacation on 206 sites. Children's playground, fishing pond, basketball, volleyball, pool, snack bar, planned activities.

WHERE TO EAT

DINING OUT
In Litchfield

West Street Grill (860-567-3885), West Street, Litchfield, overlooking the green. Nationally acclaimed since its opening in the late 1980s, the Grill has become a favorite with celebrities, who flock down from the hills for very pricey but excellent meals. A unique marriage of ingredients: roasted eggplant, squash, pepper with wilted greens on peasant bread with fresh basil aioli! $85-plus for a complete dinner for two.

Ming's Chinese (860-567-0809), US 202 South, Litchfield. Open year-round for lunch and dinner; Sunday 1–8:30; closed Monday. The entrance is at the rear of the building. No crowding; spacious booths, tables well separated from each other, plain decor. Cantonese, Szechuan, and Hunan specialties. A particularly excellent General Tso's chicken. Hot and sour soup is, whew, hot! A favorite with the local gentry. The friendly waiters will be happy to explain that shrimp with lobster sauce does not contain a shred of lobster, in the event that you are interested. $10–17.

♿ **La Cupola** (860-567-3326), CT 202, 637 Bantam Road, Litchfield. Open Tuesday through Sunday year-round for lunch and dinner. On the southern approach to Litchfield, a landmark old stone house, overlooking the Bantam River, has been converted into a handsome restaurant, serving a full range of innovative Italian cuisine from chicken piccata and veal Genovese to tutto mare, a half dozen antipasti, and pastas of your choice. Extensive wine list. Full bar. Dining alfresco in season. Under new management, so menu and hours subject to change. $12–18.

Bantam Inn (860-567-1770) CT 202 in the Bantam section of Litchfield. A charming and attentive Balkan couple have taken over this venerable inn and decorated the walls with advertising flyers of our favorite romantic movies of the '30s and '40s. The Hungarian-style roast duck is a standout. Sizzling steaks, rack of lamb, and seafood round out the menu. $18.

  ♿ **The Bistro East Restaurant** (860-567-4503) in the Litchfield Inn, US 202, in the Harris Plains section of Litchfield. Open daily for three meals. Exuberant happy hour in the bar. Enjoy the watercolors of Litchfield scenes in the hall leading from the inn lobby to the Joseph Harris Room, the main dining room of the bistro. (Harris was the first Litchfield settler killed by the resident Indians.) The eclectic menu bears faint resemblance to the fare of a typical French bistro. Dinners encompass Pad Thai, a variety of salads, crab cakes, grilled breast of chicken, veal rack chops, and prime strip steak. The pasta dishes are exotic, to say the least. $6 for the salads to $21 for the chops.

In Morris

  ♿ **Deer Island Gate** (860-567-4622), CT 209 on the shores of Bantam Lake, Morris. Open Wednesday through Saturday for dinner, Sunday buffet and à la carte 1–7. German American specialties: jaeger schnitzel, sauerbraten with red cabbage, stuffed duckling, Dungeness crabs, and traditional seafood. Also steaks and chops. $14–22.

In New Preston

The Lakeview Inn (860-868-0563), North Shore Road, New Preston. Formerly the Inn on Lake Waramaug. This 100-year-old landmark inn was purchased in February 1998 and was scheduled to reopen the following summer as a fine-dining restaurant (it no longer accepts overnight guests). The new owner, Dorothy Hamilton, is founder and owner of the French Culinary Institute in New York City. Call for hours, costs, and menus.

Oliva (860-868-1787), CT 45 in the center of New Preston at the southern end of Lake Waramaug. Lunch Thursday through Sunday; dinner Wednesday through Sunday. Closed Monday and Tuesday. Chef Riad Aamar, formerly of the popular, now shuttered Doc's, is serving Italian and Mediterranean specialties in a new restaurant that features garden and terrace dining in season. Try the stuffed eggplant with prosciutto and fontina cheese, white beans, and sage, or the gnocchi à la Romano. BYOB. Reservations recommended. $22.

The Birches Inn (860-868-1735), 233 West Shore Drive, New Preston. Chef Frederic Faveau offers the ultimate dining experience high above beautiful Lake Waramaug. The cuisine is basically American but touches of French and Asian spices and herbs enhance the steaks, chops, and veal and lamb dishes. Memorable salads and desserts. Outdoor dining in season. $18.

Le Bon Coin (860-868-7763), US 202, New Preston (west of Litchfield). Varying hours for lunch and dinner Thursday through Monday; call ahead. Closed Tuesday and Wednesday. In a state becoming blanketed with pizza purveyors, it's a treat to still be able to dine on authentic French country cuisine. There are two intimate dining rooms in this old white house. Try the Dover sole or the fish mousse. The chef has an unusual affection for sweetbreads and does wondrous things with them. Sip and savor the lobster bisque. For dessert, crêpes suzette, anyone? Blackboard specials change daily. Extensive wine list. $12.45–19.95.

Hopkins Inn (860-868-7295), 22 Hopkins Road, off North Shore Road, New Preston. Open May through October; closed Monday except holidays. Breakfast, dinner, and Sunday luncheon in April, November, and December. Continental cuisine with an Austrian flair on a lovely, tree-shaded terrace overlooking beautiful Lake Waramaug. Guests rave about the view as much as the food. Best roast duck à la orange in the hills. Wiener schnitzel, sweetbreads. Take home a bottle of the inn's own Caesar or spinach salad dressing. $17–23.

Boulders Inn (860-868-0541), East Shore Road, New Preston. Open year-round, except Tuesday in winter. Fresh vegetables, soups garnished with edible flowers and seasoned with herbs—all grown in the inn's garden by co-owner Ulla Adema. Home-baked rolls have guests clamoring for the recipe. Start your dinner with asparagus and wild rice soup with toasted pecans, followed by a most un–New England, Cajun-style crab cake with red pepper sauce or a more traditional roast pork rib chop with warm chunky applesauce and potato pancake. Named in 1991 as one of the "ten best country inns of the year." $17.50–23.50. Guest rooms.

In and around Washington

   ♿ **G.W. Tavern** (860-868-6633), 20 Bee Brook Road, Washington Depot. Lunch and dinner Monday through Sunday; brunch and dinner Saturday and Sunday. American and English favorites from meat loaf and chicken potpie to fish-and-chips and duck with apple chutney. Thick juicy burgers. Start your meal with that traditional Anglo-Indian favorite, mulligatawny soup. Fireside dining in winter, outdoors in summer. $8–18.50.

The Mayflower Inn (860-868-1497), CT 47, Washington. Open daily for the ultimate in dining in the Litchfield Hills, if not the entire state. Tables are set with Limoges china, crystal, and silver, and gourmets enjoy inspired meals that include house-smoked salmon, game sausage, and seafood from the fishing banks of New England. The chef need go no farther than the inn's organic gardens for the freshest vegetables. Breads, pastas, and pastries flow from the inn's own bakery. $15.50–24. Guest rooms.

In Woodbury

   ♿ **Carole Peck's Good News Café** (203-266-4663), 649 Main Street, Woodbury. Lunch 11:30–2:30, dinner 5–10, except Tuesday. Carole Peck, one of the first female graduates of the Culinary Institute of

America, has created a combination restaurant, bar, and art gallery in a former steak-and-potato house. Peck was chosen by *Eating Well* magazine as one of the 10 best chefs in the country for healthy gourmet food. The café is eminently accessible, on CT 6, just off I-84. On the edge of one shopping mall and across the road from another, it's hardly dining among the honeysuckles. No matter; it's become a magnet for celebrities and lovers of fine food. You enter the rather undistinguished, rambling clapboard building from the rear. To your right is a takeout bar offering gourmet delights such as peppered pappadam, buckwheat kasha cakes, and sun-dried cherry splash, or Shirley MacLaine baked macaroni and cheese (hot or cold). The list goes on. Directly in front is a bar, popular at happy hour. The lower-cost café anchors the south end of the building; the trendy dining room is on the north. Reservations are recommended. For an entrée, try the wok-seared shrimp with garlic, herb potatoes, and olives. The crispy fried onion bundle is a popular appetizer. $5.75 for take-out sandwiches, $12.50–25 for dinner entrées.

    Curtis House (203-263-2101), 506 Main Street, Woodbury. Open for lunch Tuesday through Saturday; dinner daily. Dependable American cuisine in the oldest inn in the state. The owners boast that they offer 38 entrées on the menu, ranging in price from $13.50 to $19.75 for roast turkey, trout, bluefish, shrimp, lamb chops, prime rib, and chicken. Enjoy happy hour in the **City Hall Pub and Tavern.** Guest rooms.

    Olive Tree Restaurant (203-263-4555), US 6 & CT 64, Woodbury. Lunch and dinner Tuesday through Saturday, dinner Sunday noon to 9. Closed Monday. Seafood, steaks, and prime rib expertly prepared in the Continental style. Olive oil–based Mediterranean dishes—pastas and veal—are welcome additions to the menu. $18.

In New Milford

    Rudy's (860-354-7727), 122 Litchfield Road, New Milford. Dinner only and Sunday brunch. On the main road on the outskirts of town, Rudy's has been a Litchfield County favorite for more than a decade. Here's where you fill your tummy with such reliable Swiss and German classics as sauerbraten, Wiener schnitzel, and veal eminence. And they don't prepare flan any better in Basel. Waitresses in dirndls ring cowbells on your birthday! Sorry, no yodeling. $15.70.

    The Bistro Cafe (860-355-3266), 31 Bank Street, New Milford. Open for lunch, dinner, and Sunday brunch. Changing menus reflecting available fresh foods feature contemporary American cuisine. Hearty portions; friendly staff. One of the premier eateries in town. Also operates the new **Bistro East Restaurant** in the Litchfield Inn (see *Lodging*). $13.

In Kent

    Fife 'N Drum (860-927-3509), Main Street (US 7), Kent. Open year-round for lunch and dinner; Sunday brunch. Closed Tuesday. Just inside the door is a grand piano. It's not for decoration—Dolph Traymon, the genial owner, plays while you enjoy French and Italian specialties in a barnlike setting. Rack of lamb, steak *au poivre,* roast duck flambé prepared tableside. All topped off with the queen of desserts, crème brulée. Taproom menu available. Popular with Kent School faculty and visiting parents of students. $8.95–23.

In Sharon

   West Main Cafe (860-364-9888), 13 West Main Street, Sharon. Open daily for dinner; lunch Friday through Sunday. Would you believe a gourmet restaurant located in a building that started its life as a small A&P grocery? Matthew Fahrner, former chef at the West Street Grill in Litchfield, is filling a gap in a pretty village where fine dining was in short supply. Nori-wrapped salmon is a luncheon specialty; for dinner, shrimp dumplings. Red tomato sauces are rare in the pasta dishes, which are seasoned more in Asian fashion, with ginger and other spices. More traditional is strip steak with yummy "smashed" potatoes. Dining on covered deck in season. Takeout available. $14.95–19.95.

In Norfolk

The Pub & Restaurant (860-542-5716), CT 44, Norfolk. Open for lunch and dinner, Tuesday through Friday 11–9; Saturday 11–10; Sunday 11–8:30. Located across from the Norfolk Music Festival (see *Entertainment*) in one of the country's first multipurpose buildings, the ambience is English pub. The menu belies the setting, however, ranging from chili with corn bread to burgers with a variety of toppings (including portobello mushrooms), spicy Buffalo wings, and such innovative sandwiches as apple, ham, and Gruyère cheese with honey mustard. Soups are made fresh daily, and you can make a meal of one of the salads. The lunch pizza is garnished with artichoke hearts, red onions, sun-dried tomato pesto, and three cheeses. Locals say the Pub is the second best reason to visit Norfolk. (The first? The Norfolk Music Festival.) A roast suckling pig for six or more diners can be ordered—with 6 days' advance notice. $5.75–18.95.

In Salisbury

White Hart Inn (860-435-0030), CT 41 and US 44, Salisbury. Known locally as The Porch because of the wide, old-fashioned veranda that fronts the green. Its restaurant, **Julie's New American Grill,** and its well-prepared seafood dishes are earning additional praises for this charming old wayside inn. Lunch in the Garden Room; visit the taproom for a lively happy hour. $16–25.

Under Mountain Inn (860-435-0242), CT 41, Salisbury. A British husband and an American wife have joined forces to create a little outpost of Britain in an 18th-century New England home. An authentic English holiday dinner with roast goose as the centerpiece is the highlight for Christmas holiday guests. During the rest of the year, the general public can enjoy dinners on Friday and Saturday nights. English favorites include steak and kidney pie and bangers and mash (sausages and mashed potatoes). Guest rooms. Entrées $12–17.

In Winsted

✐ **The Tributary** (860-379-7679), 19 Rowley Street, Winsted. This renovated 1860s warehouse sits on the banks of the Mad River, just off Main Street. Open Tuesday through Sunday for lunch and dinner. Awards for its fresh seafood since 1979 have made the Tributary one of the most popular restaurants in northwestern Connecticut. Usually a fresh-grilled fish highlights the three daily specials; or, from the full menu, choose fresh veal, chicken, beef, or a vegetarian dish. Children's menu. Chocolate cakes, pies, and bread puddings flow from the in-house oven, along with seasonal fruit breads and low-fat options. Reservations are suggested. $14–20 includes salad, bread, vegetable, and starch.

Jessie's Restaurant (860-379-0109), 142 Main Street, Winsted. Dinner only, starting at 4. Closed Tuesday. An impressive turn-of-the-century mansion is the setting for fine dining year-round on an enclosed porch, indoor dining room, or on the patio in season. Start your meal with a homemade soup, followed by fresh pasta, a creative pizza, or any other Italian specialty. Don't pass up the desserts. Early-bird specials at $9.95, à la carte entrées average $16.

In Canaan

The Cannery Cafe, an American Bistro (860-824-7333), 85 Main Street, Canaan. Lunch and dinner, Tuesday through Saturday. The modest storefront belies the culinary treats inside. New owners Lisa Sullivan and William O'Meara are creating unique dishes such as eggplant ravioli with caramelized onions and grilled sea scallops and sautéed lamb with wild straw mushrooms on a bed of salad greens. $13–18.

In Torrington

The Venetian (860-489-8592) 52 East Main Street, Torrington. Year-round; open 11–10, Sunday noon–9; closed Tuesday. Genial host Michael Dilullo greets visitors in what is arguably the temple of Italian cuisine in the county. That said, if you tend to go out of your way for thick, juicy lamb chops, this is the place. For years the house salad dressing was a well-kept secret; now you can pick up a bottle on the way out after your meal. If you give credence to current medical advice about the efficacy of garlic, the Venetian's linguine with white clam sauce affords a month's ration of this heart-sustaining bulb. All this and the friendliest waitresses in town. $10–20.

✐☞**DiLeo's** (860-496-7330), 545 Winsted Road, Torrington. Open Tuesday through Thursday 7:30 AM–9 PM; Friday through Sunday to 9:30 PM. Closed Monday. Conveniently located in the north end of town across from a major shopping center. A roadside restaurant with wood paneling and comfortable booths, DiLeo's is a cut above the typical family eatery. The lavish menu runs the gamut from specialty salads such as The California (three garden greens, mandarin oranges, walnuts, and cukes) to Extraordinary Sandwiches. How about Hot Turkey Supreme? Pastas, burgers, grinders, and a nice children's menu round out your choices. Easy on the pocketbook: $4.75–12.

In Watertown

Golden Palace (860-274-6779), 544 Straits Turnpike, Watertown. Open daily. Well-prepared favorites from two of China's classic cuisines: the better-known Cantonese and the more highly spiced Szechuan. The chef also recommends Polynesian duck and chicken fingers fried in egg batter on a bed of vegetables. Pleasant Old World atmosphere. $14.50.

In Waterbury

Diorio Restaurant and Bar (203-754-5111), 231 Bank Street, Waterbury. Open Monday through Friday for lunch 11:30–2:30; dinner 5:30–9 or 10; Saturday for dinner only. Closed Sunday. Italian and Greek cooking combined with a happy hour make dining here a very pleasant experience. Linguine topped with fish in a red sauce and ravioli with vegetable fillings give you an idea of the pasta treats that await you. Veal is a favorite. Pasta dishes $16.95–18.95; meat dishes $15.95–22.

Drescher's (203-573-1743), 25 Leavenworth Street, Waterbury. Open for lunch and dinner; closed Sunday. A venerable eatery that has been pleasing local and visiting palates since 1868, which makes it older than probably half the states in the union. High, old-fashioned metal ceiling, polished wooden bar. Vintage photographs on the wall tell the story of Waterbury. The menu offers a wide array of German, Italian, and American dishes. Shrimp with fettuccine, grilled pork chops, and veal and lobster combinations. Daily specials. $9.95–14.95.

Cafe 4Fifty7 (203-574-4507), 457 West Main Street, Waterbury (a few blocks west of the town green). Open Monday through Saturday for lunch and dinner. This eatery has all the feel and atmosphere of an Irish pub, but the owners describe it as a "retro '40s café." The cuisine is predominantly Italian, but a favorite dish is seafood Portuguese, a nice combination of shellfish in marinara sauce over pasta. Other choices are sea scallops in a mustard and dill sauce, and grilled chicken topped with roasted peppers and spinach. The roast tenderloin is for unreconstructed meat-eaters. Popular happy-hour bar. $16.95.

1249 West Restaurant (203-756-4609), 1249 West Main Street, Waterbury, exit 18 off I-84. Open for lunch and dinner; closed Monday. Specializes in northern Italian cuisine, which translates into veal and steak dishes, and rice dishes and bolognese sauce with hardly a trace of the ubiquitous tomato of the south and Sicily. $12–20.

EATING OUT

In Litchfield

The County Seat Restaurant (860-567-8069), 3 West Street on the green, Litchfield. Open Monday through Thursday 7 AM-9:30 PM; Friday and Saturday 8–midnight; Sunday 8–8:30. An all-purpose restaurant–cum coffeehouse–cum ice cream bar! The County Seat gives you a choice: Enjoy a repast at the counter on a high stool or relax in a comfortable stuffed chair where you can sip your latte and peruse the newspapers or one of the many books on Connecticut collected by hosts Bob and Linda Calabrese. There's chess and cribbage, but no dartboard. The fountain has a complete range of ice cream delicacies, from cones to sundaes. The full menu offers such treats as pan-seared salmon topped with a spinach-horseradish crust, grilled chicken tenderloins with asparagus spears, bourbon-barbecued pork, and, for a southwestern touch, roast turkey quesadilla. There are burgers, chili, and tasty salads. Entertainment Friday and Saturday nights. $14.95. If Paul Robert Blackman is playing his African drums, join the crowd.

Main Course Family Restaurant (203-482-6246), US 202, Litchfield, just east of Torrington. Daily except Christmas Day and New Year's Eve. Best meat loaf for miles around. On Wednesday night, steak in all its variety dominates the menu. Juicy hamburgers. You don't have to settle for french fries, for you get your choice of mashed or steak fries. Children's menu. Popular with seniors and families.

Aspen Garden (860-567-9477), 51 West Street, at the south end of the green, Litchfield. Open daily. Pleasant atmosphere; you'd never guess this was a Ford showroom for years. As in so many "Italian" restaurants in Connecticut, the chefs are talented Greeks. So it's no surprise that, in addition to the Italian specialties, you'll find on the menu gyros and bountiful Greek salads garnished with feta cheese. Try the mussels. Specialty pizzas; seafood and veal dishes. Popular summer terrace with umbrella-shaded tables.

DiFranco's Restaurant and Pizzeria (860-567-8872), 19 West Street, on the green, Litchfield. Open daily 10:30 AM–11 PM. A popular family restaurant, in the center of the village, that doesn't pretend to be anything but a satellite of Naples in a colonial setting. The decor needs updating, but the food is good and plentiful. Most of the entrées—veal, chicken, and seafood—are sautéed or fried. The pasta dishes are particularly flavorful. Ample children's menu. $5.50–12.50.

Grappa (860-567-1616), 26 Commons Drive, US 202, Litchfield. Dinner; lunch sometimes. Uncommon appetizers—julienne fried zucchini, for one—and mouthwatering desserts complement innovative pizza from the wood-burning oven. Outdoor dining in season. A less expensive satellite of the West Street Grill (see *Dining Out*) up the street.

Elsewhere

Popey's Ice Cream Shoppe, at the junction of CT 61 and CT 109, Morris. When the kids' tummies are growling after a day of swimming and boating at nearby Bantam Lake or Mount Tom State Park, this is the place to stuff them with bulging burgers and fries, clams, sandwiches, and ice cream. A popular Litchfield Hills pit stop for nearly a quarter century.

Painted Pony (203-266-5771), CT 61, Bethlehem. Open daily 11–11. This inauspicious eatery in the center of a sleepy colonial town should be approached with caution: Eat lightly the day before—portions are enormous. Would you believe a baked potato the size of a small football, fillets of sole that cover a huge platter, 20-ounce prime ribs? Oh, if you insist, you can order a 12-ounce cut. Pastas, chicken, and seafood round out the menu. Happily, all this food is expertly prepared. But be ready to take home a doggy bag. Salads are a nice mix of greens, onions, and peppers. Scrumptious desserts in the event there's still room in your tummy. Children's menu. $13.50.

Wood's Pit B.B.Q. & Mexican Cafe (860-567-9869), 123 Bantam Lake Road (CT 209), next to the Bantam Cinema, in Bantam. Open for lunch and dinner, Monday through Friday and Sunday, 11:30-9; Saturday until 10. In the extensive menu that samples the cattle ranges of Mexico and the Southwest, owner-chef Paul Haas takes pains to warn that outdoor "grilling New England style" is *not* the same as barbecuing, which is the very slow cooking of meat. The results speak for themselves: The pulled pork barbecue sandwich ranks with the best in the Southwest. Choose from a variety of sandwiches or platters. In the unlikely event your ribs and meat dishes aren't flavorful enough, each table is adorned with a half-dozen bottles of serious hot sauces. Mexican, Canadian, and even Dutch beers. $6.50 for sandwich baskets to $13.50 for platters.

Hold the Pickle (860-567-0084), 722 Bantam Road (US 202), Bantam. Open Monday through Friday 10–6, Saturday and Sunday 10–3. A gourmet deli in a modest former home that serves a dazzling array of sandwiches and soups. No burgers, dogs, or pizza, thank you. Choose a sandwich from the extensive menu or build your own. One mouthwatering example: the Squish Squash, a medley of zucchini sautéed in garlic and olive oil and served with olives, leeks, roasted red peppers, and feta cheese. Super-rich desserts. $2.75–4.75.

Salsa (860-355-5860), 54 Railroad Street, New Milford. Open for lunch and dinner; closed Sunday and Monday. A Mexican restaurant with authentic Mexican food. Goat cheese rellenos with butternut squash, venison, chimichangas, and homemade moles.

✎ **The Villager** (860-927-3945), Main Street (US 7), Kent. Open for breakfast, lunch, and dinner, varying hours. With an ambience that can only be described as "crowded and busy," the Villager's popularity rests on the variety and virility of its sandwiches, bagels, burgers, and croissants. The chili burger is topped with cheddar cheese, chili, and sour cream. House specialty sandwiches run from "shaved steak" to vegetarian melts, authentic Reubens, ingenious salads, and much more. Half-sandwiches for the youngsters. And they will do almost anything with an egg except give you an egg shampoo. $2.95 for breakfast to $9.95 dinner.

Chaiwalla (860-435-9758), Main Street, Salisbury. Open daily in summer; Thursday through Sunday in the off season—except March, when it's closed. Owner Mary O'Brien ("I'm the chatty one," she says) has gathered unblended teas from around the world. Simple food, sandwiches, crumpets, and scones are served in the tearoom.

Chatterley's (860-379-2428), Two Bridge Street, New Hartford. Lunch and dinner. Small musical combos on weekends in the back room. Located in the landmark former New Hartford Hotel in the center of the village,

Chatterley's ambience is pure Victorian—but its food is artful 20th century. The Caesar salad, for example, is garnished with shrimp. A sweet-and-sour sauce enhances the grilled medallions of pork loin. Hefty burgers are listed under the "Lighter Side of the Menu." Save space for cheesecake for dessert. Chatterley's is popular in winter with athletic folk just off the slopes of nearby Ski Sundown (see *Downhill Skiing*). $11.50.

✐ **Log House Restaurant** (860-379-8937), US 44, Barkhamsted. Open daily starting with breakfast at 6 and serving dinner until 9:15; 7 AM–8:15 PM Sunday. Antlers on the wall, rustic furniture, a fast-food counter, and two spacious dining rooms, plus an all-American menu make this one of the most popular roadside eateries on the Albany Turnpike. Specialties range from corned beef or turkey-pastrami Reuben sandwiches to Yankee pot roast, from seafood specials, steaks, and chops to grinders and the ubiquitous pasta dishes. And the most you can spend on an entrée is $13.95, except for the Alaskan King Crab Legs, which are priced to market. A favorite with traveling families.

Monaco's Ristorante (860-379-6648), 380 Main Street, Winsted. Lunch and dinner. Don't pass up this inauspicious-looking storefront restaurant; it was the favorite of former Gov. Lowell Weicker and his wife, Claudia. They made the trip out from Hartford for the ziti in cognac sauce. Spaghetti puttanesca is another house specialty.

Collins Diner (860-824-7040), US 44, Canaan. Extended hours. Full breakfast is served all day. One of five classic diners in the United States to be listed on the National Register of Historic Places. Traditional, down-to-earth American food: thick steaks, juicy burgers, shrimp, meat loaf with rich mashed potatoes. An MIT geology professor has been trying for years, in vain, to buy the marble countertop streaked with fossils.

☞ **Central Lunch** (203-496-0297), 31 Hungerford Street, Torrington. Breakfast, lunch, and dinner. A dining counter popular with the locals. Best hash browns in town. Homemade basic Italian classics. Nothing fancy, but more than your money's worth. Four booths.

ICE CREAM

Stosh's Ice Cream (860-927-4495), Main Street (US 7), Kent. Open April through October. Located in the restored Kent Railroad Station. Gallerygoers, prep school students, and tourists mingle in line to savor delicious ice cream served here on the west bank of the Housatonic River. Enjoy your confections under umbrellas at upscale white picnic tables, and watch the passing parade. Gourmet hot dogs. The other half of the station is an art gallery.

Peaches 'n Cream, US 202, Litchfield. Year-round. Well into the evening this unpretentious building on the outskirts of Litchfield dishes up 40 flavors of rich, luscious ice cream concoctions—cones, sodas, sundaes, ice cream bars. Tables.

(See also *The County Seat* in Litchfield and *Popey's Ice Cream* in Morris.)

ENTERTAINMENT

Warner Theatre (860-489-7180), 68 Main Street, in the heart of Torrington. Open year-round. One of the state's few remaining grand old Art Deco movie theaters, now under restoration. Showcases Broadway musicals, top solo artists, and the internationally renowned local Nutmeg Ballet.

Thomaston Opera House (860-283-6250), Main Street, Thomaston. Year-round. A classic community opera house, once slated for the wrecking ball but restored by state and local funding. Family fare, highlighting seasonal holidays, with local and traveling troupes.

Litchfield Performing Arts (860-567-4162), a homegrown management group, without a theater of its own, that stages classical music series, piano competitions, selected readings, jazz, Christmas house tours, and a variety of outreach cultural programs in local theaters, auditoriums, schools, and churches.

Norfolk Music Festival (860-542-3000), US 44 and CT 272, Norfolk. What Tanglewood is to Massachusetts, Norfolk is to Connecticut, with a few differences: size and the scope of music. Where 25,000 souls can crowd the lawn in front of the Tanglewood Shed, the Shed at Norfolk entertains only 1,000 music lovers. And here the repertoire is limited to chamber music, an annual choral concert, and an occasional jazz concert. The **Music Shed,** an acoustically superb hall lined with redwood, was built in 1906. Prior to that, Ellen Battell Stoeckel and her husband, Carl, held musical gatherings in Whitehouse, their estate's 35-room mansion. They brought to Norfolk on specially chartered trains such luminaries as Fritz Kreisler, Rachmaninoff, Caruso, Paderewski, and cousins of the Laschever author of this book, violinist Efrem Zimbalist and his wife, Metropolitan Opera star Alma Gluck. Jean Sibelius made his only visit to the United States in 1914 at the request of the Stoeckels and, while a guest at Whitehouse, composed his tone poem *The Oceansides.* The estate was left to the Yale Music School, which now sponsors chamber music, jazz, and choral music concerts from June through August. Concertgoers enjoy picnic suppers on tree-shaded grounds beside a gurgling brook.

Music Mountain (860-824-7126), Falls Village off US 7. June through early September, 16 string quartet concerts are presented in the oldest continuing summer chamber music festival in the country in a specially designed hall. US and international artists are featured; Saturday-night jazz festivals are held. Picnic and stroll in the woods on this 120-acre hilltop aerie. Take a good look at the houses on the grounds. They were purchased sight unseen years ago through Sears-Roebuck catalogs! These unique architectural oddities now house staff and visitors. Adults $15; children $5.

✎ **Sharon Playhouse,** (860-364-6066), CT 343 just west of the center of the village of Sharon. Summer season of Broadway family musicals are staged in a revitalized and renovated traditional summer theater. Children's theater series, live one-hour musicals in the morning and early afternoon, and a theater workshop for youngsters. $18–22.

In addition, the Litchfield Hills are alive with the declamations of amateur actors, expressing themselves year-round in a variety of local theater groups. The **Goshen Players,** with its annual, 3-weekend Broadway musical in spring, is the granddaddy of the area's thespians. Check listings in local papers for current offerings. The **Torrington Civic Theatre** takes a more serious stance toward the stage and, in the main, presents heavy drama, with an occasional comedy. Performances are in Coe Park Center on the Torrington green. Watch the local papers for performances by Torrington's internationally recognized **Nutmeg Conservatory for the Arts.** Ballet dancers trained by director Sharon Dante have won international competitions and have been invited to join European companies.

SELECTIVE SHOPPING

ANTIQUES SHOPS

What cars are to Detroit, airplanes are to Seattle, and jazz is to New Orleans, antiques are to the Litchfield area. Until recently, New Preston was a sleepy little town whose grocery store served summer residents and campers on nearby Lake Waramaug. It has suddenly blossomed into a major antiques center, with 10 dealers offering everything from kerosene lamps to Native American rugs from Santa Fe. All are on CT 45 (Main Street), off US 202. Woodbury has long held the title of "antiques capital" of the state, but in recent years antiques dealers have opened shops in almost every village, including on the main street of Torrington, formerly a bustling brass-manufacturing town.

In and around Litchfield

Tillou Antiques (860-567-9693), West Street on the Litchfield green. Rare, quality colonial antiques are gathered for connoisseurs who prize authenticity above all else. Furniture, dinnerware, wall decorations, clothing accessories.

Bantam Antiques (860-567-4587), US 202 south of Litchfield, on the Riverside. Open year-round; closed Wednesday. Ten rooms of 18th-, 19th-, and 20th-century American country furniture in a 1756 house.

The Old Carriage Shop Antiques (860-567-3234), 920 Bantam Road, Bantam. Open Wednesday through Friday 10–5; Saturday 11–5. One of the largest antiques centers in the region: Some 20 dealers offer for sale an eclectic array of antiques and collectibles ranging from silver to furniture, from glassware to pottery, from mirrors to accessories—and even this guidebook!

In Kent

The Bittersweet Shop (860-354-1727), US 7 south of Kent, Gaylordsville. Open daily. Restricted winter schedule. You're certain to find something to your taste. A consortium of 14 dealers, who've joined the choice pieces they've collected in their world travels, from portrait and landscape paintings to prize quilts, along with the traditional antique formal and country furniture.

Pauline's Place (860-927-4475), Main Street (US 7), Kent. If fine jewelry is the language of love, it's spoken here in every tongue. Earrings, bracelets, chains, rings of precious stones, and pins, many from dispersed estates and from every period—Victorian, Georgian, art deco, Edwardian, and contemporary.

Kent Antiques Center (860-927-3313), Kent Station Square, Main Street, Kent. Eighteenth- to 20th-century antiques and collectibles—displayed in a 19th-century farmhouse—are offered for your browsing pleasure by eight dealers.

In New Preston

Black Swan (860-567-4429), CT 45, Main Street, off US 202, New Preston. Country English, American, and European furniture from the 17th and 18th centuries crowds the floors of this popular dealer. Accessories and prints.

J. Seitz & Co. (860-868-0119), CT 45, Main Street, off US 202, New Preston. Open daily. Original and reproduction southwestern furniture. Also Native American crafts and an extensive collection of men's and women's clothing. Saves you a trip to Santa Fe.

The Village Barn and Gallery (860-868-0501), CT 45, Main Street, off US 202, New Preston. Closed Tuesday. The emphasis is on original paintings—oils, watercolors, and acrylics—along with decoys, pewter, pottery, brass, glassware, lighting. Nicely displayed in a restored barn and attached gallery.

In Woodbury

Monique Shay Antiques & Design (203-263-3186), 920 Main Street (US 6), Woodbury. The focus is on country antiques, tables, armoires, chairs, and cupboards from Canada. Open daily.

Robert S. Walin American Antiques (203-263-4416), 547 Flanders Road, Woodbury. Folk art along with 18th- and 19th-century American furniture.

West Country Antiques (203-263-5741), US 6, off Main Street, Woodbury. Two barns bulging with 18th- and 19th-century French and English furniture. Design service available.

Elsewhere

Remember When (860-489-1566), 111 Main Street, Torrington. Two floors of most anything from the 1920s to the 1950s: jewelry, lamps, linen, furniture, china, pottery. Large selection of lighting fixtures and remnants from estate sales.

Salisbury Antiques Center (860-435-0424), 46 Library Street, Salisbury. An unusually large and varied collection of formal and country American and English furniture, along with antique silver and unique prints.

ART GALLERIES

Paris–New York–Kent Gallery (860-927-3357), Kent Station Square, US 7, Kent. One of New York's foremost furriers, Jacques Kaplan, persuaded by his conservation-minded children to abandon the sale of animal pelts, has established an art gallery based in Kent that has been described as "international class." Works of only the highest quality have won Kaplan a clientele of the most discriminating art connoisseurs. Now Jacques, an artist in his own right, has persuaded 10 other outstanding artists to set up their easels in Kent, making the town a major art center.

Carol Wallace Fine Art Studio (860-379-4286), 437 Main Street, New Hartford. Open by appointment. Carol Wallace has achieved a reputation throughout New England for her watercolor paintings and pen-and-ink sketches of regional scenes, particularly landscapes of the Litchfield Hills and the Berkshires. She was the producer a few years back of a series of promotional TV spots for the state tourism office.

Bachelier-Cardonsky Art Gallery (860-927-3357), Main Street (US 7), Kent, atop the House of Books (see *Bookstores*). Open Saturday and Sunday 11–5 and by appointment. Contemporary and Connecticut artists displayed in a charming setting. Ranks with the most attractive galleries in New England.

Artwell Gallery (860-482-5122), 51 Water Street, Torrington. Open Thursday through Sunday. A well-concocted Russian salad of art exhibits, classes, lectures, poetry readings, and musical and theatrical performances. Check area newspapers for happenings when you're in town.

ARTISANS

Cornwall Bridge Pottery Store (860-672-6545), CT 128, West Cornwall. A hop, skip, and jump from the covered bridge that spans the Housatonic. Award-winning pottery designed by Todd Piker and fashioned in his huge Korean kiln down the road. The store also sells works of other local artisans—plates, mugs, tiles and lamps, toys, glassworks, containers for indoor bulbs, and a variety of Australian outerwear.

Ingersoll Cabinetmakers (860-672-6334), CT 128, West Cornwall. Ian Ingersoll, son of the late, famed journalist Ralph Ingersoll, meticulously crafts replicas of the famous furniture made in New England and New York in once thriving Shaker villages. Tables, chairs, and benches, simple but just as functional as the day they were designed.

Susan Wakeen Doll Company (860-567-0007), US 202, Litchfield (across from the Litchfield Inn). Open weekdays 10–5, Sunday 11:30–4:30. Susan Wakeen designs and sculpts her own dolls and is one of the most honored doll artists in the country. In the cozy retail store you can choose a limited-edition baby doll—or create your own: Pick out an already sculpted face, then select eye color, hair, and handmade dress, and your doll is assembled while you watch. Group tours of the studio are available by appointment. Limited-edition dolls range in price from $199 to $250; create-your-own dolls are $98. Tea sets, doll clothing, and related doll items are also for sale. Definitely a class act!

The Country Doll House (860-824-7739), Seven Sodom Road, Canaan. Call for directions. Open Tuesday through Saturday 10–5, Sunday 1–5. Yvonne Clarke has collected dolls from all over the world and invites you and your children to bring out "the child in all of us" and come to her 200-year-old farmhouse on a back country lane. In addition to exquisite dolls of boys and girls, you can choose from a wide selection of bears and plush animals. Need we say it? Of course, Barbie is here!

Guy Wolff Pottery (860-868-2858), US 202, in the Woodville section of Washington. This talented potter copies the designs of clay flowerpots from 17th- and 18th-century paintings. He also incorporates into his work shards sent to him by archaeologists. He "antiques" the pots with leaf mold and other natural stains. From his "little shop by the road," long a favorite of a select group of local pottery fans, Wolff has been discovered and now has a national clientele.

BOOKSTORES

Barnidge & McEnroe (860-567-4670), Seven West Street, on the Litchfield green. Three floors of books, from the latest fiction to specialty works on cooking, gardening, music, and art. World and local travel guides. Enjoy pastry and a cup of coffee in the Caffe Espresso Bar just inside the entrance.

John Steele Book Shop (860-567-0748), 15 South Street (CT 63), Litchfield. Open Tuesday through Saturday 11–5, Sunday 10–5, and by appointment. Bill Kiefer, a former newspaper editorial writer, invites you to browse in the pleasant Colonial house he's converted into a specialty bookstore. While his stock-in-trade is old books, he'll order new ones for you and promises prompt delivery. A wide collection of books on legends and lore of New England.

Hickory Stick Bookshop (860-868-0525), Green Hill Road (CT 47), in the center of Washington Depot. Open Monday through Saturday 9–6, Sunday 11–5. An attractive, sprawling, full-service bookstore with an unusually large section devoted exclusively to children's books. At Hickory Stick's frequent book signings, you can meet the famous authors who labor over hot computers in their Litchfield Hills farmhouses.

House of Books (860-927-4104), Main Street (US 7), Kent. Open Monday through Saturday 10–5, Sunday noon–5. A midtown landmark, this cozy shop stocks cards, CDs, tapes, maps, and calendars to complement its comprehensive selection of the latest books.

FACTORY OUTLETS

Hitchcock Chair Company Factory Store (860-379-4826), CT 20, Riverton. Open daily. Lambert Hitchcock achieved a national reputation in the early 1800s with his hand-stenciled maple and oak furniture. Originals are prized antiques, but the factory on the banks of the Farmington

River is still producing the same attractive, quality furniture designed by the founder.

Woodbury Pewter Factory Outlet (203-263-2668), 860 Main Street South, Woodbury. Open Monday through Saturday. Museum reproductions and factory "seconds." Dinnerware, lamps, and accessories.

SPECIALTY FOODS

Litchfield Food Company, West Street, on the green, Litchfield. Gourmet meats, cheeses, condiments, imported goodies. Dried cèpe and porcini mushrooms, chutneys, Devon cream. Exotic deli counter. Try the take-out and make your own sandwich; enjoy lunch in the small dining area.

Dutch Epicure, US 202, southwest of Litchfield. Pastries, cakes, muffins, cookies. The cook is a miracle worker with chocolate you would kill for.

Superior Foods, West Street, on the green, Litchfield. A pre-supermarket village center grocery store has been deftly converted by Kathleen Ellsworth into a specialty food purveyor-cum-eatery. Enjoy scrumptious sandwiches at a community table or at counters; shop for exotic coffees, fish so fresh you'd think it was just caught, and a variety of ethnic foods. A favorite of the locals.

The Pantry (860-868-0258), Five Titus Road, Washington Depot. Open Tuesday through Saturday 10–6. In the heart of a pretty little town, this gourmet shop is a favorite for a take-out lunch or dinner. No exotic herb or seasoning extant has escaped the attention of the chef when concocting exciting sandwiches and salads. Or you can order a late breakfast, lunch, or snack to eat at a table.

Nodine's Smokehouse, North Street (CT 63), Goshen. One of two smokehouses in the state. Smoked chicken, turkey, beef, andouille and other sausages, bacon without nitrites. Supplier to major New York City gourmet food stores.

The Egg & I Pork Farm (860-354-0820), 355 Chestnutland Road, New Milford. Open weekends 10–5. During high season, April to New Year's, children can watch several hundred piglets and porkers gambol about the farm, their snouts always on the alert for food. Cases in the retail store offer a tempting array of fresh and smoked pork products. Here's one place where you can really go to "bring home the bacon"! Gift packages and baskets.

Harney & Sons (1-800-TEA-TIME), on the village green, Salisbury. Open Monday through Saturday 10–5, Sunday noon–5. A major tea importer and supplier to the finest hotels in America, Harney & Sons invites you to sample its choicest blends in the elegant new Tasting Room. Teas, accessories, and books on tea are also for sale.

Hedgerows Market & Deli on CT 128 just east of the covered bridge in West Cornwall is filling the gap caused by the demise of two restaurants. A variety of deli sandwiches may be taken out, or you can order light meals for the table from the menu on the second floor.

SPECIAL SHOPS

The Workshop, on the green, Litchfield. Open Monday through Saturday 9:30–5:30, Sunday 11–5. If you're furnishing your home or looking for the dress or ensemble that matches your sophisticated tastes, don't pass up this outstanding boutique. Glassware, rugs, pottery, and handmade furniture, plus women's clothes.

Kitchenworks & Gourmet Gifts, 23 West Street, on the green, Litchfield. Open Monday through Saturday 10–5, Sunday noon–5. Garlic peelers, sturdy whisks, and a variety of other cookware, bakeware, and tableware, all designed to take the work out of cooking and serving family and friends.

SPECIAL EVENTS

Late January: **Woodbury Antiques Show**, Woodbury. **Bald Eagles** at Shepaug Bald Eagle Observation Area, Southbury, through March (see *To Do—Birding* in "The Housatonic Valley").

Mid-February: Olympic hopefuls vie for berths on the US team during the annual **US Eastern Ski Jumping Contest** in Salisbury on one of the most beautiful ski jumps in the country.

Mid-March: **Maple Syrup–Making Demonstration** of Flanders Nature Center, Woodbury. **Maple Sugaring Festival** in Norfolk.

Spring: **Eastern Women's Intercollegiate Crew Races** on Lake Waramaug, New Preston. Women from a dozen eastern colleges and universities compete in the big shells for the Governor's Cup. Watch the determined young women race their hearts out from the shores of Lake Waramaug State Park.

End of May: Traditional **Memorial Day parade** in Litchfield winds down historic North Street and around the southern part of town, then back to the green for patriotic oration. The parade is kicked off with cannon blasts by colorfully garbed troopers of the 1st Litchfield Artillery Regiment. Advise your children to put their hands over their ears. Fireworks at night at the high school off US 202. Bring a picnic supper and blankets or lawn chairs. **The Covered Bridge Dance** is West Cornwall's way of ushering in the summer. Barbecued specialties, clowns, comedians, fire eaters, and musical groups (Elvis has been sighted) attract several thousand people to the banks of the Housatonic. Dancing *inside* the historic covered bridge recalls old customs.

Early June: **Laurel Festival** in Winsted, celebrating the state flower. Three-day festival features the crowning of a queen, who rides a float in the parade. Laurel ball, sidewalk café. For more information and a road map of the best viewing areas of the thousands of bushes in bloom in the surrounding hills, call 860-379-1652.

June to September: **The Twisters,** Collegiate Baseball League team, play

home games in the newly refurbished Fussenich Park field in downtown Torrington. Mostly night games with excellent lighting, comfortable benches. Bulging hot dogs. Great fun—and at only $2 a seat!
Waterbury also fields a summer collegiate team.

Late June: **Litchfield 10K Road Race**—This annual race starting in the
center of the village now attracts the best runners in the world. Festive
social event on the town green. **A Taste of the Litchfield Hills**—A 2-
day celebration, at Litchfield's Haight Vineyard, of the distinctive culinary creations of the region's best restaurants, bistros, gourmet food
shops, and caterers. Wine tastings, country and classical music, and
demonstrations. Hayrides for the children.

Early July: **Litchfield House Tour**—Unique, elegant estates and gardens
are opened to visitors as a benefit for the Connecticut Junior Republic.

Late June–mid-August: **Norfolk Chamber Music Festival** in an
accoustically perfect redwood shed on the beautiful grounds of the
Battell Stoeckel estate in Norfolk.

Midsummer: **Lime Rock Race Track**—varied schedules of weekend stock-
car races on one of the country's most beautiful racetracks.

Mid-June–early September: **Music Mountain,** Falls Village off US 7—
string quartet concerts (see *Entertainment*).

Mid-August: **Morris Bluegrass Festival,** center of Morris. **Litchfield Jazz
Festival,** Goshen Fairgrounds.

Labor Day weekend: **Goshen Fair**—Tiny rural village hosts 60,000 visitors
for 3 days at one of the state's top 10 old-fashioned country fairs. Oxen
pull, wood-cutting contests, children's midway with a variety of rides,
competitions for vegetables, flowers, baked goods, arts and crafts.
Enough food to feed the 82nd Airborne for a week.

Second week in September: **Bethlehem Fair**—If you miss the Goshen Fair,
Bethlehem stages the second largest fair in the county the following week.

Late September: **Scottish Games** on the Goshen Fairgrounds, CT 63. Tossing the caber, bagpipes, the clans marching in their colorful tartans,
Scottish souvenirs, and plenty of food. Sorry, no haggis.

Early October: **Riverton Country Fair,** the last of the season.

Mid-October: **Witches Dungeon—a Horror Festival,** Bristol.

Thanksgiving: **Turkey Trot**—A grueling 6-mile road race up and down hill
and dale, starting at 10 AM at the Goshen Fairgrounds. Runners and
spectators work up a great appetite for the big bird.

Autumn: **Crew races** on the Housatonic at Kent by the champion rowers
of the Kent School.

Early December: Carol singing, a visit with Santa, and browsing for collectible
treasures displayed by 75 craftspeople at the annual **Christmas Town
Festival** in Bethlehem. Thousands annually have their holiday greeting
cards stamped in the village post office with the Bethlehem postmark.
Litchfield Performing Arts invites visitors to a candlelight tour of a half-

dozen historic Litchfield homes, all decorated in their Christmas finery. One house usually features a fine arts and crafts showcase. Children can pet the reindeer and give Santa their wish list in the **Torrington Christmas Village,** second Sunday through December 24.

☞ *Mid-December:* The **Christmas House** on Main Street in Torrington, a private home, is annually decorated inside and out with a massive display of colored lights and animated figures. Model trains. Hot chocolate for the kids. A donation is suggested for an inside visit.

December: **Candlelight service** in the Congregational church on the Green (fire marshal permitting), Litchfield. Annual performance of the ***Nutcracker*** by the Nutmeg Conservatory for the Arts, Warner Theatre, Main Street, Torrington.

☞ *December 31:* **Torrington First Night,** nonalcoholic evening of fun and games, ballet, country singing, playlets, food, and even a family night in the YMCA pool, all staged in a variety of venues around the core city. Modeled after Boston's First Night, granddaddy of all the First Nights now being held throughout the country.

III. HARTFORD AND CENTRAL CONNECTICUT

The City of Hartford
West of the River
East of the River

KIMBERLY GRANT

Connecticut's gold-domed state Capitol Building has been described as a "Gothic Taj Mahal." It houses the governor's office and legislative chambers.

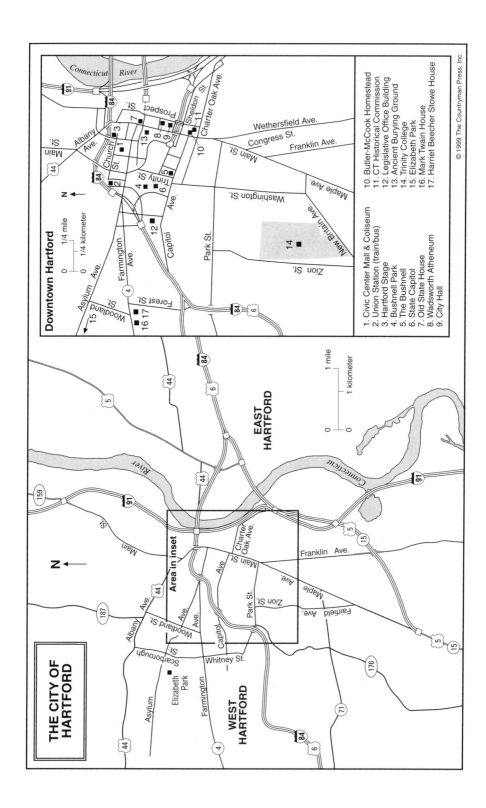

THE CITY OF HARTFORD

WEST HARTFORD

EAST HARTFORD

Area in inset

Connecticut River

Main St.
Albany Ave.
Scarborough St.
Woodland St.
Asylum
Elizabeth Park
Farmington
Whitney St.
Capitol Ave.
Woodland Ave.
Main St.
Charter Oak Ave.
Park St.
Zion St.
Maple Ave.
Fairfield Ave.
Franklin Ave.

0   1 mile
0   1 kilometer

187
159
91
44
5
91
15
5
15
176
71
84
6
4
44
84
6

© 1999 The Countryman Press, Inc.

Downtown Hartford

Connecticut River

Prospect St.
Sheldon St.
Charter Oak Ave.
Main St.
Church St.
Albany Ave.
Trinity St.
Capitol Ave.
Farmington Ave.
Asylum Ave.
Woodland St.
Forest St.
Park St.
Washington St.
Maple Ave.
New Britain Ave.
Zion St.
Wethersfield Ave.
Congress St.
Franklin Ave.

0   1/4 mile
0   1/4 kilometer

N

91
84
44
84
84
6
4

1. Civic Center Mall & Coliseum
2. Union Station (train/bus)
3. Hartford Stage
4. The Bushnell
5. State Capitol
6. Old State House
7. Wadsworth Atheneum
8. City Hall
9. City Hall
10. Butler-McCook Homestead
11. CT Historical Commission
12. Legislative Office Building
13. Ancient Burying Ground
14. Trinity College
15. Elizabeth Park
16. Mark Twain House
17. Harriet Beecher Stowe House

The City of Hartford

In 1868 Mark Twain wrote:

I think this is the best built and handsomest town I have ever seen . . . What a singular country it is! At the hospitable mansion at which I am a guest, I have to smoke surreptitiously when all are in bed, to save my reputation and then draw suspicion upon the cat when the family detects the unfamiliar odor. I never was so absolutely proper in the broad light of day in my life as I have been for the last day or two. So far I am safe; but I am sorry to say that the cat has lost caste.

The Dutch fur traders who arrived here in 1623 would hardly recognize their Fort New Hope today. Later, Thomas Hooker and his following of Puritan dissenters from Massachusetts founded Hartford. The colony's Fundamental Orders of 1639 is regarded as the world's first written constitution, lending Connecticut its status as the Constitution State.

Hartford was the hometown of notables from J.P. Morgan in the 19th century to Katharine Hepburn in the 20th. Its manufacturing heyday produced the Colt revolver, the pay telephone, Columbia bicycles, and the Pope Motor Car. Its distinguished sons include the inventor of anesthesia and the founder of the world's first permanent school for the deaf. Mark Twain built himself a grand Victorian home in Hartford and lived there during his most prolific years. Among the other literary celebrities who chose to live in Hartford are Harriet Beecher Stowe, Sinclair Lewis (briefly), and Wallace Stevens.

Connecticut's capital city has its share of history and suitably imposing public buildings. Served by two interstates and four bridges, it's a river town that has just in time remembered its waterway. Frederick Law Olmsted, the father of American landscape architecture, lived here for a time and designed the state capitol grounds. His son devised the city's system of parks, most of which still serve the changing population.

By the turn of the century, immigrants from around the world brought their speech, customs, and ideas, creating a diverse cultural mosaic. Ethnic city neighborhoods include the still largely Italian section around Franklin Avenue, where grocery stores, bakeries, and restaurants maintain Old World traditions and standards of taste.

Downtown, the heart of the city's social and cultural life, is the best place to begin exploring. Among the choices are a visit to the Wadsworth Atheneum, the country's oldest public art museum; a performance at the award-winning Hartford Stage Company; the 1798 Old State House, first in the nation; the Ancient Burying Ground, where city founders are memorialized; a ride on the 1914-vintage carousel in Bushnell Park to the tunes of a 1925 Wurlitzer organ; and lovers of American literature shouldn't miss the Mark Twain and Harriet Beecher Stowe homes at Nook Farm.

The proximity of its larger neighbors, New York and Boston, keeps Hartford abreast of urban trends, but the city has an identity and a charm of its own. A revitalized coffeehouse-and-bar scene is emerging downtown, along with art galleries, experimental theater, myriad culinary options, and clubs that draw nationally known musicians to their stages.

Bear in mind that Hartford's history-rich outlying towns are nearby and easily accessible. Check the mileage scale on your map: Hartford makes an excellent base for exploring the whole state, but do take a good look at the city itself—the local events, the neighborhoods, and the people.

Entries in this section are arranged in alphabetical order.

AREA CODE
860

GUIDANCE

For information on attractions, events, lodgings, and more, write to or call the **Greater Hartford Tourism District** (860-244-8181; 1-800-793-4480), 234 Murphy Road, Hartford 06114 (Web site: www.travelfile.com/get/ghtd). The **Hartford Downtown Council** (860-522-6400, events hotline; 860-728-3089, office; Web site: www.hartford-hdc.com) sponsors events and provides assistance to visitors, such as participation in a Park/Shop/Dine program offering discounted parking (860-727-1090).

Privately run visitors centers are found at the **Old State House** (860-522-6766) on Main Street in downtown Hartford; in the **Hartford Civic Center Coliseum** (860-727-8010), Trumbull and Asylum Streets; and at the **State Capitol,** west entrance (860-240-0222), Monday through Friday 9–3. **Heritage Trails Tours** (860-677-8867), PO Box 138, Farmington 06034, offers guided tours of Hartford and a variety of sight-seeing and exploration trips, from 2-hour to all-day affairs.

GETTING THERE

By air: **Bradley International Airport** (860-292-2000), Windsor Locks, 12 miles north of Hartford off I-91, serves the region with daily flights scheduled by American, Carnival, Continental, Delta, Midway, Northwest, TWA, United, and USAir. Commuter lines into Bradley are Air Alliance, Air Ontario, American Eagle, Business Express, Conti-

nental Express, Downeast Express, Northwest, TWA Express, United
Express, and USAir Express. Rental cars are available at the airport,
and there is limousine service to Hartford hotels.

By bus or limo: **Greyhound** (860-247-3524; 1-800-231-2222), **Peter
Pan Trailways** (1-800-343-9999), and **Bonanza Buslines** (1-800-556-
3815). **Connecticut Limousine Service** (1-800-472-5466) serves Bradley, JFK, and La Guardia airports. All train and bus lines connect at
Union Station downtown.

By rail: **AMTRAK** (1-800-872-7245) serves Hartford and connects at
Union Station.

GETTING AROUND

Taxi service in Hartford: **United Cab Co.** (860-547-1602), **Yellow Cab**
(860-666-6666). Taxis are available at Union Station and on call.

City bus service is available and reliable in Hartford; most routes
operate daytime only. A **Connecticut Transit** (860-525-9181) information booth is at State House Square and Market Street. It's open
weekdays only, 7–6. (*Note:* Unless you plan to limit your visit strictly to
downtown Hartford, you will need a car.)

Hartford Guides (860-275-6456; 860-522-0855) are uniformed
men and women who patrol the streets downtown from Union Station
to Constitution Plaza and from Church Street to Bushnell Park.
Dressed in khaki, red, and white, with HARTFORD GUIDES lettered on the
backs of their shirts, they'll give you free directions to anywhere in the
area; provide you with information on events, services, shopping, and
attractions; escort you to your car or bus; and, in emergency situations,
get help. They also lead walking tours of the city's historic sites; call
ahead. The guides are headquartered at 101 Pearl Street in the **Hartford Police Services Museum.**

MEDICAL EMERGENCY

The statewide emergency number is **911.**

Hartford Hospital (860-545-5000), 80 Seymour Street. The emergency number is 860-545-0000.

Mount Sinai Hospital (860-714-4000), 500 Blue Hills Avenue. The
emergency number is 860-714-2644.

St. Francis Hospital (860-714-4000), 114 Woodland Street. The
emergency number is 860-714-4001.

TO SEE

THE CONNECTICUT RIVER

Hartford has a new attraction, one that's been there all along—the **Connecticut River.** In the grip of progress, the city abandoned its waterway in
favor first of the railroads and later of the interstates, but now all that is
changing. Parks and walkways have been created along both banks of the
river, and excursion boats are back in business. There are picnic areas and

playgrounds, quiet spots for reflection, and, on the East Hartford side, an amphitheater. A full schedule of fishing tournaments, athletic competitions, rowing lessons, jazz concerts, and occasional fireworks keep the riverfront bustling with activity. More attractions are on the way—a 3-mile loop for walkers and bicyclists, making use of two bridges, and a landscaped plaza leading from downtown Hartford to the riverfront are slated for completion in 1999. For information on facilities, activities, and special events, call **Riverfront Recapture Inc.** (860-713-3131).

Hartford's revitalization may not end there, however. An ambitious $1 billion development plan to remake the city and transform the riverfront calls for a convention center and stadium, hotel, an entertainment and shopping complex, residential areas, and parks. Planners have high hopes.

INSURANCE COMPANIES

The insurance industry was born when a city resident had his home insured against fire in 1794. This first written policy led to the establishment of the Hartford Fire Insurance Company (1810), whose reputation soared after a devastating New York City fire in 1835. Policies covering shipping (shippers set aside a portion of their profits to insure against losses incurred by fire, wrecks, and storms) were followed later in the century by automobile and home insurance; hence, Hartford became known worldwide as the Insurance City. A reminder of the city's ties to the industry is the **Travelers Tower** (860-277-4208) in the center of the downtown area at One Tower Square. Once the tallest building in New England, the tower still offers a spectacular view of the countryside in all directions. Free tours, weather permitting, May through October, Monday through Friday 10–3. *Caution:* After you get off the elevator, you still have 100 steps to climb. Nearby on Constitution Plaza, the **Phoenix Home Life Mutual Insurance Company** inhabits a two-sided (done with curves) green-glass wonder—the first of its kind in the world—known locally as the boat building. Crosstown at 151 Farmington Avenue, **Aetna** is headquartered in what has been called the world's largest Federal-style building, across the street from Saint Joseph's Cathedral. The **Hartford Insurance Group** (860-547-5000), 690 Asylum Avenue, houses **The Hartford Exhibit,** a collection of insurance memorabilia and artifacts (including a 200-year-old fire pumper) that traces the company's pivotal role in the history of the nation's insurance industry. Open Monday through Friday 8:15–4:15.

MUSEUMS

Connecticut Historical Society (860-236-5621), One Elizabeth Street. Open year-round, Tuesday through Sunday noon–5. Its library is open Tuesday through Saturday 9–5. Adults $6, seniors $5, students $3; children under 6 free. An outstanding collection of Connecticut furniture and other local items; changing exhibits on selected topics in state history. The library specializes in history and genealogy. Musical events, lectures, and family programs throughout the year. Bookstore. Call for schedule and information.

Connecticut Resources Recovery Authority Visitors Center (860-247-4280), 211 Murphy Road. Open September through June, Wednesday through Friday noon–4; July and August, Tuesday through Saturday 10–4; other times by appointment. Free admission. See what happens to your recyclables after you leave them at the curb. Hands-on exhibits and games reinforce the importance of recycling. Visitors can watch as bottles, cans, and plastic are sorted, crushed, and shipped away to become something new. The "Temple of Trash" exhibit illustrates the evils of old-fashioned garbage dumping. The gift shop features items made of recycled materials.

Menczer Museum of Medicine and Dentistry (860-236-5613), Hartford Medical Society Building, 230 Scarborough Street. Open year-round, Monday through Friday 10–4. Adults $2, children $1. A one-of-a-kind museum with exhibits of instruments and medications in use over the past three centuries; also traces the history of anesthesia. An excellent aid to appreciation of modern methods and technology. A comprehensive medical library is on the premises.

The Museum of Connecticut History (860-566-3056), 231 Capitol Avenue, is housed along with the **Connecticut State Library** and the **State Supreme Court.** Open year-round, Monday through Friday 9:30–4. Free admission. Facing the ornate State Capitol across the street, this example of Beaux-Arts architecture adds to the monumental aspect of the neighborhood. The main reading room of the library is a handsome hall with a spectacular ceiling. Downstairs, the nationally known history and genealogy collection attracts researchers from all over. The museum has changing exhibits devoted to aspects of state history, economic life, Connecticut products, and events of note. Permanent displays include the Colony of Connecticut Royal Charter of 1662, and a collection of more than 300 artifacts covering the state's political, military, and industrial history.

Wadsworth Atheneum (860-278-2670), 600 Main Street. Open year-round, Tuesday through Sunday 11–5, 11–8 on the first Thursday of each month. Adults $7; seniors and college students with ID $5; ages 6–17, $3; children under 6 free. Admission is free on Thursday and until noon on Saturday. Free tours; call for schedule. The country's oldest continuously operating public art museum (since 1842) is nationally recognized for the excellence and scope of its collections, which include more than 50,000 works covering 5,000 years of sculpture and painting, china, furniture, and textiles. Traveling exhibitions, national and international, are scheduled. Specialties are the MATRIX Gallery of contemporary art, the Amistad Foundation Gallery of African-American Art, Hudson River School paintings, 19th-century Impressionist works, and 18th-century furniture. The Atheneum Theater presents lectures, films, and concerts. The **Museum Café** (860-728-5989) is open for lunch and on Sunday for brunch. Of course there's a quality gift shop.

HISTORIC HOMES

Butler-McCook Homestead (860-247-8996; 860-522-1806), 396 Main Street. Open May through October, Tuesday, Thursday, and Sunday noon–4. Call for admission price. Though the home dates back to 1782, it was expanded, "improved," and finally "Victorianized" by successive generations of the same family. It has thus become a living history and is indeed one of a very few surviving historic homes in the city. Formal gardens designed by Jacob Weidenmann are maintained out back, and mementos of the Reverend Mr. McCook and his large and active family enliven the tour. Among the treasures are a collection of Japanese armor, a Bierstadt landscape, antique furniture, toys, and clothing. The house is a property of the Antiquarian and Landmarks Society, which has restored and continues to maintain a number of historic buildings throughout the state.

Governor's Residence (860-566-4840), 990 Prospect Avenue. Open every Tuesday and Wednesday for a tour at 10 AM, by appointment only. Free admission. Visitors are guided through the carefully restored first-floor public rooms in the 1909 Georgian Revival home where the state's first families have resided since 1945. Special events take place here throughout the year; call for schedule.

Harriet Beecher Stowe House (at Nook Farm) (860-525-9317), Farmington Avenue at Forest Street. Open year-round Tuesday through Saturday 9:30–4; Sunday noon–4. Open also Monday from June through Columbus Day and during December; closed holidays. Adults $6.50; seniors $6; children $2.75. Across the way from Mark Twain's mansion, the more modest "cottage" of the Stowes was home to the "little lady that started this big war"—in the words of Abraham Lincoln. The author of the 1852 abolitionist classic *Uncle Tom's Cabin* was one of a group of creative souls who settled in and around Nook Farm in the latter part of the 19th century, when it was a semirural area, nearly a mile from the crush of downtown Hartford! Mrs. Stowe's views on housekeeping and decorating are evident in the house, which is quietly Victorian and comfortably human-scaled. The **Katharine S. Day House** (860-522-9258), at Nook Farm, itself a striking example of Victorian taste, is primarily devoted to the Stowe-Day research library. The collection emphasizes events and issues surrounding Mrs. Stowe, her family, and her times. The Day house and its changing exhibits are accessible by appointment.

Isham-Terry House (860-247-8996), 211 High Street. Open year-round; call for schedule. This dignified Italianate 1854 mansion—property of the Antiquarian and Landmarks Society—was purchased in 1896 by a doctor whose two sisters lived there well into their 90s (the second died in 1979). The sisters left the house in mint condition: ornate Victorian gaslight fixtures, stained-glass panels over the French doors, a mam-

Mark Twain composed some of his greatest masterpieces while living in Hartford.

moth carved mirror, heavy carved mantel, and coffered ceilings.

Mark Twain Memorial (at Nook Farm) (860-493-6411), 351 Farmington Avenue (at Woodland Street). Open year-round Monday through Saturday 9:30–5; Sunday noon–5. Closed Tuesday January through May, and Columbus Day through November. Adults $7.50; seniors $7; children $3.50 (under 6 free). Determined to live up to the standards of the Gilded Age, Mark Twain moved to Hartford with his new wife and in 1874 built this flamboyant, many-gabled mansion, which added his own unique whimsy to the quirkiness of the era. He spared no expense— interiors were by Louis Comfort Tiffany. His specifications included a room shaped like a pilot's house and a kitchen at the front of the house, so servants could view the goings-on in the street. The mansion has been restored with great care—artisans were brought here from Germany for the project—and docents are prepared with anecdotes and sidelights to help you imagine a time when Sam Clemens's world was a happy one. He composed some of his greatest masterpieces here, including *Tom Sawyer, Huckleberry Finn,* and *Life on the Mississippi.*

HISTORIC SITES

Ancient Burying Ground (860-244-8181), at the corner of Main and Gold Streets, remains a remarkably peaceful enclave even though it's in the middle of the city. In use from 1640 to the early 1800s, it is the resting place of the town's first settlers, and of many who came after. The carvings and inscriptions on a number of the headstones and monuments have been restored or replicated. A sober epitaph found on several stones is typical of the Pilgrim Fathers' views: "Behold my friend as you pass by, / As you are now so once was I / As I am now, so you must be / Prepare for death and follow me."

Armsmear, 80 Wethersfield Avenue. Open to visitors by appointment only (860-246-4025), this was the home of Samuel Colt. The grand Italianate exterior indicates the scale of the original estate, which included a lake, fountains, and a deer park. The inventor of the "gun that won the West" founded his factory in Hartford in 1855. The building is still there, with its distinctive blue onion dome visible from I-91 as you come into Hartford from the north.

Cedar Hill Cemetery (860-956-3311), 254 Fairfield Avenue. Open year-round, daily 7–5, Cedar Hill is an example of the possibilities of the picturesque in landscaping. Founded in 1864, it is the last resting place for many of the city's important Victorian citizens. J.P. Morgan, Samuel and Elizabeth Colt, Isabella Beecher Hooker, and James G. Batterson (founder of the Travelers Insurance Company) are among the notables buried here. Its 270 acres provide a pleasant place to walk, despite the reminders of mortality. However, a note of hope is inscribed on the tombstone of Horace Wells, inventor of nitrous oxide: "There shall be no pain."

Center Church (860-249-5631), 675 Main Street. Open May through October, Wednesday and Friday 11–2, and by appointment. This is the church that Thomas Hooker began when he brought his band of dissenters from Massachusetts in 1636 to found Hartford. The first meetinghouse was on the site of the Old State House, across Main Street. The church site was moved in 1737, and the present church, patterned after St. Martin in the Fields in London, dates from 1807. The elegant, barrel-vaulted ceiling and the remarkable stained-glass windows—six of them by Tiffany—would no doubt surprise Thomas Hooker, whose original meetinghouse was a simple square wooden building. Visitors are welcome to attend services and tour the church. Concerts are often held here; call for information.

Charter Oak Cultural Center (860-249-1207), 21 Charter Oak Avenue. Gallery is open September through July, Tuesday through Thursday noon–5; closed August. Listed on the National Register of Historic Places, this Romanesque Victorian brick building was Connecticut's first synagogue, built in 1876. Irish-born Hartford architect George Keller used rounded arched windows to echo its domed twin towers, and the recently restored interior features remarkable stenciling and other ornate touches. The center presents a variety of performances and concerts featuring local artists; call for schedule.

Charter Oak Marker. Not many cities boast a legend featuring a tree, but as mentioned earlier, Hartford has its own character. Charter Oak Place is near the spot where the Charter Oak stood. Strictly undocumented legend says that when the mother country sent a new governor, Edmund Andros, to take control of the New England colonies in 1687, the Connecticut colony balked. Still, Hartford city fathers gathered, on

Andros's command, in Joseph Wadsworth's tavern to turn over their original and very generous charter, thus relinquishing their freedom to govern themselves. At the moment of transfer, however, the lights were extinguished, confusion set in, and when the candles were relit, the charter was gone. It had been concealed—by Wadsworth, they say—in the hollow of an enormous oak. By the time the tree blew down in 1856, it was 33 feet in circumference and had become an icon of state history. Objects made or said to be made from its wood were considered precious, and they proliferated. Mark Twain remarked, typically, that he himself had seen "a walking-stick, dog collar, needle-case, three-legged stool, bootjack, dinner table, tenpin alley, toothpick, and enough Charter Oak to build a plank road from Hartford to Salt Lake City."

Church of the Good Shepherd (860-525-4289), 155 Wyllys Street. Open by appointment. Edward Tuckerman Potter designed this Victorian Gothic church of red and yellow sandstone, with intricate carvings, stained-glass windows, and a decorative motif of crossed pistols. It was commissioned by Mrs. Colt as a tribute to her entrepreneur-manufacturer husband and to their three children who died in infancy.

Connecticut State Capitol (860-240-0222), 210 Capitol Avenue at Trinity Street. Open Monday through Friday 9–3, Saturday 10:15–2:15. Designed by Richard Upjohn and completed in 1878, it has evoked strong opinions—Frank Lloyd Wright declared it a monstrosity. In fact, it's a perfect statehouse, combining elements of the Gothic, classical, and Second Empire styles. For its 100th birthday, the building was cleaned, restored, renovated, and polished to a high shine. Under its massive gold dome are elaborate Gothic facades front and back, and decorative sculpture depicting historical events; it's no less impressive inside, with towering granite columns, stained-glass windows, atriums with lofty ceilings, and ornate chambers for the governor and the two houses of the legislature. Displays of bullet-riddled battle flags, Lafayette's camp bed (a hard choice for a night's sleep), a larger-than-life statue of Coventry native Nathan Hale, and numerous other historical mementos share space with state governing bodies. Adjacent is the **Legislative Office Building,** completed in 1988 and designed to echo architectural features of the capitol in a 20th-century manner. Members of the League of Women Voters lead free tours of both buildings hourly.

Old State House (860-522-6766), 800 Main Street. Open Monday through Friday 10–4, Saturday 11–4; closed the last two weeks of August. Admission is free. The nation's first statehouse built specifically for that purpose, the 1796 Federal-style Old State House was the first public building designed by Boston's Charles Bulfinch. Careful renovations have not only saved the building from collapse, but also added features that bring its history to life—including costumed guides playing historical roles. This is the site of the first written constitution, as well as the *Amistad* and Prudence Crandall trials. Inside, visitors can follow the

KIMBERLY GRANT

The Old State House hosted the Amistad *trial.*

building's changing role in Hartford: The Court Room looks as it did in 1796; the upstairs chambers show where the city council met in the early 19th century; upstairs, Joseph Steward's gallery combines art and curiosities of the late 1800s. The Old State House is the scene of farmer's market days, public meetings, official and private events, arts and crafts shows, and performances of all sorts. An exceptional gift and bookshop features Connecticut goods.

Stegosaurus is a monumental and unmistakable Calder stabile, in the center of downtown Hartford on Main Street. He perches between the **Hartford Municipal Building,** a 1915 Beaux-Arts beauty with a grand atrium that runs the length of the building, and the **Wadsworth Atheneum.** This bright orange monster dominates **Alfred E. Burr Memorial Mall,** a vest-pocket park with plantings and benches where you can sit and watch the birds that nest on the giant steel creature's infrastructure.

Trinity College (860-297-2000), 300 Summit Street. A compact and self-contained campus located at the city's highest elevation, Trinity (founded in 1823) is a good browsing ground for architecture buffs. The "Long Walk" is made up of three connected brownstone buildings in the Victorian Gothic style. The college chapel, considered by many to be the finest example of Victorian Gothic in America, is the setting for organ and chamber concerts. The college sponsors showings of films both old and new and presents lectures, dance programs, and other performance events open to the public. Call for schedules.

TO DO

BOAT EXCURSIONS
Charter Oak Landing (860-526-4954). Follow signs from exit 27 off I-91 or from Wethersfield Avenue. Riverboat cruises offered daily on the Connecticut River, Memorial Day through Labor Day; call for additional spring and fall schedules. The *Lady Fenwick* makes two 1-hour lunchtime cruises, a longer downriver cruise at 2:30, and a cocktail cruise at 5:30.

CANOEING
Huck Finn Adventures (860-693-0385), Collinsville. For an otherworldly adventure, don a headlamp and paddle a canoe under the city on a guided 2-mile outing on the Park River which runs through a 20-foot concrete tunnel. You won't see them, but you'll pass under the Hartford Public Library, the State Capitol grounds, Bushnell Park, I-84, and other Hartford landmarks on your way to the confluence of the Park and Connecticut Rivers. Trips leave from Charter Oak Landing and run from June through September. Call for reservations.

FISHING
There are boat-launching sites on the Connecticut River at **Charter Oak Landing** (860-713-3131), exit 27 off I-91, and at **Riverside Park** (860-293-0130), exit 33 off I-91. Anglers can also cast their lines from the riverbank. The bass population here is thriving, and the city hosts fishing tournaments at these sites; call for schedule.

GOLF
Goodwin Golf Course South (860-525-3601), 1130 Maple Avenue. Par 70, 18 holes, 5,638 yards.
Goodwin Golf Course North (860-525-3601), 1130 Maple Avenue. Par 35, 9 holes, 2,544 yards.
Keney Park Golf Course (860-525-3656), 280 Toner Avenue. Par 70, 18 holes, 5,969 yards.

ROWING
Riverfront Recapture Inc. Community Boating (860-713-3131), at Riverside Park, exit 33 off I-91. Open June through August; call for schedule. Programs on the Connecticut River for rowers of all abilities, from 1-hour lessons to multiday clinics on sculling (using a single-person shell) and sweep rowing (with a four- or eight-person crew).

SIGHT-SEEING TOURS
Heritage Trails Sightseeing Tours (860-677-8867), PO Box 138, Farmington 06032. Daily tours of the city depart from hotels; imaginative tours of area towns and attractions are also scheduled. Call for information.

SPECTATOR SPORTS
Connecticut Pride (860-678-8156), Hartford Civic Center Coliseum, Trumbull and Asylum Streets. Continental basketball team plays at the

civic center and other arenas November through March. Call for schedule.

✐ **Hartford Wolf Pack Hockey Club** (860-246-PUCK), Hartford Civic Center Coliseum. American Hockey League, an affiliate of the New York Rangers. Games October through April. Call for schedule.

✐ **New England Blizzard** (860-522-4667), Hartford Civic Center Coliseum. American Basketball League, and the area's first professional women's team. Call for schedule.

GREEN SPACE

✐ **Bushnell Park** (860-232-6710), one block west of Main Street, at Gold and Jewell Streets. Hartford's downtown green space, the park is named for Rev. Horace Bushnell, who advocated creation of the park to counter the rapid urbanization of the city—in the 1850s. Its 37 acres are embellished with bridges—although the streams no longer flow under them—a pond, varied plantings (call for tours of Memorial Arch and guided tree walks), a playground, and benches. The performance shell hosts summer concerts of all sorts. **The Pump House Gallery** (860-722-6536; 860-543-8874), on the park grounds, is open year-round, Tuesday through Friday 11–2; weekends by appointment. Works of Connecticut artists are shown in this 1947 Tudor-style pumphouse, and in summer there is a noon music series (call for schedule; see *Entertainment—Theaters*). To the west of the gallery is the handsome pavilion that houses **The Carousel** (860-246-7739; 860-249-2201), an authentic 1914 Stein and Goldstein merry-go-round with rampant hand-carved horses prancing to the music of a 1925 Wurlitzer under hundreds of twinkling lights. It operates on weekends 11–5 mid-April through mid-May and during September; Tuesday through Sunday 11–5 in summer. The park extends north of the State Capitol, where the dominant feature is the **Corning Fountain,** memorializing the Native Americans who were the original inhabitants of the region. The handsome brownstone **Soldiers and Sailors Memorial Arch,** designed by local architect George Keller, frames the entrance to the park on Trinity Street. For a self-guided tour, get a copy of the brochure *Bushnell Park Tree Walks,* available from the **Department of Environmental Protection,** 165 Capitol Avenue, Room 555, Hartford 06106.

✐ **Charter Oak Landing** (860-713-3131), Brainard Road exit off I-91; follow signs. The park, one link in the chain of attractions strung along the banks of the Connecticut River, is in the shadow of the Charter Oak Bridge. Set with picnic benches, walkways, a gazebo, a small playground, and a boat launch, it's the site of fishing tournaments and athletic contests from swimming to rowing sprints (contact Riverfront Recapture, 860-713-3131, for a schedule). It serves as the departure point for a boat ride (see *Boat Excursions*) that further opens up Hartford's traditional waterway.

Elizabeth Park in Hartford was the nation's first municipal rose garden.

Elizabeth Park (860-722-6514), Prospect Avenue at Asylum Avenue. Open
year-round, dawn to dusk. Greenhouses open daily, except holidays,
10–4. This 100-acre park, straddling the Hartford–West Hartford town
line, has many features—vistas, plantings, and activities—to recommend it, but it's best known as the site of the nation's first municipal
rose garden. Upwards of 15,000 roses grow in beds and over archways,
on fences, and up around a perfect wedding-picture gazebo. If you're
lucky enough to visit in late June or early July, you'll catch these beau-
ties at their peak. Other features are the Perennial Garden—designed
by Frederick McGourty, a nationally known gardener based in Norfolk
(See "Litchfield County"—*Nurseries/Gardens*)—the Rock Garden, and
the Annual Garden, as well as some 120 varieties of trees. There is a
snack bar and a lounge; ask about planned activities.

LODGING

BED & BREAKFAST

In addition to the listing below, a number of bed & breakfast reservation
services offer access to rooms available in establishments throughout
the state. For a list, see *What's Where—Bed & Breakfasts*.

The 1895 House B&B (860-232-0014), 97 Girard Avenue 06105. In the
old and still very good residential section of the city, this substantial
Victorian home was designed by a female architect, Genevra Buckland.
The former billiard parlor on the third floor has become a suite, with a

combined bed- and sitting room (with refrigerator) and a large private bath; an attractive guest room on the second floor has its own bath. Continental breakfast. $70–85; senior discounts available.

HOTELS

 ♿ **Goodwin Hotel** (860-246-7500; 1-800-922-5006), One Haynes Street (opposite the Civic Center) 06103. Hartford's luxury hotel—a National Historic Landmark—with 124 units, 11 suites (some on two levels), a full concierge service, lounges, entertainment, an elegant restaurant, room service, health and exercise facilities, and valet garage parking. Rising behind the elaborate, red, Queen Anne facade of the 1881 Goodwin Building, the hotel, with its four-story atrium, is all new but well up to the standards of Gilded Age magnificence. Weekend rates $99–159; $189–225 during the week; packages available.

 ♿ **Sheraton-Hartford Hotel** (860-728-5151; 1-800-325-3535), 315 Trumbull Street 06103, connected to the Civic Center and a block from the Hartford Stage Company (see *Theaters*). A downtown hotel with a comfortable, deeply upholstered lobby and direct indoor access to the shops, restaurants, and performance and trade show spaces of the Civic Center. One of the most convenient of the city's hotels, with 388 rooms, nine suites, and a restaurant, lounge, health club, and indoor pool. Up to $100.

OTHER LODGING

 ♿ **The Hastings Hotel & Conference Center** (860-727-4200), 85 Sigourney Street (off Farmington Avenue) 06105. Originally a conference center for the use of employees and visitors to the Aetna insurance company, the Hastings has a businesslike air but a sure touch with basic amenities. Located near the Cathedral of Saint Joseph and the Mark Twain and Harriet Beecher Stowe houses (see *Historic Homes*), just outside the main downtown area, it's worth considering as a base for exploring the city. There are 271 recently refurbished rooms, each with private bath and also a desk, PC modem hookup, cable TV, radio, alarm clock, and coffeemaker. Suites are equipped with kitchen appliances. There's a casual restaurant on the premises, as well as a fitness center, gymnasium, and pocket billiards and table tennis. Around $95 for rooms; more for suites.

WHERE TO EAT

DINING OUT

Franklin Avenue is Hartford's Italian district. You'll find dozens of places for elegant dining, not to mention pastry, pizza, pasta, and grinders (the local name for heroes, subs, whatever you call the big sandwich). Most places are Italian, most have a coterie of regulars, and the quality is uniformly high.

 ♿ **Carbone's Ristorante** (860-296-9646), 588 Franklin Avenue. Lunch and dinner Monday through Saturday; closed Sunday. Full bar. In business since 1938, this is probably Hartford's best-known Italian restaurant, serving both northern and southern specialties. Service is masterful; menu choices, elegant. Table-side preparation, pasta (of course) and veal, but they also have inventive ways with sweetbreads, poultry, and tenderloin tips. Reservations recommended. $14–26.

  ♿ **Gaetano's** (860-249-1629), One Civic Center Plaza. Lunch Monday through Friday; dinner Monday through Saturday. Bistro open 11:30–10. A first-class restaurant among the shops at the Civic Center. Full bar. Distinguished for its service as well as the food, which concentrates on northern Italian dishes: sautéed filet mignon with stuffed cherry peppers, roasted sweet peppers, and sausage; veal stuffed with prosciutto and cheese, accompanied by polenta; grilled house-made ravioli with portobello mushrooms in an asagio cream sauce. The bistro section has faster, less expensive service. Reservations recommended. $16–25.

  ♿ **Max Downtown** (860-522-2530), 185 Asylum Street, in City Place, opposite the Civic Center. Open every day; closed Sunday from Memorial Day through Labor Day. Lunch 11:30–2:30; dinner 5–10, Sunday 5–9. The centerpiece of the three Max restaurants in the area, this is the former Max on Main in a new location. An airy, high-ceilinged dining room, white linen, and knowledgeable staff add to the savvy air of this home of "world cuisine." A sample dinner entrée: oak-grilled salmon with Israeli couscous, served with vegetable fondue, arugula, and lobster-basil sauce. Asian-barbecued pork chops are another possibility, as is a roasted vegetable platter. For dessert: crème brûlée, sorbet, or try the chocolate hazelnut torte. Dinner entrées $15–25.

  ♿ **No Fish Today** (860-244-2100), 80 Pratt Street. Lunch Monday through Friday, dinner daily. Full bar. In the heart of downtown, on a one-block street connecting Main Street with the Civic Center, No Fish is a friendly eatery in what appears to be a real house, with seafood as a specialty and Italian as a leitmotiv. Popular entrées include salmon, scampi crostini, and seafood Portugais—clams, scallops, mussels, and more, over pasta. Reservations recommended. $14–20.

  ♿ **Pierpont's Restaurant** (860-522-4935; 860-246-7500), in the Goodwin Hotel, One Haynes Street. Breakfast daily starting at 6:30; lunch Monday through Friday; dinner Monday through Saturday; brunch Sunday. Under a pale grillwork ceiling and surrounded by polished wood and spacious windows, diners are served on hushed white linen befitting a room named for onetime resident J.P. Morgan. Exceptional treatment and saucing of American regional cuisine—steak, poultry, seafood—prepared and presented with gourmet flair. You could start with pancetta-wrapped shrimp over shaved fennel and basil–red pepper puree, then continue to smoked salmon with butternut squash risotto, or duck with cider vinegar jus and parsnip whipped potatoes. $14–25.

The Savannah (860-278-2020), 391 Main Street. Serving dinner Monday through Thursday 5:30–9; Friday and Saturday 5:30–10; closed Sunday.

Eclectic cuisine accented by the exotic flavors of Africa, the American South, and the Far East, at some of the city's trendiest tables. Surrounded by an atmosphere of cool sophistication—exposed brick walls, African sculpture, fluted columns, and candlelight—diners can delve into such innovations as Louisiana crab cakes with lemon pepper remoulade; grilled sesame-crusted tuna with a salad of warm curried bananas and papaya; and sweet potato ravioli sauced with chive butter. Desserts are no less spectacular: pumpkin crème brûlée, or a bread pudding of apricots and port wine. Meals are artful presentations; service is attentive. Reservations recommended. Entrées $16–26.

EATING OUT

   The America's Cup (860-246-7500; 1-800-922-5006), at the Goodwin Hotel, One Haynes Street. *The* place for upscale snacking: a lounge of leather and wood for relaxing with a cocktail and/or light fare. Moderate prices.

   Black-Eyed Sally's BBQ & Blues (860-278-7427), 350 Asylum Street. Open for lunch Monday through Friday from 11:30; dinner Monday through Wednesday until 10, Thursday until 1 AM; the kitchen is open until 2 AM on weekends; closed Sunday. A little slice of Memphis in New England, serving up food that is as red-hot as the blues legends who grace the stage. Cajun and Creole cuisine—étouffée, jambalaya, and pan-blackened catfish, to name a few—with such classic southern accompaniments as collard greens, black-eyed peas, and cornbread. Live blues in the evening, Thursday through Saturday (see *Nightlife*). Entrées $9–16.

   Coach's Sports Bar & Grille (860-52-COACH), 187 Allyn Street. Open daily for lunch and dinner, with appetizers served after the dinner hour. Full bar. A huge square bar dominates one side of the brick-walled space; the other is set with tables and booths. DJ on weekend evenings, after the game. From every seat, we're told, you can see 6 of the 32 TV monitors that emphasize the restaurant's theme. Jim Calhoun, coach of the University of Connecticut men's basketball Huskies, is part owner, and is in attendance as much as his schedule permits. Local sports commentators regularly broadcast from the bar. The menu has Mexican hints, Italian favorites, all-American standards, and options for the health-and-fitness crowd. Steak, barbecued ribs, fajitas, tuna melt, veggie pocket, shrimp stir-fry, and meat loaf. For dessert, selections include the colossal hot fudge sundae. Dinner entrées under $15.

   Congress Rotisserie (860-525-5141), 208 Trumbull Street, across from the Civic Center. A carryout lunch place specializing in sandwiches and roast chicken. Everything is fresh; portions are generous, choices enormous. Go in and read the menu—capicola and provolone with imported peppers and red onions on French bread; Southwest rotisserie chicken salad with tortilla strips, cilantro, and honey-lime vinaigrette, garnished with light peanut sauce. Sandwiches up to $6; salads under $7; soups, cookies also to round out your meal. Small portions on request. Congress Rotisserie is a local chain, with a restaurant at 691 Silas Deane Highway

(860-563-4300) in Wethersfield and other carryout places—at 274 Farmington Avenue (860-278-7711) and at 333 North Main Street (860-231-7454) in West Hartford.

☞ **Gathering Place** (860-278-4090), 100 Allyn Street. Open Monday through Friday for breakfast and lunch; brunch on Sunday. A converted storefront with a high ceiling, tall windows (plenty of light), and plain but inviting decor, this Catholic-sponsored haven welcomes people of all beliefs, for both meals and programs. A book section specializes in religious and spiritual titles (see *Bookstores*). Worship services and music, poetry, and storytelling in adjoining rooms; ask for a schedule. A full breakfast is available, as well as muffins, bagels, and scones; lunch brings excellent soups, sandwiches, pastas, salads, and desserts. Popular items include the chicken-cashew salad sandwich, chicken potpie with puff pastry crust, turkey chili, and veggie pocket. $7 and under.

& **Hartford Brewery, Ltd.** (860-246-BEER), 35 Pearl Street. Lunch and dinner served Tuesday through Saturday; closed Sunday and Monday. They make their own, right here: ales, stouts, porters; dark, light, and golden—35 recipes; 7 on tap every day. Food is hearty—roast chicken, pot roast, manly sandwiches. Tours of the brewery are available, by appointment. Sandwiches around $7; dinner entrées $9–16.

& **Hot Tomatoes** (860-249-5100), One Union Place. Open for lunch Monday through Friday 11:30–4; dinner nightly from 5. Full bar. A lively Italian restaurant decorated in a tomato motif, adjacent to the train station. The exposed kitchen puts out innovative Italian dishes: Pan-seared chicken breast topped with prosciutto and sauced with a sage vinegar cream; Gulf shrimp with hot sausage, olives, and spinach on a bed of linguine; and grilled chicken with sun-dried tomatoes and pesto with house-made ricotta gnocchi are standouts. The garlic bread, stuffed with four cheeses, is to die for. Patio dining in summer. Entrées $13–25.

& **Museum Cafe at the Atheneum** (860-728-5989), 600 Main Street. Serving lunch Tuesday through Saturday; brunch on Sunday. Overlooking a courtyard that may be described as bleak, the café provides art to look at and food to delight in. Casual but elegant, with small tables and a menu that ranges from familiar to exotic, it's the way you want a museum café to be. Selections vary with the seasons but run to salads, soups, creative pasta combinations, and omelets featuring such ingredients as wild rice, duck, and pea pods—always accompanied by good bread.

✐☞**Oasis Diner** (860-241-8200), 267 Farmington Avenue. Open daily for lunch and dinner; brunch 10–3 on Sunday. The original 1948 Art Deco dining car is actually three cars joined, and the feel of the old diner has been nicely preserved, along with the original wall clock. Full bar. There are two banks of clean, comfortable booths, and a bar area. The large number of regular customers confirms the manager's claims of good food and friendly service. The menu remains true to form: tasty, wholesome, no-nonsense platters, cherry Coke, meat loaf and pot roast, open-face turkey sandwich with mashed potatoes. Generous portions, everything fresh; good bread and biscuits. Desserts in the same vein: strawberry Jell-O, rice pudding, deep-dish apple pie. The popular Sunday brunch is an elaborate breakfast—French toast, quiche, huevos rancheros, steak and eggs—although you can have soup, salads, and sandwiches if you like. Brunch dishes $5–10; dinner platters up to $9.50; sandwiches under $6.

Pancho's (860-527-2188), 267 Farmington Avenue; downstairs at the Oasis Diner, serving dinner only, from 5. Full bar. Neon strips, colorful tile tabletops, and corrugated-metal wall accents create a cozy, friendly Mexican roadhouse, with mole, jalapeños, quesadillas, black beans, jicama, chorizo—and other authentic hot stuff from south of the border. Flan de naranja and tequila lime pie appear on the dessert menu. Hearty salads around $7; platters $9–15.

 ♿ **Peppercorn's Grill** (860-547-1714), 357 Main Street. Lunch Monday through Friday, dinner Monday through Saturday; closed Sunday. They call it New Italian, and this means stylish pasta combinations, with broccoli rabe pesto, say, and scallop-and-lobster ravioli. Risotto, pizza, veal, seafood, and lots more to choose from. Waiters are friendly and helpful, the surroundings are informal. Salads $4–10; appetizers $7–9; entrées up to $22.

 ♿ **Skywalk/Lord Jim's Pub** (860-522-7623), 242 Trumbull Street, upstairs on the second level. Skywalk serves three meals on Thursday, Friday, and Saturday; breakfast and lunch Monday through Wednesday. The big attraction here is the view from the skywalk of the busy street below—a new way of looking at Hartford. The pub offers some 35 imported beers and ales. There's an inclusive, mostly American menu: steaks, pasta, chicken, seafood, salads. Lunch $5–12; dinner entrées $8–17.

 ☞ **Timothy's** (860-728-9822), 243 Zion Street. Across the street from the Trinity College campus, in the area known as Back of the Rocks, this little wonder serves huge portions of comfort food three times daily except Sunday. Casual American cuisine means inventive soups (a specialty) and unusual treatments of standard entrées. The restaurant occupies two separate buildings, so your server will carry your meal from the kitchen and onto the sidewalk before arriving at your table. Many meals under $10.

COFFEEHOUSES

 ♿ **Pumpkin's** (860-278-1600), 54 Pratt Street. Open Monday through Saturday; closed Sunday. Coffee and pastry in the morning; hearty sandwiches for lunch; fancy coffee drinks and limited bar offerings in the evening. Retreat to the softly lit lounge to curl up on a sofa before the fireplace and sip a cappuccino or, if you're really brave, a quadruple espresso. Sandwiches around $6.

 ♿ **Zuzu's Coffee Bar** (860-244-8233), 103 Pratt Street. Open daily, serving a coffee of the day, various blends to order, espresso, and lattes. Pastries are available in the morning, and panini—grilled sandwiches on Italian bread—wraps, and other sandwich options later in the day, along with tempting desserts. Full bar in the evening. The tiny but colorful storefront conceals a larger operation than you think: tables in the front, comfortable seating beyond, and an art gallery on the lower level. Outdoor patio seating in season.

SNACKS

&☞**Heidi's** (860-247-8730), 221 Main Street. Open for breakfast and lunch, Monday through Friday 5:30 AM–2:30; Saturday 7–1; closed Sunday. Tasty eat-in or take-out deli foods, sandwiches, specials, and sweets. Breakfast under $5; sandwiches $2.25–6.

Mozzicato–De Pasquale's Bakery and Pastry Shop (860-296-0426), 329 Franklin Avenue. Don't even try to compute fat grams or caloric content: This is a place for pure hedonism. Traditional Italian pastries, each more sinfully tempting than the next, fill gleaming glass cases in this tidy South End shop. Cannoli, biscotti, eclairs, marzipan, cookies, cakes, and imported Italian confections. They also make stuffed breads and pizza slices mounded with toppings.

ENTERTAINMENT

Before going out, pick up a free copy of the *Hartford Advocate*, available at stores and restaurants all over the city, for listings of concerts, exhibits, films, and events. **The Hartford Civic Center Coliseum** (860-727-8010), Trumbull and Asylum Streets, is the venue for sports contests (see *Spectator Sports*), popular and rock concerts, and trade shows of all sorts.

MUSIC

Bushnell Memorial Hall. See *Theaters.*

Concerts and recitals are held in many of the city's churches and in public buildings such as the **Old State House,** Main Street; **Connecticut Historical Society,** One Elizabeth Street; and the **Hartford Conservatory** (860-246-2588), 834 Asylum Avenue, for vocal and instrumental recitals and dance performances as well. Check local newspaper listings for more information.

Outdoor concerts are held during the summer in Bushnell Park, Elizabeth Park, and elsewhere around the city (see *Green Space*).

Charter Oak Cultural Center (860-249-1207), 21 Charter Oak Avenue. A variety of concerts and performances mounted year-round. Call for schedule. (See also *Historic Sites.*)

Meadows Music Theatre (860-548-7370), 61 Savitt Way. Hartford's newest venue, designed to allow both indoor (seats for 7,500 and outdoor (seating for 18,000) performances. Schedule includes pop, rock, blues, country, and classical artists as well as comedy and family shows. Food and drink concessions; a tree-lined plaza with patio tables and concessions.

Webster Theatre (860-525-5553), 31 Webster Street. Rock, blues, jazz, and more in a well-preserved 1937 art deco movie house. Call for schedule.

THEATERS

Aetna Theatre (860-278-2670), 600 Main Street. This attractive little theater on the lower level of the Wadsworth Atheneum (see *Museums*) presents a variety of live entertainment and films, including innovative concerts and programs designed to illuminate current exhibits; family activities that combine theater and artworks for parents and children together; film festivals; and live drama by local theater companies.

Austin Arts Center at Trinity College (860-297-2199), 300 Summit Street. September through May, drama, music, lecture events. Trinity also presents a regular series of popular and classic films. Call for schedule.

Bushnell Memorial Hall (860-987-6084), 166 Capitol Avenue. The city's major center for both local and touring performance artists and companies; events virtually every night. Performance home of the Hartford Ballet, Connecticut Opera, and Hartford Symphony. The building, with its distinctive Art Deco auditorium, is a national historic landmark. Free tours of the hall are offered September through June, Wednesday and Thursday 11–3. Call for a schedule of events.

Hartford Stage Company (860-527-5151), 50 Church Street. Downtown Hartford's prestigious, Tony Award–winning theater, at home in a Venturi & Rauch–designed redbrick block of a building, slashed with bold zigzags of darker brick. The three-quarter-thrust stage in a 489-seat auditorium provides flexibility for a wide range of offerings: Shakespeare, Molière, and other classics, along with new plays and frank experiments. The season is late September through June, with performances Tuesday through Sunday nights and two matinees a week. Call for schedule.

Real Artways (860-232-1006), 56 Arbor Street. Open year-round, with gallery hours Monday through Friday 10–5, Saturday noon–5. Performances scheduled evenings; call for information. Devoted to new and experimental art and art forms; exhibits, concerts, performances, and video presentations. A café and 125-seat cinema are on the premises.

Theaterworks (860-527-7838), Bronson & Hutensky Theater, 233 Pearl Street. New and contemporary works presented by a local professional company at this off-Broadway-style venue. Several productions a year. Call for information.

NIGHTLIFE

Arch Street Tavern (860-246-7610), 85 Arch Street. Friday and Saturday nights feature rock. Cover charge varies; neat attire required.

Black-Eyed Sally's BBQ & Blues (860-278-7427), 350 Asylum Street. When nationally known blues legends come to Hartford, this is where they play. Also a good restaurant, with New Orleans and Cajun specialties.

Bourbon Street North (860-525-1014), 70 Union Place (near the train station). Live music Friday and Saturday nights.

Brick Yard Cafe (860-621-2112), 113 Allyn Street (downtown location). Thursday-, Friday-, Saturday-night schedules; live bands.

Cafe 880 Jazz Club (860-956-0880), 880 Maple Avenue. Hartford's oldest jazz club, and a neighborhood icon in the city's south end for nearly two decades. Live music almost every night—mostly jazz, sometimes blues. Cover varies.

City Steam Brewery (860-525-1600), 942 Main Street. A many-level restaurant and gathering spot, in a landmark Romanesque brownstone. Blues, jazz, zydeco, and live comedy acts on weekends. Cover varies.

Hartford Brewery Ltd. (860-246-2337), 35 Pearl Street, next to the Gold Building. Open until 1 AM weeknights, 2 AM Friday and Saturday; closed Sunday. Just off Main Street, in the heart of downtown, a chummy place featuring beer brewed on the premises and eclectic pub offerings. (See also *Eating Out.*)

Municipal Cafeteria, aka "the Muni" (860-527-5044), 485 Main Street. Wednesday through Saturday nights. Informal, cafeteria-style club with wooden booths and lively sessions: blues, jazz, bluegrass, and more. Cover charge varies; casual dress.

Russian Lady Cafe (860-525-3003), 191 Ann Street. Strictly a nightclub operation; live music Thursday, Friday, and Saturday nights. This historic building across from the Civic Center has a European feel—dark wood, antiques, and mirrors. In good weather you can enjoy the view from the rooftop patio, enhanced by the ornate stone sculpture capping the facade. On the first floor is a bartender-DJ, downstairs a no-smoking area; reggae is on the roof.

Scarlett O'Hara's (860-728-8290), 59 Pratt Street (downtown location). Open nightly. DJ; live bands Thursday, Friday, and Saturday nights.

Velvet (860-278-6333), 50 Union Place (near the train station). DJ; live bands Thursday, Friday, and Saturday nights.

SELECTIVE SHOPPING

ART GALLERIES
Artworks Gallery (860-247-3522), 233 Pearl Street. Exhibitions, lectures, workshops, and performances throughout the year.

100 Pearl Gallery (860-233-1932), 100 Pearl Street. Changing exhibits focusing on the work of artists from the greater Hartford area and throughout Connecticut.

Small Walls Gallery (860-728-0861), 1841 Broad Street. Open September through July. Group and solo shows featuring the work of contemporary Connecticut artists.

BOOKSTORES
Gallows Hill Book Store (860-297-5231), 300 Summit Street, on the Trinity College campus (use Broad Street entrance). A former maintenance building has been transformed with carpets, woodwork, and taste into a

book lover's paradise. An exhibit is devoted to works by Trinity faculty, and the general level of offerings befits a college campus. There's a good children's section and good travel coverage; coffee and cookies are available, as well as comfortable chairs to sit in.

Gathering Place (860-278-4090), 100 Allyn Street. Bookstore and café. Spiritual, religious books, tapes.

Hartford Seminary Bookstore (860-509-9500), 77 Sherman Street. In the pristine and unusual white building that houses the seminary, the bookstore serves those interested in religion, theology, and related fields.

Reader's Feast (860-232-3710), 529 Farmington Avenue. Bookstore and café. Book sections emphasize feminist, gay, and lesbian literature.

SPECIAL SHOPS

The **Civic Center Shops,** in the Civic Center, Asylum and Trumbull Streets, occupy an attractive space, not overwhelmingly large, with commendable variety, including restaurants and a food court. There are several good antiques shops, a comprehensive audio store—from equipment to tapes and CDs—a bookstore, an import shop devoted to Russian crafts, the mandatory health-food emporium, and a mini-museum of sports—just for a sampling.

Main Street Market in the heart of downtown, at Main and Asylum Streets. Outdoor space for vendors of fresh-from-the-farm produce, flowers, and a variety of wares, from Ecuadoran sweaters to framed posters.

The Unique Antique (860-522-9094), Civic Center. Small as antiques shops go, but worth a trip. An impressive selection of antique and estate jewelry, as well as glassware and porcelain collectibles.

SPECIAL EVENTS

February: **Hartford Flower Show** (860-529-2123), at the Connecticut Expo Center, Weston Street. Landscape displays, floral and garden tools, garden appliances and aids, advice, crafts, workshops.

March: **Connecticut Spring Antiques Show** (207-767-3967), at the State Armory, Broad Street. Nationally recognized event. **Connecticut Home Show** (860-563-4565), at the Hartford Civic Center. Hundreds of the newest products and services to enhance your domain.

June: **Taste of Hartford** (860-728-3089), the largest food fest in New England, with samplings from hundreds of city restaurants. Held on Constitution Plaza.

July: **Riverfest** (860-293-0103), Hartford's regional Fourth of July celebration. A traditional community gala in Hartford and East Hartford, embracing the Connecticut River, with events, performances, food, fun, clowns, and balloons on either side of, and even in, the water. Fireworks. **Mark Twain Days** (860-247-0998), a celebration of the author's legacy and Hartford's Victorian heritage. More than 100 events, including concerts, encampments, riverboat rides, and tours of the Twain house.

October: **Antiquarian and Landmarks Society Antiques Show** (860-247-8996), Connecticut State Armory, Broad Street and Capitol Avenue. Museum-quality pieces dating from the early 1600s.

November–December: **Festival of Light** (860-728-3089), on Constitution Plaza, celebrates the holiday season with thousands of tiny white lights on trees, buildings, and fountains, with silhouetted angels in midair.

December: **Christmas Crafts Expo,** two weekends at the Civic Center.

December 31: **Hartford First Night** (860-728-3089), a strictly nonalcoholic celebration to greet the new year with music, mime, drama, dancing, and children's activities, including a parade and early fireworks.

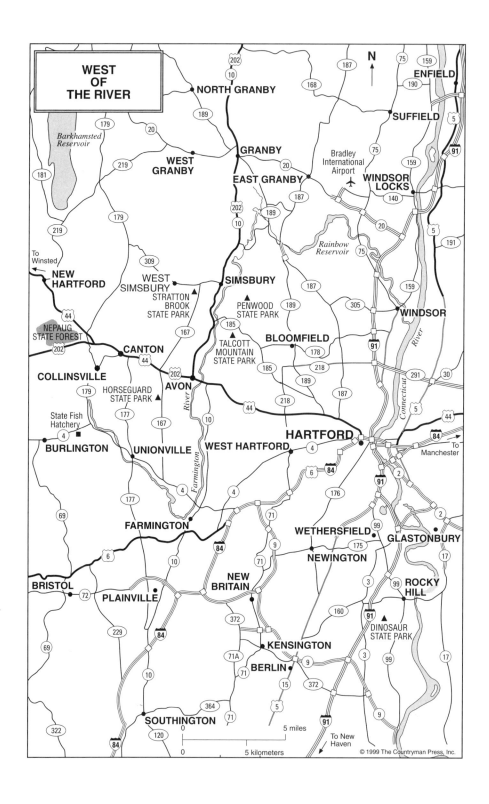

West of the River

Hartford's neighboring towns have been able to preserve much of their New England flavor thanks to the foresight—and what some call the stubbornness—of tradition-conscious citizens. West Hartford, immediately west of the city, invites you to visit Noah Webster's birthplace as well as the house where a group of Tories spent the Revolutionary War. For contrast, West Hartford Center is a mecca for all things hip, and its art galleries, cafés, and boutiques make for unparalleled people-watching. In Farmington, a scenic and historic town, the elegant turn-of-the-century Hill-Stead mansion is a virtual museum of fine arts. The town also remembers local sites where refugees from the slave ship *Amistad* found homes in the early 19th century. Farmington is perhaps best known as the site of Miss Porter's School, where young women are prepared for college, life, and, in many cases, celebrity. Major antiques, crafts, and horse shows are held on the Farmington Polo Grounds during warm weather.

Avon, Simsbury, and Canton successfully tread a careful path between commercialism and historic integrity. In Avon the cubicles of a former explosives plant have been turned into a series of artists' and craftsworkers' studios, while in Simsbury a complex of historic buildings traces the town's progress from the earliest contacts between colonists and Native Americans. In the Collinsville section of Canton sits the former site of the world's first ax factory, now home to a sprawling antiques center and artists' studios.

The historic district of Old Wethersfield boasts the house where George Washington not only slept but, along with Rochambeau, also planned the campaign that ended the Revolutionary War. A number of homes—one open as a museum—date from the Pilgrim century, and a pre-1691 warehouse on the cove testifies to the town's importance once as a shipping port. In the town center stands the handsome redbrick church funded by the sale of locally grown red onions. In his diary, John Adams describes the view from its steeple as "the most grand and beautiful prospect in the world." Wethersfield was once dubbed Oniontown because of the pungent scent of the town's famous red bulbs that pervaded the air. A vestige of Wethersfield's agricultural past is Comstock, Ferre & Company, the oldest continually operating seed company in the United States, and a Main Street landmark since 1820.

New Britain belongs to another age, the industrial 19th century. It's known as the Hardware City, where the Stanley Works, P. and F. Corbin, North and Judd, and the New Britain Machine Company distributed hardware, builders' tools, locks, ball bearings, and much more to the whole world. With the factories less of a presence in town these days, New Britain points to other attractions: the Central Connecticut State University campus—home to one of the country's largest public telescopes—a lively performing arts community, and a first-rate museum of American art.

Winding through the northern section, the Farmington River stakes out a generous loop of territory west and north of Hartford, where the traprock ridge lends variety to the landscape. The river itself offers white water during the spring thaw, as well as a cool venue for kayaking, tubing, and canoeing in midsummer. Anglers, birders, and those seeking solitude will enjoy a tranquil stretch of the river from Farmington to Simsbury that parallels the old Farmington Canal, which linked New Haven with Northampton, Massachusetts, from about 1828 to 1848. Cave-in problems plagued the operation, but the coming of the railroads sealed its doom.

The natural beauty of the countryside and its proximity to Hartford have attracted many who work in the city to establish their homes and develop community life in towns that not long ago were remote rural villages. As a result, elegant inns, antiques shops, and restaurants—many among the bright stars on the state's culinary scene—abound on and around busy US 44, which cuts through the heart of the valley. Others are tucked away on scenic country roads and other pleasantly out-of-the way places.

Tobacco Valley is the local name for the land alongside the Connecticut River, where shade tobacco was once the major cash crop. Native Americans were cultivating it when the first English settlers arrived, and by 1640 the skill had been passed on to the newcomers. Later it was discovered that the climate in the Connecticut River Valley was similar to that of Sumatra, where broadleaf tobacco—used for cigar wrappers—came from. Proper humidity, however, was lacking, and when this problem was remedied by covering the crops with white fabric tents over the fields, the valley blossomed with a new industry. Much less tobacco is raised nowadays, but in summer you'll still see fields around Windsor covered with billowy white cloth—a puzzling sight to strangers. As recently as 20 years ago, area youngsters got their first jobs "working on tobacco" during school vacations. The leaves had to be picked, inspected, sewn into bundles, and carried into the huge barns for drying. The barns, two of which, in Bloomfield and Windsor, now house museums, were designed to help control humidity—in this instance, to reduce it. Huge doors opened above and below, and every other plank along the sidewalls was loose and could be propped open to allow air to circulate around the tobacco to cure it properly. Today, the land has been claimed for other uses, with only an occasional farm remaining.

Suffield, Windsor, and the Granbys retain their picturesque flavor with charming B&Bs, historic homes, museums, and parks. Windsor was founded in 1633, which makes it arguably the oldest town in the state. In 1777, the nation's first Christmas tree was trimmed and illuminated in Windsor Locks, a town better known today for Bradley International Airport, which serves Hartford and virtually all the rest of Connecticut. On the grounds of the airport, the New England Air Museum has an impressive array of aircraft—historic to ultramodern—to see, and a cockpit simulator to climb into.

Entries in this section are arranged in alphabetical order.

AREA CODE
860

GUIDANCE
Central Connecticut Tourism District (860-225-3901), One Grove Street, Suite 310, New Britain 06053, can supply information on attractions and events in New Britain, Berlin, Southington, Plainville, and Cheshire. Ask for the brochure for a self-guided walking tour of New Britain's downtown area.

Connecticut's North Central Tourism Bureau (860-763-2578; 1-800-248-8283), 111 Hazard Avenue, Enfield 06082 (Web site: www.cnctb.org). The source for information on Bloomfield, Windsor, Suffield, the Granbys, and Windsor Locks.

Farmington Valley Visitor Association (1-800-4-WELCOME), 15 Farm Springs Road, Farmington 06032. This local organization can supply information on special seasonal promotions as well as visitor attractions and lodgings in Avon, Canton, Simsbury, Farmington, and West Hartford.

The Greater Hartford Tourism District (860-244-8181; 1-800-793-4480), 234 Murphy Road, Hartford 06114 (Web site: www.travelfile.com/get/ghtd), can provide brochures, events listings, maps, and answers to questions about travel and lodging in the area.

Travels with a Connecticut Yankee (800-243-1630), 533 Cottage Grove Road, Bloomfield 06002. Year-round narrated tours via motorcoach. Anecdotes, history, and horticultural information on the region.

Heritage Trails Tours (860-677-8867), PO Box 138, Farmington 06034. If you enjoy guided tours with historical notes, this operator offers a variety of trips ranging in length from 2 hours to all day, some with meals and all including narratives on local background. Hartford, West Hartford, and towns of the Farmington Valley are included in the offerings. Sight-seeing is enhanced by specially designed vans. Theme trips are featured from time to time, such as Graveyard Tours in October.

Wethersfield Historical Society (860-529-7656), 200 Main Street, Wethersfield 06109, at the Keeney Memorial, has brochures with maps; information on museums, historical sites, and shopping in town; and a guide to the town's ancient burying ground.

GETTING THERE

By car: I-84 and I-91 intersect in Hartford, providing access from all directions. CT 9 is a divided, limited-access route connecting I-84 in Farmington with I-91 in Hartford, and continuing south to Old Saybrook. US 44 and CT 4 are good routes heading west from Hartford.

By air: **Bradley International Airport** (860-292-2000) serves the entire state.

By train: **AMTRAK** (1-800-USA-RAIL) stops at Windsor, Windsor Locks, and Berlin.

GETTING AROUND

From **Bradley International,** you'll find ground transportation by taxi and limousine to other parts of the state. For sight-seeing or traveling in the state, a car is necessary.

MEDICAL EMERGENCY

The statewide emergency number is **911.**

Bradley Memorial Hospital and Health Center (860-276-5000), 81 Meriden Avenue, Southington.

John Dempsey Hospital/University of Connecticut Health Center (860-679-2000), 263 Farmington Avenue, Farmington. The emergency number is 860-679-2588.

New Britain General Hospital (860-224-5011), 100 Grand Street, New Britain.

Total Medical Care Family Walk-in Center (860-688-8888), 340 Broad Street, Windsor.

Windsor Locks Walk-in Medical Care Center (860-627-0161), 556 Elm Street, Windsor Locks.

TO SEE

HISTORIC HOMES AND SITES

American School for the Deaf (860-570-2307), 139 North Main Street, West Hartford. Guided tours once a month, October through April; call for schedule. Free admission. The first school of its kind in the nation (established 1817) and the birthplace of American Sign Language. Visitors can tour the 57-acre campus, see a classroom, view historical artifacts, and meet professionals in the field.

Amistad **Tour** (call 860-678-1645 for schedules and location). Farmington's role in African-American history is explored in a tour conducted by the Farmington Historical Society, available by special arrangement. The connection has to do with the takeover of the slave ship *Amistad* by the slaves on board. After a series of trials, 38 mem-

The Buttolph-Williams House in Wethersfield was built in 1700.

bers of the Mende tribe were declared free men and came to stay in Farmington while funds were raised to return them to their homes in Sierra Leone. The quarters where they lived, their school, and their farmlands are now privately held but available to interested visitors. Also included on the tour are authenticated stops on the Underground Railroad, the network of safe houses run by pre–Civil War abolitionists to assist runaway slaves on their way north to freedom.

Barnes Museum (860-628-5426), 85 North Main Street (CT 10), Southington. Open Monday through Wednesday, Friday 9–3; Thursday 2–8; weekends by appointment. Free. The building is the 1836 Amon Bradley house, home of a distinguished local family for more than a century. Many of the original furnishings remain, with collections of Orientalia, glassware, and furniture. Down the street at 239 Main Street is the **Southington Historical Center,** where local industry forms the major theme of the exhibits—including the facade of the nation's first bolt factory.

Buttolph-Williams House (860-529-0460; 860-247-8996), 249 Broad Street, Wethersfield. Open May through October, Wednesday through Monday 10–4. Call for admission charge. Built in 1700, this is one of the truly early homes; it has dark clapboards and small windows, and inside is an enormous fireplace and period furnishings. Exposed beams upstairs show the solid framing methods of the first settlers. If the houses didn't catch fire, they could last virtually forever. A property of the Antiquarian and Landmarks Society, it is a compelling introduction to life in early Connecticut.

First Church of Christ, Congregational (860-529-1575), 250 Main Street, Wethersfield. Connecticut's only remaining brick Colonial meetinghouse, completed in 1764. Funded by the sale of red onions—Wethersfield's principal crop and main claim to odorous fame in early times—it's a noble example of church architecture. The cupola is an exact replica of that on Boston's fabled Old North Church. George Washington and John Adams appear on the roster of worshipers here.

First Company Governor's Horse Guard (860-673-3525), Military Reservation, 232 West Avon Road (CT 4 and 44), Avon. Drills every Thursday at 7:30 PM. Special weekend events; call for schedule. Free admission. Watch the nation's oldest cavalry unit in continuous service (since 1658) practice its precision maneuvers. Now serving primarily a ceremonial function, the unit has a noble history, from acting as an honor guard when President Washington visited town, to service in the War of 1812, the Spanish-American War, and the two World Wars.

Hatheway House (860-247-8996), 55 South Main Street (CT 75), Suffield. Open mid-May to mid-October, Wednesday, Saturday, and Sunday 1–4; July and August, Wednesday through Sunday 1–4. Adults $4, children $1. One of the prime properties of the Antiquarian and Landmarks Society, this commodious white-clapboard Colonial, with its added wings, provides a quick tour of 18th-century Connecticut. The midcentury parlor is sparsely furnished with elegantly simple tables and chairs, the wide-board floor is bare, and the curtains are plain white hangings. In the later section of the house, dated about 1790, there's a lavish look to the rooms. The French wallpaper—reproduced in all its elaborate splendor—the heavy red window hangings, damask-covered wing chairs, and intricately designed Oriental rugs stand in striking contrast to the 1760s section. On the grounds, enjoy a formal garden, 19th-century barns, and a carriage house.

Iwo Jima Memorial (860-666-5521), CT 9 at exit 29; off CT 175, Newington–New Britain town line. The famous flag-raising scene on Iwo Jima is reproduced in bronze and granite statuary, set in a simple park. On national holidays, special memorial events are held, attended by many local veterans of the Pacific Theater battle.

King House Museum (860-668-5256), 232 South Main Street (CT 75), Suffield. Open May through September, Wednesday and Saturday 1–4, and by appointment. Adults $1, children free. A 1764 center-chimney mansion noted for its long porch, the King House is an upscale Colonial: smooth, painted walls inside, drapes that hang to the floor, ornate mirrors, crewel-embroidered bed linens, a shell corner cupboard in the dining room. Of special note are the exhibit on the local cigar and tobacco industry, the collection of Bennington pottery, and an antique flask and bottle collection.

Lieutenant Walter Fyler House/Windsor Historical Society (860-688-3813), 96 Palisado Avenue, Windsor. Open April through November, Tuesday through Saturday 10–4; December through March, Monday through Friday by appointment. Adults $3; seniors $2; children with adult, free. The society headquarters are in the Lieutenant Walter Fyler House, built in 1640, seven years after Windsor's first settlers arrived. One of New England's oldest survivors, the Fyler House is an oxblood, clapboard-sided house with gables, a distinctive broken roofline, and fairly ornate pediments over the windows—clearly the home of an important citizen. There are nine antiques-furnished rooms, a small "fancy goods" shop, and a vest-pocket post office. You can also arrange a walking tour of the adjoining Palizado (palisaded against the Pequots) area and the settlers' burying ground. Museum exhibits change periodically; a library is available for historical and genealogical research.

Massacoh Plantation (860-658-2500), 800 Hopmeadow Street (CT 10), Simsbury. Open year-round, with guided tours daily 10–4; **Phelps House** office open all year, Monday through Friday 1–4; closed holidays. Adults $6; children $3; seniors $5. This village complex, maintained by the Simsbury Historical Society, covers some 300 years of local history: a replica of the 1683 meetinghouse; museum exhibits in the Phelps House that include rare Higley coppers, the first coins struck in the colonies; a tin peddler's cart that represents the heyday of the Yankee trader; and a one-room schoolhouse and Victorian carriage house that bring you through the 19th century.

Newington Historical Society (860-666-7118), Newington, has two properties that offer special insights into early times, when Newington was an outpost of nearby Wethersfield. **The Enoch Kelsey House,** 1701 Main Street, was saved from demolition when valuable trompe l'oeil floral wall paintings were discovered and identified as authentic period decorations. Fireplaces, a beehive oven, and paneling are all original to this 1799 home built for a tinsmith. The house is open May through October, weekends 1–4. Admission $2. The **Kellogg-Eddy Museum,** 679 Willard Avenue, is an 1808 three-story home, with furnishings from local collectors, a changing display of quilts, noteworthy mantelpieces, and a ceiling frieze. Open March through December, weekends 1–4; January and February, Sunday only, 1–4. Donation requested.

Noah Webster House (860-521-5362), 227 South Main Street, West Hartford. Open year-round, Thursday through Tuesday 1–4, closed Wednesday; July and August, Monday through Friday 10–4, weekends 1–4. Adults $5; children $1; seniors $4. The restored colonial farmhouse where Noah was born in 1758 is a saltbox with an added-on lean-to that sports proper period furnishings and an especially good hearth restoration. His *Blue-Backed Speller,* published in 1783, sold 24 million copies in his lifetime. His groundbreaking *American Dictionary* was published in 1828, when he was 70. The museum, with guides in colonial garb, mounts changing exhibits related to local history and excellent programs—notably Noah's birthday party each September, featuring a hard-fought, herculean spell-down for local students.

Noden-Reed Farm Museum (860-627-9212), 58 West Street, Windsor Locks. Open May through October and early December, Sunday and Wednesday 1–5, and by appointment. Free admission. The period artifacts housed in the 1840 early-Victorian home and the 1826 brick barn are of considerable interest, but the real attraction here is the story. According to legend, the first Christmas tree in Connecticut—who knows, perhaps in the country—was set up at the Noden-Reed house by a Hessian soldier captured during the Revolutionary War. He remembered, it's said, the customs of his homeland and introduced what became a lasting practice in the new country.

Old New-Gate Prison and Copper Mine (860-653-3563; 860-566-3005), Newgate Road, East Granby. Open mid-May through October, Wednesday through Sunday 10–4:30. Adults $3; children and seniors $1.50; children under 6 free. The first chartered copper mine in North America (1707) did not produce much copper. Perhaps the Pilgrim fathers were just trying, in Yankee style, to make use of the tunnels when they converted it into the colonial government's first prison in 1773. During the Revolutionary War, Tories were housed here. Walking through the underground caves, hearing the water dripping on the stones, imagining the prospect of spending time there in the damp darkness, is enough to make you think twice about wanting to live in the Pilgrim century. Guides have fascinating tales of escapes and of prison life in colonial times.

Oliver Ellsworth Homestead (860-688-8717), 778 Palisado Avenue (CT 159), Windsor. Open mid-April through mid-October, Tuesday, Wednesday, and Saturday noon–4:30. Admission $2; children under 12 free. This Georgian manse was the home of one of the state's most distinguished public figures: Oliver Ellsworth was a delegate to the Constitutional Convention, a chief justice of the Supreme Court, Connecticut's first senator, and minister plenipotentiary to France. George Washington and John Adams both visited him here. Inside are many of Ellsworth's personal belongings and a piece of a Gobelin tapestry presented to him by Napoleon Bonaparte.

Plainville Historic Center (860-747-6577; 860-747-0081) 29 Pierce Street, Plainville. Open May through December, Wednesday and Saturday noon–3:30. Donation $1. Built in 1890 as the Town Hall, the structure that houses the center has both permanent and changing exhibits devoted to Plainville history. Settled as part of Farmington, the town enjoyed a short-lived boom in the 1820s when the Farmington Canal opened, and a century later was a manufacturing center. The historic center collection illuminates the story through artifacts and antiques—including quilts, toys, tools, clocks, paintings, and clothing. There is a museum shop.

Sarah Whitman Hooker Homestead (860-523-5887), 1237 New Britain Avenue, West Hartford. Open year-round, Monday and Wednesday 1:30–3:30; closed holidays. Adults $3; children $2. This house started

Visitors to the Webb-Deane-Stevens Museum can tour three different 18th-century homes.

out simply as one room with a chamber above. Like many colonial homes, it underwent a series of changes, serving as an inn for a time, and ended as a large and sturdy representative of the period 1720–1807. The meticulous restoration traces changes in the size and appearance of the house, with ingenious "windows" enabling the visitor to see construction details ordinarily out of sight. Look for reproductions of original wallpapers and fabrics, a good collection of Staffordshire, and a tale of Tories quartered here while under house arrest during the Revolutionary War.

Stanley-Whitman House (860-677-9222), 37 High Street, Farmington. Open May through October, Wednesday through Sunday noon–4; November through April, Sunday noon–4. Adults $5; children $2; seniors $4. Built in 1720, the house retains some of the very early medieval characteristics of Colonial architecture: for example, the narrow casement windows with small diamond panes, the 18-inch overhang in front (embellished with four pendant drops), the lean-to in back creating the classic saltbox. A restoration project created hinged panels to allow examination of construction details. There's period furniture and a museum exhibit outlining the results of an archaeological investigation. Special programs for adults and children on spinning, weaving, open-hearth cooking, and candlemaking are held periodically; call for schedule.

Trinity Episcopal Church, 300 Main Street, Wethersfield, may seem a stranger among all the colonial-era saltboxes and hewn overhangs; it came into town with the Victorian age in 1871–1874. Designed by

Edward Tuckerman Potter, architect of Mark Twain's Hartford mansion, it's of Portland (Connecticut) brownstone and enhanced by three Tiffany windows.

Webb-Deane-Stevens Museum (860-529-0612), 211 Main Street, Wethersfield. The museum consists of three 18th-century houses, side by side, each telling a different story. Properties of the National Society of Colonial Dames in Connecticut, they are open May through October, Wednesday through Monday 10–4; November through April, Saturday and Sunday 10–4. Well-briefed guides conduct tours of the three properties: adults $8; children and students $4; seniors $7. **Joseph Webb House.** Built in 1751 and expanded as his business prospered, Joseph Webb's home is an example of the mid-18th-century style known as Connecticut River Valley. The wide central hall, well-proportioned rooms, and interior paneling are typical. This is where George Washington, in 1781, met with Rochambeau and others of his staff to plan the campaign that led to the Battle of Yorktown—a recent restoration uncovered murals in the house depicting the conflict. Another chapter concerns Mrs. Webb, who rose to the challenge of a visit from the commander of the Continental Armies by selecting, buying, and hanging fancy new French flocked wallpaper in an upstairs bedroom for his gratification—all on very short notice. The paper is still on the walls for our gratification. **Silas Deane House.** Dating from 1766, this house was home, at least for a time, to a lawyer who quickly moved into circles of power in the emerging United States. He served as a member of the First Continental Congress and in 1776 went to Paris to negotiate with the French government for help for the Revolutionary forces. **Isaac Stevens House.** In 1788 this house belonged to a leatherworker and saddler who built it for his bride, Sarah. Of interest to gardeners is a period herb garden behind the house.

Wethersfield Historical Society (860-529-7656) manages the following: **The Old Academy** (860-529-7656), 150 Main Street, Wethersfield. Open Tuesday through Friday 10–4, Saturday 1–4, and by appointment. You can pick up information on museums and historic sites either here or at the Keeney Memorial down the street. The academy houses research archives and a library of local and state history, specializing in genealogy and architecture. **Keeney Memorial** (860-529-7161), 200 Main Street, Wethersfield. Open Tuesday through Saturday 10–4, Sunday 1–4. Admission to the galleries: adults $2; children under 16 free. An 1893 structure, clearly designed to be a school, served first as a high school and later as a location for elementary classes. It's now a museum and lecture-recital hall, with a permanent exhibit of local history and changing displays, generally of arts and crafts by local artists, as well as special events throughout the year. Visitor information on area events and attractions is available. **Hurlbut-Dunham House** (860-529-7656), 212 Main Street. Open mid-May through October, Thursday through Saturday 10–4, Sunday 1–4; November and December, weekends 1–4.

Call for admission prices. A resplendent brick Georgian mansion with Palladian window, marble fireplaces, painted ceiling, chandeliers, furnishings, and artwork reflecting three centuries of its inhabitants. The **Cove Warehouse,** at the end of Main Street, on the Cove, Wethersfield. Call 860-529-7656 for days and times to visit. Built around 1690, the warehouse was used to store goods brought upriver by sea-going merchant vessels. What's now the cove was just a bend in the river until the flood of 1692, which swept away the other warehouses, leaving this one survivor.

Windsor Historical Society (860-688-3813), 96 Palisado Avenue, Windsor. April through October, Tuesday through Saturday 10–4; November through March, Monday through Friday 10–4. Adults $3; children free; seniors $2. Two homes are owned and managed by the society: the **Lieutenant Walter Fyler House** (circa 1640), one of the oldest frame houses remaining in the state, and the **Dr. Hezekiah Chaffee House** (circa 1765), a Georgian, brick-sided, three-story house. Both are enhanced with period furnishings. Changing exhibits are devoted to local history; there is a library for genealogical and historical research, as well as a gift shop.

MUSEUMS

American Radio Relay League (860-594-0200), 225 Main Street, Newington. Open Monday through Friday 8–5. Mecca for some 160,000 ham radio operators throughout the country. Members may tour the headquarters at any time; others can call and make reservations. A state-of-the-art ham station is a tour highlight.

Canton Historical Museum (860-693-2793), 11 Front Street, Collinsville. Open April 1 through November 30, Wednesday through Sunday 1–4, Thursday until 8; December through March, Saturday and Sunday 1–4. Adults $3; children and seniors $2. On the site of the world's first ax factory, established in 1826 (until then, blacksmiths made them to order). John Brown, the fiery abolitionist, bought the pikes he used at Harpers Ferry here. Museum exhibits cover various aspects of Victorian life, from fire-fighting equipment, to locally produced machetes, to the gown milady wore to tea and the teapot she poured from.

✐ **Copernican Space Science Center Planetarium and Observatory** (860-832-3399; 860-832-2950), 1615 Stanley Street, campus of Central Connecticut State University, New Britain. Adults $3.50; children and seniors $2.50; children under 5 free. Programs scheduled year-round. Shows Friday and Saturday 8:30 PM; children's shows Friday 7 PM, Saturday 1:30. One of the country's largest public telescopes, with imaginative programs for all age groups.

Day-Lewis Museum (860-678-1645), 158 Main Street, Farmington. Hours limited; call ahead for schedule and admission prices. At the site of an archaeological dig in the 1970s that turned up evidence of more than 10,000 years of human habitation, this Yale-owned archaeology museum specializes in Native American artifacts. The house itself, with

KIMBERLY GRANT

The Hill-Stead Museum's Beatrix Farrand–designed Sunken Garden is the site of an acclaimed summertime poetry festival.

its gambrel roof and clapboard siding, is an example of the post-and-beam construction used in colonial times.

Farm Implement Museum (860-242-1130), 434 Tunxis Avenue Extension, Bloomfield. Open April through October, Tuesday through Saturday 9–5. Call for details. One man's lifelong collection of handmade tools used in field, house, barn, and garage. Some date as far back as 1790. The museum building itself is of historic interest: It's one of the tobacco barns in which the leaves were dried. There's a small petting zoo and a picnic area on the grounds.

Hill-Stead Museum (860-677-9064), 35 Mountain Road, Farmington. Open year-round, Tuesday through Sunday 10–5. Adults $6; children 6–12, $3; seniors and students $5. The 1901 Colonial Revival mansion, home of industrialist Alfred A. Pope, was designed by his daughter, Theodate Pope. As a student at Miss Porter's School, she fell in love with Farmington and prevailed upon her parents to move here from Cleveland. One of the country's first female architects, she designed and built her family's elegant Farmington home with noted architect Stanford White. Subsequently, she designed two of Connecticut's private schools and other private homes. In 1915 she was a passenger on the *Lusitania* bound for England when the torpedo struck. As the ship sank, she refused to leave without her friends and wound up in the water clinging to an oar. Naturally, she was rescued; Theodate survived several brushes with death. William and Henry James were among the distinguished visitors she entertained at her home. The interior remains as it was when lived in, with exceptional European and American fur-

nishings and an outstanding collection of Impressionist paintings—
Monet, Manet, Degas, Cassatt, Whistler—as well as exquisite 16th- and
17th-century Italian majolica, Japanese prints, and Chinese ceramics.
The grounds have walking paths through wooded areas and a Beatrix
Farrand–designed sunken garden, the site of an acclaimed summer-
time poetry festival (see *Special Events*).

Luddy/Taylor Connecticut Valley Tobacco Museum (860-285-1888),
135 Lang Road, in Northwest Park, Windsor. Open March to mid-
December, Tuesday, Wednesday, Thursday, Saturday noon–4. A barn
where tobacco was cured now houses exhibits explaining how the crop
was cultivated, harvested, and subsequently prepared for use in cigars. A second, modern building supplies more background photos
and documents. Tobacco was once the chief agricultural product of
the Connecticut River Valley from upper Connecticut north into Massachusetts. Visitors may watch a 28-minute film on tobacco growing.

Museum of American Political Life (860-768-4090), University of
Hartford, 200 Bloomfield Avenue, West Hartford. Open year-round,
Tuesday through Friday 11–4; Saturday and Sunday noon–4; closed
major holidays. Donation. A virtual history course. Artifacts—buttons,
posters, badges, and more—from the campaigns of US presidents
from George Washington on. Also memorabilia from such movements
as women's rights and temperance-Prohibition. Exhibits illuminate
various cogs in the politcal machine, such as the history of presiden-
tial elections and the role of the press in politics. Visitors may watch a
brief film on the history of political campaigns.

New Britain Industrial Museum (860-832-8654), 185 Main Street, New
Britain. Open year-round, Monday to Friday 2–5; Wednesday noon–5.
Free admission. Still known as the Hardware City, New Britain commemorates its industrial giants with changing exhibits devoted to Stanley
Works, Fafnir Bearing, American Hardware, and other manufacturers
that brought prosperity and jobs to the city in its heyday. Local residents
have contributed items their fathers and grandfathers helped make, from
saddle hardware to Art Deco kitchenware. There are also glimpses of the
future, focusing on electronics and the new technologies.

New Britain Museum of American Art (860-229-0257), 56 Lexington
Street, New Britain. Open year-round, Tuesday through Friday 1–5;
Saturday 10–5; Sunday noon–5; closed Monday and holidays. Adults
$3; seniors and students $2; children under 12 free. Housed in a 19th-
century mansion, an impressive collection of American artworks, (the
oldest such collection in the country), from Thomas Hart Benton murals to Borglum bronzes to Sol LeWitt line drawings. Copley, Stuart,
Whistler, Sargent, Wyeth, Cole, and Church are represented. Gift shop.
Special events; ask for schedule.

✐ **New Britain Youth Museum** (860-225-3020), 30 High Street, New Britain.
Open year-round, Tuesday through Friday 1–5; Saturday 10–4; extended

summer hours. Donation requested. A small but winning spot for children. Exhibits of Americana and of other cultures, circus miniatures, dolls, and many hands-on opportunities.

✐ **New England Air Museum** (860-623-3305), CT 75 at Bradley International Airport, Windsor Locks. Open year-round, daily 10–5; closed Thanksgiving and Christmas. Adults $6.50; children $3.50; seniors $6. When you walk into the hangar (actually there are two buildings of displays), you walk into aviation history: trainers, gliders, fighters, bombers, helicopters—more than 70 US aircraft dating from 1909 to the present. For a multimedia experience, climb into the jet fighter cockpit simulator. Aviation films are shown—ask about special events. Gift shop.

✐ **Science Center of Connecticut** (860-231-2830), 950 Trout Brook Drive, West Hartford. Open year-round, Tuesday through Saturday 10–5; Thursday 10–8; Sunday noon–5. Closed major holidays. Adults $6; children and seniors $5; children under 3 free. Additional charge for planetarium and laser shows. On the grounds is the popular, life-size, walk-in sperm whale replica. Inside, for the younger set, the Discovery Room is devoted to hands-on exhibits. Besides a live animal center, there are displays on the wonders of physics, electricity, electronics, and technology. Daily star shows in the planetarium and laser light demonstrations.

TO DO

AIRPLANE RIDES
Interstate Aviation (860-747-5519; 1-800-573-5519), 62 Johnson Avenue, Plainville. Sight-seeing flight over central Connecticut, year-round.

BALLOONING
&. **Airvertising & Airventures** (860-651-4441; outside Connecticut: 1-800-535-2473), PO Box 365, West Simsbury 06092. Balloons that are handicapped-accessible, others that hold up to 20 people. Year-round, weather permitting.

Berkshire Balloons (203-250-8441), PO Box 706, Southington 06489. Reserve in advance. Available daily for 1-hour rides. Specializing in foliage tours.

KAT Balloons Inc. (860-678-7921), 40 Meadow Lane, Farmington. Champagne charter flights over the Farmington Valley. Call for brochure.

Livingston Balloon Co. (860-651-1110), 70 West Street, Simsbury. Champagne flights over the Farmington River Valley.

Sky Endeavors Inc. (860-242-0228), 4 Brown Street, Bloomfield. Champagne flights over the Farmington Valley. Reservations required.

Windriders Balloon (860-677-0647), 314 South Road, Farmington.

BOAT EXCURSIONS
Glastonbury–Rocky Hill Ferry (860-563-9758), CT 160, either town. The nation's oldest ferry in continuous operation, in business since 1655. Drive your car onto the barge and get out to watch the tugboat nudge you across the Connecticut River. Lovely views, short trip.

Tubers stay cool in the Farmington River.

CANOEING/KAYAKING/WHITE-WATER RAFTING

Collinsville Canoe & Kayak (860-693-6977), 41 Bridge Street (CT 179), Collinsville. Canoe and kayak rentals for flat-water sections of the Farmington River, as well as for area ponds and lakes. Guided tours and instructional programs available; call for schedule.

Farmington River Tubing (860-693-6465), Satan's Kingdom State Recreation Area, US 44, Canton–New Hartford town line. Specially designed river tubes are available for the 2.5-mile ride downstream through three sets of rapids. The ride back is provided. Rentals daily Memorial Day through mid-September, 10–5.

&. **Huck Finn Adventures** (860-693-0385), Collinsville section of Canton. Canoe rentals for groups and families on a scenic, wooded, flat-water section of the Farmington River; guides provided. Services available for wheelchair-bound passengers.

Main Stream Canoe Corporation (860-693-6791), New Hartford. Offering canoe and kayak excursions—white-water, flat-water, moonlight trips—as well as instruction, rentals, and sales.

FISHING

Connecticut River shad fishing is permitted, in season, in Suffield along the Windsor Locks Canal below the Enfield dam (there's no fishing in the canal, however). This is a controlled area, and posters mark the limits within which fishing is allowed.

The **Farmington River** winds through the area, replete with brown, brook, and rainbow trout, large- and smallmouth bass, pickerel, yellow perch, and others. For specifics, contact the **Farmington River Anglers Association** (PO Box 147, Riverton 06065).

Quiet Sports (860-693-2214), 100 Main Street, Collinsville, offers fly-fishing equipment, lessons, clinics, and guided trips.

Rainbow Reservoir, Windsor, is recommended for largemouth bass, and you can also expect sunfish, chain pickerel, and brown bullhead. Access is on foot through Northwest Park (see *Green Space*) or, if you have a boat, at the state boat launch off Merriman Road.

GOLF

Bel Compo Golf Club (860-678-1679), US 44, Avon. Par 72, 18 holes, 7,028 yards.

Buena Vista Golf Course (860-521-7359), 56 Buena Vista Road, West Hartford. Par 32, nine holes, 2,050 yards.

Millbrook Golf Course (860-688-2575), 147 Pigeon Hill Road, Windsor. Par 70, 18 holes, 6,050 yards.

Pattonbrook Country Club (860-793-6000), Pattonwood Drive, Southington. Par 60, 18 holes, 4,433 yards; dress code (no tank tops).

Pine Valley Golf Course (860-628-0879), Welch Road, Southington. Par 71, 18 holes, 6,325 yards.

Rockledge Country Club (860-521-3156), 289 South Main Street, West Hartford. Par 72, 18 holes, 6,436 yards.

Simsbury Farms Golf Club (860-658-6246), Old Farms Road, Simsbury. Par 72, 18 holes, 6,421 yards.

Stanley Golf Course (860-827-8144), 245 Hartford Road, New Britain. Par 36/36/35, nine/nine/nine holes, 3, 313/3, 140/3, 106 yards.

Suffield Airways Golf Course (860-668-4973), South Grand Street, Suffield. Par 71, 18 holes, 5,900 yards.

Tunxis Plantation Country Club (860-677-1367), 87 Town Farm Road, Farmington. Par 72/72/35, 18/18/9 holes, 6, 101/6, 241/2, 999 yards.

HAYRIDES AND SLEIGH RIDES

✎ **Brown's Harvest** (860-683-0266), CT 75, Windsor. In the fall, take a hayride out to the pumpkin patch to pick out your jack-o'-lantern.

✎ **Flamig Farm** (860-658-5070), 7 Shingle Mill Road, West Simsbury. Horse-drawn hay-, sleigh, pony, and carriage rides; petting zoo. Open year-round.

HIKING

See also *Green Space*.

Lamentation Mountain, off Spruce Brook Road, which abuts the Berlin Turnpike (US 5 and CT 15) in Berlin. The mountain is reached by the Mattabesett Trail. Part of the traprock ridge that runs down the center of the state, the 720-foot mountain is named for the plight of poor Mr. Chester, an early settler who, lamentably, was lost here for two days. The views from the mountain include the lopsided, so-called "hanging hills" of Meriden, to the west, and to the east the Connecticut River and its gorge at Middletown. The blue-blazed trail runs along Spruce Brook Road briefly, then turns south to take you up the rise through hardwoods and hemlocks. The slope is moderate, and the views from the top are far from lamentable. Another part of the trail intersects the loop around 761-

foot **Ragged Mountain** on the Berlin-Southington town line. The loop is accessible from either West Lane or Reservoir Road, both of which run west from CT 71A. See the **Connecticut Forest and Park Association**'s *Connecticut Walk Book* for guidance (860-346-TREE).

McLean Game Refuge (860-653-7869), Salmon Brook Road (CT 10 and US 202), Granby. This spot has been set aside to preserve the trees and flowers and to safeguard the wildlife that lives here or migrates through. Hiking, birding, cross-country skiing, and general nature lore are what the McLean is for. You have the Barndoor Hills to climb, excellent views, a picnic grove and recreation field, and some 3,400 acres in all to explore.

Metacomet Trail runs from Sleeping Giant State Park in Hamden (see "The New Haven Area"—*Hiking*) up to Mount Monadnock in New Hampshire, with just one break in Massachusetts. A good entry point is in Granby at CT 20. Watch for the blue oval sign that marks Connecticut hiking trails. If you go north, the trail goes near Old New-Gate Prison; if you turn south, it takes you to the dramatic Tariffville Gorge of the Farmington River and on down through Penwood Park.

MOUNTAIN BIKING

Despite its proximity to Hartford, the suburbs to the west offer riders plenty of trails to explore.

Winding Trails Cross-Country Ski Center (860-677-8485), 50 Winding Trails Drive, Farmington. Open May through October. Its 400 acres offer 12 miles of well-marked trails, mostly hard-packed ski trails with some technical singletrack. Trail fee.

The **Metropolitan District Commission Reservoir** (860-231-9023), Farmington Avenue, on the West Hartford–Farmington town line, will satisfy riders of all abilities with a 3.5-mile paved loop, a network of fire roads, and—for the adventurous—miles of challenging singletrack trails on **Talcott Mountain.**

Central Wheel (860-677-7010), 62 Farmington Avenue, Farmington, rents mountain bikes and has an extensive line of cycling equipment and accessories.

CROSS-COUNTRY SKIING

Cedar Brook Cross Country Ski Area (860-668-5026), 1481 Ratley Road, West Suffield. Ten km of trails, ski shop for sales, rentals, food service.

Winding Trails Cross-Country Ski Center (860-678-9582), 50 Winding Trails Drive, Farmington. 20 km of trails in a 400-acre recreation area. Rentals, lessons, and food service available in the ski shop.

DOWNHILL SKIING

Mount Southington Ski Area (860-628-0954; 1-800-982-6828), 396 Mount Vernon Road, Southington. Modest mountains characterize Connecticut's ski areas; Mount Southington offers good family skiing, easily accessible, with snowmaking capability to extend the season. There are 14 trails, two chair lifts and five surface lifts, a ski shop, lessons, food service, and night skiing.

ICE SKATING

International Skating Center (860-651-5400), 1375 Hopmeadow Street (CT 10), Simsbury. Public skating Wednesday and Friday 8:15–10:15 PM; Saturday 1–3 and 8:15–10:15; Sunday 1–3 and 6–8 PM. Rental skates on the premises. Visitors are admitted daily 6 AM–midnight. This is a first for Connecticut: a world-class twin-rink ice skating facility for learners and pros. One rink is Olympic-sized; the other meets National Hockey League specifications. If you're lucky, you may see Olympic medalists practicing and/or legendary hockey stars on the ice. Restaurant/coffee shop allows visitors a view of both rinks. Pro shop.

SPECTATOR SPORTS

✐ **Connecticut Wolves Soccer** (860-223-0710), Veterans Memorial Stadium, Willow Brook Park Complex, New Britain. Division II professional soccer team plays April through September. Call for schedule.

✐ **New Britain Rock Cats** (860-224-8383), Willow Brook Park Complex, South Main Street, New Britain. Class AA minor league affiliate of the Minnesota Twins. Games April through September. Call for schedule and prices.

WINDSURFING

Windways (860-651-8696), Simsbury. Windsurfer instruction and rentals offered at many sites, from area lakes to the shoreline. Mid-May to mid-October.

GREEN SPACE

Pinchot Sycamore, the largest tree in the state, is worth a stop just to contemplate what nature can do in the way of size. In a little park on the banks of the Farmington River in the Weatogue section of Simsbury, the Pinchot Sycamore is visible as you cross the steel bridge over the river on CT 185 south of Simsbury center. At last measurement, its gnarled and noble trunk had a circumference of 25 feet, 8 inches. It stands 93 feet high, and its average branch spread (the diameter of the canopy formed by its branches) is 138 feet. Depending on the size of your family, you may be able to join hands around its massive base.

NATURE CENTERS

✐ **Hungerford Outdoor Center** (860-827-9064), 191 Farmington Avenue (CT 372), Kensington (Berlin) 06037. Open year-round, Tuesday through Saturday; closed Sunday, Monday, and holidays. Adults $2; children $1; seniors $1.50. Operated by the New Britain Youth Museum, the center offers activities year-round, with animal programs Saturday at 1:30 and 3:30. In this natural-history haven especially designed for family visits, there are animals both familiar and exotic, trails for hiking, gardens, a pond with an observation station, and changing exhibits on natural history, geology, and more. Picnic area and gift shop.

✐ **Roaring Brook Nature Center** (860-693-0263), 70 Gracey Road, Canton. Open year-round, Tuesday through Saturday 10–5, Sunday 1–5; open Monday July and August. Adults $3; children and seniors $2. Native

While in Simsbury, stop to contemplate the Pinchot Sycamore, the largest tree in the state.

American exhibits, including a longhouse; nature displays, live animals, self-guiding nature trails, and wildlife-attracting areas. With 115 acres of natural terrain and woodland trails, this is an inviting place (a stream runs through it) to visit, especially with children. Call for information about the many tours, guided walks, and family activities. Live entertainment by renowned national and international acoustic folk musicians; call for schedule.

Tomasso Nature Park (860-747-6022), Granger Lane, Plainville. Open daily mid-March through mid-November. Free admission. An 11-acre home to nearly 600 painted turtles, as well as other animals, which can be viewed from trails, bridges, and observation areas. Prime area for birding.

Westmoor Park (860-232-1134), 119 Flagg Road, West Hartford. Open daily; free admission. Agricultural, horticultural, and environmental education center. A demonstration farm has barnyard animals; also on site are herb, perennial, and organic gardens, a nature center with live animals and exhibits, and nature trails. Demonstration farm open daily 9–4.

PARKS

Dinosaur State Park (860-529-8423), West Street, Rocky Hill. The feature of this 70-acre park is the treasure trove of Jurassic-era footprints embedded in the ancient mud. The exhibit center, a geodesic dome enclosing a museum and some of the footprints, is open Tuesday through Sunday 9–4:30; the park itself is open daily 9–4:30. Call for admission charge. A dramatic discovery by a bulldozer operator in the 1960s resulted in the establishment of this park, where 185-million-year-old tracks are on display. You can make a plaster cast to take home: Bring

along 10 pounds of plaster and ¼ cup of cooking oil. Special programs
are offered; call for schedule. There are hiking trails, an interpretive
nature walk, and picnic tables.

Northwest Park (860-285-1886), 145 Lang Road, Windsor. A town park,
these 500 green acres border the Farmington River's Rainbow Reservoir. It's a good place for birders: Bluebirds and other species are
encouraged to settle here. There are 6 miles of walking trails, and a
nature center with live animals. Open summers only is the **Luddy/
Taylor Connecticut Valley Tobacco Museum** (see *Museums*).

Penwood State Park (860-424-3200, state parks office), CT 185, on the
Simsbury-Bloomfield line. Curtis H. Veeder, industrialist, outdoors-
man, and inventor, originally developed this 787-acre paradise as his
own estate. His home no longer stands, but the park is a tribute to his
love for the woods. Roads, small lakes, shelters, picnic areas, a bikeway,
trails (part of the Metacomet Trail comes through), small bridges, scenic overlooks. *Veeder* is Dutch for "pen," and Veeder's ancestors came
from Pennsylvania—the official explanation for the name of the park.
Drinking water is available, as are flush toilets.

Stratton Brook State Park (860-424-3200, state parks office), CT 309, 2
miles west of Simsbury. A small park—148 acres—where you can swim
in the brook, hike, fish, and picnic. There are facilities for changing
clothes, a concession, drinking water, and flush toilets.

Talcott Mountain State Park (860-424-3200, state parks office), CT 185,
south of Penwood Park and 3 miles south of Simsbury. The main attraction here is what many consider the state's best viewing spot. Talcott
Mountain is 1,000 feet above the valley of the Farmington River. On
the mountain is the **Heublein Tower,** built as a summer place by the
family that owned Heublein Liquor Distributors. The four-story square
white tower is visible from up to 50 miles away. A society dedicated to
its preservation opens it to visitors on a seasonal basis. It's a good climb,
and worth it—your reward at the top is a view of four states. The park
has a picnic shelter and toilet facilities.

Walnut Hill Park (860-826-3360), West Main Street, New Britain. Open
daily. A 90-acre retreat designed by Frederick Law Olmsted—
Manhattan's Central Park is another of his claims to fame. Walking and
exercise paths, a band shell, World War I monument, and rewarding
vistas at the crest of the park.

LODGING

INN
& **Simsbury 1820 House** (860-658-7658), 731 Hopmeadow Street (CT 10),
Simsbury 06070. A spacious manor house of early-19th-century vintage—
before Victorian tastes took over. The common rooms are classic, with
dark walls and white woodwork, leaded-glass windows, fine paintings,
authentic antiques, and reproductions throughout. The huge, open porch

with its wooden swing makes you want to linger. The rooms are up to the same standards: the charm of an old-fashioned country inn but with modern amenities such as private bath and TV. There are 32 rooms, all with private bath and continental breakfast. Outstanding restaurant (see *Dining Out*). $115–185.

BED & BREAKFASTS

In addition to the listings below, a number of bed & breakfast reservation services offer access to rooms available in establishments throughout the state. For a list, see *What's Where—Bed & Breakfasts*.

Barney House (860-674-2796), 11 Mountain Spring Road, Farmington 06032. An elegant 19th-century mansion just off the main road, with seven large guest rooms and spectacular views. There's a Victorian greenhouse and comfortable common rooms; each guest room has a private bath, TV, and air-conditioning. Facilities include tennis courts and an in-ground pool. Continental breakfast included. Rooms $102 and up.

Captain Josiah Cowles Place (860-276-0227), 184 Marion Avenue, Southington 06489. Two guest rooms in a genuine center-chimney Colonial home, built in 1740 and listed on the National Register of Historic Places. The amenities here are comfortingly up-to-date, with private bath, air-conditioning, TV, and outdoor pool. One room has a fireplace, the other a king-size four-poster. Full breakfast is served, and snacks. Room rates around $75.

Charles R. Hart House (860-688-5555), 1046 Windsor Avenue, Windsor 06095. A Victorian painted lady, with gables, a Palladian window, turret, and a wraparound veranda. The interior is comfortably elegant and furnished with antiques. Four guest rooms, all with private bath, one with fireplace; full breakfast featuring homemade breads. $65–90.

Chester Bulkley House (860-563-4236), 184 Main Street, Wethersfield 06109. This elegant 1830 Greek Revival home is a perfect base from which to explore Old Wethersfield. Common space includes working fireplaces, wide-pine floors, hand-carved woodwork, and period antiques. There are five rooms, three with private bath; guests are served a full breakfast. Innkeepers Frank and Sophie Bottaro are gracious hosts, and will arrange for special needs. Rate for room with shared bath, $70; with private bath, $85.

Merrywood (860-651-1785), 100 Hartford Road (CT 185), Simsbury 06070. Michael and Gerlinde Marti's elegant Colonial Revival home, set on 5 wooded acres, has a pleasing mix of period antiques, Oriental carpets, and original artwork. Guests can explore hiking trails, stroll through the garden, or relax on the sunporch, in the library, or by the fire in the living room. There are two guest rooms and two suites, each with private bath. Breakfast at Merrywood is splendid, with candlelight, handmade linens, and antique English porcelain. Afternoon tea is also served. Rates $120–200.

The Red House on the Road (860-620-0059), 1460 Meriden Avenue, Southington 06489. The Avery Clark Homestead was one of the town's first homes, and a stop on the Underground Railroad. Today innkeepers Donald and Suzanne Myler welcome guests to their lovingly restored 18th-century home, listed on the National Register of Historic Places. Four guest rooms furnished with queen beds and quilts, two with private baths and fireplaces. The Mylers also offer an apartment-style portion of the house, a great option for families. Guests can relax and enjoy goodies in the rustic keeping room. Full breakfast. $89 and up.

HOTELS/MOTELS

Avon Old Farms Hotel (860-677-1651; outside Connecticut: 1-800-836-4000), CT 10 and US 44, Avon 06001. There are 161 rooms and three suites. At the foot of Avon "Mountain," this is a 20th-century place with a spectacular lobby and curved staircases leading to mezzanines. Mindful of its New England past, it's furnished with antiques, embellished with traditional architectural touches, and thoroughly comfortable. Rooms are in the main building and in the outbuildings on the 20-acre site. Amenities include an outdoor pool and a health club. **Seasons Restaurant** offers excellent food. $90 and up.

    Centennial Inn (860-677-4647; outside Connecticut: 1-800-852-2052), 5 Spring Lane (US 6 and CT 177), Farmington 06032. For families who prefer to settle into a homelike arrangement including a kitchen, here are 112 suites, each with fireplace in the living room. Other amenities include an exercise room, an outdoor pool, a whirlpool, barbecue grills, and continental breakfast. Suites start at $115 in spring and fall; reduced rates on weekends and in winter.

    Farmington Inn (860-677-2821; outside Connecticut: 1-800-648-9804), 827 Farmington Avenue (CT 4), Farmington 06032. There are 72 rooms and suites featuring original paintings by area artists, fresh flowers, and luxury amenities—same-day valet service, covered parking. Also a gourmet Italian restaurant on the premises. This is an excellent base for a Farmington Valley visit. Continental breakfast. $110 range.

    Hartford Marriott Hotel—Farmington (860-678-1000), 15 Farm Springs Road, Farmington 06032. With 375 rooms, six suites, a parklike setting, and a jogging trail, this is a model of a suburban hotel. Restaurant, health club, indoor and outdoor pools, tennis, and easy access to the interstate. Rates start at $100.

    Homewood Suites Hotel (860-627-8463), 65 Ella Grasso Turnpike (CT 75), Windsor Locks 06096. For travelers who require the comforts of home—132 apartment-style suites with kitchen and TV; amenities include an exercise room, outdoor pool, and whirlpool. Continental breakfast and free shuttle service to Bradley International Airport. $125–160.

    Sheraton Hotel at Bradley International Airport (860-627-5311), One Bradley International Airport, Windsor Locks 06096; located between two terminals. While many fine motels ring the airport, this is, no contest, the most convenient; it's right there, with 237 units, one suite, and a host of amenities: restaurant, coffee shop, lounge, entertainment, TV in the rooms, health club, sauna, indoor pool. $99–175.

  &. **The Simsbury Inn** (860-651-5700; 1-800-634-2719), 397 Hopmeadow Street, Simsbury 06070. This full-service hotel looks like a resort: a redbrick, white-trimmed central building with wings on either side, a circular drive, and flags flying at the entrance. Besides two restaurants (see *Dining Out*) and 100 guest rooms, there are tennis courts, an indoor pool, and health club facilities. $100 and up.

  &. **West Hartford Inn** (860-236-3221), 900 Farmington Avenue, West Hartford 06119. Just two blocks from West Hartford center, with its nice shops and restaurants, this 50-room in-town accommodation offers laundry and room service and enclosed parking spaces. Thermasol steam baths and king-size beds are available. Adjacent is the **Shangri-La Restaurant** (860-523-8829), specializing in gourmet Chinese cuisine. Continental breakfast is included with the moderate price: around $70.

MOTOR INN

  &. **Hawthorne Inn** (860-828-4181), 2387 Wilbur Cross Highway (US 5 and CT 15), on the Berlin Turnpike, Berlin 06037. Open year-round; 70 rooms, all with private bath. Managed by the Grelak family for more than 50 years, the Hawthorne is known for quality service. Recently renovated, its amenities include an outdoor pool, an exercise room, minigolf, shuffleboard, volleyball, and horseshoes. The Grelaks run an excellent restaurant next door (see *Dining Out*). Continental breakfast is included; rates under $75.

WHERE TO EAT

DINING OUT

  &. **Apricots** (860-673-5405), 1593 Farmington Avenue (CT 4), Farmington. Serves lunch and dinner daily, brunch and dinner on Sunday. Views of the Farmington River—floodlit at night—are a bonus with this elegant dining experience. There's an English-type pub downstairs, with piano Wednesday through Saturday. Upstairs are three dining rooms with formal lighting and decor and contemporary American cuisine, all under the management of Ann Howard—a respected name among Connecticut restaurant buffs. You may find such temptations as baked Maine crabcakes with a mango glaze (as an appetizer), pan-seared rack of spring lamb with ratatouille and lamb jus, or grilled swordfish dressed with an asparagus vinaigrette and accompanied with rösti potatoes. The menu changes seasonally. Exquisite desserts, including the signature apricot mousse. The pub menu is in the moderate range; upstairs, entrées up to $26.

  &. **Avon Old Farms Inn** (860-677-2818), CT 10 and US 44, Avon. Open daily for lunch and dinner, brunch on Sunday. Looking the way you expect an inn to look—low, rambling, and comfortably colonial (a 1757 core building)—the Avon Old Farms is proud of its reputation for award-winning food. Several additions over the years have produced a series of dining spaces, most with exposed beams, wide-board floors, and New England memorabilia. In winter you'll welcome a seat in the Forge Room, under wagonwheel light fixtures and near the fireplace, or across the room in the booths that were once horse stalls. The cuisine is New American—crispy shrimp in a pineapple-ginger sauce, and portobello mushrooms stuffed with goat cheese are examples—and tried-and-true: baked stuffed shrimp, pan-seared sirloin steak, and other classics. Entrées at dinner $16–28.

&. **Evergreens Restaurant** (860-651-5700), at the Simsbury Inn, 397 Hopmeadow Street, Simsbury. Full bar; serves lunch Tuesday through Friday and dinner Tuesday through Saturday; Sunday brunch. Linen on the tables, carpeting underfoot, greenery throughout, and tall windows to bring in the light. Continental fare: chicken roulade, Black Angus sirloin with three-onion confit, Dover sole, fresh vegetables, a good hand with herbs. $20 range.

The Frog and the Peach (860-693-6352), 160 Albany Turnpike (US 44), Canton. Lunch Tuesday through Saturday; dinner Tuesday through Sunday; closed Monday. This charming eatery, set in a pale green Victorian house, is enthusiastically praised by locals and food critics. Creative dishes are expertly prepared and artfully presented. You might start with a salad of mixed greens studded with pine nuts, Michigan dried cherries, and goat cheese; continue to ginger-crusted salmon with roasted fennel, leeks, and lotus chips, or pulled five-spice duck with a crispy noodle cake, peppers, and sliced grapes in an Asian plum sauce; and finish with a delicate lavender crème brûlée. The dining rooms can get noisy when times are busy, but the exceptional food, attentive staff, and intimate surroundings more than compensate. Reservations suggested. Entrées $17–23.

&. **The Gristmill Restaurant** (860-676-8855), 44 Mill Lane, Farmington. Open daily for lunch and dinner; brunch on Sunday. Reservations suggested. Dine on northern Mediterranean seafood and pasta specialties in this converted 17th-century flour mill. Entrées $12.50–26.50. An inviting bookshop is upstairs (see *Selective Shopping—Bookstores*).

&. **Hawthorne Inn** (860-828-3571), 2421 Wilbur Cross Highway (US 5 and CT 15, also called Berlin Turnpike), Berlin. Serving lunch and dinner daily. Before the interstates came through, the turnpike was the main road from Hartford to New Haven, crowded with motels, fast-food restaurants, and all kinds of dealerships. The turnpike is still a "strip," but the Hawthorne is different: quiet rooms, muted colors, wood paneling, leather banquettes, and an air of serious dining. Known for prime rib and seafood—lobster and swordfish; also roast duckling and other American specialties. A "lite" menu is available. Reservations suggested. Up to $30.

J. Timothy's Taverne (860-747-6813), 143 New Britain Avenue (CT 372), Plainville. Open daily for lunch and dinner. This rambling Colonial structure, with its wide-plank floors, wall sconces, and fireplaces, harks back to 1789, the year President Washington was inaugurated and the tavern first opened for business. Traditional American fare is served in several hushed, softly lit dining rooms. The lunch menu offers hearty sandwiches and salads; the dinner menu includes satisfying and well-prepared steak, chicken, and seafood dishes. Lively pub. Sandwiches around $7; entrées $10–18.

  ♧ **Madeleine's Restaurant** (860-688-0150), 1530 Palisado Avenue, Windsor. Dinner Monday through Saturday from 5. Full bar. On the Connecticut River—close enough to allow you to see the ripples in the water from your window. A very haute French dining room, with white tablecloths to underscore the Continental and French cuisine. The restaurant itself and its wine selection have received awards of excellence. Specialties are lobster bisque, rack of lamb, and berries au gratin. Dieters take heart: Madeleine's offers "Spa Cuisine" with calibrated sodium, cholesterol, and calories content: good stuff like salmon steamed with leeks, chicken pot-au-feu, and grilled veal rib Marengo. Adventurous diners can reserve a table right in the kitchen, where they're served a tasting menu to sample while the chef and crew go about their alchemy. Reservations suggested. Entrées $19–25.

  ♧ **Max A Mia** (860-677-6299), 70 East Main Street (US 44), Avon. Open for lunch and dinner daily. A roadside restaurant with a superior northern Italian menu. Popular with the boomer set, a gathering place both at lunch and in the evening. The dozen varieties of stone pies—pizzas baked in a wood-burning stone pizza oven—are worth a trip. Other menu features: risotto, portobello mushrooms, shrimp with basil, seafood, and red meats, along with vegetarian concoctions, distinctive and tasty. Desserts are amazing, from tiramisu to apple tart with puff pastry. Reservations are suggested for lunch; accepted only for parties of six or more for dinner. Luncheon entrées under $10. Pasta at dinner under $15; stone pies under $10; other entrées all under $20.

  ♧ **Simsbury 1820 House** (860-658-7658), 731 Hopmeadow Street (US 202 and CT 10), Simsbury. Open for dinner Monday through Saturday, closed Sunday. Full bar. Set in a New England manor house that has been transformed into a country inn, the decor is dignified, softly lit. Dishes are imaginatively prepared: You might begin with roasted duck atop a bed of fennel and oranges, then dine on salmon stuffed with spinach, sun-dried tomatoes, and Parmesan cheese, or grilled chicken breast sauced with a peach and jalapeño glaze. For dessert, dark rum chocolate bread pudding or a triple chocolate terrine. Reservations suggested. Entrées $19–27.

EATING OUT

  ♧ **Bamboo Grill** (860-693-4144), 50 Albany Turnpike (US 44), Canton. Open for dinner daily. No liquor license. A small, plain storefront, not easy to find, the Bamboo Grill dazzles with variety. Vietnamese takeout or eat in, with soups, appetizers, salads, main dishes, and desserts, totaling more than 70 choices. Some are familiar from acquaintance with Chinese dishes—some not. Rice-batter crêpes, flan caramel, or this satisfying one-dish concoction: grilled chicken (or beef or pork) on rice noodles with lettuce, fried onions, peanuts, and house sauce. Main dishes to $15; desserts $3 and $3.50.

& **Bistrot Gabrielle** (860-688-2616), 1530 Palisado Avenue, Windsor. Dinner only, Tuesday through Saturday. Full bar. Located alongside Madeleine's Restaurant (see *Dining Out*), the Bistrot shares a splendid view of the Connecticut River. The cuisine is French-Mediterranean, with attention paid to fresh ingredients in combinations both classic and original. You may find on the menu such specialties as escargots with browned butter, and fricasseed mushrooms; among the entrées are poultry, veal with sauces both classic and rewarding, and beef bourguignonne. Reservations are a good idea. Entrées $9–15.

✐&☞**Brannigan's Restaurant and Gathering** (860-621-9311), 176 Laning Street, Southington. Lunch and dinner daily; Sunday brunch; full bar. A much-loved and easy-to-find destination for barbecue fans. The house specialty is baby back ribs, but there are charbroiled steaks, seafood, chicken specialties, salads, soups, or Very Big Sandwiches. Key lime pie is the dessert of choice. Reservations are a good idea. Modest pricing: lunch $6–11; dinner $10–16; early-bird specials Monday through Thursday.

✐&☞**Congress Rotisserie** (860-563-4300), 691 Silas Deane Highway, Wethersfield. Open daily for lunch and dinner. A friendly eatery, favored by locals for its generous salads and sandwiches. Carry-out locations at 333 North Main Street (860-231-7454) in West Hartford; and 208 Trumbull Street (860-525-5141) and 274 Farmington Avenue (860-278-7711) in Hartford. Sandwiches $6; entrées around $10.

☞&**Connecticut Culinary Institute** (860-677-7869), 230 Farmington Avenue (in Loehmann's Plaza), Farmington. Future chefs help produce a variety of dishes, beginning with continental breakfast (consisting of breads and pastries baked, of course, on the premises) and luncheon (soups, salads, sandwiches, and a selection of entrées). Open Monday through Friday 8–4; Saturday 9–3. Closed Sunday. Entrées top off under $7.

☞&**Great Taste** (860-229-7373; 860-827-8988), 597 West Main Street, New Britain. Open daily for lunch and dinner. Locally famous Chinese fare: Try the tangerine beef or General Tso's chicken, or any of the seafood preparations. Dishes are generally around $10, but with special orders—Peking duck, for instance—you can spend more.

& **La Trattoria** (860-673-5000), US 44, Canton. Open for lunch Monday through Friday, dinner daily, for brunch on Sunday. Watch for the sign; the restaurant is well back from the road on the side of a hill. An old, established eatery with a reputation for good food, not necessarily fancy but well prepared and familiar. Broiled scrod, baked stuffed shrimp, veal tenderloin, steak Diane, veal cutlet parmigiana or Marsala. Entrées up to $20; desserts $3 and $4, except for cherries jubilee and crêpes Suzette—$10 each. There are early-bird specials until 6, priced $10–12.

& **Lemon Grass** (860-233-4405) Seven South Main Street, West Hartford. Open for lunch Monday through Saturday, for dinner daily. In the center of West Hartford, this storefront oasis manages to create a calm spot in a busy shopping area. It serves Thai cuisine, as hot as you can stand it or serenely mild if you prefer. The house specialty is Lemongrass Treasure, combining shrimp, scallops, squid, and fish with hot chiles, mushrooms, onions, green peppers, and mysterious spices and herbs on top of steamed clams. There are simple salads, fiery curries, barbecued chicken dishes, and pad Thai—the classic noodle dish with shrimp, tofu, ground peanuts, and vegetables. Entrées $6.50–14.

& **Maharaja** (860-233-7184), 964 Farmington Avenue, West Hartford. Lunch and dinner daily. It's little wonder that this calm, softly lit restaurant is a favorite with locals. The staff is warm and attentive, and the menu reflects the diversity of Indian cuisine, from fiery curries to fragrant rice dishes, perfumed with cumin, saffron, and cardamom. Try the channa batura, a large, puffed lentil-flour bread stuffed with chickpeas; or dosai, a large, thin pancake served with grated coconut chutney and sambar, a curry of toasted lentils and spices. Exotic desserts include cream dumplings dipped in honey syrup and rose water. Entrées $8–14.

☞✐**Newport Blues Cafe** (860-676-2583), 51 East Main Street (US 44), Avon. Open daily for lunch and dinner; both menus are available at all times. Live music Thursday, Friday, and Saturday evenings. Set in a complex of buildings that house mostly upscale shops and boutiques, the café is upstairs, a sprawling, casual place with fun decor devoted to transportation nostalgia—a railway car, lots of auto memorabilia, and (upside-down on the ceiling) a rowboat occupied by two fishermen. Specialty sandwiches with tortillas, pita pockets, club rolls, some with old-fashioned bread. You can have Spanish "Oh" rings as an appetizer; entrées of chicken, scallops, tenderloin tips, or fajitas; and burgers, salads, quiche, meat loaf, and chicken potpie to round things (you) out. Desserts? Key lime pie, deep-fried ice cream, excellent cheesecake, and fudge brownie monster. Entrées $10–16; sandwiches generally $6–8.

&☞**Olympia Diner** (860-666-9948), 3413 Berlin Turnpike (US 5 and CT 15), Newington. Open year-round, 5:30 AM to midnight. The diner of your dreams: Bright neon guides you to the super-long, silver-bullet core car with added-on dining rooms. Dependable diner fare—burgers and dogs, home fries, black coffee. Booths with slick plastic, Formica tables, a voluminous menu offering serious food dished out in generous portions.

&☞✐**Pagliacci's Restaurant** (860-793-9241), 333 East Main Street (CT 10), Plainville. Open daily for lunch and dinner. The heady aroma of garlic and fresh-baked bread is the first thing you notice as you enter this bustling restaurant. Generous portions of traditional Italian specialties—veal scaloppine, chicken parmigiana, and shrimp scampi, to name a few—impossibly huge bowls of house-made pasta, hearty pizzas, and calzones. Be prepared to wait for a table, especially on the weekends—Pagliacci's has a loyal following. Entrées $8–17.

COFFEE BARS

The Beanery Bistro (860-688-2224), 697 Poquonock Avenue (CT 75), Windsor. Open daily. A likable little store, 5 minutes from Bradley International Airport. Seating outdoors on the patio in warm weather; pastries, breads, and muffins are baked on the premises. The menu includes desserts and "savory sandwiches"—for example, one with arti-choke hearts, Parmesan cheese, and mild chiles in a spread. The spe-cialty is a roast turkey and stuffing with tomato and Swiss sandwich on crispy French bread. As for the coffee, choose espresso or one of sev-eral flavored brews. There's a gift store as well, with gift baskets to give (or keep and enjoy). $3–5.

    ఈ **Gertrude and Alice's Coffee Bar & Bookstore** (860-693-3816), 10 Front Street, Collinsville. Open Tuesday through Sunday; closed Monday. Elaine Marchese and Lilias Keszycki have turned a former freight station into an eclectic coffeehouse that actively supports the local arts commu-nity. Aromatic coffees, pastries, soups, and sandwiches are served inside or, in good weather, out back on the deck. New and used books, cards, and gifts. Blues, folk, and acoustic musicians play here on weekends; call for schedule.

    ఈ **Peter B's Espresso Bar** (860-231-9390), 984 Farmington Avenue, West Hartford. Open daily. The back room of the coffeehouse is a little island of luxury—small tables, soft music, and heavenly imported cakes and pastries to accompany your exquisite brew. Take your java to a sidewalk table if you prefer to watch the passing scene.

SNACKS

The Ann Howard Cookery, Ltd. (860-678-9486), Brickwalk Lane, Farmington. Open Monday through Saturday. A changing blackboard menu offers fixings for gourmet picnicking: hearty breads (three-cheese, cranberry multigrain, for example), excellent soups and entrées, tempting desserts. Another location at 981 Farmington Avenue (860-233-5561) in West Hartford.

    ☞ **The Spicy Green Bean Deli** (860-563-3100), 285 Main Street, Wethersfield. Open Monday through Friday 7:30–3; Saturday 8–3; closed Sunday. This cheery little deli in the historic district is the perfect place to stop while touring Wethersfield's many notable homes and sites. Offerings are simple yet satisfying: breakfast sandwiches in the morning; soups, salads, and sandwiches for lunch; cookies, tarts, muffins, and other sweets for a snack. Indoor seating can feel cramped; take your meal to an outdoor table, in season. Everything under $5.

ENTERTAINMENT

MUSIC

Lincoln Theater (860-768-4228; 1-800-274-8587), University of Hartford, 200 Bloomfield Avenue, West Hartford. The showcase for perfor-mances by students, faculty, and guest artists at the University's Hartt School of Music. Call for schedules—chamber and orchestral concerts, recitals, opera, musical comedy, and more.

Miller Band Shell (860-826-3360), Walnut Hill Park, New Britain. A long-standing summer music festival featuring jazz, blues, country/

western musicians, and other performers. Concerts every Monday and Wednesday evening at 7:30 during July and August. Call for schedule and information.

THEATER

Beckley Dinner Theater (860-828-7630), 197 Episcopal Road, Berlin. Weekly performances year-round: professionals performing favorite musicals, with a buffet dinner, wine, tables for eight, and friendly staff. Call for reservations and information.

Centennial Theater Festival (860-408-5300), 995 Hopmeadow Street, Simsbury. An 8-week summer festival of professional theater, music, and dance in a replica of a European opera house in downtown Simsbury. Call for schedules.

Hole in the Wall Theater (860-229-3049), 10 Harvard Street, New Britain. Ambitious amateur productions; year-round schedule. Call for information.

DRIVE-IN

Southington Drive-In (860-628-2205), 935 Meriden-Waterbury Turnpike, Southington. One of only 100 or so left in the country. Two screens, snack bar.

NIGHTLIFE

Maple Tree Cafe (860-651-1297), 781 Hopmeadow Street, Simsbury. Live local and nationally known blues acts on weekends; cover varies. Hearty American fare: steak, chicken, seafood.

Newport Blues Cafe (860-676-2583), 51 East Main Street (CT 44), Avon. Live blues, jazz, rock on weekends (see *Eating Out*).

SPECTATOR SPORTS

Bradley Teletheater (860-623-0380), 11 Schoephoester Road (near Bradley International Airport), Windsor Locks. Open year-round. Live simulcasts of jai alai, horse- and greyhound racing.

SELECTIVE SHOPPING

ANTIQUES SHOPS

Antiques at Canton Village (860-693-2715), 220 Albany Turnpike (US 44), Canton. A multidealer shop featuring 18th- and 19th-century furniture, accessories.

Antiques on the Farmington (860-673-9205), 218 River Road, at the junction with CT 4, Unionville. A huge barn divides space among many dealers, with a nice variety of quality goods.

Balcony Antiques (860-693-6440; 860-693-4478), 81 Albany Turnpike (US 44), Canton. Connecticut's oldest group shop in continuous operation—some 60 dealers offer accessories, furniture, fine art, and jewelry.

Collinsville Antiques Company (860-693-1011), One Main Street (CT 179), Collinsville. Two floors in old Collins Axe Factory, with 94 dealers offering variety in furnishings, mirrors, china, silver, lamps, and rugs.

Olde Windsor Antique Center (860-249-4300), 184 Windsor Avenue, Windsor.

Red Barn Christmas Shop (860-563-2121), 133 Main Street, Wethersfield. Open August to January 1; but adjacent, in the house at 135 Main Street, **Enchanted Heart** collectibles shop is open year-round. A treasure trove of figures, town scenes, ceramic, porcelain, and bisque objects; name brands, many imported.

The Vintage Shop (860-224-8567), 61 Arch Street, New Britain. Clothing, costume jewelry, accessories, as well as furniture, lamps, glassware, and more. Coffee shop.

William III Antiques (860-658-1121), 21 Wolcott Road, Simsbury. Victorian and Empire furniture, fine china, glassware, collectibles.

ART GALLERIES

Barker Animation Art Gallery (860-232-TOON), 60A LaSalle Road, West Hartford. Open Tuesday through Saturday 10–5:30; Thursday until 8. Original cels, model sheets, prints, and drawings. Some rare treasures: from Betty Boop to the Simpsons; works from the studios of Disney, Hanna-Barbera, Warner Brothers, and Universal. Also collectibles such as T-shirts, mugs, jewelry, dolls, stuffed animals, wall hangings, watches, posters, and more, bearing the comic grins of the likes of Popeye and Minnie Mouse.

Fisher Gallery Shop (860-678-1867), in Farmington Valley Arts Center, Avon (see *Artisans—Farmington Valley Arts Center*). Located in the brownstone complex of artists' studios, the shop carries only works by American artists and craftspeople: pottery, glass, toys, pewter, jewelry, and so on.

Gallery on the Green (860-693-4102), US 44, Canton. Open March through December, Wednesday through Sunday 1–5. Exhibits of work by members of the oldest artists' guild in the state. The gallery also schedules invitational and open shows.

Petrini Art Gallery (860-677-2747), Four East Main Street, Avon. Nationally known fine art and custom framing.

Saltbox Gallery (860-521-3732), 37 Buena Vista Road, West Hartford. Call for exhibition schedules. Home of the **West Hartford Art League,** which also maintains the **Clubhouse Gallery** (860-521-1138) and **Chimney Gift Shop** (860-521-3732), both adjacent. Outstanding works by local artists in various media.

ARTISANS

Farmington Crafts Common (860-674-9295), 248 Main Street, Farmington. Some 200 artists and craftworkers. Café and gift shop.

Farmington Valley Arts Center (860-678-1867), 25 Arts Center Lane (US 44), Avon. A stretched-out, 19th-century brownstone, formerly an explosives plant, makes an ideal studio complex: Each artisan has a private space, with access provided by an exterior walkway. The 20-odd studios are open at varying times at the artists' discretion, and visitors are invited to come in and watch, and to ask questions. Workers in ceramics, stone, textiles, wood, metal; portrait and landscape painters, water colorists, and photographers. The center also offers classes in arts and crafts, and in the **Fisher Gallery Shop** exhibits works of resident artisans, with American-made arts and crafts for sale (see *Special Events*).

Spirited Hand (860-677-5153), 315 West Main Street, Avon. Widely known for contemporary handcrafted gifts, doodads, and essentials in ceramic, glass, wood, and more.

BOOKSTORES

The Amity Bookstore (860-529-7733), 825 North Cromwell Avenue (CT 3), Rocky Hill. Both new and used books, children's section, special orders.

Bookworm (860-233-2653), 968 Farmington Avenue, West Hartford. A full-service, locally owned bookstore in the center of town and known throughout the area. Book signings, special orders, advice, suggestions, play area for children.

The Jumping Frog (860-523-1622), 585 Prospect Avenue, West Hartford. Antiquarian bookseller specializing in special orders and out-of-print searches. The largest seller of used books in the state. Frogs everywhere.

Millrace Books (860-677-9662), 40 Mill Lane, Farmington. Set in a former mill building, a succession of large and small rooms, quirky and comfortable, upstairs over a very good restaurant. Accommodating, knowledgeable staff.

On the Road Bookshop (860-693-6029), 163 Albany Turnpike (US 44), Canton. A comfortable storefront place, excellent for browsing, specializing in fine used, rare, and out-of-print books.

West Hartford Bookshop (860-232-2028), 322 Park Road, West Hartford. A small, friendly shop specializing in used, out-of-print, and rare books.

FARMS AND GARDENS

Pickin' Patch (860-677-9552), Nod Road, Avon. Open daily May through December. Connecticut's 10th oldest family farm, since 1666. Pick your own fruits and veggies; later in the season, tractor-drawn hayrides to the pumpkin patch; Christmas trees. Bedding plants in spring.

SPECIAL SHOPS

Comstock, Ferre & Company (860-571-6590), 263 Main Street, Wethersfield. The oldest continuously operating seed company in the United States (since 1820); the late-1700s chestnut post-and-beam structure is a National Historic Landmark. Seeds, plants, and good, reliable advice.

Old Avon Village (860-678-0469), East Main Street (US 44), Avon. One-of-a-kind shops and boutiques in a complex of Colonial buildings, originally the center of the village of Avon.

Patrick Baker and Sons (860-628-5566), 1650 West Street, Southington. New England's largest religious supply and gift store, featuring books, music, candles, and more.

Riverdale Farms Shopping (860-677-6437), CT 10 North, Avon. It's a quarter mile north of busy US 44, but it feels like the country. A former dairy farm turned into an unusual shopping complex—a series of buildings inhabited by 30 or more gift and specialty shops. Clothing, gifts, jewelry, kitchenware, furnishings—along with boutiques and restaurants.

SPECIAL EVENTS

For details, contact the Greater Hartford Tourism District (1-800-793-4480).

March: **Professional Bowlers Tournament,** Bradley Bowl, Windsor Locks.

May: **Shadmaster Tournament** in Windsor at the CT 159 boat ramp; **Craft Fair** (860-871-7914), at the Polo Grounds, Town Farm Road, Farmington.

June: **Main Street U.S.A.**—New Britain street festival. **Craft Fair** (860-871-7914), at the Polo Grounds, Farmington. **Antiques Weekend** (508-839-9735), at the Polo Grounds, Farmington. The state's largest antiques event, with more than 600 dealers.

Summer: **Horse shows** at the Farmington Polo Grounds, Simsbury Folly Farm, and First Company Horse Guard Grounds. Call 1-800-4-WEL-COME for more information. **Sunken Garden Poetry Festival** (860-677-4787) at the Hill-Stead Museum, Farmington. Local and world-renowned poets read their works.

September: **Antiques Weekend** (508-839-9735), at the Polo Grounds, Farmington. **Craft Fair** (860-871-7914), at the Polo Grounds, Farmington.

October: **Berlin Fair,** Berlin. **Apple Harvest Festival,** Southington.

November–December: **The Art of Giving/The Giving of Art** (860-678-1867; 860-674-1877), Farmington Valley Arts Center, Avon. Handmade American crafts representing more than 200 artisans, including artists working in studios on the premises.

November–December: **Holidayfest** in Connecticut's North Central Tourism Bureau area. Open houses, special events in historic homes, trolley rides, visits with Santa, and more.

East of the River

The Connecticut River effectively divides the state, east and west. To get from Hartford to East Hartford, Windsor to East Windsor, Rocky Hill to Glastonbury, you need a bridge or a ferry. And that may be why East of the River has come to have an identity all its own, distinct from West of the River. In the northern half of the state, the barrier is spanned, so to speak, by a ferry and five bridges—three of them in Hartford.

The East of the River character was built on industrial development as much as on farming. The many swift streams encouraged farmers to turn to water-powered milling operations instead of plowing the rock-filled hills. By the 19th century, industrialization had come to the region, and the many textile mills attracted workers from Ireland, Germany, Britain, Sweden, Canada, and elsewhere, to find themselves part of what was called the nation's melting pot.

East Hartford is the home of Pratt and Whitney aircraft engines, but it has its share of remembrances of earlier times, including 18th-century gunpowder factories, a possibly haunted house, and a one-room school built in 1820. In neighboring Manchester are reminders of the Cheney silk mills that made the town famous in the last century. The Cheney brothers at one time imported silkworms in order to control the means of production; indeed, Cheney was one of the most renowned silk manufacturing empires in the world. Manchester today boasts a delightful children's museum, parks inviting quiet reflection, summertime bandshell concerts, and a restaurant that consistently ranks at the top of the charts statewide.

South Windsor, just above East Hartford, and its neighbor East Windsor were major tobacco farming areas when this whole region was called Tobacco Valley. Earlier, it was the site of fierce battles during the Mohawk and Podunk Wars. The first settlers built no homes here and used the land only for hay and pasture crops because of the danger from unfriendly Pequots. South Windsor was the birthplace of Jonathan Edwards, whose sermon "Sinners in the Hands of an Angry God" stands as a statement of the beliefs of New England's founding fathers. East Windsor's most popular attraction is the Trolley Museum, where you can climb aboard a streetcar and take a ride.

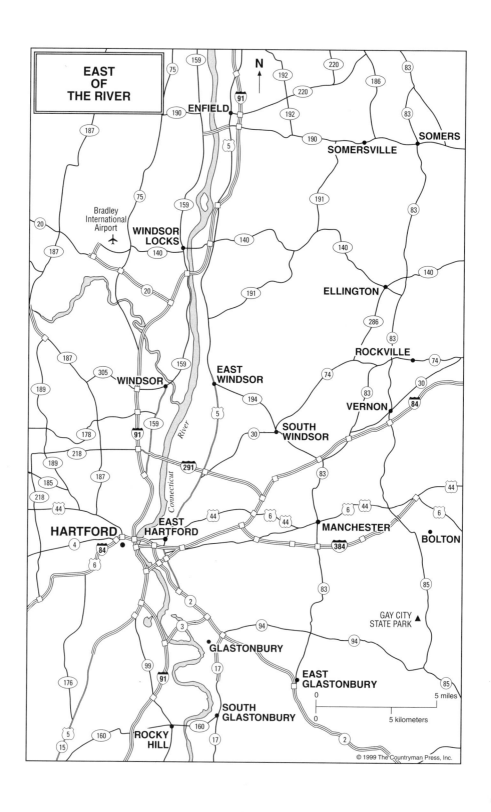

EAST
OF
THE RIVER

N

75
159
220
192
220
186
83
91
190 ENFIELD
192
220
83
190
187
5
SOMERSVILLE
SOMERS
75
159
191
83
Bradley
International
Airport
WINDSOR
LOCKS
140
140
140
20
140
187
20
191
ELLINGTON
140
286
187
83
305
WINDSOR
159
EAST
WINDSOR
ROCKVILLE
74
189
74
30
178
5
194
83
30
VERNON
84
91
159
SOUTH
WINDSOR
218
30
189
291
83
185
6
44
44
218
187
6
44
44
HARTFORD
44
EAST
HARTFORD
6
44
MANCHESTER
6
4
84
BOLTON
6
384
85
River
83
2
GAY CITY
STATE PARK
3
94
176
99
91
94
GLASTONBURY
EAST
GLASTONBURY
17
85
5
160
SOUTH
GLASTONBURY
0   5 miles
15
160
ROCKY
HILL
160
17
0   5 kilometers
2
Connecticut

© 1999 The Countryman Press, Inc.

Continuing east, you'll find the town of Vernon, named for George Washington's Virginia home. Vernon's textile mills were the first to weave satinet, a fabric developed to simulate satin. Both here and in Rockville the mill buildings remain, as well as much of the workers' housing.

Glastonbury, south of East Hartford, is accessible from the western side of the river by the Putnam Bridge or by the nation's oldest ferry service, in operation since 1655. Today it's powered by a small tug, surpassing the wooden poles, steam engines, and horse-powered treadmills employed in the past. Out of the manufacturing mainstream, Glastonbury runs more to orchards than to industry, and has blossomed into an upscale suburb, with new homes supplanting the apple and peach trees of earlier times.

Entries in this section are arranged in alphabetical order.

AREA CODE
860

GUIDANCE
The Greater Hartford Tourism District (860-244-8181; 1-800-793-4480), 234 Murphy Road, Hartford 06114 (Web site: www.travelfile.com/get/ghtd), includes in its literature many of the towns east of the river, as does the **North Central Tourism Bureau** (860-763-2578; 1-800-248-8283), 111 Hazard Avenue, Enfield 06082 (Web site: www.cnctb.org).

GETTING THERE
By car: I-84, I-384, and CT 2 are the major arteries through this section. *By air:* **Bradley International** in Windsor Locks serves the whole state as its major airport.

GETTING AROUND
From Bradley International, you'll find good ground transportation by taxi and limousine to other parts of the state.

MEDICAL EMERGENCY
The statewide emergency number is **911.**

Enfield Ambulatory Care Center (860-745-1684), 15 Palomba Drive, Enfield.

Manchester Memorial Hospital (860-646-1222), 71 Haynes Street, Manchester. The emergency number is 860-647-4777.

Rockville General Hospital (860-872-0501), 31 Union Street, Vernon. The emergency number is 860-872-5291.

TO SEE

MUSEUMS
Cheney Hall (860-647-9824), 177 Hartford Road, Manchester. A splendid example of the benefits of a one-industry town when the management is motivated by mankind's better impulses. This elegant French Second Empire monument, with mansard roof, circle windows, arches,

The Connecticut Fireman's Historical Society Museum has hand-pulled and horse-drawn fire engines on display.

and fancy cornices, has an equally fine interior, resplendent with carved oak and chestnut woodwork and paneling. Listed now as a National Historic Landmark, it was built in 1867 by the Cheney family as Manchester's theater and cultural center. The building serves the same function today, part of the legacy of the silk mills that employed, housed, educated, and watched over 19th-century Manchester. A local theater group presents various productions here (see *Entertainment*), and tours of the building can be arranged.

✐ **Connecticut Fire Museum** (860-623-4732), 58 North Road (CT 140) behind the Trolley Museum, East Windsor. Open June, July, and August, Tuesday through Friday 10–4, Saturday and Sunday noon–5; May through June and September through October, weekends only, noon–5. Adults $2; children and seniors $1. A century's worth of fire trucks, 1850–1950, and other historic fire-fighting apparatus and memorabilia are displayed in a hangarlike building. A good combination with the Connecticut Trolley Museum (see *Trolley Ride*).

✐ **Connecticut Firemen's Historical Society Museum** (860-649-9436), corner of Hartford Road and Pine Street, Manchester. Open April through November, Friday and Saturday 10–5, Sunday noon–5. Adults $4; seniors and children 12–18, $2; children 5–12, $1. Who can resist the lure of the fearless firefighter, the trucks and sirens, dangers and rescues? Hand-pulled and horse-drawn wagons and early motorized apparatus are on display, as well as leather fire buckets, helmets, tools, badges, and lanterns, all in a 1901 firehouse.

✐ **Lutz Children's Museum** (860-643-0949), 247 South Main Street (CT 83), Manchester. Open Tuesday and Wednesday 2–5, Thursday and Friday

9:30–5, Saturday and Sunday noon–5. Adults $3, children $2.50. Their watchword is "Do touch." The museum covers science, history, and natural history, with live animals and exhibits geared to catch and hold youngsters' interest. Ask about special events and programs.

Museum on the Green (860-633-6890), 1944 Main Street, at the corner of Main and Hubbard, Glastonbury. Open year-round, Monday and Thursday 10–4, or by appointment. Free admission. The former Town Hall has become a museum of local history, with artifacts from area Native Americans and memorabilia of local industry—soap, glass, silver plate. Changing exhibits, a costume collection, and other displays. The ancient burial ground for this 300-year-old town is adjacent.

✎ **Somers Mountain Museum of Natural History and Primitive Technology** (860-749-4129), 332 Turnpike Road, Somers. Open Memorial Day through Labor Day, Wednesday through Sunday 10–5; April, May, and September through December, weekends 10–5. Adults $2; children and seniors 99¢. A private collection of authentic artifacts of many Native American tribes dating back more than 10,000 years. Items include war bonnets of the Mohawks, baskets made by Navajo, moundbuilders' pots, masks of the Iroquois, bows of the Lakota Sioux, and other weapons of the Apache and Algonquian. Outside, visitors can tour an eastern woodlands–style wigwam and a Native American herb garden, and explore a trail system lined with edible and medicinal wild plants.

Vintage Radio & Communications Museum of Connecticut (860-675-9916), 1231 Main Street, East Hartford. Open Thursday and Friday 10–2; Saturday 11–4; Sunday 1–4. Adults $4; seniors $2; students $1.50. Exhibits trace the history of radio from the 1920s to 1970s. The museum also features a sound effects room, and examples of motion picture projection from silent crank to sound on film. There's a library and video viewing room on the premises.

HISTORIC HOMES AND SITES

Cheney Homestead (860-643-5588), 106 Hartford Road (US 44), Manchester. Open year-round, Thursday and Sunday 1–5, and by appointment; closed holidays. Adults $2; children under 16 free if accompanied by an adult. Farmer-clockmaker Timothy Cheney built this relatively modest home in 1780; the furnishings and paintings date from the 18th and 19th centuries. Cheney's sons, born here, launched the silk industry that put Manchester on the world map in the 1800s. Also on the grounds is a restored schoolhouse of the 18th century.

Huguenot House, Goodwin One-Room School, and **Burnham Blacksmith & Tool Shop** (860-568-6178; 860-568-5032), Martin Park, Burnside Avenue (US 44), East Hartford. Free admission. Open Memorial Day through September, Thursday, Sunday, and holidays 1–4, and by appointment. A concentration of local history. The Huguenot House, built circa 1761, is atypical of the homes built by the English and their descendants; it stands out with its gambrel roof and vaulted dormer windows. Furthermore, there's a ghost story connected to the builder, a saddlemaker. The school is of later vintage, 1820, and the blacksmith shop dates from about 1825.

Jonathan Edwards Marker, next door to the Montessori School at 1370 Enfield Street (US 5), Enfield. In a church that stood on this site, the legendary preacher delivered his blistering sermon "Sinners in the Hands of an Angry God" in 1741, giving new strength to the Great Awakening. Edwards's father, the Rev. Timothy Edwards, was pastor.

Martha A. Parsons House (860-745-6064), 1387 Enfield Street (US 5), Enfield. Free admission. Open May through October, Sunday 2–4:30, and by appointment. Built in 1782 and lived in by the same family for more than 180 years, the house neatly covers most of the country's lifetime. "George Washington Memorial" wallpaper is a unique feature. The house is decorated for Christmas and open the first weekend in December (see *Special Events*).

Shaker Monument, Shaker Road and CT 220, Enfield. The Enfield Shaker community that flourished here in the 19th century is no more, although some of the buildings remain.

Welles-Shipman-Ward House, 972 Main Street, Glastonbury. The house is open May through October, Sunday 2–4; Wednesday 2–4 in July. Admission $4. Built in 1755 and cited by the Department of the Interior for "exceptional architectural interest," it also incorporates much of local history. Children's animal drawings from the 19th century are preserved on a chamber wall, and the kitchen fireplace and elaborate paneling are among points of interest in the house. There's an 18th-century herb garden on the grounds.

SCENIC DRIVE

CT 160 in Glastonbury for a little over a mile—from Roaring Brook Bridge to Ferry Lane, then to the Connecticut River—is one of the state's official scenic roads. You'll travel through low-lying bottomland, set with houses built two centuries ago for farms, some of them still working, and open land. The ride ends at the dock where you drive onto the ferry for the trip to Rocky Hill. This is the operation that began in 1655, propelled by a hardworking ferryman pushing a long pole.

TO DO

BALLOONING
Emerald City Balloon Co. (860-647-8581), Manchester. Reservations required; year-round, weather permitting.

BOAT EXCURSIONS
Glastonbury–Rocky Hill Ferry (860-443-3856), CT 160. The nation's oldest continuously operating ferry: Drive onto the barge and watch as the tugboat nudges you across the sometimes mighty Connecticut River. It's difficult to describe how satisfying this simple trip can be.

The Rocky Hill–Glastonbury vehicle ferry on the Connecticut River is the oldest continuously operating ferry service in the US.

FISHING

There's a boat-launching site on the Connecticut River at **Great River Park** (860-713-3131), East River Drive, East Hartford, exit 53 off I-84 east. Anglers can also cast from the docks on shore.

GOLF

Cedar Knob Golf Course (860-749-3550), Billings Road, Somers. Par 72, 18 holes, 6,734 yards.

Manchester Country Club (860-646-0226), 305 South Main Street, Manchester. Par 72, 18 holes, 6,167 yards.

Tallwood Country Club (860-646-1151), 91 North Street, CT 85, Hebron. Par 72, 18 holes, 6,366 yards.

MOUNTAIN BIKING

A 10-mile network of well-groomed fire roads is open to riders at **Gay City State Park** (860-424-3200), CT 85, Hebron. Bikes are also allowed on the **Charter Oak Greenway,** a 7.5-mile paved bike path that follows I-384 from Manchester to East Hartford. A parking lot and trailhead is located at Hartford Road and Main Street in Manchester. **The Bike Shop** (860-647-1027), 681 Main Street, Manchester, carries a complete line of cycling accessories; repair shop on the premises.

SKYDIVING

Connecticut Parachutists Inc. (860-871-0021), Ellington Airport, off CT 83, PO Box 507, Ellington 06029. It's fun to watch, and if you yearn for adventure, this may be it. Certified instructors offer training Saturday and Sunday mornings at 8:30, April through November.

SPECTATOR SPORTS

Shallowbrook Equestrian Center (860-749-0749), Hall Hill Road (CT 186), Somers 06071. A family-owned complex of stables, rings, arenas, and polo fields, this 50-acre compound also contains one of the world's largest indoor hippodromes. Primarily a training school for riding and polo, Shallowbrook presents a year-round schedule of spectator events: ASHA horse shows, carriage shows and sleigh rallies, dressage and 3-day events, and polo tournaments—national and international, collegiate, and professional. Call or write for schedule.

TROLLEY RIDE

Connecticut Trolley Museum (860-627-6540), 58 North Road, East Windsor. Open Memorial Day through Labor Day, Monday through Saturday 10–5, Sunday noon–5; Labor Day through Memorial Day, Saturday 10–5, Sunday noon–5. Free admission to museum; charge for trolley ride (call for fares). More than 50 cars have been restored or are in the process; visitors may watch. Three miles of track allow for a taste of old-time fun. Trolleys were the mass transit of the late 19th century, and tracks crisscrossed New England and many other parts of the country. The wheels still clack along the rails and the conductor-engineer still keeps that guide wheel on the overhead wire; bumping along, you can sit and read the period advertisements on the curve between the windows and the roof.

GREEN SPACE

NATURE CENTER

Connecticut Audubon Society at Glastonbury (860-633-8402), 1361 Main Street, Glastonbury. Open year-round, Tuesday through Friday 1–5, Saturday 10–5, Sunday 1–4; closed Sunday in January. A 38-acre park with a trail system to explore in an area known for scenic views, soft hills, and a rural feel. The society's museum building has exhibits on the Connecticut River ecosystem and local plant and animal life; also a shop catering to naturalist interests.

PARKS

Gay City State Park (860-424-3200, state parks office), CT 85, 3 miles south of Bolton center in the town of Hebron. The ruins of an abandoned, 18th-century mill village are concealed by the second-growth forest. Some 1,569 acres in all, with lots of hiking opportunities, swimming, picnicking, fishing, cross-country skiing, mountain biking, flush toilets, drinking water, telephone.

Great River Park (860-713-3131), East River Drive, East Hartford. A small, grassy retreat—one link in the chain of parks along the Connecticut River—with walking paths and a fishing dock, sits across the river from Samuel Colt's 19th-century arms factory. A 500-seat amphitheater hosts children's entertainment and concerts.

Oak Grove Nature Center (860-647-3321), 269 Oak Grove Street, Manchester. Open daily year-round. A 53-acre, soul-soothing park operated by the town of Manchester, complete with ponds and streams, fields, and nature trails.

Wickham Park (860-528-0856), 1329 West Middle Turnpike, Manchester. Formerly The Pines, the estate of a prominent Manchester industrialist, this 215-acre park straddles the East Hartford–Manchester border, with a variety of gardens, wooded areas, ponds, picnic area, playgrounds, aviary, sports facilities, walking trails.

LODGING

BED & BREAKFASTS

In addition to the listings below, a number of bed & breakfast reservation services offer access to rooms available in establishments throughout the state. For a list, see *What's Where—Bed & Breakfasts.*

Butternut Farm (860-633-7197), 1654 Main Street, Glastonbury 06033. Welcome to the 18th century: a 1720 homestead furnished with period antiques. Host Don Reid (a superb cook and model innkeeper) will give you a tour of the livestock if you wish—prizewinning goats, pigeons, chickens. There are five guest rooms, including one apartment, and two suites (with fireplaces), all strictly New England in character and appearance. Eight fireplaces, an herb garden, imaginatively landscaped grounds. A full breakfast is served, featuring homegrown eggs and other treats, in the original colonial kitchen. Rates $70–90.

✐ **Cumon Inn** (860-644-8486), 130 Buckland Road, South Windsor 06074. The Krawski family has opened its working farm to those seeking a peaceful country setting. A rustic Colonial reproduction saltbox has eight guest rooms that share six baths. The 20-acre grounds include orchards, a birch grove, and 100-miles views. Children and some pets (there's a barn and paddock for horses, and a kennel for dogs and cats) are welcome. A full country breakfast featuring homegrown ingredients is served. $50–100.

Old Mill Inn (860-763-1473), 63 Maple Street (CT 190), Somersville 06072. This three-story Greek Revival home, built in the mid-19th century, has been enlarged and a roomy sunporch added. Guests have a choice of king- or full-size beds; some baths are shared. A gourmet breakfast is served, and in the evening guests enjoy hors d'oeuvres and wine. There's a pond and a Jacuzzi in the back, a game room with TV, fitness room, and a comfortable parlor with hardwood floors and fireplace. Six rooms for guests, continental or full breakfast available. Rooms with king beds $95; full-size, $85.

✐ **Udderly Woolly Acres** (860-633-4503), 581 Thompson Street, Glastonbury 06033. Share in the life of a 20-acre working farm: The 1820 farmhouse is authentic but comfortable. The generous breakfast would adequately fuel the most energetic of farmhands. Suite with private bath, $75; two

smaller rooms (available only if suite is rented) with shared bath, $45.

  ᜪ **The Watson House** (860-282-8888), 1876 Main Street, South Windsor 06074. A circa-1788 Palladian mansion in the historic district, an area so charming that, after a visit, John Adams was inspired to pen in his diary, "Today I rode through paradise." The two guest rooms and one suite all have working fireplace, private bath, TV, and phone. Full breakfast. $95–125.

WHERE TO EAT

DINING OUT

  ᜪ **Cavey's** (860-643-2751), 45 East Center Street, Manchester. Serves lunch and dinner; closed Sunday and Monday. Cavey's is ambitious and successful on two levels—Italian cuisine upstairs, French downstairs. Many believe this is the best: The service is authoritative, the food exquisite, the surroundings suitably tasteful. Reservations recommended. The French restaurant is the more expensive, although neither is cheap. Choice of à la carte or prix fixe menu in the French venue. An all-vegetable prix fixe menu—a superb blend of textures and tastes— requires 24-hour advance notice. À la carte entrées—seasonal choices of seafood, meat, fowl—are $23–30; prix fixe (three courses), $55. In the Italian restaurant upstairs, equally creative northern Italian cuisine can be found—risotto, veal wonders, game entrées; the menu changes seasonally. Italian entrées $16–19.

Main and Hopewell (860-633-8698), corner of Main and Hopewell, South Glastonbury. One of those 200-year-old structures that convey authentic New England—candles on the tables, exposed beams overhead. Standard American steaks and roasts, and novel but sound treatments of both meat and seafood. **The Pub** offers informal dining and live jazz on weekend nights. Serves lunch Tuesday through Friday; dinner Tuesday through Sunday. Reservations are a good idea. Entrées up to $22.

  ᜪ **Max Amore** (860-659-2819), 140 Glastonbury Boulevard (Somerset Square), Glastonbury. Open daily for lunch and dinner, except on Sunday, when there's dinner only, 5–9. "Lite" menu served 2:30–5 daily. Full bar; good wines. One of a family of Max restaurants in central Connecticut, all loosely Italian but each with its own flair. This one, in an upscale shopping center, features stone pies with wild toppings—for instance, goat cheese, mozzarella, Parmesan, fontina, tomato, prosciutto, and red onions; or another with escarole and mashed potato, dotted with pancetta, wild mushrooms, and mozzarella. There is a special "per Bambini" edition with tomato sauce and mozzarella for the under-10 crowd. Pastas are equally inventive, as are seafood, vegetarian, poultry, and meat entrées. A daily special is listed on the menu, and the waiter will outline others. Entrées $12–18; stone pies are under $10.

  ᜪ **Somers Inn** (860-749-2256), 585 Main Street, Somers. Serves lunch Tuesday through Friday; dinner Tuesday through Sunday, as well as Sunday brunch; closed Monday. Reservations are a good idea. Facing a major intersection in the center of Somers, the inn announces its existence since 1769: It looks important, and in this part of the state it is. No longer offering lodging, it comforts the traveler with good food. The menu is comprehensive if not lengthy, featuring all-American favorites—lobster, shrimp, and other seafood; roast prime rib; pork and lamb chops; roast duckling; veal. Appetizers may be stuffed mushrooms, escargots, cherrystones, or a fresh fruit cup. Entrées $15–22. Lunch under $13.

EATING OUT

The Eatery (860-627-7094), 297 South Main Street, East Windsor. Open for lunch Monday through Friday; dinner Monday through Saturday. Full bar. Reservations suggested. The Eatery has a distinctly elegant tone, part New England manor house, part American cuisine. The menu offers solid favorites like American rack of lamb along with some unusual creations, such as stuffed filet mignon and potato-crusted salmon. Appetizers include grilled bruschetta with mozzarella and basil. Lobster bisque, French onion soup, and good old New England clam chowder are among the soups offered. Entrées $13–22.

& **John Harvard's Brewhouse** (860-644-2739), 1487 Pleasant Valley Road, Manchester. Open daily, this is the Connecticut version of an English pub, complete with a vague allusion to a beer recipe with a connection to W. Shakespeare. Legends aside, the food is sturdy, tasty, and traditional: bangers and mash even, with homemade sausages and chicken pie. Entrées around $10.

& **Jonathan Pasco's** (860-627-7709), 31 South Main Street, East Windsor. Open daily, serving dinner only, except brunch on Sunday. Named for an officer in Washington's army in the Revolutionary War, the house, a late-18th-century brick, has been refurbished but preserved. The bar and half-dozen dining rooms in the original house are cozy and intimate. You can dine fireside in winter, or on the patio in summertime. The menu includes steaks from the grill, Cajun-inspired pork chops, seafood in many presentations, chicken, and pastas plain and fancy. $11–20.

The Lotus (860-871-8962), 409 Hartford Turnpike (CT 30), Vernon. Open Tuesday through Saturday for lunch 11:30–2; dinner 5–9. Closed Sunday and Monday. In a suitably serene dining room, Vietnamese cuisine is presented in impeccable style. Lemongrass chicken is surrounded by fresh-cooked onions, carrots, green peppers, and lemongrass, and zinged with chili peppers. The seafood basket contains shrimp, scallops, and crabmeat stir-fried with vegetables, served in a basket of deep-fried matchstick potatoes. Reservations suggested. Dinner entrées are under $15.

& **Mill on the River** (860-289-7929), 989 Ellington Road (CT 30), South Windsor. Open Monday through Friday for lunch, daily for dinner; brunch on Sunday. Full bar. Reservations are a good idea. A big, sprawling building—indeed, once a gristmill—with choice seating overlooking the millstream. A local favorite for romantic dining, there's also a greenhouse overlooking the millpond. Specialties from the very large menu include blackened swordfish, sauerbraten, and redfish nouvelle, blackened and topped with Mornay sauce, shrimp, scallops, and spinach—the house signature dish. There are chicken, beef, and pasta entrées as well. Chocolate mousse cake and tiramisu are among the desserts. Entrées are around $15.

☞&✐**Rein's New York Style Deli** (860-875-1344), 435 Hartford Turnpike (CT 30), in the "Shops at 30" plaza, Vernon. Open daily 7 AM–midnight, for breakfast, lunch, and dinner. Full bar. They seat and serve you in a New York minute, and start you off with crisp garlic pickles. At a word from you they pile savory pastrami or corned beef on rye, layer hand-cut lox onto cream-cheese-laden bagels, and tempt you with blintzes until you think you're in Manhattan. The menu is long and light-hearted: borscht, chopped liver, roll mop, noodle pudding, knishes; also tuna melts and peanut butter and jelly. Famous for breakfast combos. Be prepared for a line if you go at mealtime (regulars travel across the state to dine here), but it moves fast. The cheesecake and cold cuts are superb. Moderate prices: sandwiches around $5; omelets around $5; entrées under $10.

☞   **Saigon Restaurant** (860-528-2722), 242 Burnside Avenue (US 44), East Hartford. Open Monday through Saturday for lunch and dinner. Closed Sunday. Don't let the unassuming tiny brick storefront fool you: From an even tinier kitchen comes Vietnamese cuisine that gets rave reviews from a loyal following. Entrées around $7.

Silvia's (860-741-6969), 32 Pleasant Street, Enfield. Open Tuesday through Saturday for lunch and dinner; serving beer and wine. Silvia is Romanian, and her soups are both aromatic and legendary. Sauerkraut, Romanian sausage, kielbasa, schnitzel, pork, chicken—lots of choices and hearty portions, intriguing spices. Dessert selections include fruit-filled cakes. Dinners including soup, salad, and dessert are around $12.

SNACKS

&☞**Natural Rhythms** (860-645-9898), 964 Main Street, Manchester. Open Monday through Saturday for lunch and dinner; closed Sunday. When cardiologist Stephen Sinatra couldn't find a lunch spot with healthy cuisine, he opened this cheery health food store/café. Several soups, sandwiches, and entrées are offered daily, all low in sodium, cholesterol, and fat, and many are vegan, meaning no eggs or dairy products. Complete line of health food products and vitamins. Sandwiches around $4; entrées around $5.

ENTERTAINMENT

MUSIC

Manchester Band Shell (860-647-8811; 860-646-4900), campus of Manchester Community College, 60 Bidwell Street, Manchester. The Manchester Bicentennial Bandshell Corp. sponsors a summertime series of concerts and presentations by a wide variety of instrumentalists and singers, with programs several nights a week. Call for information about schedules.

THEATER
Little Theatre of Manchester/Cheney Hall (860-647-9824), 177 Hartford Road, Manchester. Plays produced in March, May, and November; a year-round performing arts series features jazz, folk, world music, dance, and family programs. Call for schedule.

SELECTIVE SHOPPING

ANTIQUES SHOPS
Hazardville Antique Center (860-763-0811), 287 Hazard Avenue (CT 190), Enfield. Furniture, jewelry, glassware, toys, silver, and other collectibles.

Scantic Country Barn (860-623-5327), 169 Wells Road, East Windsor. Three levels of country antiques, crafts, and gifts in a converted 1798 barn.

Somers Shoppes (860-749-6197), CT 183, south of Somers Center, Somers. More than 20 shopkeepers offering antiques, folk art, gourmet foods, equestrian art, and so on.

Tobacco Shed Antiques (860-657-2885), 119 Griswold Street, Glastonbury. Forty dealers; antiques and collectibles.

BOOKSTORE
Books & Birds (860-649-3449), 519 East Middle Turnpike (US 6 and 44), Manchester. Buy, sell, old, new, used, antique—virtually any book on any subject is here, along with a special interest in decoys and bird art. A warehouse of a place, with shelves higher than you can reach, and stacks that go on forever. They will search for out-of-print books.

FACTORY OUTLETS
Cohoes Common (860-623-2591), 10 Prospect Hill Terrace (off US 5), East Windsor. Open daily. Two outlets: Cohoes is an attractive store, especially for a factory outlet, offering "top designer" menswear and womenswear. Cohoes Kids has clothing and items for children.

JCPenney Outlet Store (860-647-1143), exit 62 off I-84, Manchester. Regular merchandise reduced 25–75 percent.

FARMS AND GARDENS
Fish Family Farm Creamery and Dairy Farm (860-646-9745), 20 Dimock Lane, Bolton. Tractor-drawn hayrides in fall by appointment. Tours of the farm, where milk is pasteurized and bottled on the premises; homemade ice cream.

Rose's Berry Farm (860-633-7467), 295 Matson Hill Road, South Glastonbury. South Glastonbury is known as a prime spot for raising fruit, and many orchards and berry patches remain. Here's a good chance to pick your own strawberries, raspberries, blueberries, and, later in the season, pumpkins and Christmas trees. Seasonal hayrides, country store, Christmas shop.

Udderly Woolly Acres (860-633-4503), 581 Thompson Street, Glastonbury. An 1820 homestead on 20 pastoral acres with farm-fresh produce, milk, eggs, and cheese. Kids will love the sheep, goats, and geese. (See *Lodging—Bed & Breakfasts*.)

SPECIAL SHOP

✎ **New England Hobby Center** (860-646-0610), 71 Hilliard Street, Manchester. Open daily year-round. Specializes in model railroad equipment and layout materials and in dollhouse furnishings. On the first and third Sundays of each month, 2:30–4, the Silk City Model Railroad Club invites you to marvel at a mega-layout and watch the trains run. All this occurs in the building where Bon Ami cleanser was originally made.

SPECIAL EVENTS

July: **Podunk Bluegrass Music Festival** (860-282-7577), East Hartford.

September: **Chili Festival** at the Four Town Fairgrounds, Somers. **Four Town Agricultural Fair,** Somers. **Wapping Agricultural Fair** (860-644-8989), Rye Street Park, South Windsor. Know what a wapping is? Find out here.

October: **Apple Harvest Festival** (860-659-3587), on the Hubbard green, Glastonbury.

Thanksgiving Day: **Manchester Road Race** (860-649-6456), Manchester. More than 10,000 runners in the second oldest race in the East.

November–December: **Holidayfest** in Connecticut's North Central Tourism Bureau (860-763-2578); see *Guidance*. Open houses, special events in historic homes, trolley rides, visits with Santa, and more.

IV. THE QUIET CORNER

The Villages of Northeastern Connecticut

KIMBERLY GRANT

Working dairy farms are still a common sight in the Quiet Corner.

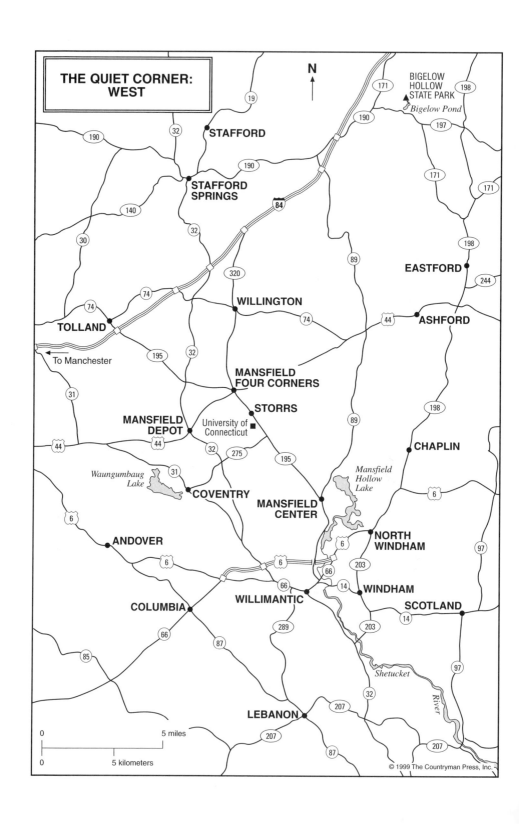

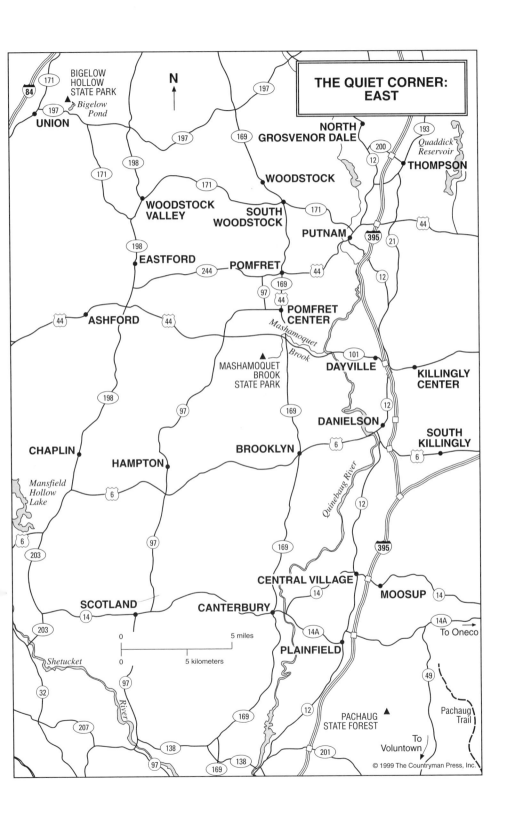

N

BIGELOW
HOLLOW
STATE PARK
▲ *Bigelow
Pond*

THE QUIET CORNER:
EAST

84
171
197

UNION

197

198

171

198

EASTFORD

244

POMFRET

97

44

169

197

169
NORTH
GROSVENOR DALE

WOODSTOCK

WOODSTOCK
VALLEY

SOUTH
WOODSTOCK

171

171

200
12

193
*Quaddick
Reservoir*

THOMPSON

44

PUTNAM

395
21

12

44

POMFRET
CENTER

*Mashamoquet
Brook*

101

DAYVILLE

KILLINGLY
CENTER

44

ASHFORD

44

MASHAMOQUET
BROOK
STATE PARK ▲

198

97

169

12

DANIELSON

6

SOUTH
KILLINGLY

6

CHAPLIN

HAMPTON

BROOKLYN

*Mansfield
Hollow
Lake*

6

97

6
203

97

169

12

395

CENTRAL VILLAGE

14

MOOSUP

14

SCOTLAND

14

CANTERBURY

14

14A
To Oneco

203

0   5 miles

0   5 kilometers

14A

PLAINFIELD

49

32

97

Shetucket

207

138

97

169

River

138

169

12

PACHAUG
STATE FOREST ▲

201

To
Voluntown

Pachaug
Trail

© 1999 The Countryman Press, Inc.

The Villages of
Northeastern Connecticut

If there's a part of Connecticut that can be considered undiscovered, the aptly named Quiet Corner is it. One way to savor the quiet is by means of CT 169, the scenic road that runs north to south through peaceful towns, abundant orchards, and meadows dotted with cattle and horses. Along the way you spot 250-year-old, center-chimney houses still at home in the dappled light of changing times. The area is a perfect setting for prep school campuses—Pomfret School and The Rectory in Pomfret on US 44, and Marianapolis in the center of Thompson. While there are no large hotels or motels, you will find a profusion of B&Bs, the lodgings best suited to the neighborly character of the region.

This is the Connecticut of long ago—its big events took place in earlier centuries. There was the local hero, Israel Putnam, the tough old co-commander at Bunker Hill: "Men, you are all marksmen; don't fire until you see the white [sic] of their eyes!"—did he say that? You'd better believe it in northeastern Connecticut. Left his plow in the furrow there in Brooklyn when the news came of Lexington and Concord. Old Put had fought with the British in the French and Indian Wars, escaped burning at the stake, helped capture Havana. After Bunker Hill he commanded colonial troops on Long Island and in the Hudson Highlands, evaded the Redcoats in Greenwich, survived a brutal winter with his troops at the Redding encampment known as Putnam's Valley Forge, and finally retired to run a tavern back at home. And all of this happened long after he crawled into the dark cave to kill the she-wolf that was decimating local sheep herds.

Speaking of history, the Quiet Corner has the distinction of serving as home for both the state hero, Nathan Hale, and the state heroine, Prudence Crandall. The town of Coventry was the birthplace of Hale, the patriot-spy whose only regret was that he had but one life to lose for his country. In Canterbury, 30 years before the start of the Civil War, Miss Prudence Crandall defied popular opinion by admitting young black women to the school she ran in her home. Miss Crandall was vilified and arrested; her home-school was attacked by angry neighbors; and eventually she was run out of town. A series of legal actions ultimately vindicated her, and she has recently been named the state's official heroine. Still more pictures from the past: The sleepy town of Lebanon hosted General Washington numerous times, and the French general Rochambeau, on his march across the state to meet Cornwallis, paused for a brief respite on Lebanon's green.

Prosperity visited eastern Connecticut in the 19th century, as textile manufacturers found ways to harness the region's abundant water-power. They turned out cotton, silk, and thread in abundance, but when the mills began to move south, the huge mill buildings were left empty, challenging developers to find new uses. Indeed, some of the mills have been imaginatively converted into housing and office space. Good examples of mill architecture stand along the Quinebaug River in Putnam, Killingly, Plainfield, Wauregan, and Central Village, and on the Willimantic and Natchaug in Willimantic.

The manufacturing interests are long gone, for the most part; the hills, still crisscrossed with stone walls, are green again; and the towns no longer tell time by the mill whistle. For the visitor, northeastern Connecticut feels remote and relaxing. It seems to be—and perhaps is—designed for hiking, fishing, and history. A look at some of the Quiet Corner towns provides a sampler for visitors.

Coventry benefits from both history and geography: You can visit the home of Nathan Hale's family and walk in the neighboring forest named for the official state hero. There is open space and farmland here, the scenic interest of New England hills, and a lake with an ancient name, Waungumbaug. Coventry is known for its self-styled good witch, the late Adelma Grenier Simmons, whose Caprilands Herb Farm has put the town on the map for gardeners and herbalists world-wide. For a small town, Coventry has a generous selection of restaurants and unique shops, a good bookstore, and, to help you find your way around, a Visitors Information Center staffed by the local historical society. If you explore the village area, you'll discover the streams and falls that powered the mills here, and, at Patriot's Park, an impressive monument to Nathan Hale. And maybe you'll pass the yard where a piecework quilt is draped over the owner's precious motorcycle.

Lebanon has as long a green as any town can seriously claim— 1 country mile top to bottom, along CT 87. If you're a walker, go ahead and stretch your legs on the new walkway; it's the way to get acquainted with Lebanon's New England identity. The green was the site of an encampment of Hussars under the Duc de Lauzun in the winter of 1780–1781, awaiting Rochambeau and his troops for the final push of the Revolutionary War. The reason they picked Lebanon was not so much the size of the green as the fact that facing it was the home of Jonathan Trumbull, royal governor of the colony, who sided with the Continentals. He was, in fact, the only colonial governor to do so. Referred to as "Brother Jonathan" by Washington, Trumbull proved a valuable source of supplies. During the winter of 1780, Connecticut sent some 3,000 barrels of pork and 1,500 barrels of beef to feed the starving troops. Washington wrote in his diary, "No other man than Trumbull would have procured them and no other state could have furnished them." Connecticut was Washington's "Provision State." In the War Office, a modest two-room frame building, Washington, Lafayette, Rochambeau, Adams, Jay, Benjamin Franklin, and other dignitaries gathered to plan strategy and decide on ways and means. The artist John Trumbull, whose paintings of historic Revolutionary War scenes grace not only the halls of Congress in Washington but also the nation's one-dollar bills, was a son of Governor Trumbull. The Trumbull homes and the War Office are open to visitors, as are other historic sites in town. William Williams, one of the signers of the Declaration of Independence, was also a native of Lebanon. A new large museum is planned for the green to tell Lebanon's story.

Putnam, one of the area's busier towns, was named for Gen. Israel Putnam, and reportedly served as a stop on the Underground Railroad in pre–Civil War times. The city's peak of activity came with the water-powered textile mills: One of the largest silk thread factories in the country operated here into the 1940s. While the milldam and Cargill Falls in the center of town, and the railroad station up the hill, now serve only as reminders of an industrial past, new interests have seen Putnam's potential. The town has become a center for antiques buyers and sellers, with a dozen or more shops—several representing many dealers—clustered downtown. Along with the dealers have come restaurateurs and operators of numerous bed & breakfasts to encourage the dedicated browser to settle in.

Tolland presents the visitor with an idyllic green, ringed by the white-clapboard houses associated with New England towns, as well as some striking Victorian gems. Among them are the Congregational church, a historic home open to visitors, a souvenir and gift shop, the old jail museum, the town library, a research library devoted to French Canadian settlers in this country, and a charming B&B. Through the summer and into fall, the green—less than a mile from the interstate—is the setting for crafts shows, rallies, pancake breakfasts, and other town events.

Woodstock has a quiet presence, with most of its area devoted to farms. As you drive north on scenic CT 169, look sharp and you'll see, on your right, close to the road, a one-room stone schoolhouse that operated from 1745 to 1946—the longest run in the country. In the mid-19th century, when wealthy city dwellers began to look for summertime respite from the heat and bustle, northeastern Connecticut became a resort area. Henry Bowen, publisher of the *Independent*—an influential abolitionist weekly edited for a time by Henry Ward Beecher—chose Woodstock as the site of his summer "cottage." Roseland, now open to the public, appears frequently in guidebooks on American domestic architecture as an outstanding example of the carpenter Gothic style. The scenic road also takes you past many antiques shops, a grand country inn, several orchards, and the local fairgrounds, where one of the state's best-known and -attended country fairs is held each Labor Day weekend.

Entries in this section are arranged in alphabetical order.

AREA CODE
860

GUIDANCE

Northeast Connecticut's Quiet Corner (860-928-1228; fax 860-928-4720; Web site: www.webtravels.com/quietcorner; e-mail: quietcorner@snet.net), PO Box 598, Putnam 06260. This district, which includes *most* of the towns discussed in this section, publishes guides to lodgings, attractions, restaurants, events, and antiques and crafts shops, as well as a calendar of events, a bicycling guide, and a list of "learning vacations" (B&B packages that incorporate how-to sessions of various kinds). For fishing enthusiasts, the district publishes *The Waters of the Quinebaug and Shetucket Rivers Heritage Corridor*, with complete information on the ponds, lakes, streams, and rivers of the northeastern corner of the state, and on the activities— canoeing, swimming, hiking, and fishing—permitted at or on each.

The towns of Andover and Tolland are part of the **Greater Hartford Region** (860-244-8181), One Civic Center Plaza, Hartford 06103. The remaining town, Stafford, is in **Connecticut's North Central Tourism Bureau** (860-763-2578; 1-800-248-8283), 111 Hazard Avenue, Enfield 06082. Both districts publish informative materials and will supply them on request.

Coventry Visitors Center (860-742-1085) on Main Street, CT 31. Housed in a picturesque 1876 redbrick building, first a post office and later the local probate court, the center is open mid-May through mid-October, Monday through Friday 10–2, Saturday and Sunday 10–3. Local maps, directions, folders, and suggestions are all provided by friendly staff.

GETTING THERE

By car: Major routes into the area are I-395, which connects I-95, the shoreline route, with the Massachusetts Turnpike, running north–south through eastern Connecticut; and I-84, which connects New York (through Hartford) with the Massachusetts Turnpike in Sturbridge, Massachusetts, running in a northeasterly direction through the district. US 6 and US 44 are good connectors, linking Hartford and Providence, US 44 being the more northerly route.

By bus: **Bonanza Bus Lines** (401-331-7500) makes scheduled stops in Willimantic (860-456-0440) and Danielson (860-779-2704; 860-774-7512) on runs connecting Providence and New York. **Arrow Bus**

(1-800-243-9560) serves Willimantic from Hartford. Mostly it's a charter company.

GETTING AROUND

Colchester Cab (860-423-5700) serves Colchester, Willimantic, Norwich, and surrounding towns.

Community Cab (860-774-9484) serves Putnam, Pomfret, Danielson, Killingly, Ashford, Thompson, and other northeastern towns, 6 AM–10 PM.

MEDICAL EMERGENCY

The statewide emergency number is **911.**

Day-Kimball Hospital (860-928-6541), 320 Pomfret Street, Putnam.

Johnson Memorial Hospital (860-684-4251), 201 Chestnut Hill Road, Stafford Springs.

Manchester Memorial Hospital (860-646-1222), 71 Haynes Street, Manchester.

Windham Hospital (860-456-9116), 112 Mansfield Avenue, Willimantic.

TO SEE

COLLEGES

Eastern Connecticut State University (860-465-5000), 83 Windham Street, Willimantic. A small and friendly campus, with concerts and theater productions, sports events, and art exhibits scheduled throughout the academic year. The new **Akus Art Gallery,** in Shafer Hall, is open Wednesday, Thursday, and Friday 11–5. Call or write for information.

University of Connecticut (860-486-1001; 860-486-3530), main campus, CT 195, Storrs. Spread over more than 3,000 acres and offering a full range of academic study, the university campus, fields, and barns appeal to visitors as well as students and scholars. As you approach the campus, a sign will direct you to University Parking Services. Stop in to pick up a parking permit, campus map, and other information. The attendants will advise you on the best routes to reach the buildings you want to see. (If you come on the weekend, you can pick up maps at the Student Union or the library.) Some of your choices are: **Gampel Pavilion,** the new facility where the basketball Huskies have been generating excitement—particularly the women's team, which won 35 straight games in the 1994–95 season and captured the NCAA championship. They have continued their winning ways ever since, just short of the national title. For information on sports events, call 860-486-5050. A short distance east of the sports arena is the **Homer Babbidge Library,** with close to 2 million volumes. Opposite the library is the **UConn Co-op,** source of books of all sorts and campus souvenirs: T-shirts, sweats, baseball caps, mugs, totes. For tree fanciers, the university offers a publication, *A Tree-Walking Tour, University of Connecticut.* To get a copy, call the Department of Ecology and

Evolutionary Biology at 860-486-4322. In the center of the campus, in the Wilbur Cross Building, look for the Connecticut State Museum of Natural History, especially if you've brought along youngsters (see *Museums*). The William Benton Museum of Art (see *Museums*) features changing exhibits devoted to Connecticut-based artists. The **Atrium Gallery** in the Fine Arts Building shows contemporary art. You may want to inquire about what's on at Jorgensen Auditorium (see *Entertainment*) and the **Von der Mehden Recital Hall,** which present programs through the year—music, dance, and drama. Off in another direction, on the other side of CT 195 just south of Parking Services, are the **Floriculture Greenhouses,** a wonderland of plants and flowers, open weekends when classes are in session. On down the road you can take the children to visit the **Kellogg Dairy Barn** (there's a short video on milking and cow-tending), and last but often foremost, the Dairy Bar (see *Snacks*), with ice cream that is simply the best, according to on-campus experts. See the appropriate listings below for details on these campus attractions.

MUSEUMS

Brayton Grist Mill & Marcy Blacksmith Museum, US 44 at the entrance to Mashamoquet Brook State Park, Pomfret (see *Hiking* and *Green Space*). May through September, Saturday and Sunday 2–5. Free admission. Billed as the last mill in Pomfret. Here's a chance to see the machinery that milled the grain into flour for our forebears. Also an exhibit of blacksmithing tools used by a local family for three generations.

Connecticut State Museum of Natural History (860-486-4460), Wilbur Cross Building, University of Connecticut campus, CT 195, Storrs. Open year-round, Monday, Thursday, Friday, and Saturday noon–4; Sunday 1–4. Free admission. Exhibits cover Connecticut's Native Americans and a variety of birds, butterflies, mammals, and insects. Lectures, family activities, field trips, and other activities are scheduled. Call for information.

Mansfield Historical Society Museum (860-429-6575), 954 Storrs Road (CT 195), Mansfield. June through September, Thursday and Sunday 1:30–4:30. Donation. Mansfield's former (1843) Town Hall and adjacent office building now house the museum and library facilities of the historical society. Changing exhibits showcase clothing, furnishings, and other items—photographs and decorative objects. In the library are documents on local history and genealogy, emphasizing 19th-century town life.

New England Center for Contemporary Art (860-774-8899), CT 169, Brooklyn. Open May through November, Tuesday through Sunday 1–5. Free admission. One man's lifework, the center's gallery, in a refurbished barn, is devoted to the works of living artists around the world. Exhibits change every six to eight weeks. On permanent display, according to museum founder Henry Riseman, is the largest collection of contemporary Chinese art anywhere outside China.

KIMBERLY GRANT

The Prudence Crandall House, a National Historic Landmark, was the site of the first academy in New England to accept an African American woman.

Old Tolland Jail Museum (860-875-9599; 860-875-3544), Tolland green, junction of CT 74 and CT 195, Tolland. Open mid-May through mid-October, Sunday 1–4. Donation. The iron bars still clang shut on the cells (the jail was in use until 1968), and the form of a prisoner under the gray blanket on a narrow cot lends authenticity. Other displays feature the local historical society's collection of furniture, farm tools, and Native American artifacts.

Prudence Crandall House (860-546-9916; 860-566-3005), at the junction of CT 14 and CT 169, Canterbury. Open mid-January through mid-December, Wednesday through Sunday 10–4:30. Adults $2; children and seniors $1. This was New England's first academy to accept African American women, in 1833–1834. A handsome 1805 home fronted with a fine Palladian window, the house is famous as the site of a dramatic confrontation over racial issues some 30 years before the Civil War. Prudence Crandall, a Baptist schoolmistress, opened a school for girls here in 1831. She later accepted among her students a young black woman, precipitating an angry response from both townspeople and the families of her other students. When Miss Crandall stood her ground, the school was stoned and finally closed, and she was arrested and held overnight in prison. Released the next day on a technicality, she and her husband left the state and settled in Kansas. When she was in her old age, Mark Twain, then a resident of Hartford, urged her to return to Connecticut. She declined. The Connecticut Legislature thereupon awarded her a lifetime stipend.

A portion of the house is furnished as it would have been in the 1830s, and a permanent display covers the story of the woman who has been named state heroine. Changing exhibits deal with topics suggested by Prudence Crandall's struggle: African American history, women's history, and local history. The house is a National Historic Landmark.

William Benton Museum of Art (860-486-4520), University of Connecticut, 245 Glenbrook Road, main campus (CT 195), Storrs. Open Tuesday through Friday 10–4:30, Saturday and Sunday 1–4:30; closed major holidays and during some college recesses. Free admission. A small space but the scene of excellent exhibits, many featuring Connecticut artists and movements. The permanent collection includes European and American paintings, drawings, prints, and sculptures, 16th century to the present. The shop has a variety of books, toys, and giftware.

Windham Textile and History Museum (860-456-2178), 157 Union Street, corner of Main (CT 66), Willimantic. Open Friday, Saturday, and Sunday 1–5, and by appointment. The museum that tells the story of the textile industry in this part of the state occupies a building that belonged to the Willimantic Thread Company, one of the (former) giants of the industry. Along with changing exhibits are displays on mill operations—showing machinery used in making thread—and the homes of workers—showing typical rooms in workers' and managers' houses. The gift shop has articles reminiscent of 19th-century life and the industry that flourished here.

HISTORIC HOMES

Benton Homestead (860-870-9599), Metcalf Road, Tolland. Open May through mid-October, Sunday 1–4. Donation. A 1720 center-chimney Colonial, remarkably preserved; low ceilings, original paneling, and a history of Hessian prisoners kept in the cellar during the Revolutionary War.

Dr. William Beaumont House (860-642-6744), on the Lebanon green, Lebanon. This is a modest 1760 "cottage" and the birthplace of the "father of the physiology of digestion." Open May 15 through October 15, Saturday 1–5. Donation. While caring for soldiers during the Revolutionary War, Beaumont pioneered studies of digestion by inserting a glass window in the stomach of a wounded man; he watched the digestive process through it for years. Displays of early surgical instruments instill an appreciation of current medical practice. The Lebanon green itself is remarkable, being nearly a mile long and still held and mowed in common by the householders who live adjacent to it.

Hicks-Stearns Museum (860-875-7552), 42 Tolland Green, Tolland. Open mid-May through mid-October, Sunday and Wednesday 1–4. Donation. Recording changes in taste, this house was originally a Colonial and over time was transformed into a Victorian home with such improvements as taller windows, a wide veranda, and an ornamental turret. Furnishings are family heirlooms, mostly 19th-century pieces. Summer concerts are held on the lawn.

Jillson House Museum (860-456-2316), 627 Main Street, Willimantic. Open July and August, Sunday 2–4 and by appointment. Built from

Roseland Cottage is a gem of the carpenter Gothic Revival style.

stone quarried nearby, this was the home of a mill owner (1825), and is furnished in keeping with his position. Besides changing exhibits, the house contains local memorabilia and period artifacts.

Jonathan Trumbull House (860-642-7558), 169 West Town Street (CT 87), Lebanon. Open May 15 through October 15, Tuesday through Saturday 1–5. Adults $2; children under 12 free. In 1776, at the outset of the Revolutionary War, Jonathan Trumbull had been governor of the colony of Connecticut for seven years. He was the only colonial governor to defy the Crown and support the War of Independence. He continued in office until 1784. His home, on the Lebanon green, was built in 1735 and is furnished with period pieces.

Jonathan Trumbull Jr. House (860-642-6100), another stop on the Lebanon green, just down the way from the Trumbull homestead. Open May 15 through October 15, Saturday and Sunday 1–5. Adults $1; children under 15 free. Built in 1769, this is a foursquare example of a center-chimney farmhouse, boasting eight corner fireplaces.

Nathan Hale Homestead (860-742-6917; 860-247-8996), 2299 South Street (off US 44), Coventry. Open May 15 through October 15, daily 1–5. Adults $4; children $1. Ironically, Nathan Hale never lived in the house, although he was born on this site. Nathan, whose five brothers also fought in the war, was already in the Continental Army in 1776 when the present house was built by his father, Deacon Richard Hale. Period furnishings include memorabilia of the patriot-spy, whose only regret was that he had but one life to lose for his country.

Roseland Cottage (860-928-4074), CT 169, Woodstock. Open Memorial Day through Labor Day, Wednesday through Sunday noon–5; Labor Day to mid-October, Friday through Sunday noon–5. Tours on the hour; last tour at 3. Adults $4; children under 12, $2; under 5 free; seniors $3.50. A perfect gem of the carpenter Gothic Revival style, with crockets, pointed arches, and stained-glass windows. Built in 1845 by wealthy New York publisher and avid abolitionist Henry Bowen as a summer home, it shares the property with formal gardens, a summer-house, a vintage bowling alley, an icehouse, and an aviary. Bowen loved roses: The cottage is painted a wild and rosy pink, and the garden between the residence and the carriage house features his chosen flower. Bowen also loved the Fourth of July: His annual celebrations included fireworks and refreshments for the town and visits by every US president from Grant through McKinley.

The Strong-Porter House Museum (860-742-7847), 2382 South Street, Coventry. Open mid-May through mid-October, weekends only, 1–5. Adults $1; children free. Joint admission to Strong-Porter and Nathan Hale homes is also available. A staff of volunteers maintains this near neighbor of the Nathan Hale Homestead. Half the large frame farmhouse dates from circa 1730 and was built by a great-uncle of Nathan Hale, Aaron Strong. On the grounds and open to visitors are a carpenter's shop, carriage shed, and barn.

HISTORIC SITES

Daniel Putnam Tyler Law Office (860-774-7728), CT 169, Brooklyn. Open Memorial Day through Labor Day, Wednesday and Sunday 1–5. Free admission. Furnished as it would have been in the mid-19th century for use by a small-town lawyer. The lawyer, a great-grandson of Revolutionary War hero Gen. Israel Putnam, became clerk of the county and superior courts and a county court judge, and he also held state elective offices.

Gurleyville Grist Mill (860-429-9023), Stone Mill Road, Storrs. Open late May to Sunday of Columbus Day weekend and by appointment. (The office is open Thursdays 1:30–3:30, or leave a message for a return call.)

Free admission. A mill has stood on this site since 1720. The existing structure and machinery are of 19th-century vintage; the mill is said to be the state's only remaining stone gristmill. The miller's house nearby is open as a museum of local history. Wilbur Cross—author, Yale professor of literature, and governor of the state during the 1930s—once lived here.

Revolutionary War Office (860-449-1110), on the green, Lebanon, near the Trumbull House. Open Saturday from May 30 to the last Saturday in September, 1:30–5; May 30 through August 31, Sunday 1:30–4. Free admission. General Washington, Governor Trumbull, and other key officials met here periodically to plan strategy. Before the war, this simple structure served as the Trumbull family store. Nutmeggers call it the "Pentagon of the Revolution."

Wadsworth Stable, on the green, Lebanon, near the Trumbull House. Surely the only structure to claim that George Washington's *horse* slept there. The stable was brought to Lebanon from Hartford, where Revolutionary partisan Jeremiah Wadsworth lived. He and Trumbull managed Connecticut's major contribution to the war effort—the supply of provisions to Washington's Continental troops. Washington referred to Trumbull as "Brother Jonathan" and to Connecticut as the "Provision State." For admission, inquire at the Jonathan Trumbull House.

TROUT HATCHERY

Quinebaug Valley Trout Hatchery (860-564-7542), Cady Lane off CT 14, Central Village. The visitors center is open daily 10–4. Free admission. Here visitors can glimpse the scale (no pun) of the job of making sure there will be trout in the state's rivers and ponds for all fishing enthusiasts. A special visitors pond allows you to view various species. Two fishing ponds (open March through May) and a third for children (open mid-April through September) provide the opportunity to drop in a line.

WINERY

Nutmeg Vineyard (860-742-8402), 800 Bunker Hill Road (off US 6), Coventry. Telephone before you visit to make sure the winery is open and to get directions. The blue-gray barn is at the end of a steep, mile-long ascent. Visitors are offered tours and tastes on weekends. This is a small but well-established vineyard, with wine made by old-fashioned methods. Varieties include reds and whites as well as fruit wines—raspberry and strawberry.

SCENIC DRIVE

CT 169, the north–south route from Norwich into Massachusetts, takes you through farmland and hilly wooded areas interspersed with villages seemingly untouched by time—Canterbury, Brooklyn, Pomfret, and Woodstock—each with its historic landmarks and all with an air of another era. The section of road from Norwich to Woodstock has been chosen as one of the 10 "most outstanding scenic byways" of the United States, and the 32-mile stretch from Lisbon to the Massachusetts line is one of the state's designated scenic roads.

George Washington didn't *sleep at the Wadsworth Stable—but his horse did.*

TO DO

BALLOONING
Brighter Skies Balloon Company (860-963-0600), 33 Butts Road, Woodstock. Open year-round, daily—depending on conditions, of course. Balloon rides with breakfast and the traditional champagne toast. Reservations required.

BICYCLING
Suggested bicycle routes are outlined in Northeast Connecticut's Quiet Corner brochure, *Bicycle Guide.* Copies are free on request from the district (see *Guidance*). Most of the roads in this part of the state are accessible to bicyclists; the terrain is varied and often hilly, but not daunting.

Clark Cottage, a B&B in Pomfret, offers bicycles for the use of their overnight guests (see *Lodging—Bed & Breakfasts*).

BOATING
You can launch a boat on **Morey Pond** at the Ashford-Union boundary (CT 171); in Coventry on **Coventry Lake;** in Griswold on **Glasgo Pond, Hopeville Pond,** and **Pachaug Pond;** in Hampton on **Pine Acres Lake;** in Mansfield on **Mansfield Hollow Lake;** in Plainfield on **Moosup Pond;** in Preston on **Amos Lake** and **Avery Pond;** in Thompson on **Quaddick Reservoir** and **West Thompson Lake;** in Voluntown on **Beach Pond, Beachdale Pond,** and **Green Falls Reservoir;** and in Woodstock on **Black Pond** and **Roseland Lake.**

Center Marine (860-423-1497), 457 Storrs Road, Mansfield Center. Canoe and rowboat rentals.

Quaddick State Park, East Putnam Road, Thompson. Canoe and paddleboat rentals at park concession, daily 10–5 (see *Green Space*).

Rent-Me-Canoes (860-974-2886), 118 Westford Road, Eastford.

River Bend Campground and Canoe Sales (860-564-3440), Pond Road off CT 14A, Oneco (see *Campgrounds*).

Water Works (860-456-0558), 351 Boston Post Road, US 6, North Windham.

FISHING

This is a prime freshwater fishing area. Streams and lakes abound, and all locals have their favorite spots. In **Eastford** and **Chaplin,** along CT 198, is access to trout fishing areas on the Natchaug River. In **Willington,** a fly-fishing catch-and-release area on the Willimantic River can be reached from either CT 74 or the state welcome center on I-84 between exits 70 and 69 westbound; trout are stocked. In **Plainfield,** at the trout hatchery on CT 14, there's access to trout fishing on the Moosup River. In **Union,** in Bigelow Hollow State Park, trout and bass fishing are found in Mashapaug Lake; access is at the boat-launch site (see *Green Space*). In **Mansfield Center,** Mansfield Hollow Lake, in Mansfield Hollow State Park off CT 195, is a favorite spot for bass and northern pike. In **South Coventry,** Waungumbaug (some call it Coventry) Lake off CT 31 has good bass fishing.

GOLF

Harrisville Golf Course (860-928-6098), Harrisville Road, Woodstock. Par 35, nine holes, 2,814 yards.

Raceway Golf Club (860-923-9591), Thompson Road, Thompson. Par 72, 18 holes, 6,550 yards.

Skungamaug River Golf Club (860-742-9348), 104 Folly Lane, Coventry. Par 70, 18 holes, 6,085 yards.

Twin Hills Country Club (860-742-9705), CT 31, Coventry. Par 71, 18 holes, 6,000 yards.

HAYRIDES AND SLEIGH RIDES

Most hayrides and sleigh rides are offered on a group basis. Call to inquire about the date in which you are interested. **Stoneybridge Farm** (860-423-0665), Lebanon; **Windy Hill Farm** (860-642-6188), Lebanon; **Wrights Mill Tree Farm** (860-774-1455), Canterbury; **Ye Plain Ole Farm** (860-546-1079), Canterbury.

HIKING

The state parks as well as many private parks and land preserves mark and maintain hiking trails. Northeast Connecticut's Quiet Corner (see *Guidance*) can supply information, or you can call the **Connecticut State Bureau of Parks and Forests** (860-424-3200) for maps.

Mashamoquet Brook State Park, off US 44, Pomfret. Of all the hikes in Connecticut, this is the one most fraught with local myth: It takes you to Israel Putnam's wolf den. Putnam is an important presence in this part of the state. Born in Massachusetts, he came to Brooklyn and took up farming at a fairly early age, and later ran an inn. He also saw a good deal of military service—escaped death more than once in the French and Indian War, led the colonial troops at the battle of Bunker Hill (Breed's Hill, really), and later in that same war escaped capture by making a daring dash on horseback down a precipice in Greenwich. But here in Pomfret is where he began his larger-than-life career. An old she-wolf was ravaging local flocks of sheep, and the farmers had no luck catching her. Israel Putnam crawled in the dark of night into her den, shot the wolf, and dragged her out to the cheers of his lantern-lit friends. Various versions of the tale elaborate on the struggle and supply details on the roistering, all-night vigil at the mouth of the wolf's lair, but the upshot is that before he was 20 years old, Old Put had manifested the stuff of greatness. To follow in his footsteps, then, begin at the junction of US 44 and CT 101 in Pomfret. Wolf Den Drive will take you to the park's second parking area, where the trail leads past the campground down to the scene of the struggle. You can continue on a 5-mile loop with some mild climbs, through woodlands and marsh, past the rock formation Indian Chair, across Mashamoquet Brook, and, finally, back to the parking lot.

HORSEBACK RIDING

Horseback riding is offered at the following: **Cherry Ledge Farm** (860-928-1016), Putnam; **Coventry Meadows** (860-742-5540), Coventry; **Diamond A Ranch** (860-779-3000), Dayville; **Hawthorne Farm** (860-684-5487), Willington; **Hillside B&B** (860-974-3361), Pomfret; **Renaud Farms** (860-564-8901), Plainfield; **Trapalanda Stables** (860-974-1064), Woodstock; **Woodcock Hill Riding Academy** (860-487-1686), Willington; and **Woodstock Acres Riding Stable** (860-974-1224), Woodstock (English saddles).

HORSE CAMPING

Diamond A Ranch (860-779-3000), Dayville 06241. One- and 2-hour rides, 1½-hour ride with cookout, overnight expeditions. Call for schedule.

SKYDIVING

Woodstock Airport (860-963-7004), Woodstock.

SPECTATOR SPORTS

Plainfield Greyhound Park (860-564-3391) Lathrop Road, Plainfield. Open year-round, Tuesday through Sunday; for schedule, call 1-800-RACES-ON. Both greyhound racing (live) and simulcast horse racing.

Stafford Motor Speedway (860-684-2783), CT 140, Stafford Springs. Open April through November. NASCAR auto racing on a 0.5-mile paved oval track; modified late-model pro stocks; monster trucks late July, early August.

Thompson International Speedway (860-923-9591), East Thompson Road, Thompson. Open March through October. Professional, street, and modified stock car racing on a ⅝-mile NASCAR Winston Racing Series track.

University of Connecticut (860-486-2724), main campus, CT 195, Storrs. Athletic events at Gampel Pavilion and playing fields on campus. Basketball, soccer, football, baseball, men's and women's team events.

SWIMMING

The lakes and ponds of the Quiet Corner provide ideal swimming for those who prefer fresh water and minimal wave action. Most of the swimming areas are in state parks, with shelters for changing and lifeguards on duty during the summer. In most cases there's a fee for parking, swimming, or both. Swimming is permitted and lifeguards are on duty at **Bicentennial Pond,** Mansfield; **Coventry Lake,** Coventry; **Moosup Pond,** Plainfield; and **Quaddick Reservoir,** Thompson. There are indoor pools at **Koinonia School of Sports** (860-928-6420), Thompson; and **Plainfield Recreation** (860-564-6447), Plainfield. (See also *Green Space.*)

GREEN SPACE

Albert E. Moss Forest, CT 195 and CT 275, Storrs. Open to the public, this wildlife and wildflower sanctuary serves as an outdoor classroom for botany students at the University of Connecticut.

Bigelow Hollow (860-928-9200), CT 197, Union. More than 500 acres of woodlands with two popular trout ponds, Mashapaug Lake and Bigelow Pond. Activities include picnicking, fishing, hiking, boating, hunting, cross-country skiing. Outhouses, boat launch.

Laurel Sanctuary in Nipmuck State Forest, exit 72 off I-84, CT 190, Union. In late June and early July, walk through clouds of pink and white laurel blooms.

Mashamoquet Brook State Park (860-928-6121), US 44, Pomfret. A good trail system (the park is nearly 1,000 acres) for hikers; picnicking, fishing, swimming; nature trail, concession, and camping sites. Changing houses for swimmers, flush toilets.

Pachaug State Forest (860-376-4075), CT 49, Voluntown. At 23,115 acres, this area is a sizable preserve, highlighted by a rare rhododendron sanctuary.

Quinebaug and Shetucket Rivers Valley, A National Historic District (860-424-3540, ext. 2875). The National Park Service, together with state and local agencies, has designated an unprecedented 850-square-mile region that extends from Mystic in the south almost to the Massachusetts border as one of the country's "last green valleys." It is a region of small towns, villages, farmland, and forests in what once was a thriving, bustling complex of fabric mill towns. Its major artery is CT 169, but the full-color illustrated map/brochure published by the National Park Service suggests byways and small highways inviting you to explore at your leisure. The mission is to hold back the developers who would plant their urban malls on this inviting open space. Call for a copy of the brochure.

Quaddick State Park (860-928-920; 860-424-3200, state parks office), 7 miles northeast of Putnam on East Putnam Road, off US 44, Thompson. Originally a fishing area for the Nipmuck tribe, we're told, this popular 116-acre space contains a reservoir with a separate swimming pond. The sandy beach and cool water are major attractions; activities include hiking, fishing, and boating. There's a concession for food and drink during summer, and drinking water is available, as are telephone, changing houses, flush toilets, and a boat ramp.

Trail Wood (860-455-0759) on Kenyon Road (off CT 97), Hampton. Open daily, dawn to dusk. Three miles of trails on a 140-acre farm, formerly the home of birder and naturalist Edwin Way Teale. Hikers are welcome anytime; guided walks and other activities are scheduled. Teale's study and a museum are open by arrangement. Call for appointment, information, hours, or to receive regular mailings. Trail maps (and a donation box) are at the information shed. Maintained by the Connecticut Audubon Society.

NURSERY/GARDEN

University of Connecticut Greenhouses (860-486-4052), 75 North Eagleville Road, Storrs. Open Monday through Friday 8–4. There are tours for the public on weekends in March and April. Talk about diversity— UConn's internationally recognized greenhouses contain more than 3,000 kinds of plants, from aquatic carnivores (yes! underwater meat-eaters) to a redwood tree. There are 900 varieties of orchids, as well as ferns, cacti, palm trees, passionflowers, cinnamon, lavender, violets, and exotic forms, scents, and colors from around the world.

LODGING

RESORT

☞ **Spa at Grand Lake** (860-642-4306), CT 207, Lebanon 06249. Individualized programs for weight loss and stress reduction: pool, sauna, massage, aerobics, swimnastics, tennis, yoga, special diet, beauty salon; 51 rooms with private bath. Under $90.

INNS

Altnaveigh Inn (860-429-4490), 957 Storrs Road (CT 195), Storrs 06268. Located in a historic district, this is a 1734 wayside inn; it's close to the University of Connecticut campus but in a country setting. Six rooms, two with private bath; continental breakfast, restaurant (see *Dining Out*). Under $90.

Inn at Woodstock Hill (860-928-0528), 94 Plaine Hill Road (just off CT 169), South Woodstock 06267. With views of unspoiled rural Connecticut, this former country estate has been transformed into a romantic getaway, offering 22 rooms and suites, some with fireplaces and four-poster beds, all with private bath, TV, and air-conditioning. The lavish cabbage roses of the wallpaper and the abundance of crisp floral chintz give the decor a decidedly British flavor. Continental breakfast is included; lunch and dinner are served in the restaurant daily; brunch on Sunday (see *Dining Out*). Rates, based on double occupancy, in high season (May through October) are $75–150; from November through April, $65–140.

   ♿ **Plainfield Yankee Motor Inn** (860-564-4021), Lathrop Road, exit 87 off I-395, Plainfield 06374. Greyhound Park is within walking distance. This inn has 49 comfortable rooms; free in-house movies. $50–89. Ask for senior discounts.

   ♿ **Sleep Inn** (860-684-1400), 327 Ruby Road, exit 71 off I-84, Willington 06279. Easy ride to the University of Connecticut. Sixty-two up-to-date rooms, all with bath. Outdoor pool, restaurant, and convenience store. Continental breakfast. Seasonal rates, $69–89.

BED & BREAKFASTS

In addition to the listings below, bed & breakfast reservation services offers access to rooms available in establishments throughout the state. For a list, see *What's Where—Bed & Breakfasts.*

In Brooklyn

Friendship Valley (860-779-9696), 60 Pomfret Road (CT 169), Brooklyn 06234. An 18th-century Georgian country house, listed on the National Register, combines 12 acres of woods and open land with evocative local connections to national events, notably the abolitionist movement—the house was the scene of the wedding of William Lloyd Garrison to Helen Benson, who lived here. Today's guests enjoy five rooms and suites decorated with antiques, working fireplaces, private baths, and swimming pool, as well as full breakfast and afternoon tea. Rates from $75 (single) to $195 for family suite.

☞ **Tannerbrook B&B** (860-774-4822), 329 Pomfret Road (CT 169), Brooklyn 06234. An 18th-century saltbox on a hill overlooking a private, spring-fed lake—good fishing. Two rooms with private bath, full breakfast. $75; senior discounts.

In Coventry

Bird in Hand (860-742-0032), 2011 Main Street, Coventry 06238. Antiques, fireplaces, stone walls, rolling landscape, perennial flower beds. Three rooms, two with private bath and fireplace; full breakfast served. Up to $90.

Maple Hill Farm (1-800-742-0635; fax 860-742-4435), 365 Goose Lane, Coventry 06238. Ten minutes from the University of Connecticut campus at Storrs. Putting together the old and the new, this restored 1730s farmhouse, behind an ancient stone wall, has welcoming fireplaces, books to read, screened porch, picnic areas with hammocks, and 7 acres of open land to hike. It also has an outdoor pool and a hot tub in the solarium. Bicycles are available, as are maps for those who want to explore the nearby hills. Horses, goats, and chickens on the premises. There are four rooms, one with private bath. A full country breakfast is served with eggs fresh from the nest. $50–85 per room.

Mill Brook Farm (860-742-5761), 110 Wall Street, Coventry 06238. An Italianate-style farmhouse with a wraparound veranda, fronted by a stone wall, this cozy spot is also the home of Rose Fowler's handmade Farm Bears. Real animals can be found as well, on the generous, 7-acre grounds.

Two double rooms and one single are available; a country breakfast is served. Weekend workshops are scheduled. $45 single, $60 double.

Special Joys (860-742-6359), 41 North River Road, Coventry 06238. With a hexagonal tower front and slightly off-center, a veranda across the front, and pink as its signature color, Special Joys makes you smile before you're out of your car. As you enter, you see the museum-shop of Joy Kelleher, who, with her husband, runs the inn. Antique dolls, stuffed animals, and toys of all sorts, sizes, and ages, some for sale, all for enjoying (see *Special Shops*). B&B guests have their own entrance and a choice of porches, parlors, and gardens. Three handsome guest rooms, two with private bath, equipped with TV and phone jacks; a full breakfast is served in the new conservatory. $62, double occupancy, with senior discounts.

In Mansfield

The Fitch House (860-456-0922), 563 Storrs Road (CT 195), Mansfield Center 06250-0163. Massive Ionic columns and a classical pediment announce the Greek Revival taste of the architect-builder of this 1836 home. There are two large rooms, each with private bath. One room can be connected to a third to create a suite; the other room offers a working fireplace. A classical garden enhances the experience, as does the elegant breakfast in the two-story solarium. $75–95, double occupancy.

Still Waters B&B (860-429-9798), 129 Summit Road, Mansfield 06269. A hop, skip, and a jump to the University of Connecticut campus. Contemporary fieldstone house with two bedrooms with bath in a wooded setting overlooking a sylvan pond. Full breakfast. $80-plus.

In Plainfield

☞✐**French Renaissance House B&B** (860-564-3277), 550 Norwich Road (CT 12), Plainfield 06374. Dating from 1871, an unusual—for this neck of the woods—Second Empire–style home. Four rooms, not all with private bath; full breakfast. Children welcome. Under $90; special winter rates.

☞✐**Isaac Shepard House** (860-564-3012), 165 Shepard Hill Road, Plainfield 06332. A restored 1750 Colonial; the screened porch is a later and happy addition. The adjacent wildlife reserve adds greenery and birdsong to the experience. Three guest rooms, shared baths, continental breakfast. A kitchenette and an exercise room are also available. Children welcome. $50 and up.

In Pomfret

Chickadee Cottage B&B (860-963-0587), 375 Wrights Crossing Road, Pomfret 06259. Great location for serious birders, across from Audubon preserve. Two rooms, one with private bath, in traditional Cape furnished with family antiques. Sunroom, screened porch. Walking trails on 10 acres of private land. Continental-plus breakfast. $70-plus, depending on the season.

☞✐**Clark Cottage at Wintergreen B&B** (860-928-5741), 354 Pomfret Street (CT 169), Pomfret 06259. This 18-room cottage was a satellite structure on a former estate. Lordly old trees, mature gardens, a soothing country setting. Four rooms, full breakfast. Children are welcome. Up to $90; senior discounts.

Cobbscroft B&B (860-928-5560), 349 Pomfret Street (CT 169), Pomfret 06258. Two artists are at work in this 1780 manor house. Tom McCobb's paintings enliven the walls, and Janet's bold decorating flair is evident everywhere—in the green-and-white-striped bathroom with gold-footed tub, in the deep red walls of the parlor, as well as in the note cards and other items offered in the studio shop. There are three guest rooms, all with private bath; one is actually a suite with a fireplace. A full breakfast is served in the sunny dining room. Senior discounts. Accommodations are for adults only. Under $90.

Grosvenor Place B&B (860-928-4633), 321 Deerfield Road (CT 97), Pomfret 06258. An early-18th-century, center-chimney Colonial with winding stairway. Three rooms with period furnishings, continental breakfast. $90.

Karinn (860-928-5492; fax 860-928-6026), 330 Pomfret Street (CT 169), Pomfret Center 06259. This 100-year-old, 20-room Victorian mansion was first a school for girls and later an inn. Now refurbished, it makes a comfortable and inviting B&B, with four rooms (two suites) with private bath and fireplace. Antiques and Oriental rugs lend authenticity to the New England flavor, while the grand scale of the foyer and the availability of TV and vintage recordings add a distinctive twist. Game room and library. Outdoors, the porch, deck, and gardens invite guests to relax. "Well-mannered" pets are welcome, and a full breakfast is served. Afternoon refreshments. Rates for double occupancy are $85–100 for double rooms, $150–155 for suites.

☞✎**Quail Run** (860-928-6907), One Townhouse Drive, Pomfret 06259. All to yourself, a guest apartment including living room, dining room, full kitchen, two bedrooms, bath, TV, phone. Children are welcome, and continental breakfast is served. $100.

In Putnam

27 Church Street B&B (860-928-9333), 27 Church Street, Putnam 06260. Unpack and prepare to enjoy the view of the Quinebaug River, Cargill Falls, and even downtown Putnam. One room with private bath, living room and kitchenette; continental breakfast. Up to $90.

☞✎**Felshaw Tavern** (860-928-3467), Five Mile River Road, Putnam 06260. An extraordinary restoration of a 1742 tavern where, legend says, militiamen gathered during the Revolutionary War. Among the elegant but comfortable furnishings are many antiques. The Kinsmans are the kind of innkeepers who make you feel not merely welcome but also at home. Two rooms, each with bath. Children welcome. Full breakfast. Under $90.

Thurber House (860-928-6776), 78 Liberty Way (CT 21), Putnam 06260. On the village green; a traditional Colonial, formerly the home of artist

T.J. Thurber. Two guest rooms, private bath, full breakfast. $70 double.

In Thompson

☞𝒜**Corttis Inn** (860-935-5652), 235 Corttis Road, Thompson (North Grosvenor Dale) 06255. A genuine Colonial—1758—with cozy fireplaces. The outdoors is complete with stone walls, and the 900 acres encourage you to explore, hike, bike, cross-country ski, and ice skate. Four rooms and a suite, private bath. Children are welcome. A full breakfast is served. $75–100, double occupancy; senior discounts.

Lord Thompson Manor (860-923-3886), CT 200, Thompson 06277. A spectacular country estate with a 0.5-mile approach, 62 acres of grounds. Nine rooms, some with private bath; luxury suites, fireplaces. Full breakfast. Up to $100.

In Tolland

English Lane Bed & Breakfast (in-state, 1-888-871-6618; out-of-state, 1-888-871-6618), 816 Old Post Road, Tolland 06084. A beautifully restored 1840 farmhouse typical of the Colonial style brings a British flavor to Tolland. Rick and Sheryl King, innkeepers, serve a gourmet breakfast either in the chestnut-beamed dining room or, in warm weather, outdoors in the gazebo. Two guest rooms are elegantly decorated, each with queen-size bed and private bath. Seasonal rates, $60–75.

Old Babcock Tavern (860-875-1239), 484 Mile Hill Road (CT 31), Tolland 06084. Three rooms with private bath in a 1720 Colonial manse, originally a tavern, now listed on the National Register of Historic Places. The interior puts you in another era: dark wood siding, exposed timbers, and furnishings of the 18th century, including a spinning wheel. Innkeepers Barbara and Stuart Danforth offer a lecture on the restoration work on request. A wedge of pie adds a regional flavor to the full breakfast. $70–85, double occupancy, tax included.

☞ **Tolland Inn** (860-872-0800), 63 Tolland Green (CT 74), Tolland 06084-0717. Standing at the end of the town green, this former inn returned to its original calling after a long hiatus. Innkeepers Susan and Steve Beeching have reworked and expanded, adding a sunroom, a massive fireplace, and new porches. There are books everywhere, lovely gardens, and a pair of birds that nest on the front porch. The rooms, individually decorated, are furnished with a combination of antiques and custom furniture designed and built by Steve Beeching. Seven rooms, all with private bath; one with fireplace and hot tub; and two suites, one with sitting room and fireplace, the other with sitting room and hot tub. Full breakfast with home-baked bread and scones. $70–130.

In Woodstock

☞𝒜**Beaver Pond B&B** (860-974-3312), 68 Cutler Hill Road, Woodstock 06281. If you can tear yourself away from the cozy fireplace in the comfortable sitting room, you'll find, in this country setting, fishing, boating, nature trails, and herb gardens. There are just two guest

rooms with shared bath; continental breakfast. Children are welcome. Under $90.

☞ **Taylor's Corner** (860-974-0490; fax 860-974-0498), 880 CT 171, Woodstock
06281. An 18th-century Colonial, listed on the National Register and
restored to its original look. There are eight fireplaces, and herb and
spectacular flower gardens. Three cozy air-conditioned rooms, each with
private bath. Full breakfast served on weekends; children over 12
welcome. $80; personal check accepted.

In Other Quiet Corner Towns

Buck Homestead (860-429-4568), 630 Westford Road (CT 89), Ashford
06076. An 18th-century home on 13 acres; two guest rooms with shared
bath, full breakfast. Under $90.

Woodchuck B&B (860-546-1278), 256 Cemetery Road, Canterbury
06331. This is what the Quiet Corner is all about: a rural getaway in an
attractive home set on 13 wooded acres with brooks, fishing, gardens.
Close to the historic Prudence Crandall House (see *Museums*). One
large bedroom with bath and private entrance. Continental breakfast.
Up to $85.

☞ **Nathan Fuller House** (860-456-0687), 147 Plains Road, Scotland 06264.
On a real country road, set on a lot trimmed by a stone wall, its clapboards
a reserved beige, the Nathan Fuller House invites getaways. If you crave
peace and quiet, it's here. Two rooms, one with fireplace, share a bath;
full breakfast is served. Game room with fireplace. Children over 10 are
welcome. Rates under $75.

Olivia's Garden Bed & Breakfast (860-228-8070), 256 CT 66, Columbia
06237. Three rooms, two double and one single, in a 1750 Cape Cod–
style home set among gardens of fruit, vegetables, and flowers. Porches
surrounding the house invite relaxation. Guests are served continental
breakfast. Rates are $60 single occupancy, $80 double.

☞✐**Empty Nest** (860-423-7196), 267 High Street, Windham (Willimantic)
06226. A Greek Revival home, revised and expanded over the past 100
years, offers comfortable surroundings adjacent to Eastern Connecticut
State University and is 10 minutes from the University of Connecticut at
Storrs. Two rooms with shared bath; one with queen, the other with
double bed. $40 single, $50 double; children over 3 welcome; continental breakfast served. Pay by personal checks, not credit card.

☞✐**Storrs Farmhouse** (860-429-1400), 418 Gurleyville Road, Storrs 06268. A
short way from the University of Connecticut campus, this generous
Cape Cod house in a genuine rural setting also offers access to nearby
hiking and fishing. Four rooms, private bath; one apartment. Children
over 4. Full breakfast. $40 single, $60 double.

☞✐**Stoughton Brook Farm** (860-684-6510), 510 Buckley Highway (CT 190),
Union 06076. If you're looking for early New England, here's a sample.
What's called the new section is actually the 1815 addition, built onto a
1740 Cape Cod home. Many antiques, three generous-size rooms with

private bath; children welcome; continental breakfast. Under $90.

HOTEL

   King's Inn (860-928-7961; 1-800-541-7304), Five Heritage Road, Putnam 06260. A hotel on 7 landscaped acres, with a pond, swimming pool, 40 rooms, TV, telephone; restaurant, theater packages with Bradley Playhouse (see *Entertainment*). Near Putnam antiques district and Old Sturbridge Village, just across the border in Massachusetts. Continental breakfast. $60–90; senior discounts.

MOTELS

   Ashford Motel (860-487-3900), 26 Snow Hill Road, Ashford 06278, exit 72, just off I-84. Modern facility in a wooded setting with 45 rooms. Near the University of Connecticut. Children welcome. $50–89.

   Best Western–Regent Inn (860-423-8451), 123 Storrs Road, Mansfield 06250. Another modern facility close to the UConn campus; golf and a restaurant within walking distance. Eighty-eight clean and bright rooms. No frills, but offers athletic facility, indoor pool, TV, laundry. $75.

   Plainfield Motel (860-564-2791), CT 14, exit 89 off I-395, Moosup 06354. Close to dog track, equidistant from Mystic Seaport and Old Sturbridge, Massachusetts, offering 35 unpretentious rooms, some efficiencies. Outdoor pool. Laundry. $80 plus.

CAMPGROUNDS

There are 20 campgrounds in northeastern Connecticut: Two are in **Mashamoquet Brook State Park,** Pomfret, and offer inexpensive rustic camping with open sites, centrally located flush toilets, and dump stations. For information and reservations, call 860-928-6121 or the Connecticut State Bureau of State Parks and Forests (860-424-3200). Among the other properties are the following—all members of the Connecticut Campground Owners Association (CCOA; 860-521-4704), all with some sewer hookups and other basic amenities.

Brialee R.V. & Tent Park (860-429-8359; 1-800-303-CAMP), 174 Laurel Lane, Ashford 06278. Grassy and shaded, 150 sites, planned activities, boating, swimming, hiking, fishing, and more. Under $20.

Charlie Brown Campground (860-974-0142), 100 Chaplin Road (CT 198), Eastford 06242. On the Natchaug River; 97 seasonal sites, planned activities, swimming, fishing. Rates vary: some under $20, some over.

Lake Williams Campground (860-642-7761; in Connecticut, Rhode Island, and Massachusetts, 1-800-972-0020), 1742 Exeter Road (CT 207), Lebanon 06249. Eighty-three seasonal sites on the lake, sunny and shady; boating, swimming, fishing, planned activities. Under $20.

Nickerson Park (860-455-0007), CT 198, Chaplin 06235. Open year-round; 100 sites, planned activities, swimming, boating, fishing.

Peppertree Camping (860-974-1439), CT 198, Eastford 06242. Forty-five sites.

River Bend Campground (860-564-3440), 41 Pond Street (CT 14A), Oneco 06373. Seasonal; 160 sites, planned activities, boating, swimming, fishing. Canoes and kayaks for sale and rent; tent trailers, log cabins, and on-site trailers for rent. Under $20.

WHERE TO EAT

DINING OUT

Altnaveigh Inn (860-429-4490), 957 Storrs Road (CT 195), Storrs. Lunch served Monday through Friday 11:30–2:30; dinner Monday through Thursday 5–9, Friday and Saturday 5–10; Sunday brunch 11–2, dinner 2–8. A legendary country inn setting; dinner by the fireplace or, in summer, on the patio. Continental fare—prime rib of Angus beef, veal Oscar, roast glazed duckling citron, filet of sole Parisienne. $14–25.

Chez Pierre (860-684-5826), 179 West Main Street (CT 190), Stafford Springs. Open Wednesday through Friday 5–9, Saturday 5–10, Sunday 3:30–8; closed Monday and Tuesday. This is a carpenter Gothic marvel of a building, with the Victorian theme continued inside. The food, however, is distinctively French. A four-course prix fixe dinner is $28–32.

The Depot (860-429-3663), 57 Middle Turnpike (US 44), Mansfield Depot. Open seven days a week: lunch Monday through Friday; dinner every night and Sunday brunch. Full bar. Once in a while a train rumbles past the west-facing windows, and between trains the decor reminds you of the Age of Steam. A giant mural features an oncoming locomotive, and toy trains are tucked into convenient corners here and there. The food is American with northern Italian leanings, and much admired by the locals. You might encounter potato gnocchi with a fresh herb cream sauce, prosciutto, and other improvements; or grilled salmon with black beans and rice. There are always vegetarian dishes and seafood specials. Desserts run the gamut from cheesecakes and chocolate fantasies to wholesome fresh fruit. Dinner entrées under $20.

Golden Lamb Buttery (860-774-4423), 499 Bush Hill Road, off CT 169, Brooklyn. Open May through December, the Golden Lamb serves dinner on Friday and Saturday only at 7. Lunch is served Tuesday through Saturday noon–2:30. This is more than a restaurant; it is an experience. The proprietors, Bob and Jimmy (a tomboy from childhood) Booth, also manage a working farm; each had a career in business but switched allegiance to Hillandale Farm years ago. Jimmy is the cook; Bob is your genial host. Reservations are essential, since you're truly treated as a guest. For dinner, you'll assemble at 7 in the barn, where an assortment of antiques, heirlooms, and whimsical gleanings promote conversation. On the walls are ecstatic reviews of the restaurant's recent triumphs. You're invited to go on a hayride to view the grounds, with grazing sheep, transient deer, and ancient stone walls. Music is provided on the hayride and during dinner by a singing guitarist, Susan Lamb (no kin). Meals are prix fixe and include a choice of soups, clear or creamy (Jimmy is famous for her pear-and-pineapple invention), along with an entrée that might be pork roasted with apricots, garlic, and Calvados in mushroom–cream cheese sauce, or fresh salmon rolled in herbs and served in puff pastry with Mornay sauce, lime, and dill. The nation's top food critics have praised the cuisine here. The vegetable courses are prepared in as many as five different ways—braised celery, baked zucchini casserole, and the like. Finally, dessert may be poppy-seed cake with praline frosting, flourless chocolate cake, exquisite cheesecake with raspberry sauce. In December there are special holiday festivities. Dinner is about $60 per person; lunch under $20.

The Harvest (860-928-0008), 37 Putnam Road (US 44), Pomfret. Fine dining in a 1785 homestead to which considerable space has been added; three dining rooms of varying sizes and a lounge. Full bar. Extensive wine list and adventurous cuisine. Bistro menu Monday to Friday, lunch and dinner. Dinner served seven nights; regular menu offers beef, lamb, chicken, seafood, and vegetarian entrées. Specials range from Thai to Southwestern to French inventions. No lunch served on Saturday, but brunch available Sunday 11 to 2. Entrées $12 to $25; bistro items under $10.

   ら **Inn at Woodstock Hill** (860-928-0528), 94 Plaine Hill Road (just off CT 169), South Woodstock. Lunch Tuesday through Saturday. Dinner daily. Sunday brunch. The grand piano provides tranquil background music, the pale pink table linen promises careful service and properly prepared dishes. This is the restaurant of an upscale country inn, and the cuisine, described as American Continental, bears out the claim. Oysters Rockefeller, New England seafood chowder, and smoked Norwegian salmon are among the appetizers. Entrées feature seafood: poached or grilled salmon with tarragon butter or dill hollandaise; or shrimp and sea scallops with artichoke hearts, orange zest, garlic, and herbs. For meat fanciers, there's filet mignon with Madagascar green peppercorn sauce, or duck, pork tenderloin, veal dishes, or rack of lamb. Cap off your meal with a scrumptious chocolate mousse cake. Soups are around $3.50; appetizers $9.50–13.50; entrées up to $28.

White Horse Inn at Vernon Stiles (860-923-9571), 351 Thompson Road (CT 193 at its junction with CT 200), Thompson. A 200-year-old inn on the town common, now a restaurant serving dinner Monday, Wednesday, Thursday 5:30 to 9; Friday and Saturday 5 to 10; Sunday 4 to 8; also Sunday brunch 11 to 2. Known for the Wednesday "Stew and Story" presentations featuring local storytellers and hearty stews, February to April. Another unique feature: wines in two price ranges suggested for each entrée. Entrées under $20.

EATING OUT

In step with the latest national trend, the Quiet Corner invites you to sample homemade beers in two microbreweries, both in downtown Willimantic: the **Olde Wyndham Brewery** (860-423-0444), at 322 Main Street, and the **Willimantic Brewing Company & Main St. Cafe** (860-423-6777), at 967 Main Street. The latter also has an extensive menu of pub fare. Call for scheduled tours of the vats, pipes, whistles, and gongs where the beer is actually brewed.

At the same time, two Chinese restaurants in the Quiet Corner get our nod of approval: the **Jade Garden** of Plainfield, 1019 Norwich Road, featuring an all-you-can eat buffet, and its counterpart, the **Jade Garden** of Putnam, at 243 Kennedy Drive. Both serve "Exotic Island" drinks.

Bar-B-Q Hut (860-928-6499), 1 Mechanics Street, Putnam. Closed Monday and Tuesday. Open Wednesday through Saturday noon to 8, Sunday noon to 7. Hickory-smoked barbecue: ribs Texas-style, pulled pork sandwiches, beef and chicken sandwiches.

Bidwell Tavern (860-742-6978), 1260 Main Street (CT 31), South Coventry. Open daily for lunch, dinner, and evening snacks. Full bar and live entertainment. Built in 1822 as a tavern, the Bidwell has changed and grown, but maintains its historic flavor, enhanced by the patient horse out front—not a real one. Among the latter-day additions is a two-level double porch and garden room, perfect for snacks or mealtimes. Specialties of the house include 20 varieties of chicken wings—Buffalo, Louisiana, Santa Fe, teriyaki—and the interesting choice: mild, hot, or complicated. There are 14-ounce steaks to be had, baby back ribs, veal, seafood, and vegetarian dishes. Appetizers $3.75–7; dinner entrées $10.25–15. A Bidwell burger is $5.25.

Fitzgerald's Pub & Grille (860-774-0603), 1086 North Main Street, Dayville. Open daily 11 to 10, until 11 Friday, midnight Saturday. Rub shoulders with the locals as you munch on hearty burgers, dogs, pasta, and chicken specials in a neighborhood pub that won't strain your pocketbook. Entertainment weekend nights.

Fox Hunt Farms Gourmet Shop (860-928-0714), 292 CT 169, South Woodstock (behind Scranton's Shops; see *Antiques Shops*). Opens at 10 AM and closes 7 PM Tuesday through Friday, 5 PM on Sunday. Closed Monday. Hearty sandwiches, French bakery, a complete deli, and sweets you won't be able to resist.

George's Galley (860-774-7111), 55 Main Street in the heart of Danielson. Open Monday through Saturday 5 AM–8 PM, Sunday 6 AM–1 PM. Stop in at this in-town restaurant for breakfast any hour of the day. Otherwise choose from one of the standard family classics, served promptly and with a smile. Reasonable prices.

Husky Blues (860-429-2587), 1254 Storrs Road (CT 195), Mansfield. You enter in the back. Dinner and evening entertainment; Sunday brunch; full bar. It's adjacent to the University of Connecticut campus (UConn teams are known as the Huskies), so this is a lively, youthful place. And the food is exceptionally fine: Meats and fish are smoked on the premises, and the variety represented on the menu is surprising. You may find Creole, Italian, and American dishes with many accents. There are appetizers, desserts, sandwiches, salads, and full dinners. Think of smoked bluefish with a perfect horseradish sauce, homemade bread, and deep-dish pecan pie. Although essentially a nightspot, with live music after 9, there is a children's menu available. The cover charge varies. Reservations are a good idea on weekends. Entrées up to $14.

☞ **Stoggy Hollow General Store & Restaurant** (860-974-3814), CT 198, Woodstock Valley. Opens daily at 7 for breakfast; lunch and dinner are also served daily. Closing times: Sunday through Thursday 8 PM; Friday and Saturday at 9. Close to the road, rustic, informal, and inviting, with outdoor seating in summer, Stoggy Hollow manages to combine the atmosphere of an old-time general store and bakery with a menu that defies categories. Breakfasts are hearty—for instance, Grumpy Ed's omelet blends broccoli, sausage, and cheese with a white herb sauce. Or try buttermilk pancakes with Canadian bacon, biscuits, and sausage gravy; or Grannie's apple crumb cakes. Later in the day there are even more choices: BLTs, burgers, and gourmet pizza, along with nachos, chowders, and chili. Great homemade desserts. The Hearty Breakfast is $5.25; soups are $2 and $2.95; sandwiches $5–6.

✐☞**Traveler Restaurant: The Food and Book People** (860-684-4920), on the state line, I-84, exit 74, Union. Open daily 7 AM–9 PM (8:30 PM in winter). Breakfast is served until 11, but omelets and egg sandwiches are available all day. The specialty is turkey—white meat, dark meat, or mixed—prepared five ways. The owners say they serve 12 tons a year. Desserts include hot peach cobbler with ice cream; children are welcome and prices are accommodating. The second specialty is free books. The foyer and the interior walls are lined with them; diners are encouraged to find a good one and start right in. Take it along when you leave. Wednesday is "Three Free Book Day." There are more than 30,000 volumes in the collection. An added treat: The walls of the restaurant are crowded with autographed photographs of myriad famous authors. Also on the premises is a gift and collectibles shop stocked with everything from Depression-era glass to household furniture. Entrées $4.25–14; the turkey dinner is $8.50; full bar.

Uncle D's Log Cabin (860-456-7663), 383 Trumbull Highway, Lebanon. Visit Washington's War Office and the other historic homes clustered around the green, then stop in at Uncle's for pizza, steaks, calzones, chicken, seafood, the whole gamut of Italian "comfort food." Daily 11 AM to midnight. Closed Tuesday.

♿ **Vanilla Bean Cafe** (860-928-1562), junction of CT 169 and US 44 with CT 97, Pomfret. Open Monday and Tuesday 7–3; Wednesday, Thursday, and Sunday until 8; Friday and Saturday until 9. Breakfast Saturday and Sunday. Desserts and beverages are served during the entertainment on Saturday nights. The barn features casual dining and folk entertainment, while alfresco service is offered on the patio from May through Columbus Day. Beer and wine are available. An ever-expanding menu, with daily specials posted on the board, features quiche, chili, stew, and other hearty standbys, with good French bread and fresh fruit garnishes.

The main attraction, in the view of many, is the soup menu: There are as many as six a day to choose from. Dinners $6.50–12.

& **The Vine Bistro** (860-928-1660), 85 Main Street (off US 44), Putnam. Closed Monday; lunch and dinner Tuesday through Sunday. Among the many antiques shops that have settled in downtown Putnam, here's the perfect storefront restaurant, offering savvy American cuisine and emphasizing freshness. Soups, salads, and specialties like pasta with olive oil, garlic, and herbs; a layered eggplant dish with ricotta and mozzarella; rack of lamb; vodka rigatoni; fresh fish daily and Gulf shrimp. Appetizers are $5.95; entrées, served with potatoes, salad, and bread, are $10–14.

✐☞&**Willington Pizza** (860-429-7433), CT 32, a half-mile east of the junction with CT 195, Willington. Open daily 11–11, except until midnight Friday and Saturday. Beer and wine are served. A sprawling, comfortable place built around a 200-year-old house and decorated with carousel horses. Great for families, it's recommended by the locals. All the old favorite toppings, but low-cholesterol cheese if you specify. To broaden your horizons, consider the national award–winning Red Potato Pizza (featured on network TV shows) or the white pizza, covered with fresh garlic and oil. Other menu possibilities are spaghetti, ravioli, lasagna, and chicken Parmesan; and there's a kiddie menu. Pizzas $5.50–16.50; entrées up to $10.50.

& **Willington Pizza Too** (860-429-9030), intersection of CT 74 and CT 32, Phelps Crossing, is a branch operation, attesting to the popularity of the original.

Zip's Diner (774-6335), Dayville, junction of CT 12 and CT 101. Daily 6 AM–9 PM. A good honest diner with fresh, well-cooked, traditional American specialties. Try Zip's when you're in a hurry for a quick pick-me-up. Check your "smokes" at the door.

SNACKS

Dairy Bar, operated by the University of Connecticut at the Storrs campus (CT 195), serves homemade ice cream—cones, sundaes, milk shakes— Monday through Friday 10–5, weekends noon–5. Extremely popular. In summer, you may have to stand in line; it's worth the short wait.

Kathy-John's Food & Ice Cream (860-429-0362), Mansfield. Another popular stop for great ice cream and sundaes, along with a nice selection of sandwiches, soups, and salads. Open 10 AM to 11 PM daily.

Olde English Tea Room (860-456-8651), CT 97 and CT 14, Scotland. It really is. Overlooking the town green, the house is a Colonial survivor (1759) with plastered walls above dark wood paneling and ancient wideboard flooring. The tables are dressed English-style, in layers topped by a lace cloth. The proprietress, Pearl Dexter, has wide knowledge of the world of tea and offers a dozen or more varieties. Besides a standard tea service, the menu suggests soup, sandwiches, and even a plowman's lunch—a British specialty, usually bread, cheese, and accompaniments such as cucumber or pickle. The afternoon tea, $8.50, is indeed an English tea: cucumber sandwiches, scones with cream and jam, a sweet bread, and shortbread cookies. Dainty but exquisite portions.

ENTERTAINMENT

✒ **Bradley Playhouse** (860-928-7887), 30 Front Street (US 44), Putnam. Local productions of musicals, comedy, and drama, with children's theater and classes and workshops in theater. Dinner packages are available. Operates year-round.

Jorgensen Auditorium (860-486-4226), Hillside Road, off CT 195, University of Connecticut, Storrs. Ticket office open Monday through Friday 10–6, Saturday 10–1. During fall, winter, and spring, the hall offers a variety of dance, theater, and music: internationally renowned soloists and symphony orchestras on tour. Largest hall in the area, seating 2,630. Call or write for brochure.

✒ **Mansfield Drive-In** (860-456-2578), 228 Stafford Road (CT 32), Mansfield. A survivor! Advertised as the only drive-in theater east of the Connecticut River. Three screens, first-run family films. Wednesday is family night.

Connecticut Repertory Theatre (860-486-4226), Harriet S. Jorgensen Theatre, University of Connecticut, Storrs. Professional and student actors perform one musical, six plays and an occasional puppet show during the academic season. Lighter fare is staged in the theater's **Nutmeg Summer Series.**

SELECTIVE SHOPPING

ANTIQUES SHOPS

You'll find good antiquing in this section of Connecticut, at both individual shops and multidealer venues. The Quiet Corner has so many dealers it was only a matter of time before they got together for a joint effort. The result is the area's annual Antiquing Weekend, held the first weekend of November. Lodgings packages, special events, and workshops of various kinds are scheduled (see *Special Events*). For information, call or write the Northeast Connecticut Visitors District (860-928-1228), PO Box 598, Putnam 06260.

The town of Putnam has become a major center for antiques. Because the stores are grouped within easy walking distance, we've made a separate listing for your convenience. Antiques shops elsewhere are listed below, alphabetized by name.

In Putnam

30 Front Street Antiques (860-928-4752), 30 Front Street. **Antiquary Frank Racette** (860-928-4923), 215 Park Road. **Antique Corner**

(860-963-2445), 2 Main Street. **Antiques Marketplace** (860-928-0442), 109 Main Street. **Arts and Framing** (860-963-0105), 88 Main Street. **Brighton Antiques** (860-928-1419), 91 Main Street. **Estate Jewelry** (860-928-1419), 91 Main Street. **Gallery 44—Putnam** (860-963-0200), 39 Front Street. **Grams & Pennyweights** (860-928-6624), US 44 at I-395. **Grandpa's Attic** (860-928-5970), 10 Pomfret Street. **J.B.'s Antiques** (860-928-1906), 37 Front Street. **Jeremiah's Antique Shoppes** (860-963-8989), 26 Front Street. **Mission Oak Shop** (860-928-6662), Main Street at US 4. **Mrs. Bridge's Pantry** (860-963-7040), 136 Main Street. **Pendleton's Antiques** (860-928-1242), Pomfret Street. **Playhouse Supply Company** (860-963-9030), 127 Main Street. **Putnam Antiques Exchange** (860-928-1905; 860-928-5579), 83 Main Street. **Remember When Antiques** (860-963-0422), 80 Main Street. **Toys from the Attic** (860-928-2525), 4 Pomfret Street.

In Brooklyn

Dot's Cluttered Cupboard (860-774-3783), 320 Woodward Road, Brooklyn. Linen, lace, bottles, and more.

Heirloom Antiques (860-774-7017), 10 Winding Road, Brooklyn, and (860-928-4430), 28 Mashamoquet Road, Pomfret Center. Fine antiques; lamp and clock repairs.

In Canterbury

Cackleberry Farm Antiques (860-546-6335), 16 Lisbon Road (off CT 14), Canterbury. FYI: *Cackleberry* is a Briticism for "egg," eggcups being a special interest of the owner.

Morning Glory Shop (860-546-9297), 29 Lovell Lane, CT 14, Canterbury. Victorian ornaments and other Christmas items, dolls, toys.

Stone of Scone Antiques, Books & Firearms (860-546-9917), 19 Water Street, Canterbury. Special interest in books (see *Bookstores*).

In Coventry

Blue Moon, 1197 Main Street (CT 31), Coventry. Tiny shop: antiques, handcrafted gifts, knickknacks.

Memory Lane Countryside Antique Center (860-742-0346), 2224 Boston Turnpike (US 44 and CT 31 North), Coventry. Multidealers in three buildings. Furniture, accessories, linens, china, Tiffany lamps, Fiesta ware.

Village Antiques, at the junction of CT 275 and CT 31, Coventry. Ruby glass, furniture, lamps, hats, kitchenware, chandeliers.

In Danielson

Heart & Home (860-774-2623), 86 Main Street, downtown Danielson. Furniture, collectibles, prints.

The Prop Shop (860-774-5972), 172 Hall's Hill Road, Danielson. The answer to a set designer's prayer.

In Hampton

Barbara & Don Ladd Antiques (860-455-9173), 246 Main Street, Hampton.
Bearly Making It (860-455-0389), 266 Windham Road off CT 97S, Hamp-

ton. Specialty handmade teddy bears.

In Pomfret Center

Old Stuff Antiques & Collectibles (860-928-6961), US 44, Pomfret Center. General line.

Pomfret Antique World (860-928-5006), US 44 and CT 101, Pomfret. Multidealers.

In Other Quiet Corner Towns

Barn Swallow Antiques (860-974-0461; 860-974-0323), 1719 CT 171, Woodstock Valley. A cooperative, also with the work of local artisans.

Button Box Antiques (860-429-6623), 297 Gurleyville Road, Storrs. Furniture, glassware, early prints, watercolors, and more.

Freudenwald Antiques (860-228-1245), 26 CT 87 (south of US 6), Columbia. Red Wing stoneware, pottery.

Hill Top Antiques & Refinishing (860-923-9622), CT 12, North Grosvenor Dale.

Lebanon Art Gallery (860-886-2477; 1-800-342-2477), 74 Norwich Avenue (CT 2, exit 22). Collectors' plates, decoys, prints, wildlife art.

Scranton's Shops (860-928-3738), CT 169 and CT 171, South Woodstock. Multidealers.

Still Waters Antiques (860-974-3500), US 44 and CT 198, Eastford. Antiques, textiles, clothing, hats.

The Tin Lantern (860-423-5676), 273 Back Road (off CT 14), Willimantic. Country antiques, reproduction lighting devices, tinware.

BOOKSTORES

Coventry Book Shop (860-742-9875), 1159 Main Street, Coventry. Used books, some rare.

Heart of Gold Books (860-871-7421), 12 Goose Lane, Gooseberry Corners (CT 195), Tolland. A full-line bookstore with a large children's section, toys, and tapes; also stationery, music tapes, calendars.

Stone of Scone Antiques, Books & Firearms (860-546-9917), 19 Water Street (off CT 14 West), Canterbury. Out-of-print books, book searching, and antiques.

UConn Co-op (860-486-5027), 81 Fairfield Road, Storrs. In the middle of the campus, the co-op has a huge selection of books, tapes, disks, stationery, and general dorm needs.

CRAFTS SHOPS

The Etcetera Shoppe on the Green (860-642-6847), 760 Trumbull Highway, CT 87, Lebanon. Christmas shop.

The Henhouse Weaver (860-546-9898; 860-546-6433), 10 Old Plainfield Road, Canterbury. A professional weaving studio just 0.25 mile from the town center and the Prudence Crandall House. Margaret LaRose offers custom goods, colonial reproductions, and contemporary designs. Besides handwoven textiles, looms and lessons are available. Call for an appointment to visit, browse, compare notes.

KIMBERLY GRANT

Caprilands Herb Farm features 38 gardens, each planted around a different theme.

Mansfield Art Center (860-423-1819), 285 Stafford Road (CT 32), Storrs. A cooperative with 30 artists: paintings, prints, stained glass, dolls, pottery, jewelry, quilts, and more. Tearoom.

Robin's Nest Studio (860-928-4063), 269 Child Hill Road, Woodstock. A working decorative arts studio: furniture, other locally made items, antiques.

Shiloh's Mything Link (860-742-9548), 1202 South Street, Coventry. Handcrafted jewelry, glass, copper sculpture, garden vanes, pottery, gemstones, stencil work.

NURSERIES/GARDENS

Buell's Orchard (860-974-1150), 108 Crystal Pond Road (off CT 198, via Westford Road), Eastford. Monday through Saturday 9–5; closed Sunday. Fruits and vegetables, cider in season. Farm store specializes in Buell's famous caramel apples. Also cheeses, homemade jams, and more. In fall there's a pumpkin patch and apples to pick.

Caprilands Herb Farm (860-742-7244), 534 Silver Street (off CT 44), Coventry. Open year-round, daily 10–5. Presided over for years until her death by internationally recognized author-lecturer-herbalist Adelma Grenier Simmons—the self-styled good witch of gardening. There are 38 aromatic herb gardens, each planted to illustrate a theme. Greenhouse, gift barn, basket and book shops. When she was alive, Mrs. Simmons hosted a popular herb-oriented, lecture-luncheon program Friday and Saturday, and high tea on Sunday. The tradition continues; call for information and reservations. The luncheon lecture is $18; the tea, $12.

Crooke Orchards (860-429-5336), 317 Bebbington Road (1 mile from the junction of CT 44 and CT 89), Ashford. Hours, with seasonal variations, are generally Monday through Friday 1–6, Saturday and Sunday 9–6. Pick-your-own fruits and vegetables, and a farm store with apples, peaches, pears, fresh cider, gift baskets, plants, and trees for sale; Christmas trees.

Greystone Gardens (860-455-9873), 401 Hampton Road (US 6, near Hampton border), Chaplin. Seasonal, Wednesday through Sunday 10–5. A small operation, specializing in organically grown herbs; plants are for sale, along with dried flowers and herbs. Call for open dates.

Logee's Greenhouses (860-774-8038), 141 North Street, Danielson. Open year-round, Monday through Saturday 9–4, Sunday 10–4. A family business founded in 1893, offering delight to the senses. You can stroll through eight greenhouses among more than 2,000 varieties of indoor plants: orchids, bougainvilleas, lemon trees, exotic herbs, geraniums, ferns, and an amazing 700 kinds of begonias.

Martha's Herbary (860-928-0009), 589 Pomfret Road (CT 169 at its junction with CT 97 and US 44), Pomfret. Open Tuesday through Sunday 11–5. An aromatic Victorian shop and herbal education center. Classes are offered in the uses of herbs in cooking, wreath-making, gift-giving, and more. Call for information.

Sandra Lee's Herbs & Everlastings (860-974-0525), CT 97, Pomfret Center. Open May through November, Tuesday through Saturday 10–5, Sunday noon–5; closed Monday and the month of August. A 2½-acre perennial and herb farm specializing in plants and flowers for drying. Retail shop.

University of Connecticut Greenhouses. See the entry under *Green Space.*

Woodstock Orchards (860-928-2225), CT 169, Woodstock. Pick your own, beginning with blueberries in July through the harvest season—peaches, apples, pears. Sweet cider is available at the farm stand. The happy placement of an old-time orchard on the scenic route makes a rewarding stop for hungry, road-weary travelers.

Wright's Mill Farm (860-774-1455), 63 Creasey Road, Canterbury. Open daily 9–5. The streams that plunge down the hillsides powered sawmills and gristmills back as far as the 17th century. The ruins not only remain, but also are used as staging for weddings and other ceremonies held on the 250-acre grounds. These days the farm grows Christmas trees and caters to visitors with tours, outings, special events, crafts shows, garden talks, bird walks, nature trails, and hayrides keyed to the seasons. Santa arrives on the Friday after Thanksgiving, but the Christmas shop is open year-round. Call to find out what's on the schedule when you visit.

LEARNING VACATION

Prudence Sloane's Cooking School (860-455-0596), 245 Main Street, Hampton. Top chefs are recruited to teach their specialties to men and women who enjoy surprising their friends and displaying their skills at formal dinners, picnics, and Ivy League (a.k.a. upscale) tailgate sporting events.

(Also see Martha's Herbary under *Nurseries*.)

SPECIAL SHOPS

Christmas Barn (860-928-7652), 835 CT 169 (1 mile north of Roseland), Woodstock. Twelve rooms of country Christmas wares.

P/R Fabrics Quilt Shop (860-774-7883), 837 Providence Pike (US 6), South Killingly. Fabrics, notions, books, and supplies for quilters.

Risom Mill Flea Market (860-774-4973), junction of North Street and Connecticut Mills Avenue (off CT 12), Danielson. Indoor and outdoor market; antiques, collectibles, jewelry, crafts, refreshments for sale.

Special Joys (860-742-6359), 41 North River Road, Coventry. Antique dolls, dollhouses, miniature kitchens and schoolrooms, stuffed animals, display-sized mechanicals; a museum-shop in a B&B.

Thompson Hill Gallery (860-923-2007), 355 Thompson Road (CT 193 on the common), Thompson. Original fine art in various media, traditional and contemporary.

SPECIAL EVENTS

For details, contact Northeast Connecticut's Quiet Corner (860-928-1228), PO Box 598, Putnam 06260.

June: **Wildflower Festival,** at the University of Connecticut campus, Storrs; second Sunday. Sponsored by Museum of Natural History and Audubon Society. Hundreds of living specimens, classified and labeled. Slide lectures and hands-on learning projects for children. Plant and book sales.

July: Third Saturday: **Nathan Hale Antiques Festival** (860-742-6917), on the grounds of the Nathan Hale Homestead, Coventry (see *Historic Homes*). Sponsored by the Antiquarian and Landmarks Society. Fourth weekend: **Revolutionary War Encampment** (860-742-6917), on the grounds of the Nathan Hale Homestead, Coventry. Sponsored by the Antiquarian and Landmarks Society.

July 4: **Boom Box Parade,** Willimantic. A local radio station broadcasts marching music at 11 AM, and all marchers bring radios for a wacky band-free stepoff. Seeing is believing.

August: **Lebanon Fair,** Lebanon—a major country fair in the state; second weekend. **Brooklyn Fair,** Brooklyn—the state's oldest country fair; fourth weekend.

September: **Woodstock Fair,** Woodstock. **Prudence Crandall Day** (860-546-9916). An old-fashioned family festival on the grounds of the Prudence Crandall House, Canterbury (see *Museums*). Games for children, entertainment, museum tours; Labor Day weekend Saturday.

October: **University of Connecticut Horticultural Show,** university campus, Storrs. **Walking Weekend** on Columbus Day weekend—hikes and guided walks in 25 area towns to celebrate their autumn splendor.

November: **Northeast Connecticut Antiquing Weekend** (860-928-4720). Dealers extend their hours; workshops and other events are planned; lodgings packages and restaurant specials are offered.

December: **Christmas Wonderland,** 105 Pineville Road, Killingly, at the home of a dedicated lover of the holiday; amazing display, thousands of lights, hundreds of animated figures.

V. MYSTIC AND MORE

The steel-hulled windjammer Joseph Conrad, *a student training ship, is a showpiece at Mystic Seaport, America's largest maritime museum.*

Introduction

From the days when the axes of the first English settlers bit into the trees hugging the shores of Long Island Sound to build shelters, the people of southeastern Connecticut have turned for sustenance to the sea.

After the nasty business of massacring most of the Native Americans—Pequots, Misticks, and Mohegans—was out of the way, the pioneers became fishermen, hunters of whales, and builders of clipper ships that broke speed records sailing around the tip of South America and across the Pacific to China. The goods the sea captains of Connecticut brought back are reflected in the Chinese wallpaper in Colonial homes and in the Chinese furniture and dinnerware still in use.

The heritage of those seafaring days lives on in Mystic Seaport, the country's largest maritime museum; in Mystic Marinelife Aquarium, with more than 6,000 marine specimens; and in the USS *Nautilus* Memorial and Submarine Force Museum. Visitors can embark on cruises in replicas of authentic tall ships, watch wooden-boat regattas, and dine in scores of extraordinary restaurants where fish, crabs, oysters, mussels, and lobsters are king of the table.

Here is the birthplace of the nuclear submarine, the awesome underwater craft that still slip down the ways at the Electric Boat Company. Monuments recall battles fought here during the American Revolution. Historic taverns and homes of patriots tell how Washington came here to plan strategy and obtain support for his chronically undersupplied Continental troops.

The cup runneth over for shoppers, who can fruitfully browse in shops offering nautical antiques, captain's binoculars, harpoons, ship bells, and lanterns, as well as furniture, seafaring garb and art, and books on sailing, sea life, and marine conservation.

A startling development that has attracted national attention also occurred here: A handful of Mashantucket Pequot Indians, the last descendants of the once mighty tribes that lived in and roamed this area, have made an unexpected comeback. In Ledyard, on their minuscule reservation in the forests just north of Mystic, they built Foxwoods, now the world's largest gambling casino, where the white man at long last is getting his just desserts—battling roulette wheels, card tables,

292

KIMBERLY GRANT

This colorful mural recalls the days when Mystic River shipyards launched vessels that broke speed records sailing to South America and China.

and slots. To their immediate south, the Mohegans, once enemies of the Pequots, have also built a thriving casino.

That's not the only surprise, though: Recently planted vineyards are flourishing and bottling premium wines along the continuation of Connecticut's new "Wine Trail."

It is safe to say that southeastern Connecticut is unlike any other region in the state, and there is no question that it is Connecticut's number one tourist destination.

To keep things as simple as we could, we've divided the southeastern region into two chapters: east and west of the Thames waterway.

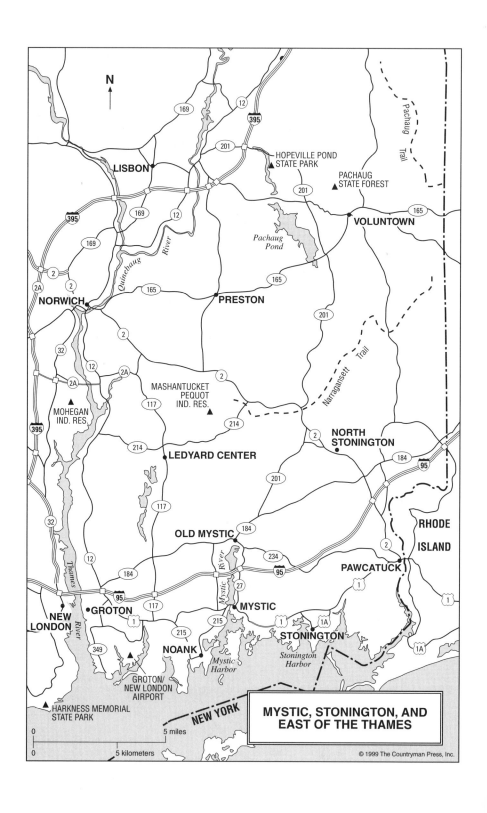

MYSTIC, STONINGTON, AND
EAST OF THE THAMES

© 1999 The Countryman Press, Inc.

Mystic, Stonington, and East of the Thames

Strictly speaking, Mystic is not a legal entity with its own government. It's a place name, a postal address spilling halfway into Groton on the west and Stonington on the east. The present Seaport was erected on the site of a former major shipbuilding yard. From the shipyards of the so-called Mystic area, numerous ships were built for the Navy and commercial fleets. A world's record, still standing, was set by the *David Crockett*, a clipper ship built by Greenman and Company, on its run around Cape Horn to San Francisco. During the Civil War, 56 transports, gunboats, and other warships went down the ways from Mystic shipyards. But when iron ships came along, shipbuilding declined in Mystic. It was only in 1929 that the nonprofit Mystic Seaport was founded to preserve the region's maritime heritage.

Bordering Fishers Island Sound between the Thames and Mystic Rivers, the popular shoreline town of Groton was home to the fierce Pequots, almost wiped out in King Philip's War but now wealthy and powerful again from an avalanche of casino money. In more recent years, Groton attained fame as the home of the North Atlantic submarine force. As a home port for nuclear subs and the site of the Navy's major submarine training school, Groton fittingly is known as the Submarine Capital of America. By no strange coincidence, the Electric Boat division of General Dynamics is located downriver in Groton on the banks of the Thames. It sent diesel subs to the Navy during World War II and is the birthplace of the USS *Nautilus,* the world's first nuclear submarine. The *Nautilus* is part of a museum complex just south of the entrance to the sub base. Visitors on the New London side of the river or when crossing the Memorial Bridge can see the hulls of emerging new giant subs poking out of the enormous factory sheds. Sub launchings are festive affairs that attract both national Navy and political dignitaries—and seaborne antiwar activists.

Entries in this section are arranged in roughly geographic order.

AREA CODE
860

GUIDANCE

Mystic Chamber of Commerce (860-572-9578), PO Box 143, Mystic 06355.

Connecticut's Mystic & More (860-444-2206; 1-800-TO-ENJOY; fax: 860-442-4257; Web site: http://www.mysticmore.com), Box 89, 470 Bank Street, New London 06320. Write for brochures, maps, and calendars of events.

State Information Center, I-95 southbound, North Stonington, just this side of the Rhode Island border. Guides, brochures, pamphlets, and maps. Full rest facilities. Open year-round daily; staffed by tourism specialists in high season.

Mystic Information Center (860-536-1641), I-95, exit 90, off CT 27 at the entrance to Olde Mistick Village.

GETTING THERE

By car: The Mystic area is accessible by I-95. The Foxwoods and Mohegan casinos, massive generators of traffic, are best reached via I-395 from the west or CT 2 from the east.

By air: The **Groton/New London Airport** (located in Groton) receives feeder service from USAir Express, Coast Air Service, and Action Airline, a charter service. **T.F. Green Airport** in nearby Rhode Island offers less-expensive fares on many routes and is becoming increasingly popular with air travelers to Mystic. Be advised that since deregulalation, airlines come and go: best to check first.

By bus: **Greyhound** (1-800-231-2222) and **Bonanza** (1-888-751-8800) bus lines serve the Mystic area. There is no local public transportation.

By rail: **AMTRAK** (1-800-872-7245) stops occasionally at the Mystic station, frequently at New London 7 miles away. The Shore Line portion of the state-owned **Metro-North** (1-800-638-7646) commuter line that links coastal towns from Old Saybrook to New Haven and then New York has been extended to New London. This extension, however, is flaky, depending on the whims of budgeteers setting taxes in the Capitol at Hartford.

MEDICAL EMERGENCY

The statewide emergency number is **911.**

Lawrence & Memorial Hospital (860-442-0711), 365 Montauk Avenue, New London.

William Backus Hospital (860-889-8331), 326 Washington Street, Norwich.

There also are walk-in medical centers in East Lyme, Mystic, North Stonington, and Norwich.

TO SEE

MUSEUMS

✐ **Mystic Seaport** (860-572-5315), 50 Greenmanville Avenue (CT 27), Mystic. Open year-round, except Christmas. A typical 19th-century New England

Seals from around the world sun and swim at the Mystic Marinelife Aquarium.

whaling village has been re-created on 17 acres of a former shipyard where clipper ships that still hold world speed records were launched. Original buildings and sailing vessels of all kinds have been gathered to help create the illusion of stepping back in time; for example, a famous cordage factory that produced the hundreds of ropes needed to maneuver a square-rigger was brought down from Plymouth, Massachusetts, and reassembled here. Today you stroll along the rope walk and watch the artisans at work. Planetarium presentations depict the starlit skies over the oceans where Yankee sailors roamed. Paintings with sea-related themes are mounted in an art gallery. Other indoor exhibits are devoted to ship models, ship gear and rigging, and, in one building, an extended graphic history of seafaring in New England. In another shed, craftspeople fashion replicas of small wooden boats. But the focus and pride of the seaport is its "tall" ships, all original and all meticulously restored: the 1841 *Charles W. Morgan,* last of the great wooden whaling ships; the *Joseph Conrad,* a steel-hulled square-rigger that served for years as a Danish cadet training ship and now hosts a summer school for young sailors; and the 1921 *L.A. Dunton,* a classic Gloucester fishing schooner. Also on exhibit are 480 small boats. Tour the ships, see how the crews lived, then board the *Sabino,* America's last coal-fired steamboat, for a cruise down the Mystic River. If you are interested, ask to see President Franklin Roosevelt's 26-foot sailboat in the storage warehouse. He was sailing in it the day he came down with polio. Seventeen major events and 160 special activities are staged at the seaport throughout the year. On the Fourth of July, marchers parade in period costumes. In the visitors center, newsman and avid sailor Walter Cronkite narrates a familiarization video. Extensive gift shop, cafeteria, and first-class restaurant. Adults $16; youth $8; reduced rates off-season and for special events.

Mystic Aquarium/Institute for Exploration (860-536-3323; 860-572-5955), 55 Coogan Boulevard, exit 90 off I-95 at the eastern end of Olde Mistick Village. Open daily 9–5 year-round, except Christmas, New Year's Day, and the last week in January, 9–5. More than 6,000 fish and other denizens of the deep, including a great white shark and Steller's sea lions, are on view in a 30,000-gallon tank and in re-created outdoor settings, such as the seal and walrus habitat. Dolphins, beluga whales, and seals gambol and leap through hoops in the Marine Theater. Formal and very dignified African blackfooted penguins strut in the Penguin Pavilion. Laboratories are geared toward rescuing and saving beached whales. Robots of the Sea allows children of all ages to steer a remote-operated device and explore a shipwreck. Gift shop. Friendly tip: Because it's first off the interstate, the aquarium is often confused with the seaport. After seeing the fishes, proceed a mile down CT 27 to the ships. Dr. Robert Ballard, the famed oceanographer who discovered the wreck of the *Titanic*, has moved his research facilities from Woods Hole on Cape Cod to the aquarium. The $45 million Institute for Sea Exploration features relics Ballard has retrieved from the ocean floors and a simulated submarine. Visitors can explore shipwrecks and oceans thousands of miles away using interactive satellite and computer technology. Adults $9.50; children 3–12, $6.50; 2 and under free. Last performance in the theater is at 4:30; doors close at 6.

Old Lighthouse Museum (860-535-1440), Seven Water Street, Stonington village. Open daily, except Monday, May through October. During the Revolutionary War, the British warship HMS *Rose* (see Captain's Cove under *Museums* in "The Bridgeport Area") appeared offshore, seeking a flock of lambs to feed its crew. Its bombardment was answered by a cannon barrage from the Stonington home guard. The battle wagon fled. During the War of 1812, another British warship, HMS *Ramilles,* showed up and made another attempt to capture the harbor town. The local folk once more trundled out their two cannons and again repelled the attack. The British later saluted Stonington as the only port that "twice repelled His Majesty's Navy." A granite column topped by the British cannonballs graces Cannon Square in the center of the village. The story of the valor of Stonington's patriots is told in this unique museum. Adults $2; children 6–12, $1.

Capt. Nathaniel Palmer House (860-535-8445), 40 Palm Street, Stonington. Open May through October, Wednesday through Monday 10–4, and by appointment. The intrepid captain and his sturdy crew are remembered and honored for discovering the Antarctic in 1820 on a sealing expedition in the 47-foot sloop *Hero*—and returning to tell about it. A versatile Yankee, the captain also was a skilled designer. A docent on the 1-hour tour of this mid-19th-century, 16-room mansion points out his architectural innovations. Adults $4; children $2.

The Captain Nathaniel Palmer House tells the story of the man who discovered the Antarctic—and returned to tell the tale

Mystic Art Association Gallery (860-536-7601), Nine Water Street, Mystic. On the banks of the Mystic River and in view of downtown Mystic's famous **Bascule** drawbridge, which is raised on schedule for tall-masted schooners, yachts, and fishing boats. Changing and permanent exhibits, including the works of William North, a modern-day Impressionist who painted many local landscapes. Free admission.

⊘ **Portersville Academy** (860-536-4779), 74 High Street, Mystic. Open late May to early October, Tuesday, Thursday, and Saturday. Varying hours. Step back more than 100 years as you sit at a tiny desk in the restored classroom of this once-active schoolhouse. Changing exhibits on the first floor. Free admission; no apple for the teacher is necessary.

⊘ **USS *Nautilus* Memorial** (860-449-3174; 1-800-343-0079), CT 12, exit 86 off I-95, Groton. Open year-round, except Tuesday in winter and major holidays. Also closed the first full week of May and the first two full weeks of December. Peer through one of three periscopes in the US Navy's **Submarine Museum** and see simulated battle scenes from World War I to the present. Trace the history and lore of sailing underwater in two minitheaters. Inspect the full-size model of the *Turtle*, invented by Connecticut's David Bushnell and the first sub to attack an enemy battleship—a British man-of-war in New York Harbor in the opening days of the Revolutionary War. Leave the museum and descend into the USS *Nautilus*, the world's first nuclear submarine, now tied up at the dock in the Submarine Capital of America. Built by Adm. Hyman Rickover and in service for 30 years, the *Nautilus* was the first submarine to sail under the North Pole and the first to journey

"20,000 leagues under the sea." Visit the control and navigation room, the crew's quarters, and the galley. The *Nautilus* joins only two other specially commissioned historic US Navy vessels as unique celebrations of American ingenuity and courage: the USS *Constitution*, Old Ironsides, still afloat in Boston Harbor, and the sunken wreck of the USS *Arizona*, at Pearl Harbor, honoring the victims of the Japanese sneak attack on December 7, 1941. Free admission.

National Submarine Memorial and Wall of Honor. A conning tower and memorial wall, both on Thames Street, Groton, honoring the 54 US Navy subs lost at sea during World War II. On the wall are engraved the names of the submariners who died in the line of duty.

Mashantucket Pequot Museum and Research Center (1-800-411-9671), exit 92 off I-95. More than 10,000 years ago Native peoples were the first inhabitants of southeastern Connecticut, home today to the Mashantucket Pequot Tribal Nation. Today their state-of-the-art museum, the newest addition to the Foxwoods entertainment complex, traces the history of the Pequots and other Northeast woodland tribes through historic artifacts, life-size dioramas, art, film, interactive media, and a 22,000-square-foot re-created village. Extensive archives are open to writers and scholars of Native American history.

Fort Griswold Battlefield State Park (860-445-1729), Groton Heights, south of I-95, Fort Griswold. Battle monument and museum. Open daily Memorial Day through Labor Day; weekends, Labor Day through Columbus Day. While Washington and his French allies were marching toward Yorktown in 1781, the British launched a diversionary attack against New London under the command of the traitor Benedict Arnold. After burning the city's bulging warehouses, a British force of 800 regulars crossed the Thames and attacked Fort Griswold, defended by only 150 militiamen led by Col. William Ledyard. In a fierce battle that lasted just 40 minutes, the defenders killed many of the British, but were finally overwhelmed. Colonel Ledyard offered his sword in surrender, in keeping with military custom. Instead of accepting the sword, the British commander, enraged at the temerity of the Americans in fighting back, plunged the blade into Ledyard's stomach, killing him on the spot. Much of the ramparts of the fort remains. The story of the battle is told in a museum building. A 134-foot-high granite obelisk commemorates the bravery of Ledyard and his men; a plaque in the ground marks where Ledyard fell.

John Bishop Museum (860-376-6866), 11 South Burnham Highway (CT 169), Lisbon. Open Saturdays, June through August, 10–noon. Ever wonder why an occasional New England home is painted white on three sides and red on the back? This house, now the home of the Lisbon Historical Society, is a good example. Historians explain that red paint was less expensive than white, but white was more prestigious. So many a thrifty Yankee saved a bit of money, showing his white face to the passersby. A remarkable early Federal structure, a unique feature of the Bishop house

Visitors to the US Navy's Submarine Museum in Groton can tour the USS Nautilus, *the world's first nuclear submarine.*

is the indoor area, with a well located in the pantry. Donations.

HISTORIC SITES

Stonington Borough extends along a narrow peninsula to the sea. It's one of the most charming seaside villages in New England. During the American Revolution and the War of 1812, courageous villagers with a pair of old cannons chased away attacking British warships that were bent on stealing sheep. (For the complete story, see Old Lighthouse Museum under *Museums.*) A colorful Blessing of the Fleet is held in summer when boats from Connecticut's only commercial fleet set out to sea. Huge lobster pound.

Clyde's Cider Mill (860-536-3354), North Stonington Road, Stonington. Watch the country's largest historic, steam-powered cider mill squeeze juice from barrels of apples. Fall operation only. Sweet and hard cider for sale.

WINERIES/BREWERY

Stonington Vineyards (1-800-421-WINE), Taugwonk Road, exit 91 off I-95, Stonington. On Connecticut's "Wine Trail." Open daily year-round. Stroll among the rows of grapevines or take a conducted tour of the winery, offered daily. Enjoy free wine tasting; buy a bottle of crisp Seaport White or Seaport Blush for your table. Browse among local crafts and gift baskets in the souvenir shop.

Heritage Trail Vineyards (860-376-0659), 291 North Burnham Highway, Lisbon. This 6-acre vineyard on the site of an 18th-century farm is located on CT 169, one of America's most scenic roads. Sample award-winning Cabernet Sauvignon and Chardonnay and French-American hybrids brewed by a native of the wine country in northern California. Gift shop.

Cottrell Brewing Company (860-599-8213), 100 Mechanic Street, Pawcatuck. Learn how Old Yankee Ale is brewed and sample the freshest beer in the area. Tours Saturday at 1 and 3 and by appointment.

TO DO

AMUSEMENT PARK

Maple Breeze Park (860-599-1232), Liberty Street, Pawcatuck. Summer only. Water slide, go-carts, and bumper boats in a small amusement park. Snack bar and gift shop.

BOAT EXCURSIONS

See also *Fishing.*

Mystic Whaler (1-800-697-8420), Box 189, Holmes Street, Mystic. Modeled after the trading schooners that served ports along the New England coast, the *Whaler* has been completely refurbished and offers adventures under sail with cruise ship amenities. Schedules have been designed to suit every taste, from 1-day on up to 5-day sails that put in at such interesting ports of call as Block Island, Shelter Island, Sag Harbor, Cuttyhunk, Newport, and Martha's Vineyard. There are lighthouse cruises, full moon cruises, and twilight sails. Not to miss is the weekday late-afternoon Atlantic sail feast: Clam chowder is served while the ship sails to historic Noank to pick up fresh lobster! Help veteran captain John Eginton and his friendly crew work the rigging or just relax as the *Whaler* heels nicely in the cooperative winds of the waters off southern New England. $60–620, depending on the sail of your choice.

Sabino (860-572-5315), Mystic Seaport. Trained guides describe coastal flora and fauna on cruises aboard this historic coal-fired vessel as it steams down the Mystic River into the Sound. The *Sabino* served Maine ports for years.

Resolute (860-572-4315), Mystic Seaport. Daily mid-May to mid-October. This antique wooden boat in mint condition—once the tender for an America's Cup defender—offers Seaport visitors another way to cruise the Mystic River. Capacity: six passengers. Small fee in addition to Seaport admission.

FISHING

See also *Green Space.*

Charter boats may be rented with or without a crew: *Lorna Anne* (860-423-9121), Shaffer's Marina, Mason's Island Road, Mystic. *Magic* (860-423-9121), at Mystic Harbor Marina, Water Street, Mystic. *Blue Heron* (860-535-3387), Skippers Dock, Stonington Harbor. There are two operators at Noank Village Boatyard on Bayside Avenue in Noank: *Reelin'* (860-449-1980) and *Trophy Hunter* (860-536-4460). *Anna R.* (860-536-0529) and *Mataura* (860-536-6970) are both on Riverview Avenue, Noank. *Hel-Cat II* (860-535-3200), Hel-Cat Dock, 181 Thames Street, Groton, has party-boat cruises.

GOLF

Elmridge (860-599-2248), Elmridge Road, Pawcatuck. Driving range. Challenging course on a cool hilltop. Modern clubhouse on the 19th hole. Full line of discounted supplies in pro shop. Lessons. Par 71, 18 holes, 6,501 yards.

HAYRIDES

✎ **Davis Farm Horse-drawn Hayrides** (860-599-5841), Greenhaven Road, Pawcatuck. Beautiful big Belgian horses pull hay wagons on 1-hour rides.

MINIATURE GOLF

Great Brook Mini Golf (860-448-0938), 850 CT 184; Groton; and **Maple Breeze Mini Golf** (860-599-1232), 311 Liberty Street, Pawcatuck.

SAILING

The Mystic River, barely long enough to show up on a state map, is nonetheless a beehive of maritime activity. Busy private marinas sit cheek by jowl alongside Mystic Seaport, whose own dock accepts reservations from out-of-town yachters in for a visit to the prestigious museum. A good area for viewing river activities is the lawn of the Mystic Art Association, which sits on the banks of the busy waterway. Windjammer cruises from river wharves are offered on a variety of Coast Guard–inspected and –approved vessels.

Four sailing vessels of various sizes with varying schedules put out from Mystic River docks: *Brilliant* (860-572-5315), Mystic Seaport; *Sylvina Beal* (860-536-8422; 1-800-333-6978), 120 School Street, West Mystic; *The Lady* (860-572-8472), Seaport Marine; and *Argia* (860-536-0416), Steamboat Wharf. (Also see *Boat Excursions.*)

SELF-IMPROVEMENT VACATIONS

✎ **Project Oceanology** (1-800-364-8472), Avery Point campus of the University of Connecticut (I-95, exit 87), just south of the Electric Boat factory. Lace up your boat shoes and bring along a sweater or windbreaker for exciting adventures on the 55-foot *Enviro-lab II* or the 65-foot *Enviro-lab III*, two research vessels sponsored by several New England schools and universities. During the summer months, family groups are invited aboard for such hands-on activities as pulling nets and identifying and recording catches of lobsters, crabs, fish, and other marine life. You and your young ones will collect plankton, test the waters of Long Island Sound, and, on the bridge, learn from the captain how to unravel the mysteries of navigation maps and charts. Visit New London's famous Ledge Lighthouse on one cruise, or book a 2½-hour Marine Science Tour on another day. Capacity of the floating laboratories is limited to 50, so reservations are a must. This could be the highlight of your visit to southeastern Connecticut. Adults $15; children under 12, $11.

CROSS-COUNTRY SKIING

Denison Pequotsepos Nature Center (860-536-1216), Pequotsepos Road, Mystic. There's no downhill skiing in southeastern Connecticut, but cross-country skiing can be found here, when nature obliges. Some area parks also may be used for limited cross-country skiing.

SWIMMING

Esker Point Beach, CT 215 and Marsh Road, Noank. Small, pretty, sandy beach, very shallow. Excellent for very young children. Plenty of parking. Nice view of offshore islands. Picnic grove.

GREEN SPACE

Pachaug State Forest, CT 49, Voluntown. More than 30 miles of the Pachaug Trail snake through this massive, 22,000-acre forest preserve, the largest in the state. Only a short distance from the busy coast, Pachaug also invites visitors to hunt, camp, picnic, and fish. Fishing is available nearby at **Beach Pond,** north of CT 165 at the Rhode Island border; **Beachdale Pond,** on the west side of CT 49 at CT 165; **Green Falls Reservoir,** south of CT 138; and **Hodge Pond,** on CT 49 south of the village center. Boat-launching ramps.

Denison Pequotsepos Nature Center (860-536-1216), Pequotsepos Road, Mystic. Open May through October, Tuesday through Saturday 9–5. Shorter hours off-season. Self-guiding trails on a 125-acre nature preserve where your children come face-to-face with great horned owls, toads, bogs of frogs, and lots of turtles. Native wildlife, birds, and small animals are on exhibit and described in a small museum. Wildflower garden. Trails are marked for the blind.

Pequot Trail, just north of Stonington. The first of 12 official state scenic trails, CT 234 climbs a steep ridge, plunges into a scenic valley, and winds through colonial villages graced by the famed maple trees whose fiery leaves turn autumn in New England into an artist's palette. The trail follows the warpath blazed by the fierce Pequots.

LODGING

The recent concentration of Native American–operated casinos in southeastern Connecticut created a demand for lodgings for thousands of people at one time, particularly in high season. This demand has led to a proliferation of modern hotels and motor inns, most of which are members of chains. While there are only a few resorts and classic inns, B&Bs are sprouting like mushrooms. Because Mystic is a major tourist destination, rates vary from wintertime lows to August highs. When possible, we have indicated the range for double occupancy in high season. Be advised that rates are always subject to change, generally upward. Most don't accept pets; children are usually welcome, with myriad age restrictions. Call ahead.

RESORT

The Inn at Mystic (860-536-9604; 1-800-237-2415), US 1 and CT 27, Mystic 06355. The former estate of a local industrialist, this unique 15-

KIMBERLY GRANT

Despite its small size, the Mystic River is a beehive of maritime activity.

acre complex, set on a plateau overlooking the sea, is a beautiful Russian salad. The first section is an upscale motor inn with 47 rooms, plus four efficiencies and five suites. In the center of the estate, the Georgian Colonial mansion of the late owner has five suites, including one in which Humphrey Bogart and Lauren Bacall spent their honeymoon. The building is on the National Register of Historic Places. There are five rooms with fireplaces and a Jacuzzi in the Gatehouse. Finally, there's the deluxe East Wing. Formal gardens, outdoor and indoor pools, tennis, boating, and a fitness room round out the facilities. Afternoon tea is served; the inn's Flood Tide restaurant is ranked with the best in the state (see *Dining Out*). $95–220 motor inn; $75–235 Gatehouse; $160–220 East Wing—deluxe rooms, with private balconies overlooking the harbor; $160–235 in the mansion. Children under 18 free.

INNS

In Mystic

☞♿ **Whaler's Inn** (860-536-1506; 1-800-243-2588; fax 860-572-1250), 20 East Main Street, Mystic 06355. There are 45 rooms by the bridge in this comfortable and homey inn in the heart of downtown Mystic. Recently renovated rooms are decorated with canopy beds, wingback chairs, humpback couches, and rich color schemes. There's an excellent restaurant on the premises, along with a gourmet bagel shop and seasonal outdoor café. $95–139; children free.

♿ **Steamboat Inn** (860-536-8300), 73 Steamboat Wharf, Mystic 06355. The location couldn't be more ideal: This small and intimate luxury inn is right on the banks of the Mystic River but close to the heart of the city and Seaport. Each of the 10 rooms has a whirlpool; 6 have fireplaces. The larger suites on dock level have wet-bar areas and refrigerators. Prints and antique furnishings decorate each room. Continental-plus breakfast and afternoon tea or sherry are served in the attractive Common Room. $110–275. Four rooms are handicapped accessible.

Residence Inn by Marriott (860-536-5150), 41 Whitehall Avenue, just north of Olde Mistick Village on CT 27, Mystic. Opened in spring 1996, the Whitehall Inn—a five-room Colonial mansion—fronts a new modern Residence Inn that features 80 fully equipped suites, all with kitchens, movies, and Nintendo games. Some suites have Jacuzzis. Complimentary breakfast. $250.

     Days Inn (860-572-0574; chain reservations, 800-DAYS INN), 55 Whitehall Avenue, Mystic. Just north of exit 90, the main exit for the Seaport and aquarium. Although a member of a chain, we include it because this Days Inn has been a mainstay for visitors to the area and has been recognized by Days Inns as a Property of Distinction. Its 122 rooms are above average, clean, and well appointed. The pool is inviting and the Eatery Restaurant serves daily three appetizing, well-prepared meals and snacks. All this, and room service. $39–139.

Elsewhere

     Randall's Ordinary (860-599-4540), Box 243, CT 2, North Stonington 06359. There is nothing ordinary (an old word for "tavern") about this splendid hostelry cum authentic old New England restaurant. Three guest rooms with wide-board floors are over the dining room in the 17th-century farmhouse; nine rooms are in the barn. There are four suites, and all rooms have private bath. Some rooms are equipped with fireplace and whirlpool. The inn is on the National Register of Historic Places. Most visitors make their way to Randall's for the unique culinary experience (see *Dining Out*). Rates start at $75 for a single room, midweek, with continental breakfast, and range up to $225 for a weekend in a deluxe suite, including dinner for two and full breakfast.

     Sojourner Inn (860-445-1986; 1-800-697-8483; e-mail: mysuite45@aol.com), CT 184, Groton 06340. Convenient to Mystic, the naval base, and the casinos. Four types of suites to accommodate families, singles, or to provide a deluxe vacation with a Jacuzzi. Each suite has cable TV and kitchenette. Special rooms welcome the tabby or the pooch.

     Thames Inn & Marina (860-445-8111), 193 Thames Street, Groton 06340. As the name spells out, the inn is perched on the banks of the river. Rooms feature range and stove, microwave oven, free HBO. Drive up or sail. The marina has 20 slips for boats up to 55 feet. Boat slip and room combination rates. Children of all ages welcome. $39–99.

     Applewood Farms Inn (860-536-2022), 528 Ledyard Highway, Ledyard 06339. "A fifth child on the way, we need room," exclaimed Hannah Gallup in 1826 to her husband, the deacon. The expanded house, listed on the National Register of Historic Places, now has six rooms for discriminating guests. Four have fireplaces. Stroll the farm's 33 acres, take a surrey ride, explore the undeveloped woods and fields in the bordering property, which belongs to the Nature Conservancy, or hop in your car to one of the area's well-known tourist attractions. Start the day with a hearty breakfast. $65–95.

BED & BREAKFASTS

In addition to the listings below, a number of bed & breakfast reservation services offer access to rooms available in establishments throughout the state. For a list, see *What's Where—Bed & Breakfasts*.

In Mystic and Old Mystic

Red Brook Inn (860-572-0349; 1-800-290-5619), CT 184 and Wells Road, Old Mystic 06372. Traditional old New England stone walls surround two Colonial buildings with 11 guest rooms, all furnished with period American antiques, some with canopy beds, 7 with working fireplaces. Innkeeper Ruth Keyes is justly proud of the full country breakfast, which she varies—walnut waffles, apple pancakes, blueberry pancakes, baked eggs, or muffins. Complimentary beverages in late afternoon and evening. Relax in one of several large parlors; enjoy the game room and terrace. Quiet location on 7 wooded acres. $125–189.

Pequot Hotel Bed & Breakfast (860-572-0390; fax 860-536-3380), 711 Cow Hill Road, Mystic 06355. A full country breakfast is served by a veteran flight attendant in this restored 19th-century stagecoach inn. The three charming rooms all have private bath, two with working fireplace. Guests can stroll in the estate's 23 wooded acres or relax on the large porch. $95–150; reduced rates January through March.

☞ **Old Mystic Inn** (860-572-9422), 52 Main Street, Old Mystic 06372. A former antique bookstore, this old home and its carriage house welcome guests in eight rooms. Three of the four rooms in the inn have working fireplaces; there are whirlpools in two of four in the carriage house. Complete country breakfast. $115–135.

The Adams House (860-572-9551), 382 Cow Hill Road, Mystic 06355. A little more than a mile from the Seaport. A charming 1750s-era house with six rooms in the main building and two in the carriage house that can accommodate eight people, an ideal setting for family groups. Hearty breakfast includes homemade entrées, baked goods, fresh fruit, and beverages. Linger in the lush flower gardens. $95–175.

Harbour Inne & Cottage (860-572-9253), 15 Edgemont Street, Mystic 06355. On the waterfront, close to the railroad depot and downtown Mystic. Each of the four bedrooms has kitchen privileges, cable TV, and air-conditioning. The cottage is decorated in cedar and offers a hot tub on the deck. Antique piano and fireplace in the social room. Inn $75–135; cottage $175–250.

In Stonington

Lasbury's Guest House (860-535-2681), 41 Orchard Street, Stonington 06378. Three rooms, one with private bath, in a secluded, small cottage in the rear of the house. Only lodging inside the village. Antique furniture; TV and in-room refrigerator. Continental breakfast. $85.

High Acres Bed & Breakfast (1-800-887-4355), 222 Northwest Corner Road, North Stonington 06359. Guests in this 1740 Colonial farmhouse can cuddle up to the fireplace in the library after enjoying a stroll on the farm's 150 acres. All four rooms have private bath. Tea and backgammon. Guided horseback trail rides available mid-April through November. Country breakfast. $125–150.

Antiques & Accommodations (860-535-1736; 1-800-554-7829), 32 Main Street, North Stonington 06359. The 1820 Garden Cottage is for families; doubles in the other four rooms, three with bath. An antiques-lover's delight; comfortable lodgings in an 1861 mansion on the National Register of Historic Places. Breakfast by candlelight recalls the early post–Revolutionary War days before New England's intrepid sailors brought back barrels of whale oil to light the lamps of America. $99–229.

   ć. **Arbor House B&B** (860-535-4221), 75 Chester Maine Road, North Stonington 06359. Located at Kruger's Old Maine Farm, this 1900 farmhouse has four rooms (one suite) for guests who prefer an unhurried life coupled with spectacular views overlooking a vineyard and the countryside. The house has a pleasant sitting room with books, magazines, and menus from local restaurants. Full breakfast. $85–145

John York House B&B (860-599-3075), 1 Clarks Falls Road, North Stonington 06359. Four rooms with bath and fireplace in a 1741 Colonial on the National Register of Historic Places. Guests will enjoy an 8-acre sylvan setting. Full breakfast. $60–140.

Elsewhere

Woodbridge Farm (860-859-1169), 30 Woodbridge Road, Salem 06420. Near the Old Lyme artists colony and other area attractions. A hilltop B&B built in 1792 set among large maples, sweeping lawns, and stones walls overlooking rolling hills and woods. Seven rooms, four with private bath. Five wood-burning fireplaces. View some of the 180 varieties of birds that flock in the fields and woods. And if you happen to have your horse in tow, you can put it up in the farm's stables. Your innkeeper, artist Marian Bingham, is the great-granddaughter of Hiram Bingham, discoverer of Machu Picchu and later governor and US senator from Connecticut. The center-chimney Colonial is on both the National Register and the Connecticut Trust of Historic Places. Continental breakfast. $75–165, suites over $200.

Hideaway Inn B&B (860-887-5059), 87 Cooktown Road, Preston 06365. Master suites on the first floor, guest rooms on the third and fourth floors, all with private bath. Your hosts, Charlie and Ellen Tinturin, invite you to enjoy a swim in the large outdoor pool and spa in summer; try the indoor spa in winter. Read by the fireplace or shoot a game of pool in the billiards room. Complimentary country breakfast in the sunroom. Five minutes to the gaming tables, 20 minutes to the resort complex at Mystic. $115–200.

Palmer Inn (860-572-9000), 25 Church Street, Noank 06340. Fine antiques greet you as you step through the doorway of this elegant, turn-of-the-century mansion. Private baths in all six rooms. Continental breakfast. Noank is a sleepy town of quiet dignity nestled between Groton and Mystic. A favorite retirement village for Connecticut CEOs and aging politicos. $145–195 weekends; lower midweek.

Captain Grant's, 1754 (860-887-7589; fax 860-892-9151), 109 CT 2A, Poquetanuck 06365. Five comfortable rooms in a charming home on the National Register of Historic Places. Two-story deck overlooks the historic village green. A mural depicting the village in 1825 spans the Grand Staircase. Full breakfast. Midway between both casinos. $80–125.

Two B&Bs are clustered around the Foxwoods casino, but still close to the Mystic area: **Stonecroft** (860-572-0771), 515 Pumpkin Hill Road, Ledyard 06339, four rooms, $130–175; **The Mare's Inn** (860-572-7556; fax 860-892-2976), 333 Colonel Ledyard Highway, Ledyard 06339, five rooms, continental breakfast, $100–150; handicapped accessible.

HOTELS/MOTELS

In Mystic

✐♿**Mystic Hilton** (1-800-HILTONS), 20 Coogan Boulevard, Mystic 06355. Unusually attractive for a chain establishment, this rambling redbrick hotel sits on a ledge overlooking the aquarium and Olde Mistick Village and is just down the road from the Seaport. You'll find 184 rooms, an indoor pool, and a fitness room. Golf, tennis, and racquetball are nearby. The hotel caters to children, with special activities including clowns and a kids' barbecue. There's also an outstanding restaurant (see *Dining Out*). $189–240 double, in season.

Seaport Motor Inn (860-536-2621), CT 27, Mystic 06355. Also slips into the hotel category with 118 rooms—all with direct dialing and color TV. Outdoor pool. $38–98.

East of Mystic

Several modest motels can be found east of Mystic. **Cove Ledge Motel** (860-599-4130), Whewell Circle, US 1, Pawcatuck 06379 (May to Columbus Day), 16 rooms, guest boat docking, pool; $45–85; **Sea Breeze Motel** (860-535-2843), 812 Stonington Road, Stonington 06378 (28 rooms, two suites; $25–95); **Stonington Motel** (860-599-2330; fax 860-599-2330), 901 Stonington Road, Stonington 06378 (12 rooms with refrigerators; $59–75); **Stardust Motel** (860-599-2261), CT 184, North Stonington 06359 (22 rooms; $40–65); **Budget Inn** (860-599-0835), 593 Providence/New London Turnpike, North Stonington 06359 (formerly Stateline Motel; 22 rooms; $35–75); **Plainfield Motel** (860-564-2791), Moosup 06354, off I-395 (30 rooms, five efficiencies, pool, close to the greyhound track and Foxwoods; $65).

In Ledyard

The following are just off I-95 on CT 27, the road leading to the Seaport. Olde Mistick Village and the aquarium are just at the bottom of the interchange.

Old Mystic Motor Lodge (860-536-9666), CT 27, Mystic 06355, has 56 rooms; $40–159.

  Taber Inn & Suites (860-536-4904; fax 860-572-9140), 66 Williams Avenue, Mystic 06355. This is another interesting ménage: There are 16 standard motel rooms; 12 luxury suites with fireplace and 2-person Jacuzzi; a luxury 1-bedroom suite with a fireplace, Jacuzzi, and balcony; and, finally, six 2-bedroom deluxe suites with canopy beds, Jacuzzis. $95–145 motel, $195–240 luxury suites. Guests can use the facilities of the private health club across the street.

The Foxwoods Resort Casino in Ledyard just keeps growing. It now offers three major hotels and the end, probably, is not in sight. Phone for all three is: 1-800-FOXWOOD. The latest lodging is the **Grand Pequot Tower,** a deluxe hotel soaring above the woods of Ledyard with 800 luxurious rooms, suites, and more gaming tables. It joins: **Two Trees Inn,** 240 Lantern Hill Road, CT 214, Ledyard 06339, a 280-room hotel built by the Mashantuckets to accommodate sporting folk and just plain tourists. Hardwood floors, wool scatter rugs, cherry paneling, and custom-made furniture greet guests in the spacious lobby. Sixty suites for the high rollers. The second 312-room luxury hostelry is called, unimaginatively, the **Resort Hotel at Foxwoods**. All three hotels have gourmet restaurants. The tribal sachem (that's the Eastern Woods Indian name for chief) have said that a casino is a casino, but when it also offers hotel rooms, it's a resort. $90–160.

In Groton

Accommodations on the Groton side of the Thames are clean and dependable but not out of the ordinary. They cater mainly to tourists lured by the maritime attractions of Mystic and the Foxwoods and Mohegan casinos, as well as to families visiting service personnel at the Coast Guard Academy and Navy submarine base.

  Clarion Inn (860-446-0660), 156 Kings Highway, Groton 06340 (formerly Gold Star Inn). The Clarion boasts 69 rooms, restaurant, indoor pool, Jacuzzi, exercise room. $99–159 double, children free.

  Groton Inn & Suites (860-445-9784; 1-800-452-2191; fax 860-445-2664), I-95 and CT 184, Groton 06340. There are 115 rooms with 35 apartments, 10 efficiencies, and 29 deluxe suites; microwaves, refrigerators, coffeemakers in all rooms. Restaurant. Handicapped accessible to restaurant and some guest rooms. $73–180 double.

  Morgan Inn & Suites (860-448-3000; 1-800-280-0054; fax 860-445-1152), 135 Gold Star Highway, Groton 06340. Near the sub base and area attractions. Fifty-two rooms in a well-appointed small hotel. Spacious swimming pool. $69–145.

CAMPGROUNDS

Seaport Campground (860-536-4044), CT 184, Old Mystic 06372. April through November. Tenting facilities, pool, miniature golf; 130 spacious, level sites; 3 miles from the Seaport.

Highland Orchards Resort Park (1-800-624-0829), CT 49, North Stonington 06359. Open year-round. Modern facilities. Wooded and grassy tent sites, large pull-through sites with full hookups for RVs. Pool, shuffleboard, fishing.

Pachaug State Forest (860-376-4075), Voluntown 06384. Two camping areas: **Green Falls Campground,** off CT 138, just 3 miles east of town (18 wooded sites, pond fishing, swimming; no concession; pets allowed); and **Mt. Misery Campground,** off CT 49 north of town (22 wooded sites, stream fishing, swimming nearby; pets allowed; no concession).

Connecticut has two campgrounds specifically designed for equestrians, both open April 16 through Thanksgiving. No reservations. Pachaug State Forest provides **Frog Hollow Horse Camp** (18 semi-wooded sites; no concession); **Natchaug State Forest** (860-974-1562) operates **Silvermine Horse Camp** (12 sites).

WHERE TO EAT

DINING OUT
In Mystic

The Mooring (860-572-0731), 20 Coogan Boulevard, Mystic (in the Mystic Hilton). Open daily for breakfast, lunch, and dinner. This popular establishment is a cut above typical hotel restaurants. Seafood pie, seared salmon, and a variety of beef, veal, chicken, and pasta dishes are tastefully served in a spacious high-ceilinged room with nautical decor. Don't pass up the banana nut bread pudding for dessert. From $10.95 for the pasta to $24.95 for rack of lamb.

☞ **Draw Bridge Inne** (860-536-9653), 34 Main Street, Mystic. Lunch and dinner. Basic menu of 26 items, ranging from fowl to veal and beef. Five specials daily but always expect lobster and other seafood. Original art on the walls. $9.95–14.95.

J.P. Daniels (860-572-9564), off the beaten path on CT 184, Old Mystic. Dinner and Sunday brunch in a historic barn. A favorite with locals. Raw bar. The tempting menu is crowded with everything from pasta to boneless duck, chicken, swordfish, salmon, lamb chops, veal Oscar, bouillabaisse, large salads, and a variety of steaks. All fresh food, elegantly prepared, and still the chef has time to concoct daily specials. Many entrées are available in lighter, less expensive portions. $5.95–17.95.

✍☞♿**Steak Loft** (860-536-2661), Olde Mistick Village. Lunch and dinner daily. The massive wooden beams have anchored this local favorite for more than a quarter of a century. Seven varieties of steaks, plus seafood and poultry. Incomparable juicy hamburgers. Salad bar with every order, even a humble tuna sandwich. Complete children's menu. Entertainment Wednesday through Sunday. $13.95–22.95.

☞♿**Seamen's Inne** (860-536-9649), CT 27, set within Mystic Seaport at the north gate. Open daily for lunch and dinner; Sunday brunch. Enjoy stuffed mushroom caps, escargots, fried clams, seafood potpies, New England–style clam chowder, baked stuffed lobster, exceptional prime ribs, and hearty steak in an English pub atmosphere. Antique ship figureheads on the wall; ales and beer. Wind up your meal with chocolate bread pudding. Covered patio. No rooms. $14.95–21.95.

☞ **Captain Daniel Packer Inne, Ltd.** (860-536-3555), 32 Water Street, Mystic. Open year-round, daily 11–4 and 5–10. Circa 1754. Seafood, veal, and duck, but if you've restrained yourself for a few days and have the stomach for it, do try the Steak Blackjack, a 16-ounce slab of beef flamed with Jack Daniels. The shrimp and scallops Provençal, as the name underscores, is redolent of garlic. Blues and classic '40s pop midweek in the downstairs pub. No rooms. The building is on the National and Connecticut Historic Registers. $10.95–22.95.

☞ **Flood Tide** (860-536-8140), US 1 and CT 27, at the Inn at Mystic. Open daily. High on a knoll overlooking the harbor and the Mystic Railroad Station, which was the model for the station in the Lionel toy train sets. The chef does wonders with duckling and beef. Here you can impress friends and/or loved ones with a spectacular Sunday brunch for a special occasion by filling your platters with lamb, stuffed pork, or steamship round from the carving station. Fresh seafood from salmon to codfish graces the Sunday menu. Sous-chef Richard Browning says the house pâté melts in your mouth. Pastas are always given special attention. Don't pass up the Belgian waffles. Delightful atmosphere—shoreline dining at its most pleasurable. $15.95–23.95 dinner, $15.95 Sunday brunch, $7.95 breakfast buffet, $10.95 luncheon buffet.

♿ **Restaurant Bravo Bravo** (860-536-3228), the Whaler's Inn, 18 East Main Street, Mystic. Open for breakfast daily; lunch and dinner, except Monday. "Wonderful" is the way locals describe the bounty of Italian food served in this pleasant eatery at the foot of the Bascule Bridge in downtown Mystic. For an appetizer, try the polenta torte or the Roman-style grilled mozzarella. Choice entrées include osso buco, champagne risotto tossed with lobster and asparagus, and zuppa, an Italian version of the Marseilles classic seafood-based soup. And if you're curious, *bascule* is French for "seesaw." $14.95–17.95.

Elsewhere

☞ **Randall's Ordinary** (860-599-4540), CT 2, North Stonington. A dining experience like no other. One dinner seating, at 7, and then the evening is yours to savor. Dinner is prepared in an old-fashioned, walk-in fireplace over an open hearth and served by waiters in Colonial attire. While the entrées are being prepared, soup is bubbling away in a caldron hung over the coals. Beef, poultry, and fish, and venison in season, are the stars, accompanied by home-baked corn bread. Inn guests first; reservations for the general public. Bountiful, English-style breakfast and luncheon. Prix fixe $30-plus for dinner.

Water Street Cafe (860-535-2122), 142 Water Street, Stonington. Only 10 tables in a 1900s post-and-beam house, but well worth a wait. Start

Diners at Abbot's Lobster in the Rough savor their crustaceans while watching the passing parade of boats on the Mystic River.

dinner with tartare of smoked salmon or gravlax or seared shrimp in pommery mustard sauce. For the main course, you might enjoy seared scallops in a ginger-scallion vinaigrette. Meat lovers rave over the grilled "hangar" steak in a red wine and blue cheese sauce. (Hangar steak is better known as butcher's tenderloin.) $15.

& **Cedars Steak House** (860-885-4252), CT 2, Ledyard. Open for lunch and dinner daily. One of the standout restaurants in the Foxwoods casino complex. Raw bar for the fearless. Picking up an innovation introduced in San Francisco, the mashed potatoes accompanying your gargantuan steak are fragrant with garlic. Enjoy these and other he-man specialties in an elegantly rustic setting. Nightly meat and fish specials. $18.75.

✑☞&**Abbott's Lobster in the Rough** (860-536-7719), 117 Pearl Street, Noank. Open for lunch and dinner, May through October. The ultimate fun place in all of New England for your lobster experience. Complete lobster meals served on rustic picnic tables on the banks of the Mystic River. Steamed and stuffed clams, lobster rolls. Watch fishermen unload lobsters at the dock and view the panorama of yachts, fishing boats, and windjammers while you enjoy your bountiful meal. Indoor facilities available. Live lobsters packed for travel or shipping. Chicken, and even peanut butter and jelly sandwiches, available for the non–lobster eater. New this year, a complete raw bar. $10–14.

Ming Garden (860-448-1793), 1041 Poquonnock Road, US 1, Groton. Open daily. Szechuan, Mandarin, and Cantonese cuisine; lunch and dinner, late supper. The chef tosses a particularly good "shrimp with lobster sauce" in his industrial-size wok. Try the Peking chicken or chicken in garlic sauce. $4.95 for fried rice to $14.95 for beef, seafood, and chicken dishes.

EATING OUT
In Mystic

✐ **Trader Jack's** (860-572-8550), 14 Holmes Street, Mystic. Dinner only, daily 5–midnight. Dining room or bar menu. The varied bill of fare includes poultry, lobster, seafood, veal, steaks, and pasta and Mexican dishes. Children's menu.

✐ **Margaritas** (860-536-4589), 12 Water Street, Mystic. Tex-Mex specialties with a nautical touch: seafood enchiladas plus the usual American Mexican dishes. No charge for children on Sunday. In a converted factory across from the Art Association Gallery (see *Museums*). As befits the establishment's name, the margaritas are marvelous.

Copperfield's (860-536-4281), CT 27, in the Best Western complex, Mystic. A better-than-average hotel restaurant. Seafood, poultry, and steaks. Pleasant atmosphere. A companion restaurant is in Niantic at 252 Main Street.

✐ **Sea View Snack Bar** (860-572-0096), 145 Greenmanville Avenue (CT 27), Mystic. Open daily. Don't pass up this unprepossessing-looking shanty on the banks of the Mystic River if you have a carful of hungry children. The menu runs the gamut from great chowder to fried clams or clam strips, lobster salad roll, cheese dogs, juicy burgers, platters, fries, milk shakes, and soft-serve ice cream. Eat on the premises or take out.

✐ **Sea Swirl** (860-532-3452), US 1, Mystic. Open daily 10–10. Not just another old-fashioned shoreline clam shack. Seafood fans rave over the whole-belly fried clams. Juicy hamburgers, rotisserie chicken, fresh vegetables, and ice cream; something for the entire family.

✐ **Angie's Pizza House & Restaurant** (860-536-7300), 25 Roosevelt Avenue, Mystic. Open daily until midnight. More than just a pizza house, Angie's will fill your plates with pasta, broiled fish, barbecued ribs, chicken wings, even shish kebob, and, of course, seafood. Children's menu. A favorite with Coast Guard Academy cadets, submariners, and their families.

✐ **Quiambaug House** (860-572-8543), Old Stonington Road, US 1, Mystic. Lunch and dinner. Family favorite. Emphasizes seafood, but serves ample portions of beef and poultry in a nautical atmosphere. Four-star rating.

Mystic Pizza (860-536-3737), 56 West Main Street, in the heart of downtown Mystic. Open daily for lunch and dinner. A few years back, a writer motoring from Maine along the East Coast stopped here for a pizza. Intrigued by both the food and the name of the restaurant, she wrote a movie script called *Mystic Pizza*. It catapulted one of the three female leads, Julia Roberts, into instant stardom. It didn't hurt the pizza shop, either. Shortly afterward, a satellite of Mystic Pizza opened in North Stonington at the rotary where CT 184 meets CT 2. You decide whether a slice of Mystic Pizza is "a slice of heaven."

In Groton

✐ **G. Williker's** (860-445-8043), 156 Kings Highway, Groton. Breakfast, lunch, and dinner until 10 PM. Sixteen-page menu, with more than

One of three deluxe hotels at Foxwoods, the world's largest gambling casino, built and operated by the Mashantucket Pequot tribal nation.

enough choices for your youngsters. Steaks and seafood. A variety of sandwiches and Mexican burgers.

* **Fun 'n Food Clam Bar, Inc.** (860-445-6186), 283 CT 12, Groton. Open daily year-round. Just the place to stuff a hungry teenager. Foot-long hot dogs, chili dogs, clam fritters, whole and strip fried clams, grinders, chowder, onion rings, all washed down with rich milk shakes.

* **Ground Round** (860-449-8650), 654 Long Hill Road, Groton. A family restaurant serving lunch and dinner daily. Complete meals, daily specials, and thick, juicy hamburgers. The usual steaks, chicken, and seafood, but the chef has a Lebanese background, so discuss the designs in the Persian carpets while he is preparing hummus, gyros, and special Mediterranean grilled meats.

Diana Restaurant (860-449-8468), 970 Poquonnock Road, Groton. Open daily for lunch and dinner. Enjoy hummus and falafel along with a variety of lamb dishes, shish kabob, and Mediterranean-style seafood. $16.50.

ENTERTAINMENT

Foxwoods Resort Casino (1-800-PLAY-BIG), CT 2, Ledyard, between I-395 and I-95. On a small Native American reservation, the Mashantucket Pequots are attracting millions of visitors to the world's largest gambling casino. Three hotels (see *Lodging*) and a large convention center. There are 22 restaurants (see *Dining Out*), plus shops, a theater, a dance club, and an amusement park with 21st-century high-tech rides to provide diversions for the rest of the family. The complex is near New London and Mystic attractions. Headliners such as Tony Bennett and Liza Minnelli, plus rock and country-music notables appear on a regular schedule in the casino's theater. Wrestling and championship boxing matches are an added draw. The newest addition: the $120 million Mashantucket Pequot Museum and Research Center (see *Museums*).

Mohegan Sun Resort Casino, (1-888-226-7711), CT 2A, Montville. Ten miles southwest of Foxwoods and only a mile from the interstate (I-395), the third largest casino in America has grouped its 180 gaming tables and 2,500 slots into one huge, circular room artfully decorated with Native American themes. Entertainment, three restaurants, child care. Reports that the Mohegans hadn't "lasted" were greatly exaggerated.

SELECTIVE SHOPPING

The streets of historic downtown Mystic, just south of the Seaport, are lined with gift shops, boutiques, and bookstores, with a heavy emphasis on items nautical.

☞ **Olde Mistick Village,** at the bottom of the I-95–CT 27 ramp, is a model shopping center. Jerry Olson has erected 60 Colonial-style "homes" around a small landscaped green with a creek and waterwheel, including an old Colonial meetinghouse. All the buildings are specialty shops, including a Wine Education Center, a satellite of the Haight Winery of Litchfield (see "Litchfield and Surrounding Towns"—*Wineries*). Myriad clothing stores offer sportswear, famous-label classics, jewelry, hats, fragrances, and casual vacationwear. Handmade crafts, gardening equipment, New England collectibles, Irish and Scottish imports, toys, scrimshaw, and nautical memorabilia. Family restaurant, bakery, candy shop, creamery, and movie theater. Weekend concerts June through October.

Georgetti's (860-536-2964), Olde Mistick Village, deserves special mention among all the shops in the village. Famed for Lladro Spanish porcelain, art glass, paperweights, and gold jewelry, the shop also sells leather handbags and fine crystal.

Mystic Factory Outlets I & II (860-443-4788), Coogan Boulevard, on a ridge overlooking Olde Mistick Village, features a full range of men's and women's clothes in 24 outlet stores, which also offer leather goods, crafts, shoes, housewares, and toys.

Mystic Emporium (860-536-3891), 15 Water Street, Mystic. This is the place for the gold-medal shopper in the family. Here you'll find everything from scrimshaw, jewelry, posters, and unique greeting cards to interesting tableware.

Mystic Seaport Museum Store, outside the south gate, so a Seaport museum pass is not needed. The emphasis here is on nautical books and paintings, marine artifacts, and ship models.

Window shopping in Stonington

Quimper Faience (860-535-1712), 141 Water Street, Stonington. We would be remiss if we neglected to direct you to this upscale shop that imports prized faience pottery from Italy.

ANTIQUES SHOPS

Antiques shops and galleries are everywhere in Mystic and Stonington. Here is a sampling.

In Mystic

Trade Winds Gallery (860-536-0119), 20 West Main Street. Six days a week, summer only; specializing in antique maps and prints. **Annette's Branche of Antiques** (860-536-0098), 18-B Holmes Street. Open daily. Furniture and accessories.

In Stonington

Orkney & Yost (860-535-4402), 148 Water Street. Open Monday through Saturday, Sunday by chance. Oriental rugs, 18th- and 19th-century American and Continental furniture. Estate jewelry.

Mary Mahler Antiques (860-535-0098), 117 Water Street. Open Monday through Saturday and by appointment; 18th- and 19th-century furniture.

Quester Gallery (860-535-3860), 77 Main Street. Open daily; ship models, 19th-century marine and sporting paintings.

Grand & Water Antiques (860-535-2624), 135 Water Street. Open year-round; formal mahogany furniture and accessories from the 19th and early 20th centuries.

Neil Bruce Eustace Antiques (860-535-2249), 156 Water Street. Open by chance or appointment; 18th-century American furniture.

Anguilla Gallery (860-535-4399), 72 Water Streeet. More than just an art gallery. A historically accurate model train tells the story of how the railroad opened up the Connecticut coast to high-speed commercial traffic.

ART GALLERIES

Stone Ledge Art Gallery (860-536-7813), 59 High Street, Noank. Features work of local artists.

Pratt Wright Galleries (860-536-9243), 48 Main Street, Noank. Landscapes, seascapes, American and European art in the center of a picturesque village.

BOOKSTORES

Bank Square Books (860-536-3795), 53 West Main Street, Mystic.

Village Booksmith (860-536-6185), Olde Mistick Village, Mystic.

Book Mart (860-535-0401), 17 High Street, Stonington.

SPECIAL EVENTS

April: **Mystic Seaport Seniors Month. Earth Day** celebrations throughout the region. Join the local folk and plant a tree or two. Plant a grove.

Mid-May: Sail along the coast on **Captain John's Lighthouse Cruises** and recall the days when sailing ships were warned of dangerous shoals by these sturdy and graceful sentinels of the sea.

☞ *End of May:* Annual **Lobsterfest,** Mystic Seaport Museum (see *Museums*). Old-fashioned lobster bake with corn and baked potatoes, behind the Seamen's Inne on the banks of the Mystic River. Put on a bib and pick the shells clean accompanied by sea-chantey singing.

Mid-June: Raise your voice and join the fun at the **Mystic Seaport Sea Music Festival.**

Early July: **Blessing of the Fleet** in Stonington Harbor.

✐ *Mid-July:* Fun for the kids, lots of good food at one of the first of more than 60 country fairs that take place throughout the state until early October at the **Pachaug Fair** in Griswold.

✐ *Late July:* Annual **Antique & Classic Boat Rendezvous.** Private owners of pre-1952 classic, all-wooden boats, speedboats, sailboats, and yachts, polished to a fare-thee-well, parade 9–5 down the Mystic River from the Seaport. View the parade from the dockside of the Seaport or from the spacious lawn of the Mystic Art Association on the southern side of the Bascule Bridge. Many of the sailors are in colorful vintage costumes. **Moby Dick Marathon Reading.** In Dublin, they read the complete *Ulysses* of James Joyce once a year. At Mystic Seaport, Herman Melville's birthday is celebrated with a 24-hour reading of *Moby Dick* on board the whaleship *Charles W. Morgan.*

Mid-August: Annual **Mystic Outdoor Art Festival.** Some 300 artists from around the country take over the sidewalks of downtown Mystic in one of the nation's finest outdoor juried shows. Food and entertainment. Saturday 10–dusk, Sunday noon–dusk.

Early September: **Living History Weekend** at Fort Griswold (see *Museums*) on a battleground site. Revolutionary War camp life—marching and musket drills, tenting, and food preparation exhibits. The **Annual Artists and Artisans Show,** Ocean Beach Park. Lion's Club **Fish Fry,** Mystic Seaport—food extra after paying reduced admission to the museum. **Meet the Artists & Artisans** at Olde Mistick Village.

Second week of September: **A Taste of Connecticut Food Festival,** downtown Mystic. Sample dishes from the area's myriad restaurants, inns, and specialty food shops.

Early October: Annual **Chowderfest.** Back to the Seaport again for clam and fish chowder ladled out of steaming caldrons. Food is supplied by local civic groups. Seaport admission; food extra.

Mid-December: **Christmas decorations, Lantern Light Tours,** and **Yuletide Tours,** Mystic Seaport. **One-day lumina**—5,000 lights illuminate paths of Olde Mistick Village. Holiday music, hayrides, costumed characters.

End of December: **First Night in Mystic.**

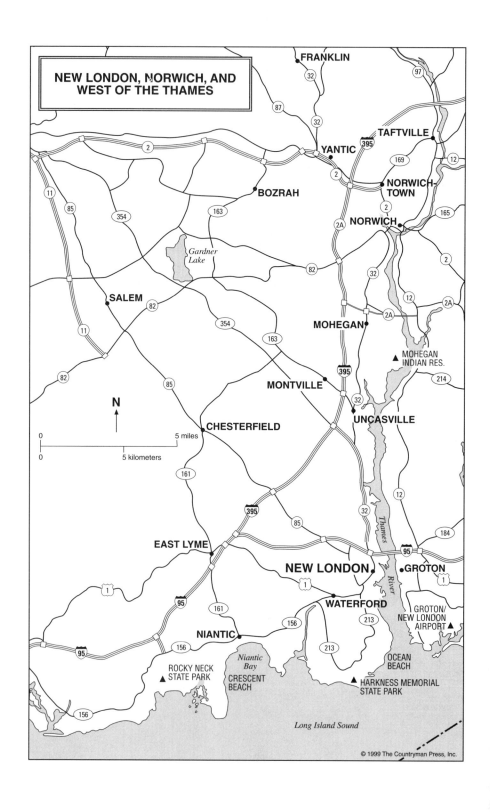

NEW LONDON, NORWICH, AND
WEST OF THE THAMES

FRANKLIN

TAFTVILLE

YANTIC

NORWICH-
TOWN

BOZRAH

NORWICH

Gardner
Lake

SALEM

MOHEGAN

MOHEGAN
INDIAN RES.

MONTVILLE

CHESTERFIELD

UNCASVILLE

N

0   5 miles
0   5 kilometers

Thames

EAST LYME

NEW LONDON

GROTON

WATERFORD

GROTON/
NEW LONDON
AIRPORT

River

NIANTIC

Niantic
Bay

OCEAN
BEACH

ROCKY NECK
STATE PARK

CRESCENT
BEACH

HARKNESS MEMORIAL
STATE PARK

Long Island Sound

© 1999 The Countryman Press, Inc.

New London, Norwich, and West of the Thames

One of the finest deep-water ports along the New England coast, New London was home base during the American Revolution for the largest fleet of New England privateers to prey on British shipping. To stem the havoc, the British dispatched a task force in 1781 under the overall command of Benedict Arnold, a native of nearby Norwich, to burn the town. The British also stormed Fort Griswold across the river in Groton.

After the war, New London mariners set out in pursuit of whales. At one time, New London was second only to New Bedford in the number of whalers seeking the elusive giants in the oceans of the world. Nantucket was third. In 1858, with the discovery of crude oil in Pennsylvania, whale oil to light the lamps of the world was no longer necessary. New London became a major commercial port, and the country's first customs house is now a museum.

Other museums in New London and at Mystic, across the Thames, recall the halcyon days when stout men pitted their individual strength against the leviathans of the deep. New London's maritime heritage also lives on in the halls, dormitories, and training ships of the US Coast Guard Academy, one of America's four military academies; and the North Atlantic sub base and submarine school across the river in Groton, to the discomfort of Grotonites, has always been called the New London US Naval Submarine Base. Among its most distinguished graduates and active officers was a young ensign named Jimmy Carter. In 1998 a new nuclear sub was named after the former president.

In New London and the other towns along the coast, you'll find a plethora of nautical sites and activities: charter fishing boats, whale-watching expeditions, oceanographic floating laboratories. Art galleries and unique museums abound: In Norwich, marvel at full-size replicas of Greek and Roman statues. In summer, outdoor art shows are combined with lobster bakes. A statue of a boy sitting on a rock in New London Harbor, reminiscent of the *Little Mermaid* in Copenhagen's harbor, depicts the young Eugene O'Neill, one of America's greatest dramatists, who spent his childhood here. The lawn (home of the Harkness Memorial) of the mansion of a partner of John D. Rockefeller

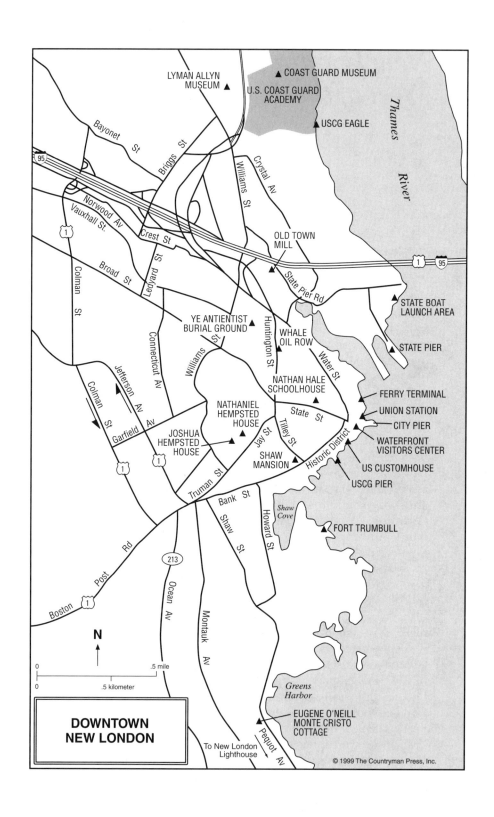

LYMAN ALLYN
MUSEUM ▲

▲ COAST GUARD MUSEUM

U.S. COAST GUARD
ACADEMY

▲ USCG EAGLE

Thames

River

Bayonet St

Briggs St

Williams St

Crystal Av

95

Norwood Av

Vauxhall St.

Crest St

Layard St

1

Colman St

Broad St

OLD TOWN
MILL
▲

State Pier Rd

1 95

STATE BOAT
LAUNCH AREA ▲

YE ANTIENTIST
BURIAL GROUND

Williams St

Huntington St

WHALE
OIL ROW

Water St

▲ STATE PIER

Jefferson Av

Connecticut Av

NATHAN HALE
SCHOOLHOUSE ▲

FERRY TERMINAL

Colman St

Garfield Av

NATHANIEL
HEMPSTED
HOUSE

State St

Jay St

Tilley St

UNION STATION

CITY PIER

1

1

JOSHUA
HEMPSTED
HOUSE ▲

SHAW
MANSION

Historic District

WATERFRONT
VISITORS CENTER

US CUSTOMHOUSE

USCG PIER

Truman St

Bank St

Shaw St

Howard St

*Shaw
Cove*

▲ FORT TRUMBULL

Post Rd

213

Ocean Av

Montauk Av

Boston 1

*Greens
Harbor*

▲ EUGENE O'NEILL
MONTE CRISTO
COTTAGE

Pequot Av

To New London
Lighthouse

N

0   .5 mile

0   .5 kilometer

DOWNTOWN
NEW LONDON

© 1999 The Countryman Press, Inc.

is the setting for a seaside summer concert series. The prestigious Yale-Harvard crew regatta on the Thames River, which separates New London and Groton, kicks off the summer social season.

Bluefish, sea bass, and flounder are the targets for the large fleet of fishing boats that put into Long Island Sound from the myriad marinas and yacht havens of southeastern Connecticut. More adventurous anglers venture into the Atlantic for tuna, swordfish, and mako shark. Charter boats are available for groups of up to six anglers, complete with rods, bait, and helpful crew. For a day of party-boat fishing, grab your gear, lace up your boat shoes, and hop aboard with the rest of the crowd. Many captains sail year-round. Connecticut does not require a license for saltwater fishing.

Norwich. You may reasonably presume that this architecturally eclectic city at the head of the Thames River carries the sobriquet the Rose City because of its garden of prize roses, the annual Rose Arts Festival, and because rosebushes adorn the gardens of every homestead. There *is* a prize rose garden, and a rose festival, but the entire town is *not* planted in roses. Like most residents, you would be wrong about the origin of its nickname. In the 19th century, the abolitionist Henry Ward Beecher, a Litchfield native, visualized the hills that rose up from the port as the petals of a rose. He declared that the city was "the Rose of New England."

Settled 300 years ago, at the turn of the century Norwich was home to more millionaires than any other city in New England. These entrepeneurs accumulated their wealth not from factories in the city, but from textile mills that drew their power from the many rivers in the valleys of south and northeastern Connecticut. The mills eventually fled south (and thence to Korea, Taiwan, and Bangladesh).

The legacy of these early industrialists can be seen in the eclectic great houses that still dot the city. One of the most interesting buildings is the spectacular City Hall, with its ornate Second Empire facade. Built in 1870, it was recently restored and still serves as the seat of government.

Benedict Arnold, our most brilliant general turned traitor in the American Revolutionary War, was born in Norwich and was a local pharmacist before he went off, first to fame and then to infamy. But the city also is the burial place of Samuel Huntingon, a signer of the Declaration of Independence and one of our most influential founding fathers.

For the visitor, Norwich offers a cornucopia of activities and attractions: an annual Rose Arts Festival, antique auto shows, Harbor Day, historic Norwichtown Days, Italian and Greek food festivals, concerts, musicals, crafts show, fairs, minor league baseball, one of the state's premier spas, a unique museum of reproductions of classical statuary—and much more. The Pequots have bought a large swath of historic buildings in the center of town in what is known as the Chelsea district and plan to restore them for businesses, shops, restaurants, and hotels.

Entries in this section are arranged in roughly geographic order.

This statue of young Eugene O'Neill overlooks New London harbor.

AREA CODE
860

GUIDANCE

Connecticut's Mystic & More (860-444-2206; 1-800-TO-ENJOY; fax 860-442-4257; Web site: www.mysticmore.com), 470 Bank Street, New London 06320. Stop in, call, or write for brochures, maps, and a calendar of events.

Southeastern Connecticut Chamber of Commerce (860-443-8332), One Whale Oil Row, New London 06320.

Norwich Tourism Commission (860-886-4683), 69 Main Street, Norwich. Story of Norwich, brochures, maps, tour guides, events.

State Information Center, I-95 southbound, North Stonington. Guides, brochures, pamphlets, maps. Full rest facilities. Open year-round daily. Staffed by tourism specialists in high season.

GETTING THERE

By car: The New London area is accessible by car from I-95, east- and westbound, and from CT 32 from the north. The Norwich area is accessible by I-395 and CT 32.

By air: The **Groton/New London Airport** (located in Groton) receives feeder service from USAir Express and Action Airline, a charter service. Many visitors also are finding less expensive flights into nearby **T.F. Green Airport** in Rhode Island.

By bus: **Greyhound** (1-800-522-9267) and **Bonanza** (1-888-751-8800) bus lines serve the area. Local public transportation is by bus.

By rail: **AMTRAK** (1-800-872-7245) stops frequently at New London and Mystic. The shoreline segment of the state-owned **Metro-North** (1-800-638-7646)commuter link to New York City has been extended to New London. But service to New London on this line is at the fickle mercy of the budgeteers in the state Capitol in Hartford. Call ahead.

By ferry: To Orient Point, Long Island: **Cross Sound Ferry Services, Inc.** (860-443-7394), Two Ferry Street, New London. Vehicle and passenger ferries leave from the Ferry Street dock. To Fishers Island: **Fishers Island Ferry District** (860-442-0165), New London Pier, Fishers Island. Auto ferries depart from New London Pier at the foot of State Street. To Block Island: **Nelseco Navigation Company** (860-442-7891), Two Ferry Street, New London. Auto ferry from the Ferry Street dock. New London to New York: **Fox Navigation High Speed Ferry** (1-888-724-5369). The Pequots are also experimenting with a large, fast catamaran between New London and Martha's Vineyard.

MEDICAL EMERGENCY

The statewide emergency number is **911.**

Lawrence & Memorial Hospital (860-442-0711), 365 Montauk Avenue, New London.

William Backus Hospital (860-889-8331), 326 Washington Street, Norwich.

TO SEE

✐ **US Coast Guard Academy** (860-444-8270), CT 32 off I-95 on the banks of the Thames River, New London. The Visitors Pavilion and a separate museum are open daily May through October. Although Connecticut is the country's third smallest state, it is proud to be home to one of America's four military academies. Cadets are trained to command ships in what is probably the true "multimission service." In addition to rescues at sea and interdicting drug and customs violators, Coast Guard personnel have served in all of this country's major conflicts. During World War II, they were assigned the dangerous mission of manning the landing craft that assaulted the heavily defended beaches of Europe and the South Pacific. They suffered heavy casualties. The Coast Guard was the first service to assign women officers to command positions on seagoing vessels. When in port, the beautiful cadet training barque USCG *Eagle* is open to the public afternoons, Friday through Sunday. The *Eagle* has been the lead ship for the past 20 years in "tall ship" parades up the Hudson River. The phone for information on the *Eagle* is 860-444-8595. Dress parades occur spring and fall on Friday afternoons. Free admission to the grounds, the museum (see *Museums*), and the ship. Visitors can eat at the Dry Dock snack bar.

✐ **Eugene O'Neill Statue,** New London. An appealing statue of the young Eugene in his schoolboy cap and first long pants sitting on a rock overlooking New London Harbor and scribbling in his notebook. America's answer to Copenhagen's *Little Mermaid* harbor statue.

MUSEUMS

US Coast Guard Museum (860-444-8511), CT 32 off I-95, New London. The museum houses some 6,000 works of art and artifacts, including a 13-foot first-order lighthouse lens from the Cape Ann Lighthouse, signatures of Presidents Washington, Lincoln, and Kennedy, and 200 ship models.

Lyman Allyn Art Museum (860-443-2545), 625 Williams Street, New London. Open Tuesday through Friday and Sunday 1–5, Saturday 11–5, Wednesday 1–9. Children will revel in the unique collection of dolls, dollhouses, and antique toys. Asian, European, and American art. Innovative, ongoing lectures and events (see *Special Events*). Adults $3; seniors and students $1.

Science Center of Eastern Connecticut (860-442-0391), 33 Gallows Lane (off Williams Street), New London. Open Monday through Saturday 9–5, Sunday 1–5; closed major holidays. Children enjoy examining local marine life in the touch tank. A salt marsh diorama and a glacier model depict the Thames River basin in ancient days. Educational programs and changing exhibits. Watch the busy bees at work in an observational beehive. Enter cyberspace through the Internet and explore the world of science. Adults $2; children $1.

Slater Museum (860-887-2506), 108 Crescent Street, Norwich. Open Tuesday through Sunday 1–4, September through June; Tuesday through Friday 9–4, Saturday and Sunday 1–4, July and August. Closed major holidays. There's nothing quite like it in the world. Packed into the Slater's relatively small space is an astonishing collection of 150 full-size, plaster-cast replicas of the most famous statuary of ancient Egypt, Rome, and Greece from Zeus to Athena, Apollo, Perseus, Julius Caesar, Medusa, and Amenhotep the Magnificent. Also Native American, Asian, African, and Early American art. Within this complex is the new **Gaultieri Children's Gallery.** Donations accepted.

Tantaquidgeon Indian Museum (860-848-9145), CT 32, Uncasville, just below Norwich. Literally the home of the "Last of the Mohegans." Small but varied collection of Native American artifacts in family-operated museum. Focuses on the life of tribes of the eastern forests. Donations accepted.

Children's Museum of Southeastern Connecticut (860-691-1255), 409 Main Street, Niantic. Open Monday, Wednesday through Saturday 9:30–4:30, Sunday 12:30–4:30. Science, arts, history, and health are illustrated in unique, interactive displays for children aged 1–12. Call for rates.

Millstone Information and Science Center (860-444-4234), 278 Main Street, Niantic. Varied hours, closed major holidays; call for schedule. A shock to first-time visitors to Crescent Beach are the towers of a nuclear reactor on the peninsula just offshore and never out of the sight of bathers. Exhibits in the nuclear power station tell the story of nuclear

Monte Cristo Cottage in New London, the boyhood home of Eugene O'Neill.

energy. Energy and computer games will interest the children. Small aquarium, small theater. Free admission.

✏ **Blue Slope Country Museum** (860-642-6413), 138 Blue Hill Road, Franklin 06254. More than 4,000 farm tools and implements are on display in a rustic, barnlike structure on a 380-acre working dairy farm. Educational programs include blacksmith and woodworking, spinning and weaving, basketmaking, butter-making, soil tillage and planting, and special activities geared to children.

HISTORIC HOMES

Monte Cristo Cottage (860-443-0051; 860-443-5378), 325 Pequot Avenue, New London. Open afternoons May through December, Monday through Friday, and by appointment; closed major holidays. Childhood home of Eugene O'Neill, America's only dramatist to be awarded the Nobel Prize and four Pulitzer Prizes. The cottage is named after a character in a classic play, *The Count of Monte Cristo,* a part played endlessly by O'Neill's actor-father. O'Neill fans will recognize the living room: the setting for two of his most famous plays—his greatest tragedy, *Long Day's Journey into Night,* and his only comedy, *Ah, Wilderness!* Mini-theater presentation; mementos of the family. Admission is charged. (See also *Entertainment.*)

Shaw/Perkins Mansion (860-443-1209), 305 Bank Street, New London. Open on a haphazard, limited schedule—call ahead. Changing exhibits and events occur here, in Connecticut's Revolutionary War Naval Office. Washington, Lafayette, and top commanders of the fledgling Continental navy met here to plot strategies. Admission is charged.

KIMBERLY GRANT

Whale Oil Row was named after the commodity that enriched its builders.

Hempsted Houses (860-443-7949), Hempsted and Jay Streets, New London. Open daily, except Mondays, May through October. Here are two important colonial houses that survived the burning of New London by Benedict Arnold. The 1678 Joshua Hempsted House is one of the oldest frame buildings in New England. The adjoining stone house was built by a grandson, constructed with a gambrel roof and an exterior projecting beehive oven. Both have been restored with family artifacts, and both are on the National Register of Historic Places. Summer programs on colonial life. Adults $3; students $2.

Whale Oil Row, east side of Huntington Street, New London. Unique group of four magnificent Greek Revival houses built in the 1830s by captains who made their fortunes on whaling expeditions.

Leffingwell Inn (860-889-9440), 348 Washington Street, Norwich. Started in 1675 and expanded over the years, the inn was the home of Col. Christopher Leffingwell, deputy commissary to the Continental Army, who did yeoman service rounding up food, arms, and clothing for Washington's troops. Restored and furnished with period antiques. Docents conduct tours. Admission is charged.

Smith-Harris House (860-739-0761), 33 Society Road, Niantic. Open July and August daily, except Tuesday, 1–5. Reduced hours in fall. Open by appointment January through March. A Greek Revival farmhouse, a popular style in America from 1820 to 1850, has been renovated with the help of local schoolchildren as a learning project. Annual Wassail Party in December (see *Special Events*). The last member of the family died in 1973, so visitors can view authentic furnishings. Picnic facilities available.

HISTORIC SITES

Old Customs House (860-447-2501), 150 Bank Street, New London. First customs house in the United States, now a museum tells the story of the customs service. Collecting duty on imported goods was the way the fledgling United States first raised funds for operating the federal government. The doors came from planks torn off the USS *Constitution* during a renovation.

County Courthouse, Huntington Street at the top of State Street, New London. An architectural treasure that escaped the torches of the British marines, this beautiful Georgian building has been a courthouse for more than 200 years. When the siege of New London Harbor was lifted at the end of the War of 1812, the citizenry staged a "Peace Ball" in this hall for the British officers.

Nathan Hale Schoolhouse, at the foot of State Street, New London. Open Memorial Day through Labor Day, Saturday 1–4. Moved from its original site, this is one of two schoolhouses in which Connecticut's state hero taught before joining the Continental Army.

Beebe Phillips Farmhouse (860-442-2707), CT 156 and Avery Lane, Waterford. June 15 through September 15, Monday through Friday 1–4. A complex of 18th- and 19th-century buildings including the **Jordan Schoolhouse, Stacy Barn Museum, Miner Education Center,** and **Village Blacksmith.** Youngsters will enjoy the early horse-drawn farm vehicles and equipment. For Mom and Dad, an authentic colonial herb garden. Free admission.

Quinebaug and Shetucket Rivers Valley National Heritage Corridor (860-928-1228), Box 161, Putnam. A unique project of the National Park system to preserve 850 square miles of what has been called "the last green valley" in the Boston-to-Washington megalopolis sprawl. Most of it lies in the Quiet Corner (see "The Villages of Northeastern Connecticut"), but its southernmost borders encompass Norwich and its historical reminders of the days when this region was first in New England in mills powered by water wheels. A traditional National Park Service full-color brochure tells the whole story. The project was spurred, in great part, through the efforts of US Congressman Sam Gedjenson of Bozrah.

TO DO

BOAT EXCURSIONS

The following offer party cruises. You may want to call for a full description, but generally reservations are not required.

Blackhawk II (860-443-3662), Niantic Beach Marina, Niantic.

Mijoy 747 (860-443-0663), Mijoy Dock, 12 River Street, Waterford.

For more serious fun, take a nature cruise with **Nature Cruises Sunbeam Fleet** (860-443-7259), Captain John's Sport Fishing Center, 15 First

Norwichtown Days Historic Encampment, on the Norwichtown green, features demonstrations of woodworking and other fading handicrafts.

Street, Waterford. Naturalists from Mystic Marinelife Aquarium perform research projects with you looking over their shoulders as the 100-foot *Sunbeam Express* comes alongside spouting whales, gamboling porpoises, or harbor seals. The *Sunbeam Express* has heated cabins, comfortable seats, and even bunks. A full galley; accommodates 149 passengers. A special treat is when Captain John is on board; he's the kindly ancient mariner with the scalloped beard of a Maine fisherman.

Bring camera and binoculars, jackets, sneakers or topsiders. Call for schedules. Rates average $20 per person; less for charter groups, seniors, and children. (See also *Sunbeam*'s eagle-watching excursions under *Boat Excursions* in "The Central Shoreline, Old Lyme to Branford.")

FISHING

Two New London docks serve the charter fleet: **Burr's Yacht Haven,** 244 Pequot Avenue; and the **Thamesport Marina** at 262 Pequot Avenue. Charters from Burr's include **'A Vanga** (860-848-0170), **Fish** (860-739-3611), **West Wind** (860-526-9453), and **White Lightning** (860-739-6906). Thamesport Marina offers **Lady Margaret** (860-739-3687), **Playin' Hooky** (413-732-2754), and **Wanderer** (860-739-2801).

The second largest charter fleet is docked in the twin towns of Niantic and Waterford, just east of New London. They are found at either the **Niantic Sportfish Dock,** Nine First Street, or **Captain John's Dock,** 15 First Street. Charters out of Nine First Street include **Dot-E-Dee** (860-739-7419) and **Osprey** (860-739-4129). The 15 First Street dock offers **Sunbeam IV** (860-443-7259) and **Sunbeam V** (860-443-7259). **Good Company** (860-443-0269) sails from Waddy's Dock, Rope Ferry Road.

MINIATURE GOLF

Yankee Clipper Mini Golf (860-739-9634), 157 West Main Street, Niantic.

Miniature golf at **Ocean Beach Park** (1-800-510-SAND), 1225 Ocean Avenue, New London.

SAILING

Parasail USA (860-442-7272), Captain John's Dock, 15 First Street, Waterford. May through September, daily, weather permitting. Act like an 82nd Airborne trooper—on the end of a tether! You're wafted off the platform of the pilot boat and soar 600 feet above Long Island Sound before landing back on the boat. Safe but scary; not for the faint of heart.

SPECTATOR SPORTS

Norwich Navigators, April to September 2, at Dodd Stadium in the Norwich industrial park. This New York Yankees AA team offers the first professional baseball in eastern Connecticut.

SWIMMING

Swimming opportunities are limited along the Connecticut shore. In the southeastern quadrant, most town beaches are restricted to residents. Ocean Beach, operated by the town of New London, is open to the public. Nearby, **Crescent Beach** at Niantic is open to anyone owning or renting a cottage in the community or staying in local lodging.

Ocean Beach Park (1-800-510-SAND), 1225 Ocean Avenue, New London, just beyond the Monte Cristo Cottage (see *Historic Homes*), is arguably the finest beach on the Connecticut coast. At the eastern end of Long Island Sound, it's washed by the rolling waters of the Atlantic but still protected enough that the surf is not dangerous. In August, jellyfish can be a problem elsewhere, but rarely at Ocean Beach. For nearly a century, Ocean Beach was a cottage colony. Wiped out in the '30s by a devastating hurricane, it was rebuilt along the lines of New York's Jones Beach. Miniature golf, Olympic-size pool, water slide, arcade, picnicking, snack bar. Parking and locker fees.

- **Rocky Neck State Park** (860-739-5471), CT 156, exit 72 off I-95, Niantic. One of three major state park beaches on Long Island Sound. The main rail line linking Boston and New York splits the park. Children and train buffs enjoy watching the occasional AMTRAK train rumble by. Mile-long sandy beach, no surf; shallow at low tide. Boardwalk, bathhouses, food concessions; also picnicking; hiking, fishing, and extensive campgrounds. Lifeguards; wonderful for infants and young children. Modest parking fee.
- **Gardner Lake Park,** 38 Lakeview Avenue, Salem. Swimming along a 325-foot strand of sand. Canoes, rowboats, and noisy Jet Skis. Snack bar and game room.

GREEN SPACE

Connecticut College Arboretum in New London is a 20-acre tract of labeled native trees and shrubs. Birders and hikers can meander by themselves or follow a self-guided tour brochure available at the main entrance. See one of the last stands of virgin pine in the state; some trees tower as high as California redwoods.

Chelsea Harbor Park and Marina, Norwich. Former decaying waterside in downtown Norwich has been landscaped into an award-winning park with walkways, lawn and flower beds, and outdoor grills.

Indian Burial Ground on Sachem Street, Norwich, recalls Uncas, the Mohegan sachem (chief) who negotiated land to the first settlers of Norwich and helped them in wars against his enemies, the fierce Pequots.

Mohegan Park Rose Garden on Judd Road, Norwich, is a small but beautifully designed formal rose garden. Here you'll find hundreds of varieties of the world's favorite flower. Summer concerts are given by the Norwich City Band.

Nearby is the **Mohegan Park Zoo,** where children may pet small domestic animals. Walking path, pool, picnicking, and children's playground.

Norwichtown green, just north of the present core city, is an ideal place to recapture the ambience of the first days of Norwich. Beautifully restored and maintained 18th- and 19th-century houses surround the green, or commons, as it was called. Revolutionary War veterans are buried in the adjacent cemetery. Brochures are available for walking tours of Norwichtown and for the 18th-century Chelsea Parade (call 860-889-9440) and Norwichtown Days (see *Special Events*) is held here.

Yantic Falls; Indian Leap, off Sachem Street, north of Norwich off CT 2. Another gorge where fleeing warriors were pushed to their deaths. Here the Narragansetts lost their final battle with the Mohegans.

Rocky Neck State Park's easy access, mile-long beach, gentle surf, and wealth of amenities makes it a family favorite.

Millstone Nature Trail. A 1-mile trail covered with wood chips leaves the Millstone Nuclear Power Plant, on CT 156, Niantic, and winds past a lagoon. Birders should bring binoculars and notebooks.

Harkness Memorial State Park (860-443-5725), CT 213, Waterford. Picnic tables on the grounds of the estate of a former oil tycoon. There's fishing off the sandy beach, but no swimming. The mansion is under restoration. Exceptional gardens. (See also *Entertainment*.)

LODGING

RESORT

Norwich Inn & Spa (860-886-2401; 1-800-ASK-4SPA outside Connecticut), 607 West Thames Street, CT 32, Norwich 06360. Built in 1929—just before the stock market crash—by the city of Norwich, the inn was abandoned and ready for the bulldozer in the 1980s. Rescued in 1983 by Edward Safdie, builder of the Sonoma Mission Inn & Spa in California, it now is the most elegant hostelry in eastern Connecticut. Probably the largest birdcage you've ever seen is the centerpiece of the lobby. A full-service spa and health club with indoor and outdoor pools has been built adjacent to the inn, which has 65 rooms and 60 villas. Tennis, hiking trails, golf, and cross-country skiing. (See also *Dining Out*.) Sunday through Thursday, $125 for rooms, $200 for duplex villas; weekends, $140–215.

INN

Lighthouse Inn (860-443-8411), Lower Boulevard, New London 06320. A restored 1902 mansion at the mouth of the Thames that takes its name from nearby New London Light. Fifty-one rooms; paneled, highly regarded dining room (see *Dining Out*). Private beach, but also just a few blocks from Ocean Beach Park (see *Swimming*). Continental breakfast. $110–180.

BED & BREAKFASTS

In addition to the listings below, a number of bed & breakfast reservation services offer access to rooms available in establishments throughout the state. For a list, see *What's Where—Bed & Breakfasts*.

The Inn at Harbor Hill Marina (860-739-0331), 60 Grand Street, Niantic 06357. A pleasant port of call for the topsider set. Mystic Seaport and other area attractions are just a short drive away. Eight rooms with baths all overlooking the marina, Long Island Sound, and the Niantic River. Transient slips are available, or arrive by car. Enjoy a continental breakfast indoors or on the wraparound porch. Italian, French, and Spanish translator available. Everyone else must speak English. $125–150.

1851 Guest House (860-848-3649), 1851 CT 32, Uncasville 06382. Four elegantly decorated nonsmoking rooms, each with private entrance and private bath. Refrigerators stocked with juices, beer, and milk. Continental basket breakfast with beverages, pastries, and cereal served in the room. $75–125. Five minutes from the Mohegan Sun (see *Entertainment* under "Mystic, Stonington, and East of the Thames").

Queen Anne Inn (860-447-2600; 1-800-347-8818), 265 Williams Street, New London 06320. Ten rooms, eight with bath. Whirlpool on the third floor is available to all guests. Full gourmet breakfast and afternoon tea. $89–185.

HOTELS/MOTELS

In New London

Red Roof Inn (860-443-0001; 1-800-843-7663), 707 Colman Street, New London 06320. Open year-round; 108 rooms, pets allowed. $35–92.

  ♿ **New London Lodgings** (860-443-3440), 380 Bayonet Street, New London 06320. Offers 24 efficiencies with stove and refrigerator; 2 one-bedroom suites, 1 two-bedroom suite with Jacuzzi. Exercise facility. Guest laundry. Outdoor pool. $49–139.

Oakdell Motel (860-442-9446; 1-800-676-REST; fax 860-447-1893), CT 85, Waterford 06385, just north of New London. Twenty-two comfortable rooms, all with microwave and refrigerator, in a semicircle centered on the pool. Continental breakfast. $42–95.

In Niantic

✎ **Connecticut Yankee Inn** (1-800-942-8466), Flanders Road, Niantic 03657. Fifty rooms with refrigerator; sauna, outdoor pool, passes to the beach. Continental breakfast. Children free. $45–120.

Elms Hotel (860-739-5545), 27–37 Ocean Avenue, Niantic 06357. The Elms is a few blocks from Crescent Beach. The venerable, 100-year-old hotel has 30 rooms. $49–60.

Niantic Inn (860-739-5451), 345 Main Street, Niantic 06357. Offers 24 spacious studios, each with dining and living room areas and refrigerators. Across the street from a sandy beach. Continental breakfast. $80–150.

Rocky Neck Motor Inn (860-739-6268), 237 West Main Street, Niantic 06357. Offers 31 rooms, including 26 efficiencies. Passes to state park beach are available. $45–95.

Starlight Motor Inn (860-739-5462; fax 860-739-0567), 256 Flanders Road, Niantic 06357. Free HBO. Restaurant, outdoor pool, 48 rooms. Continental breakfast. $45–99.

Elsewhere

Chesterfield Lodge and Country Store (860-442-0039), 1596 CT 85, Montville 06370. Offers 12 rooms with private bath and refrigerator. $49–79.

Courtyard by Marriott (860-889-2600), 181 West Town Street, Norwich 06360. Offers 120 rooms, including 24 efficiencies. Restaurant and outdoor pool. $69–139.

The Island (860-739-8316), 20 Islanda Court, Exit 74 off I-95, East Lyme 06333. Four large and two small efficiency cottages on Lake Pattagansett. Campsites. Boating, swimming, and fishing; play area for children. $250–375 weekly for cottages, $20 daily for camping.

CAMPGROUNDS

Rocky Neck State Park (860-739-5471), CT 156, exit 72 off I-95, Niantic. Extensive campgrounds; best to reserve a campsite in advance, or at least call when making a last-minute decision. Also beach with lifeguards, food concessions; hiking and fishing.

Odetah Campground (860-889-4144; 1-800-448-1193), 38 Bozrah Street Extension, Bozrah 06334. Open warm-weather seasons, with 269 sites; hookups. Sandy beach on 30-acre lake. Boating, fishing, swimming pool, tennis, recreation hall, basketball, volleyball, hiking, arts and crafts, potluck suppers, and hayrides. Cabin rentals.

Witch Meadow Lake Campground (860-859-1542), 139 Witch Meadow Road, Salem 06420. Complete family resort with a 14-acre lake for swimming, boating, and fishing. A full range of recreation facilities includes a new children's playscape and minigolf. Nature trails through 122 acres of wooded parkland. The restaurant is famous for—dare we say it—"batwings and witchburgers"!

WHERE TO EAT

DINING OUT

In New London

Bangkok City (860-442-6970), 123 Captain's Walk, New London. Lunch and dinner. Closed Sunday. Thai pepper reputedly is the hottest in the world, and if your tastes incline that way, here's a chance to scorch your stomach. A house specialty: spicy salad with seafood or meat. The pumpkin custard dessert is yummy. Milder dishes on request. $7.95–15.95.

Chuck's Steak House (860-443-1323), 250 Pequot Avenue, New London overlooking the Thames River. Open daily, dinner only, 5–10. Standard and dependable fare for the meat-and-potatoes members of your family.

The menu also features stuffed shrimp, sole, and salmon. $13.95–20.95.

Don Juan's (860-444-2884), 403 Williams Street, New London. Open for dinner Monday through Saturday. Boasts of its "International Combat-Style Cuisine," which translates into ethnic specialties from countries visited by the chef during his tours of military service. $7.95 for vegetable plate; $13.95 for the Combat Special, a medley of foods all on one platter.

☞ **Lighthouse Inn** (860-443-8411), Lower Boulevard off Pequot Avenue, New London, 0.5 mile from Ocean Beach Park. Open daily. Sixty years feeding travelers in a beautifully restored Victorian mansion overlooking the Sound. American specialties and, as befits its location, fresh seafood. Popular Sunday brunch. $13.75–18.25.

Lorelei (860-442-3375), 158 State Street, New London. Lunch and dinner specialties, chicken, seafood, steak, and (what else?) pasta. Casual dress is the order of the day. Karaoke video sing-along. More than just an eating experience. $13.

The Recovery Room Restaurant (860-443-2619), 445 Ocean Avenue, New London. Open daily for lunch and dinner. The Neapolitans who first devised the "pie" a.k.a. pizza, a circle of dough brushed lightly with a tomato sauce and a sprinkling of cheese, wouldn't recognize what the chefs here have concocted to decorate *their* version. But you will be more than satisfied. Full meals also available with sumptuous salads. Same chefs also operate the **Pizzaworks,** 12 Water Street, in Mystic, a worthy competitor to the cinematized Mystic Pizza. $6–13.95.

Timothy's (860-437-0526), 181 Bank Street, New London. Lunch and dinner daily; closed Sunday and Monday. It doesn't make the food taste any better, but in this converted old drugstore, you can watch the chefs prepare your meals. Seafoods are the specialty with unique combinations of lobster and crab to delight the palate. We also recommend the duckling. An extensive wine list. $12.50–16.50.

In Norwich

Americus on the Wharf (860-887-8555), American Wharf, Port of Norwich. Open daily 11:30–11. Closed in winter. American cuisine. Same menu all day. In keeping with the restaurant's nautical location, specialties are tagged with maritime monikers. The antipasto is "Schooner Salad"; stuffed potato skins are "Dinghies"; and for the house specialty, ask for "Americus Chicken Mediterranean." You get the idea. Raw bar; hefty burgers and sandwiches. Nice harbor view. $10.50–18.

☞ **Norwich Inn & Spa** (1-800-ASK-4SPA). The special low-cal, low-fat, low-cholesterol meals for spa guests are also available to the general public, but if you haven't yet graduated to carrot sticks and celery, ask for the all-American menu with its hearty specialties. Game in season. $16.50–24.50.

Elsewhere

Constantine's (860-739-2848), 252 Main Street, Niantic on the Sound. Lunch and dinner. Closed Monday. Extended summer hours. Everything from bulging sandwiches to lightly fried clams, swordfish, lobster.

Prime rib is a perennial favorite; sautéed seafood, pasta combinations, veal, and chicken. $5–16.95.

Modesto's (860-887-7755), 10 CT 32, Franklin. Open daily for lunch and dinner. This elegant Italian restaurant has room for authentic Mexican cuisine on its ample menu. Watching your diet? Veteran chef Modesto Moran has contrived a selection of seasoned cholesterol-free dishs. Seafood is handled consistently well. Save room for the desserts. $16.50.

EATING OUT

Flanders Fish Market and Restaurant (860-739-8866; 1-800-242-6055), 22 Chesterfield, East Lyme. Open daily; Sunday seafood brunch. Here it's "take out or eat in." Either way, the lobster and shrimp dishes have won raves from seafood lovers all over the state. The chef wields a heavy hand with garlic, except on the juicy prime rib for contrary folks who turn their backs on the sea. The seafood bisques are exceptional (and filling).

Burke's Tavern (860-739-5033), 13 Hope Street, Niantic. Open daily for lunch and dinner, serving international cuisine from great burgers to Thai chicken, coconut shrimp, Caesar salad, and a wide variety of sandwiches. Entertainment on weekend evenings.

Road Kill Restaurant (860-442-7146), 566 Colman Street, New London. Open daily for breakfast, lunch, and dinner. Caters to children. Members of the fiber generation will glory in the largest all-you-can-eat salad bar in New London. Seafood, full dinners, daily specials, and ¼-pound hamburgers. Huge lobster tanks; choose your own victim.

D'Angelo Sandwich Shop (860-443-0021), 721 Bank Street, New London. Also a Groton location at 587 Long Hill Road. Something for the entire family, from tuna sandwiches and burgers to grinders, pita pockets, and salads. Ice cream.

Ed's Kitchen & Creamery (860-848-7932), Norwich–New London Turnpike, Uncasville. Open daily. All-you-can-eat salad bar, homemade pies.

Chelsea Landing (860-889-9932), 88 Water Street, Norwich. Lunch and dinner daily. Burgers, stuffed sandwiches, seafood.

Phoenix Chinese (860-889-8868), 595 West Main Street, Norwich, exit 80 off US 395. Open daily for lunch and dinner, with an emphasis on traditional Cantonese cooking. Also serves selected Hunan and Szechuan dishes.

Yantic River Inn (860-887-2440), exit 87 off CT 2, Yantic. Closed Monday. Choice prime rib and steaks, seafood, salad bar.

ENTERTAINMENT

Concert & Artist Series (860-439-ARTS), Palmer Auditorium, Connecticut College, 270 Mohegan Avenue, New London. Classical, dance, and jazz concerts by top artists from September through April.

Garde Arts Center (860-444-7373), 325 State Street in the heart of downtown New London. The last remaining vaudeville cinema house in the region, recently restored. Annual concert series by the Eastern Connecticut Symphony Orchestra. Other Garde attractions: Broadway shows, big-screen Family Theatre Series, and a Comedy Series. Visiting artists. Seats 1,500.

☞ **US Coast Guard Band** (860-444-8468), Leamy Hall on the campus of the US Coast Guard Academy, CT 32, New London. Full schedule of concerts, but the band also performs at special events and celebrations throughout the state.

Monte Cristo Cottage (860-443-0051; 860-443-5378), Pequot Avenue, New London. Lectures of particular interest to writers and students of literature are held regularly at Eugene O'Neill's boyhood home.

Waterford Speedbowl (860-572-9395), CT 85 north of New London. Stock-car racing Saturday nights in summer; spring and fall special events.

☞ **Summer Music at Harkness** (1-800-969-3400), Harkness State Park, Waterford. July and August. Set up your table with napery and candlesticks, and listen to music ranging from classical to jazz while dining on a gourmet supper (bring your own or order by reservation). Lovely setting on the shore of the sound. As the sun sets, watch the submarines and sailing yachts.

☞ **Eugene O'Neill Theater Center** (860-443-5378), 305 Great Neck Road, Waterford. Summer theatrical colony with writers in residence. New plays, selected the previous fall, are read at the **National Playwrights Conference** in August. Many have gone on to fame and fortune on Broadway. The public is also invited to help discover new talent at the center's National Music Theater Conference and the Cabaret Symposium (also in August). Call for schedules and to make reservations. Bring a can of insect repellent for outdoor performances. Chances are excellent you'll be sharing a bleacher bench with Joanne Woodward or some other theatrical luminary. Be nice; share your bug spray.

SELECTIVE SHOPPING

Crystal Mall (860-442-8500), CT 85, Waterford. Open daily 9:30–9:30, Sunday 11–5. Major department store chains such as Sears, Jordan Marsh, Filene's, and JCPenney, along with more than 100 specialty shops. There are market pushcarts in the corridors plus enough vendors in the Food Court—Chinese, Japanese, and American—to stave off the appetite of even the most ravenous teenager.

Arrow Paper Party Store (860-447-3350), 567 Coleman Street, New London. Here you'll find colorful paper accessories for weddings, birthdays, showers, and holidays, as well as for more mundane household uses. And that's not all: Choose a take-home gourmet dessert from the freezer chest. Another outlet is at 113 Salem Turnpike, Norwich.

Elaine's Gift Shop (860-887-0053), 213 Main Street, Norwich. Figurines, napery, gadgets for the kitchen and bathroom, local mementos.

Country Feelings (860-739-5806), 253 Post Road, East Lyme. If you absolutely can't come home from a trip empty-handed, this is the place to
pick up the decorated wooden towel rack you've wanted all these years.
Napkin holders, shelves, quilting.

ANTIQUES SHOP

By the Way Antiques (860-442-3053), 293 Post Road, Waterford. Early
American items and glassware. Open by appointment only.

ART GALLERY

Ya-Ta-Hey (860-443-3204), 279 State Street, New London. Choice Native
American pottery.

NURSERY

Agway (860-859-2508), CT 85, Salem. Open daily. Stroll through 6 acres of
blooming flowers and trees. In season, view more than 800 acres of
flowering annuals. Water-garden displays. Blooming orchids in the large
greenhouse, tropical houseplants, and unique bonsai make welcome
gifts for gardeners. Large selection of garden sculptures, sundials, wind
chimes, and collectibles.

SPECIAL EVENTS

Mid-March: **Captain John's Harbor Seal Cruises** sailing out of
Waterford.

Late April: **Annual Connecticut Storytelling Festival,** Connecticut College, New London. A weekend of storytelling, afternoon workshops,
and evening concerts.

Early June: **Yale-Harvard Regatta,** Thames River, New London. Traditional
rivals in crew racing meet in the oldest intercollegiate competition in the
United States. View from shore or from charter observation boats.

Early July: **New London Sail Festival,** Waterfront, New London. Three
days of entertainment, food, games, and fireworks.

All July: **Summer Music Festival** on the shores of Long Island Sound on
the grounds of the beautiful Harkness estate.

August: **O'Neill Theater Center's Cabaret Symposium. National Playwrights Conference.** Eugene O'Neill Theater Center. Readings of new
plays; many go on to fame and fortune on Broadway. Both in Waterford.

July through August: **Ocean Beach Park Summer Festival,** New London.
Variety of special celebrations: **Annual Polkabration,** now entering its
third decade (weeklong competitions among 15 top American polka
teams, free polka lessons, fireworks); **Italian Days** (bicycle races, fashion show, beauty pageant, grand ball); **Irish Days;** and **Country Music.**
Family night every Tuesday with games, shows, movies; teen night Thursday, with dancing, DJs.

Late August: **Harbor Day,** Brown Memorial Park, Norwich.

September–June: **Food For Thought,** Lyman Allyn Art Museum (see *Museums*). Bring lunch and enjoy lectures on a wide variety of subjects.

Early September: **Annual Arts and Crafts Show,** Ocean Beach Park, New London.

mid-September: **Norwichtown Days Historic Encampment,** on the Norwichtown green. Re-enactments of life during Colonial and Civil War times. Demonstrations of lost handicrafts, woodworking, outdoor cooking, weaving, blacksmithing. Military paraphernalia and close-order drills.

Mid-October: **East Lyme Antiques Show and Sale,** East Lyme Junior High School.

Late November: **Annual Craft Sale,** Slater Museum, Norwich.

December: **Wassail Party,** Smith-Harris House (see *Historic Homes*); the house is decorated in the style of the mid-1800s.

VI. LOWER CONNECTICUT RIVER VALLEY AND SHORELINE

The Lower Connecticut River Valley
The Central Shoreline, Old Lyme to Branford

KIMBERLY GRANT

The Old Saybrook Point Lighthouse

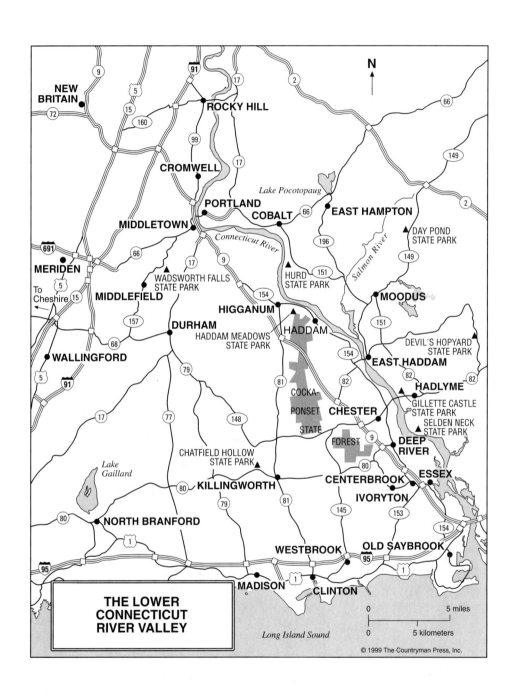

THE LOWER
CONNECTICUT
RIVER VALLEY

© 1999 The Countryman Press, Inc.

The Lower Connecticut River Valley

New England's longest river trickles out of three small lakes near New Hampshire's Canadian border and winds more than 400 miles through New England before emptying into Long Island Sound. The two waterways—the river and the sound—attracted the state's first settlers and later provided an avenue of trade for adventurous Yankee merchants and sailors.

Because the river is not much more than 15 feet deep in most spots, and since sandbars preclude the passing of deepwater ships, industry bypassed the lower valley, leaving not urban sprawl but instead an unexpectedly peaceful stretch of green and a scattering of maritime villages. In the 1970s, however, industrial dumping and general misuse polluted the river, with disastrous results for its wildlife and water quality. Thanks to a determined cleanup effort, the river underwent a renaissance; as a result, The Nature Conservancy has designated the tidelands of the Connecticut River one of the hemisphere's 40 "Last Great Places." Ospreys, bald eagles, and Atlantic salmon are now a common sight on tidal creeks and salt marshes, as are swimmers and anglers.

Along the riverbank lies the history of a region. Middletown, once the largest, busiest town on the river, has kept its splendid 19th-century mansions of successful traders and merchants, now incorporated into the Wesleyan University campus. Across the Arrigoni Bridge, east of the river, the town of Portland has given its name to the brownstone of New York City's familiar row houses. Farther downstream, on a bluff in East Haddam, broods the outlandish castle that the actor William Gillette designed as a monument to his eccentricities; its stone terraces boast one of the most spectacular vistas of the river valley. Steam-driven locomotives of the old Connecticut Valley line still rumble along the 19th-century roadbed, now hauling tourists to Deep River. Theatergoers still flock to East Haddam to savor the excellence—architectural as well as theatrical—of the Goodspeed Opera House, a Victorian gem known as the birthplace of the American musical, where theater troups used to arrive from New York by steamboat to perform. Visitors can cross the Connecticut River on an antique swing bridge, the longest such structure in the world, or board the Chester-Hadlyme ferry, a transportation option here for more than 200 years.

Chester is a quaint but upscale one-street town, home to a thriving community of artists, artisans, chefs, and others blessed with exquisite talents. On the wall of the Pattaconk 1850, a Main Street restaurant, is a lighthearted "Non-Historical Marker" announcing that on this spot on February 29, 1778, absolutely nothing happened. Essex, with a maritime legacy older than the country, was burned out by the British during the War of 1812, but the inn the Redcoats commandeered for quarters still offers lodging and hearty meals. This pristine river town, complete with clapboard homes, stately mansions, and picket fences, is classic New England. Deep River and Ivoryton once thrived by manufacturing piano keys for the ivory trade; today they are among the valley's quieter villages.

Even towns one tier removed from the river have clung to their 18th-century roots. Wooded hills are dotted with farms, historic villages, acclaimed restaurants, and charming inns tucked away off winding country roads. Lyman Orchard in Middlefield, a family enterprise dating back some 200 years, contradicts the usual New England image of rocky, barren hillsides with its bounty of apples, peaches, and berries. And Wallingford, a town that once shared with Meriden a worldwide reputation for the manufacture of pewter and silverware, has hung onto some of its orchards and farms. Cheshire, awash in greenhouses, is the self-styled Bedding Plant Capital of the World. In springtime, town roads are alive with flats of colorful blooms to brighten winter-weary yards.

Entries in this section are arranged in alphabetical order.

AREA CODES
860 and **203**

GUIDANCE
Connecticut River Valley and Shoreline Visitors Council (860-347-0028; 1-800-486-3346; Web site: www.cttourism.org), 393 Main Street, Middletown 06457-3309. The council, which represents most of the towns covered in this chapter, publishes comprehensive brochures and guides listing lodgings, attractions, restaurants, theaters, galleries, charter boats, marinas, and golf courses. It also supplies literature from individual establishments, giving excellent one-stop service that includes referrals to specific local sources.

Information centers. State centers are on I-91 in Middletown for northbound travelers, in Wallingford for the southbound. On **I-95,** the state center is at Westbrook. Open year-round, all three are staffed during the summer months by information specialists and provide state vacation guides and maps.

GETTING THERE
By air: **Groton/New London Airport** (860-445-8549) is served by USAir Express and by several charter services. **Tweed-New Haven**

Airport (203-946-8285) is served by USAir Express. Private planes may land at **Chester Airport** and at **Goodspeed Airport** in East Haddam.

By bus: **Peter Pan Trailways** (1-800-343-9999) stops in Meriden and Middletown.

By car: Get into the area from either New York or Boston via I-95 or, if you prefer more leisurely driving, by US 1, the legendary old Boston Post Road. CT 9 is the major north–south route, a limited-access divided highway connecting I-84 in Farmington with I-95 at Old Saybrook.

By train: **AMTRAK's** (1-800-872-7245; 1-800-USA-RAIL) shoreline route runs between New York and Boston with stops in Mystic, New London, Old Saybrook, and New Haven.

GETTING AROUND

Action Taxi (860-347-4222) serves Middletown, Durham, Middlefield, Cromwell, Haddam, and the central river valley area; **Yellow Cab** (203-235-4434) serves Meriden and Wallingford; **East Shore Cab** (860-388-2819) serves the shoreline from Old Lyme to Clinton. If you call ahead, you can arrange taxi service from the Old Saybrook train station to Essex, a town in which you might easily spend a weekend without need of an auto. If you plan a stay at one of the major inns or resorts, inquire about pickup service at the nearest railroad station. In Old Saybrook, a car rental agency maintains an office at the station.

MEDICAL EMERGENCY

The statewide emergency number is **911**.

Middlesex Memorial Hospital (860-344-6000), 28 Crescent Street, Middletown. The emergency number is 860-344-6686.

Shoreline Emergency Clinic (860-767-3700), 260 Westbrook Road (CT 153), Essex.

Veterans Memorial Medical Center (203-238-8200), One King Place, Meriden. The emergency number is 203-238-8399.

TO SEE

MUSEUMS

Barker Character, Comic & Cartoon Museum (203-272-2222; 1-800-995-2357), 1188 Highland Avenue (CT 10), Cheshire. Open Tuesday through Saturday 11–5. Free admission. If you like to play, this is your place. Herb and Gloria Barker have amassed a staggering collection of toys, as well as comic strip, cartoon, television and advertising memorabilia—some 10,000 items in all. About 350 lunch boxes hang from the rafters; display cases are crammed with rarities like a 1940 Fisher-Price train; a Dick Tracy wrist radio set from the 1950s; Howdy Doody talking dolls; tin toys from the early 1900s. When was the last time you saw a century-old Yellow Kid gumball machine, or found a Lone Ranger flashlight ring in your cereal box? A surreal fantasy world for the young and young at heart (see also *Selective Shopping*).

KIMBERLY GRANT

The Connecticut River Museum exhibits a replica of the world's first submarine, ca. 1775.

Connecticut River Museum (860-767-8269), at the foot of Main Street, Essex. Open year-round, Tuesday through Sunday 10–5; closed Monday and major holidays. Adults $4; children $2; under 6 free. The museum building is a well-kept 1878 Yankee dock house, situated on the water's edge at the old Essex Steamboat Dock. It's now the repository for nautical paintings, photographs, ship models, and antique objects that illuminate the maritime history of the lower river valley before and after Adriaen Block's historic voyage of discovery in 1607. Among the exhibits is a replica of David Bushnell's 1775 underwater vessel, the *Turtle*—recognized as the world's first submarine. Big enough for a crew of one (preferably smallish) human, it carries no lights and no oxygen supply and is powered by foot pedals. It was a curious precursor of the nuclear subs built nearby in Groton today.

Connecticut Yankee Information & Science Center (860-267-9279; 1-800-348-4636), 362 Injun Hollow Road (off CT 151), Haddam Neck. Open year-round, Monday through Thursday 9–4; closed Friday, weekends, and holidays. Free admission. On the grounds of the now decommissioned Connecticut Yankee nuclear power plant, the center features exhibits that detail the dismantling of a nuclear power plant. Outside are self-guided nature trails, picnic tables, and a boat dock—the center is located on the Connecticut River.

Davison Art Center (860-685-2500), Wesleyan University, High Street, Middletown. Housed in a splendid, pale pink 1838 Italianate mansion, the Davison features eight exhibits per year. Nearby in Wesleyan's Center for the Arts, the **Zilkha Gallery** (860-685-2695) shows contemporary works in various media. Both offer free admission and are open from late August to early June, Tuesday through Friday noon–4, Saturday and Sunday 2–5. Closed during academic vacations. Tours by appointment.

Lock 12 Historical Park (203-272-2743), 487 North Brooksvale Road (CT 42), Cheshire. Park open daily, sunrise to sunset; museum tours by appointment. Authentically restored section of the once bustling Farmington Canal. The success of New York's Erie Canal inspired area entrepreneurs to build their own avenue of waterborne commerce. From 1827 to 1848, barges carried passengers and cargo through 60 locks up and down the 83-mile, hand-dug canal between New Haven and Northampton, Massachusetts. The waterway eventually succumbed to the faster, more efficient locomotive. Today, the canal's quiet stillness makes it hard to believe that it was once a major transportation system. The park features a museum, lockkeeper's house, and picnic areas.

Museum of Fife & Drum (860-767-2237; 860-399-6519), 62 North Main Street, Ivoryton. Open weekends June through September, year-round by appointment; call for information. Donation $1. The Company of Fifers and Drummers is credited with preserving the tradition of mustering fife-and-drum corps for parades and concerts; this is the only museum in the world dedicated to the music of the ancient fife and drum. Exhibits trace the importance of fifing and drumming to military strategy from colonial days through the Revolutionary War. Today's civilian corps keep alive this musical symbol of American patriotism with annual musters held in Deep River, Westbrook, and Old Saybrook, drawing corps from all down the eastern seaboard and beyond. Performances are scheduled in July and August (see *Special Events*).

HISTORIC HOMES AND SITES

Amasa Day House (860-873-8144; 860-247-8996), on the green, CT 151, Moodus. Open Memorial Day through Labor Day; call for hours and admission prices. This 1816 white-clapboard classic, property of the Antiquarian and Landmarks Society, features original stenciling on the floors and stair risers. Many of the furnishings and toys belonged to the Day family, who lived here for three generations. In the restored barn, **East Haddam Historical Society** exhibits trace local twine and textile mills of the last century.

Comstock Bridge (860-267-2519) spans the Salmon River near the Colchester town line in East Hampton. Just off CT 16, this 1872 bridge is open to pedestrians only; it's one of three covered bridges left in the state. An excellent spot for souvenir pictures and for examining the lattice-truss design, devised by Connecticut architect Ithiel Town to enable early bridge builders to span rivers without suspension cables or complicated machinery. The **Salmon River State Forest** adjacent to it has picnic sites; the stocked river is a favorite spot for local anglers, so you may want to bring your pole.

General Mansfield House (860-346-0746), 151 Main Street, Middletown. Museum tours Sunday 2–4:30 and Monday 1–4; research Tuesday and Thursday by appointment. Adults $2; children $1. A Federal-style redbrick home built in 1810 and furnished with both 18th- and 19th-

William Gillette used the fortune he amassed portraying Sherlock Holmes on the stage to build this curious East Haddam mansion.

century pieces, this house has another appeal: As headquarters of the **Middlesex County Historical Society,** it contains a genealogical library that attracts visitors from all over. Exhibits focus on Middletown history, particularly during the Civil War era.

Gillette Castle (860-526-2336), 67 River Road, East Haddam. Due to extensive renovations, the castle will be open on a limited basis through 2000; call ahead for schedule and information. Adults $4; children $2; under 5 free. The 125-acre state park surrounding the castle has hiking trails and picnic tables and is open year-round. After its completion in 1919, this fieldstone oddity, perched high above the Connecticut River, was home to Hartford native and playwright William Gillette, whose fame and fortune rested on his portrayal of Sherlock Holmes from 1899 to 1932. His mansion is a collection of eccentricities, replete with such curiosities as a dining table on tracks; guests were seated on a bench against the wall, and the table was moved into place, effectively trapping them through dessert. Hidden mirrors allowed the host to spy on guests in the bar or living room, then seize the correct moment for a dramatic entrance. And what would a castle be without hidden rooms, secret passageways, and a miniature railroad that chugged around the estate? Upstairs is a replica of Sherlock Holmes's office at 221B Baker Street, with the Persian slipper of tobacco, the violin ready to play, the chemistry lab set up, and newspapers scattered about, as if the game were once more afoot and Holmes and Watson outside hailing a hansom cab.

Hitchcock Phillips House (203-272-5819), 43 Church Drive, Cheshire. Call for hours. A 1785 Georgian mansion built by a wealthy merchant, later part of Cheshire Academy, now home to the Cheshire Historical Society. The home features wood paneling, period furnishings, and a fireplace with beehive oven in the keeping room; historical exhibits highlight locally manufactured wares, such as campaign buttons, watches, and oyster kegs.

Nathan Hale Schoolhouse (860-873-9547), Main Street, behind St. Stephen's Church (see below), East Haddam. Open Memorial Day through Labor Day, weekends and holidays 2–4. Call for admission prices. Local history records that the young Yale graduate taught in this one-room Union School in 1773–1774. Later, he became a Revolutionary War hero and the school assumed his name. On display are the schoolmaster's possessions and relics of local history.

St. Stephen's Church (860-873-9547), Main Street, East Haddam. The belfry of this stone church houses an ancient bell dated 815 A.D., thought to be the oldest such bell in the New World. The bell was cast for a Spanish monastery destroyed in the Napoleonic Wars and later shipped to the colonies by a Yankee sea captain in need of ballast. The best vantage point for viewing the bell is from the hillside path to the Nathan Hale Schoolhouse, behind the church.

Thankful Arnold House (860-345-2400), Hayden Hill and Walkley Hill Roads, CT 154, Higganum (section of Haddam). Open year-round by appointment; guided tours June through October, on the second Sunday of the month. A somewhat unusual, three-story, gambrel-roof house built right on the street with entrances on two levels, dated 1794 to 1810. The deep sand color of the clapboards may surprise you if you expect all early homes to be restoration white or Colonial red. The furnishings reflect two centuries of changing tastes on the part of the owners, and like the house itself, the period herb, vegetable, and flower gardens have been carefully researched. Summer visitors can catch the **Crafters in the Garden** series of colonial crafts demonstrations by blacksmiths, herbalists, and others. Genealogists find the library well worth investigating.

TO DO

AIRPLANE RIDES

Chester Airport (860-526-4321; 1-800-752-6371), Winthrop Road, Chester. A 20-minute plane ride—a good idea at any time of year, but spectacular in fall. Passengers can choose an open-cockpit plane in spring, summer, and fall, or an enclosed aircraft year-round. With prior arrangement, you can also rent pilot and plane and create your own flight plan for a one-hour trip.

Eagle Aviation (860-873-8568; 1-800-564-2359), Lumberyard Road, Goodspeed Airport, East Haddam. Overhead views of the lower valley. Seaplanes take off from the Connecticut River in summer; land-based planes fly year-round.

BALLOONING

Berkshire Balloons (203-250-8441), PO Box 706, Southington 06489. Reserve in advance; call for a brochure. Sunrise flights let passengers take in sweeping views from Long Island Sound to the Berkshire foothills; sunset trips take off during the summer months. Launch sites—in Farmington, Cheshire, and Southington—are dictated by the day's wind conditions.

BOAT EXCURSIONS

Camelot Cruises (860-345-4507; 860-345-8591; 860-345-8592), One Marine Park, Haddam. Operates during summer months; call for schedule. Take your pick of evening Live Band or '50s and '60s Rock 'n' Roll dance cruises; Murder Mystery or New Orleans Dinner Cruises; or Sunday Brunch Cruises with live Dixieland jazz. Daylong trips travel down the river and across Long Island Sound to Greenport or Sag Harbor.

Chester-Hadlyme Ferry (860-526-2743), CT 148, either shore. Operates April 1 through November 30, daily except Thanksgiving Day, Monday through Friday 7 AM–6:45 PM; weekends 10:30–5. Car and driver, $2.25; additional passengers and walk-ons 75¢. Follow the signs to the dock and read the instructions posted there. The short river crossing on the *Selden III*—the second oldest continually operating ferry in the nation—is truly one of life's simple pleasures. During the 3- to 5-minute trip to the opposite shore, take in views of the Connecticut River and the towering hills called Seven Sisters, one of them crowned by Gillette Castle.

Deep River Navigation Co. (860-526-4954), PO Box 382, River Street, Deep River. Ply the Connecticut River or Long Island Sound on sightseeing excursions and cocktail cruises scheduled daily mid-June through Labor Day; weekends in September and October. Trips run from Hartford, Middletown, and Old Saybrook. Experience the splendor of a New England autumn with a foliage tour down the river to Gillette Castle (see *Historic Homes and Sites*), departing on weekends in October.

Valley Railroad Riverboat Ride is an optional addition to the steam train excursion that departs from Essex (see *To Do—Train Ride*). The two together produce an appealing half-day journey mixing transportation nostalgia and scenic discovery.

CANOEING/KAYAKING

Down River Canoes (860-526-1966), 189 Middlesex Square Plaza, (CT 154), Chester. Rent a canoe for a 1- to 3-day self-guided outing on smooth sections of the Connecticut and Salmon Rivers, or paddle the saltwater marshes of nearby Long Island Sound—everything from instruction to snacks provided. Call for information on specific trips, rates, and reservations.

Canoeists and kayakers can explore the **Quinnipiac River Canoe Trail** (860-225-3901), a self-guided 3-mile stretch of flat water between the towns of Cheshire and Southington. Guidebooks at the launch sites provide details about 14 natural areas marked along the route, as well as wildlife, erosion, and river ecology. Begin the trail in Southington at the

CT 322 commuter parking lot, or at the junction of CT 70 and Cheshire Street in Cheshire.

Canoe-camping enthusiasts can paddle to **Selden Neck** (860-424-3200), an island in the Connecticut River off Lyme. The primitive campsites in this 528-acre state park are accessible by water only; open May through September (see *Campgrounds*).

FISHING

There's a boat-launching site on the Connecticut River in Old Saybrook at Ferry Road. fishing is permitted in the following state parks and forests: **Day Pond,** Colchester; **Haddam Meadows,** Haddam; **Wadsworth Falls,** Middlefield; **Wharton Brook,** Wallingford; **Salmon River,** Colchester. The waterways are stocked by the Department of Environmental Protection.

GOLF

Banner Lodge Country Club (860-873-9075), Banner Road, Moodus section of East Haddam. Par 72, 18 holes, 6,300 yards.

George Hunter Memorial Golf Club (203-634-3366), Westfield Road, Meriden. Par 71, 18 holes, 6,593 yards.

Lyman Meadows Golf Club (860-349-8055), at Lyman Orchard, CT 147, Middlefield. Two separate courses, each 18 holes.

Portland Golf Course (860-342-2833), Bartlett Street, Portland. Par 71, 18 holes, 6,213 yards.

Portland Golf Course West (860-342-6111), Gospel Lane, Portland. Par 60, 18 holes, 4,012 yards.

HAYRIDES AND SLEIGH RIDES

✐ **Allegra Farm** (860-873-9658), CT 82 between the Goodspeed Opera House and Gillette Castle, East Haddam. Call for information, reservations. This 42-acre livery stable offers hayrides and sleigh rides— including its Chuck Wagon Dinner Party, a hayride to an authentic chuck wagon for a man-sized western meal. Choose from some 30 vehicles on the premises, and John Allegra and a team of horses will take you on an excursion around the 19th-century farm. Afterward, tour the post-and-beam carriage barn, which houses antique horse-drawn vehicles, including hearses and a US mail wagon.

✐ **Wimler Farm** (860-349-3190), 601 Guilford Road (CT 77), Durham. Ninety-minute hayrides or sleigh rides, depending on the weather. Call for information and to make arrangements.

HIKING

Virtually all of Connecticut's state parks (860-424-3200 for central office) have marked hiking trails; usually you'll find a map posted at the entrance, and in some cases copies are available to take on the trail. For waterfall aficionados, **Devil's Hopyard State Park** in East Haddam (see *Green Space*) has a particularly scenic one; **Wadsworth Falls State Park** in Middlefield (see *Swimming*) has two waterfalls. In Cheshire, you can hike to **Roaring Brook Falls** (203-272-2743), a picturesque set of cascades. At 80 feet, the main waterfall is the second largest in the state.

Mount Higby, Middlefield, is a good hike—about a mile to the top. The upland is a portion of the Metacomet Ridge that runs from Branford north to mid-Massachusetts. The name Hanging Hills refers to their asymmetrical shape—a gentle slope on the east, a steep cliff on the western side. To climb Higby, begin east of Middletown at the junction of CT 66 and CT 147; park behind Guida's Dairy Bar and walk along CT 66, going west, for less than ¼ mile to the blue-blazed Mattabesett Trail. Presently you'll begin to climb, by means of switchbacks, to the Pinnacle, which the *Connecticut Walk Book* calls the "best viewpoint on Mount Higby"—a nearly 360-degree sweep. From here you walk along the cliff (beware if you have trouble with heights) among laurel bushes, with unfolding views as you go. After 1½ miles or so, the trail takes you down the slope and up again to another cliff with more views and a natural bridge (nicely labeled N.B.). You can keep walking if you wish—the Mattabesett Trail continues to Chauncey Peak and Lamentation Mountain—or you can retrace your steps at any point. There's no loop trail here because of the ridge formation. (See also *Green Space* and *To Do—Swimming* for additional hiking in state parks.)

MOUNTAIN BIKING

With more than 200,000 acres of state forests and parks, Connecticut offers many opportunities for off-road cyclists. Although hiking trails are closed to mountain bikes, many miles of old logging roads, cross-country ski trails, and other paths are yours to explore. Look for maps at the entrances to these areas, or visit a local bike shop for advice on places to ride. The knowledgeable staff at **Pedal Power** (860-347-3776), 500 Main Street, Middletown, can help plan rides in the river valley.

Across the river from Middletown, **Meshomasic State Forest** (860-424-3200) in Portland offers a network of trails through 8,000 acres of hardwoods. At **Cockaponset State Forest** (860-566-2304), CT 148, Haddam, trails wind through 15,652 quiet, wooded acres in the state's second largest forest. In Cheshire, the **Farmington Canal Linear Park** (860-225-3901) features an 8.5-mile paved bike path along the historic Farmington Canal waterway. Parking lots are on Cornwall Avenue (off CT 10) and at the Lock 12 Park, 487 North Brooksvale Road (CT 42).

SWIMMING

The following state parks offer swimming as well as hiking trails, picnic tables, and rest rooms. Connecticut's state parks are well signed, well cared for, and generally well regarded by local people—a good test for any attraction.

Day Pond State Park, off CT 149, 5.5 miles west of Colchester. Especially attractive to fishing enthusiasts is the pond, which is stocked with trout. Swimming, picnicking, hiking (there's an interpretive trail), flush toilets, telephone. The pond once turned an overshot waterwheel that powered a sawmill; the stone foundations remain. There's a charge for admission on weekends and holidays.

All aboard the Essex Valley Railroad for a trip back in time.

Wadsworth Falls State Park, CT 157, two miles southwest of Middletown, in Middlefield. The falls are the main attraction in this 285-acre park but by no means the only reason to visit. Activities include picnicking, swimming, stream fishing, cross-country skiing, ice skating, and hiking (in spring, through fragrant mountain laurel to the waterfall overlook). Flush toilets, telephone. Charge for admission.

Wharton Brook State Park, US 5, two miles south of Wallingford. This small, 96-acre park started out as a rest stop for travelers in the pre-superhighway era—1918. A lovely, low-key area for swimming, picnicking, hiking, fishing, ice skating. There are changing houses and flush toilets. Charge for admission.

DOWNHILL SKIING

Powder Ridge Ski Area (860-349-3454; 1-800-622-3321), Powder Hill Road, CT 147, Middlefield. One of the oldest and most active ski areas in the state, Powder Ridge has three chairlifts, 16 trails, snowmaking, night lights, and snowboarding as well as food service. The season usually runs from November into March. There's a ski shop with rentals available, and lessons are provided for both youngsters and adults. The hills are of a size that makes for perfect family skiing—fun but not threatening.

TRAIN RIDE

Valley Railroad (860-767-0103), Railroad Avenue, Essex. The conductor wears the regulation black suit and stiff cap; the engine belches black smoke; and authentic coal-fired steam powers the mighty engine and sounds the whistle's lonesome call. If you remember real trains, or if you'd like to, here is your outing. Odds are that, after settling into your seat of rush or horsehide, you'll discover within earshot a former switchman or engineer, perhaps a news butcher from the old days, who'll spellbind you with tales of fun and danger from the heyday of the New York Central or the Wabash. When the train reaches Deep River, you can disembark and enjoy a steamboat cruise on the Connecticut River, returning to Essex by train. Special holiday trips include the **Easter Train,** hosted by the Easter Bunny and his legion of helper bunnies; and **Santa's North Pole Express,** where passengers are accompanied by elves, Mrs. Claus, and, of course, the man in the red suit himself. The train runs May through December. Call for information, fares, and departure times.

GREEN SPACE

(See also *Swimming, Hiking.*)

Devil's Hopyard State Park (860-424-3200), 3 miles north of the junction of CT 82 and CT 156 in East Haddam (east of the river). After negotiating a 60-foot drop at Chapman Falls, the Eight Mile River continues through this heavily wooded, 860-acre park, one of the river valley's most popular hiking areas. Pack a picnic lunch, find a rock at the base of the falls, and enjoy an idyllic summer day. The park's curious name is also notable as a focus for area mythology. Potholes at the base of the falls are explained by some local historians as the footprints of the Devil, hopping from one ledge to another so as not to get wet, although a plethora of legends abound. Stream fishing is permitted; there are 21 campsites. Amenities include drinking water and outhouses. Free admission.

Haddam Meadows State Park, CT 154 (still CT 9A to old-timers), 3 miles south of Higganum, in Haddam. One of the few truly flat areas in the state, this park consists of 175 acres on the banks of the Connecticut River, offering picnicking, fishing, field sports, boating (boat-launch ramp), cross-country skiing, drinking water, and outhouses. A nice way to see the river at rest. Free admission.

Hubbard Park is Meriden's green space, 1,800 acres divided by the highway, with hiking and outdoor education activities in the northern tract. The pavilion, playgrounds, and tennis courts are in the recreation area. The park's highest elevation, East Peak, 976 feet, is crowned by Castle Craig, a replica of an ancient stone castle that affords a sweeping view of the surrounding land—and of Long Island Sound on clear days. East Peak is one of Meriden's Hanging Hills, in turn part of the Metacomet Ridge, a traprock spine down the center of the state, formed by volcanic action. The park is the focus of the city's Daffodil Festival in spring (see *Special Events*), the site of summer outdoor concerts, and at holiday time festooned with lights and decorations.

LODGING

RESORTS

The Moodus section of East Haddam was the state's major resort area during the era when many families spent their vacations in a full-service summer haven. Several of these resorts remain, offering rooms or cabins, meals, swimming, a playground, and other amenities such as fishing, boating, organized activities, tennis and other games, and entertainment. For specifics, contact: **Sunrise at Frank Davis Resort** (860-873-8681; 1-800-225-9033), Box 415, CT 151, Moodus 06469; **Cave Hill Resort** (860-873-8347), 138 Leesville Road, Moodus 06469; and **Klar Crest Resort & Inn** (860-873-8649), 11 Johnsonville Road, Moodus 06469.

INNS

  ბ **Copper Beech Inn** (860-767-0330), 46 Main Street, Ivoryton 06442. A stately 1890s country house and adjacent carriage house—the former estate of a prominent ivory comb and keyboard manufacturer—have been fitted out comfortably with suitable antiques and traditional furnishings. There are 13 guest rooms, all with private bath, telephone, and air-conditioning; 9 with Jacuzzi. Guests can stroll the serene grounds and gardens (the inn's grand 200-year-old namesake resides in the front yard), or relax in the plant-filled Victorian conservatory. The dining room's French country cuisine consistently wins awards (see *Dining Out*). Honeymooners and other romantics find the inn a perfect getaway spot. Breakfast is included with overnight accommodations. $105–175; slightly lower on weekdays between November and April.

Gelston House (860-873-1411), Main Street, next to the Goodspeed Opera House, East Haddam 06423. The lobby of this romantic, white-clapboard Victorian inn is dominated by a graceful, curving staircase; splendid draperies, figured carpeting, and polished floors and woodwork all live up to the splendor of the theater next door (see *Entertainment—Theater*). For overnight guests, there are just six rooms—three of them suites—handsomely finished, each with a distinct theme and coordinated decor. The suites and one of the rooms offer breathtaking river views. The artworks are especially interesting: Paintings by local artists of local scenes are displayed, as well as Goodspeed playbills and posters. Food service includes lunch and dinner in the dining rooms (see *Dining Out*) and informal bistro fare in the outdoor Beer Garden. $100–225.

Griswold Inn (860-767-1776), 36 Main Street, Essex 06426. Claiming a history back to 1776, "the Gris" (pronounced *Griz*) is an adored landmark in the lower river valley. Standing near the riverfront at the foot of Main Street, it's essentially a three-story clapboard Colonial manse behind a latter-day wraparound porch. The building survived a British attack on the town in 1814, when it was commandeered for soldiers' quarters. Reminders of a long history are evident in the collections of Currier & Ives prints and ancient firearms, the steamboat mural (that moves), the old popcorn cart, the potbellied stove. The restaurant is especially known for its Sunday Hunt Breakfast (see *Dining Out*) and for the rousing music in the taproom—banjo, sea chanteys, and such. There are 30 guest rooms and several suites, each with private bath, telephone, air-conditioning, and classical music. Some have fireplaces. Continental breakfast is included for overnight guests. $90–185.

The Inn at Chester (860-526-9541; 1-800-949-STAY), 318 West Main Street (CT 148, on the Killingworth town line), Chester 06412. Built around a 1776 farmhouse 4 miles out of town, the inn was designed to provide full amenities and yet retain the atmosphere of a traditional hostelry. After a stroll around the 12-acre grounds, guests can lounge in a hammock by the pond, or in front of the massive fireplace at the tavern. The 44 rooms are air-conditioned; each has private bath, telephone, TV. The three-bedroom guesthouse has a private dining room, sitting rooms, a kitchenette, and three fireplaces. Tennis courts, sauna, and a gym are available, as well as The Post and Beam restaurant (see *Dining Out*). Continental breakfast provided for guests. $95–175; suites more.

BED & BREAKFASTS

In addition to the listings below, a number of bed & breakfast reservation services offer access to rooms available in establishments throughout the state. For a list, see *What's Where—Bed & Breakfasts*.

Acorn Bed & Breakfast (860-663-2214), 628 CT 148, Killingworth 06419. Hosts Richard and Carole Pleines have turned their handsome Cape Cod–style home into a quiet, wooded retreat. Two guest rooms are filled with antiques; each has a private bath. Guests can relax on a porch swing, swim in the in-ground pool, or curl up in front of the fireplace when the air gets brisk. In the morning, Carole cooks up a hearty breakfast on the woodstove, using eggs donated by their own chickens. The couple also operate an antiques shop on the premises. $105; off-season discounts.

Bishopsgate Inn (860-873-1677), Goodspeed Landing, (PO Box 290), East Haddam 06423. The Kagel family and their handsome 1818 Colonial inn have been cited for excellence by prestigious publications and by celebrities who are in town to perform at the Goodspeed Opera House. In winter, fires crackle in the fireplaces of the public rooms; four of the six very individual guest rooms also have working fireplaces, and each has a private bath. The Director's Suite boasts an outside deck, sauna, and private entrance; a two-bedroom suite is also available. A hearty breakfast is served on blue-and-white china at the long trestle table in the country kitchen; dinner can be served by candlelight in your room, with prior arrangement. Bishopsgate is about one city block from Goodspeed Opera House (see *Entertainment*), making it perfect for a theater weekend. $95–140.

The Croft (860-342-1856), 7 Penny Corner Road, Portland 06480. Host Elizabeth Hinze has perfected the art of hospitality in her rambling circa-1820 Colonial farmhouse. The B&B has three suites, each with private bath and entrance. Guests are treated to such delights as Finnish pancakes, coddled eggs, and scones, served in the breakfast room overlooking the herb garden. Catering to Wesleyan University visitors, hikers, families, and others, the Croft is a splendidly quiet retreat. $70 and up; lower rates for single travelers.

Daniel Merwin House Bed & Board (860-349-8415), 308 Main Street (CT 17), Durham 06422. A deep red, clapboard-sided mansion house, built in 1740 by a successful farmer, provides a genuine New England experience for guests. After careful renovation, the large fireplaces, exposed beams, and wide floorboards evoke an inviting mixture of authenticity and comfort. There are two guest rooms, each with private bath; one has twin beds, the other a queen. Full breakfast. Rates are in the $80 area.

Riverwind (860-526-2014), 209 Main Street, Deep River 06417. Hosts Barbara Barlow and Bob Bucknall have created a legendary country B&B, weaving together their interests in Early American crafts, antique pine furniture, stoneware, and good talk. Guests enjoy the warmth of a wood fire in winter, a breezy sunporch in summer. Four of the common rooms have fireplaces. There's a piano, and places to play checkers, read, or simply relax. Antiques are everywhere—much of the collectibles, exquisite quilts, and folk art has been in Barbara's family for generations. Guests are served a full southern-style breakfast on an antique Virginia harvest table; Barbara is a transplanted Virginian. Each of the eight guest rooms has a different decorating theme; all have private bath. $98–168.

COTTAGES

Gustine's Cottages (860-267-6254; 860-267-5300), Lake Road, on Lake Pocotopaug, East Hampton 06424. Four cottages, furnished, with kitchen facilities. Swimming and other water sports in one of the state's larger and more popular lakes. Pets okay. Per cottage, mid-June through Labor Day $390 per week; May through June 15 and through September, $250 per week.

CAMPGROUNDS

Several private campgrounds in this region are members of the **Connecticut Campground Owners Association (CCOA),** meeting that group's standards. These are:

Little City Campground (860-345-4886; 860-345-8469), 741 Little City Road, Higganum 06441, with 50 sites.

Markham Meadows Campground (860-267-9738), 7 Markham Road, East Hampton 06424, with 100 sites.

Nelson's Family Campground (860-267-5300), 71 Mott Hill Road, East Hampton 06424, with 310 sites.

Wolf's Den Campground (860-873-9681), 256 Town Street (CT 82), East Haddam 06423, with 235 sites.

State parks and forests campgrounds (860-424-3200 for brochure and reservation information) offer fewer amenities than do the private campgrounds, but they are also more rustic, less expensive, and allow for more solitude. Camping is permitted, with reservations advised, at the following state parks: **Devil's Hopyard State Park, Cockaponset State Forest, Haddam Meadows State Park.** In addition, **Selden Neck** and **Hurd State Park** offer canoe camping. Selden Neck campground is accessible only by canoe.

WHERE TO EAT

DINING OUT
In Chester

  ♿ **Chart House** (860-526-9898), 129 West Main Street. Open daily for dinner only. One of several Chart House restaurants in the state, all known for consistently high quality. This one, set beside a waterfall, is in a former brush mill and is decorated with local artifacts. Solid American fare: steaks, seafood, prime rib, rack of lamb. $15–30.

  ♿ **Fiddlers Seafood Restaurant** (860-526-3210), Four Water Street (CT 148). On your way into town, in a cluster of storefronts, Fiddlers is a small and cozy place that's often filled to capacity. Closed Monday, but serving lunch and dinner through Saturday; dinner only on Sunday. Full bar. Fiddlers is known for its way with mesquite grilling, and for its variety of seafood: crab soup, lobster, scallops of course. A prix fixe dinner is $15.95, or you can order off the menu.

🖉♿**Post and Beam at The Inn at Chester** (860-526-9541), 318 West Main Street (CT 148), on the Killingworth town line. The weathered wood and giant fireplace create a warm welcome, suggesting colonial hospitality. Both lunch and dinner are served daily; on Sunday, brunch as well. The innovative New American cuisine reaps praise from critics and locals alike. Among the specialties are Thai shrimp, breast of duck in port wine with poached pears, and, for dessert, orange crème brûlée. Full bar service is available, and special dishes are prepared for children. Entrées $18–23.

Restaurant du Village (860-526-5301), 59 Main Street. Dinner only, Wednesday through Sunday; dinner also on Tuesday, June through October. Painted a cheerful blue, this restaurant's many-paned windows are accented with well-tended flower boxes. Inside, the surroundings are quaint and charming, the service thoughtful and perfectly timed, the menu imaginative country French, the food excellent. A first-rate dining experience. The menu may offer leg of lamb marinated in herbes de Provence, and salmon pot-au-feu with fresh tomato and basil coulis. Specialties reflect authentic French country cuisine—cassoulet and choucroute garnie. Marvelous crusty breads and pastries are made on the premises. Here's just one of the desserts: chocolate génoise filled with orange-liqueur-scented chocolate mousse and raspberry jam, covered in a Belgian chocolate ganache. Excellent wine list. Reservations suggested. Appetizers $6.50–11.95; entrées $24–28.

Elsewhere

   Copper Beech Inn (860-767-0330), 46 Main Street, Ivoryton. Dinner only, Tuesday through Saturday from 5:30, Sunday dinner from 1. Full bar and award-winning wine list. Over the years the restaurant of the Copper Beech Inn has earned a reputation as an elegant establishment with an ambitious French menu, and as a prime pick for a romantic getaway. Linen, crystal, and silver table service, wall sconces for muted lighting, and a Victorian-style conservatory where you can enjoy an apéritif. The staff is extremely knowledgeable and attentive—you will be pampered. You might find on the menu French country–style appetizers such as artichoke bottoms, spinach and goat cheese in a crisp pastry shell, or fresh duck foie gras; dinner specialties include roasted venison served with a cranberry and shallot compote, or Napoleon de legumes—layers of crisp potatoes, spiced lentils, and vegetables with a grilled risotto cake on a bed of Swiss chard. Desserts range from a simple fruit-and-cheese plate to exquisite French classics like gâteau aux noisettes—delicate layers of hazelnut-rum cake and lemon curd filling. Reservations recommended. Hors d'oeuvres $9.25–30; entrées $21–27.

   Gelston House (860-873-1411), Main Street, next to the Goodspeed Opera House, East Haddam. This venerable inn offers lunch and dinner daily; brunch on Sunday. The carefully coordinated furnishings and fixtures lend an air of dignity. The dining room, with two walls given over to generous windows, allows most tables a view of the river. If you can't see the water, don't despair—you can dine before the fireplace and grand piano. Service is excellent; the large staff is intent on making sure that theatergoers are neither delayed nor rushed. Chef Thomas Grant expertly prepares creative American dishes, with hints of Asian, Italian, and Continental influences in the treatment and saucing. The bill of fare might include breast of chicken with goat cheese potato puree and lemon thyme broth; pan-seared tuna medallions over mesclun with roasted corn salsa; or grilled teriyaki filet mignon with tomatoes and snow peas in a ginger-wasabi soy sauce. The outdoor **Beer Garden** is open to diners from late spring to early fall. Reservations recommended. Entrées $16–22.

   Griswold Inn (860-767-1776), 36 Main Street, Essex. Lunch daily (Sunday Hunt Breakfast 11–2:30); dinner daily. Known far and wide as "the Gris" and renowned for its opulent Sunday Hunt Breakfast, here is the essence of Connecticut Yankee innkeeping: welcome, warmth, and bounty. Specializes in such solid fare as venison, meat pies, prime rib, and baked stuffed shrimp. Clam chowder is a tradition. The decor itself is worth the visit, with maritime art, American memorabilia, an old-fashioned corn popper, and cozy fires in the several dining rooms. The mural that covers an entire wall in the River Room undulates just enough to give you the illusion of dining on deck. Entertainment nightly in the bar: turn-of-the-century jazz, banjo pickin', sing-along encouraged. Reservations suggested. $20–25.

    ᕦ **Steve's Centerbrook Cafe** (860-767-1277), 78 Main Street, Centerbrook. Dinner only, from 5:30 daily; closed Monday. Full bar; extensive, reasonably priced wine list. Half a dozen small dining spaces, done in white and cool peach, in a mild-mannered Victorian painted lady. Formerly known as Fine Bouche, Steve's lives up to its own high standards. Chef Steve Wilkinson changes his innovative, eclectic menu seasonally. Duck soup with fall vegetables, cranberries, and cabbage might lead to a terrific grilled pork chop with a Gorgonzola-focaccia stuffing or a lamb shank braised with pumpkin ale. Pasta specials may include wild mushroom ravioli in light cream sauce with asiago cheese. Desserts are exquisite: Among Chef Wilkinson's best known is the marjolaine—almond and hazelnut torte with crème fraîche, praline, and bittersweet Belgian chocolate. Reservations are a good idea on weekends. Appetizers $4–6; entrées $10–18.

    ᕦ **Tuscany Grill** (860-346-7096), 600 Plaza Middlesex (College Street), Middletown. Open for lunch Monday through Saturday, dinner daily. Housed in what was once an opera house, the Tuscany has an intriguing interior, with a huge central bar and several dining areas including a high gallery that must have been the auditorium balcony. From the open kitchen, watch the chefs turn out creative Italian dishes with a hint of California; seared peppercorn-crusted tuna with Gorgonzola-vegetable risotto, and smoked mozzarella ravioli with chicken sausage and roasted red pepper sauce are examples. Moderate price range: lunch under $10, dinner entrées $12–16.

EATING OUT
In Middletown

America's Cup (860-347-9999), 80 Harbor Drive, Middletown. Lunch and dinner are served daily; Sunday brunch 10–2. Built in 1915 as a home for the Middletown Yacht Club, the three-level building facing the river is now part of Middletown's Harbor Park. You can stroll along the harbor, take a cruise, or just watch the river traffic ripple the water. When the mood strikes, step into the America's Cup for a meal or a snack. On the lower level is a dance area, where live music sets the beat on weekends. On the second level is the main dining room, and outdoors is a patio where drinks and light fare are served in good weather. The maritime motif extends to the menu, which features seafood and shellfish. You can get prime rib, pasta, and chicken dishes as well. Lots of choice in sandwiches and salads at lunchtime. Dinner entrées are around $15.

    ☞ **Andrzej's** (860-346-0782), 534 Newfield Street (CT 3), Middletown. Open daily for breakfast, lunch, and dinner. Authentic Polish cuisine in an unpretentious, no-frills setting. Sit at a counter stool and watch chef-owner Andrzej Cieslik (a former English professor) prepare the specialties of his homeland—potato pancakes, golabkis (stuffed cabbage), and pierogis with half a dozen fillings to choose from. The food is plentiful and reasonably priced. Breakfast $2–5; entrées around $6.

&☞**The English Tea Garden** (860-346-4086), 148 Broad Street, Middletown. Open Wednesday through Friday 11:30–2; lunch on Tuesday by reservation only; closed July and August. Much more than tea; patrons can enjoy homemade quiche, soups, and other examples of comfort food in a refurbished Victorian home. Each day cook Sharon Sheedy prepares a small menu, which might include chicken potpie, seafood quiche, or spinach–mandarin orange salad. Warm apricot cobbler with ice cream is a favorite dessert of the regulars here. The tearoom is run entirely by volunteers from the women's auxiliary of Holy Trinity Episcopal Church. A truly special place. Entrées $4.50.

&☞**It's Only Natural** (860-346-9210), 386 Main Street (behind the Main Street Market), Middletown. This vegan eatery offers inviting sights and tastes. At the deli counter, you'll find rich-tasting but very wholesome desserts, baked goods, and innovative salads. Then there's the restaurant itself, serving natural, vegan foods—no dairy or eggs. Unique culinary treats include gado gado, mixed vegetables in a spicy Indonesian peanut sauce; tasty pierogis stuffed with sauerkraut and mushrooms; and pan-fried whole wheat noodles and tofu seasoned with garlic, ginger, tamari, and toasted sesame oil. If you thought eating healthy had to be dull and restricting, you're in for a nice surprise. Restaurant critics have been impressed, and among the kudos is a gold medal for gourmet cuisine. Most dishes are under $10; meals are $6–12.95.

Mikado Sushi Bar and Grille (860-346-6655), Three Columbus Plaza, Middletown. Open for lunch Tuesday through Friday 11:30–2:30; dinner Tuesday through Sunday; closed Monday. The area's only Japanese restaurant, Mikado serves an impressive variety of tempura, teriyaki, and grilled dishes, as well as traditional sushi with flavored rice. Quilts on the walls denote common cultural ground, and the extensive menu caters to many tastes. With a bow to the current emphasis on healthy foods, chef Teddy Endo features grilled rather than fried dishes. While the cuisine is exquisite, prices are reasonable: Complete dinners are $7.50–21, and lunch is under $10.

&✐☞**O'Rourke's Diner** (860-346-6101), 728 Main Street, Middletown. Open Monday through Friday 4:30 AM–3 PM; Saturday and Sunday 4:30 AM–1 PM. The O'Rourke family has catered to a loyal following of Wesleyan University students and professors, tourists, fishermen, and locals for more than 50 years. Breakfast is any time you want it, and standard diner fare such as burgers and chili fills the menu, but Brian O'Rourke's inventive specials eclipse the traditional standbys. Try the Parmesan polenta topped with roasted portobello mushrooms and poached eggs, served with grilled eggplant; or an omelet of farmer cheese and watercress, with grilled turnips and brown bread. Other favorites have a Cajun twist—poached eggs with crawfish and spiced grits. The diner—a fixture at the end of Main Street since the 1920s—is one of only a handful in the nation listed on the National Register of Historic Places. Muffins, breads, and jams are made on the premises. Service is fast, informal, and friendly, and the portions are generous and cheap. Meals are up to $10; sandwiches and breakfast items up to $6.

   ȷ **Thai Gardens** (860-346-3322), 300 Plaza Middlesex, Middletown. Serving lunch and dinner Tuesday through Saturday; dinner only on Sunday; closed Monday. Full bar. Thai food, with its delicate and sometimes breathtaking flavorings, makes for a memorable feast. The menu lists jasmine rice, Oriental noodles, crisp steamed vegetables, and a variety of meats. For dessert, try the butternut squash custard, made with a typical Thai ingredient: coconut milk. $7–17.

In Chester

   ȷ **Mad Hatter Bakery & Cafe** (860-526-2156), 23 Main Street, Chester. Open for breakfast on weekends; lunch and dinner Wednesday through Sunday; on Sunday, brunch as well. Closed Monday and Tuesday. Former Wall Street bond analyst Maureen Higgins now works wonders in the kitchen of her eclectic village café. French, Italian, and North African–inspired dishes—escargot and Brie ravioli, Moroccan stew, and Provençal lamb, to name a few—are served up on French café tables in this intimate eatery, named for Higgins's penchant for hats of all kinds. Sunday brunch might feature banana multigrain pancakes with warm applesauce, turkey enchiladas, or Thai crab cakes with a cucumber–rice wine sauce. The bakery offers hearth-baked breads—sourdough and varied grains—and luscious pastries. Save room for some orange-cranberry bread pudding or a slice of chocolate oblivion. Breakfast $1.50–6; dinner entrées $14–21; prix fixe brunch, $9.50.

   ȷ **Wheat Market** (860-526-9347), Four Water Street, Chester. Open Monday through Saturday 9–6. A very popular, busy lunch spot: Chef-owner Dennis Welch concocts about four soups a day to choose from, perhaps chicken gumbo, clam chowder, mulligatawny, and lobster bisque; sandwiches such as French ham and Brie; imaginative salads; desserts, scones, muffins, and gourmet grocery items to carry off. Eat inside or take your prizes out to the village green and bask in the country air.

Elsewhere

✎ȷ**The Cabin** (203-237-7471), 103 Colony Street, Meriden. Open daily for lunch and dinner. Sebastian Paguni Jr., co-owner, traces his family connection to the Cabin back more than 60 years. The large but cozy restaurant faces the railroad station, and trains rumble past from time to time. A definite Italian flavor marks the offerings—fried calamari, rigatoni porcini, pasta Genovese. Also on the menu are lamb, Long

Island duckling, Maine lobster, Cajun-style swordfish steak, chicken, and veal. A bevy of appetizers, a surfeit of desserts. Dinner entrées around $15, pasta dishes around $10.

✍☞**Crow's Nest Gourmet Deli** (860-767-3288), in Brewer's Dauntless Shipyard, Pratt Street, Essex. Open daily for breakfast and lunch 7–3; in summer until 5. Mark and Judi Mannetho are now at the helm of this clean, pleasant deli (formerly known as She Sells Sandwiches) that boasts the only waterfront dining in town. Families are welcome—notice the old standbys, peanut butter and jelly and grilled cheese, on the menu. For the more adventurous, tasty homemade soups and a variety of sandwiches, as well as fresh-baked goods. Moderate prices: $1.50–5.95.

     ⛅ **Glockenspiel** (860-345-4697), CT 81, Higganum. Lunch and dinner Tuesday through Sunday; brunch Sunday from 11:30. Traditional Bavarian classics are the specialty—sauerbraten, potato pancakes, schnitzel, red cabbage, and spaetzle. Decor is alpine, highlighted by a Swiss alpenhorn overhead. Generous portions, good solid eating. $5.95–24.95

⛅✍ **Hale-N-Hearty Gillette Tavern** (860-873-2640), 381 Town Street (junction of CT 82 and CT 151), East Haddam. Lunch and dinner Tuesday through Sunday 11:30–9:30, and a late-night menu May through November, Wednesday through Saturday. There's also a summer beer garden May through September, noon–11. A big, informal roadside eatery with everything from burgers to prime rib, including escargots and meat loaf. Even the "light" specials come with fries. Another plus for impulsive travelers: The owner, Mary Ellen Klinck, is a justice of the peace.

⛅ **Shangri-Lee Chinese Restaurant** (203-250-8888; 203-272-1732), 965 South Main Street, Cheshire (CT 10, Cheshire Shopping Center). Lunch and dinner daily. Traditional Chinese American favorites such as Peking duck, moo shu pork, and General Tso's chicken are complemented by an additional selection of Buddhist vegetarian dishes designed for the health-and-fitness crowd. Dim sum, a house specialty, is served weekends. The decor is original art by Mao C. Lee, the centerpiece a huge mural in unusual ceramic tiles. A bas-relief river scene runs on three walls in the adjoining dining room. Luncheon plates are under $10; dinner specials, $9–25.

⛅✍☞**The Whistle Stop Cafe** (860-526-4122), 108 North Main Street, Deep River. Open daily for breakfast and lunch 7–2:30; dinner Friday and Saturday 6–9 during the summer. Step into this tiny house and enter a tropical oasis—the bright pastel decor is reminicent of the islands, where owner Hedy Watrous ran a Key West restaurant before returning to Deep River to continue a family tradition. (Her grandparents opened Ed's Diner on the site in 1936.) Enjoy scrumptious breakfasts and filling soups, salads, and deli sandwiches at a handful of tables and stools in this friendly, casual spot. Generous portions and prices. Breakfast $1.50–4.75; lunch $2.25–4.95.

SNACKS

Hillside Sweet House (860-873-9284), 19 Main Street, East Haddam. A walk past this colorful house is a test of willpower; all kinds of wickedly tempting sweets are on display, from decadent chocolates to old-time favorites—remember Pixy Stix and candy buttons? Other specialties are Arden's Victorian Delight Fudge and Ben & Jerry's ice cream.

Naturally, Books and Coffee (860-526-3212), 16 Main Street, Chester. A deceptively small storefront opens into a cozy, attractive bookshop with a comprehensive selection of titles. Gifts, cards, and natural foods, many varieties of tea and coffee. Italian sodas, pastries, and the aforementioned tea and (naturally) coffee are served inside or, in good weather, out back in the hanging gardens. Great place to meet local authors and artists (see *Bookstores*).

Olive Oyl's (860-767-4909), 77 Main Street, Essex. Open Tuesday through Saturday 8:30–6; Sunday 9–5; closed Monday. Extended summer hours. A friendly, bustling deli serving up hearty sandwiches, tempting desserts. Daily sandwich specials are marked on a chalkboard on the back wall; the Parmesan roll stuffed with sun-dried tomato–basil chicken salad listed here could easily feed two. Gourmet food items and a wide selection of cigars and accessories. Moderate prices: sandwiches around $5.

Our Daily Bread (860-526-2488), 439 South Main Street, Deep River. Open (you guessed it) daily; weekdays from 6 AM, Saturday and Sunday from 7 AM. A tempting array of hearty breads, pastries, cakes, cookies, sandwiches, and soup to take home or enjoy under umbrellas at picnic tables, when the weather complies. Owner Dorothea Cashman also offers a changing selection of entrées, such as fresh roasted meats, chicken and beef potpies, and lasagne.

Spencer's Shad Shack. In spring, while driving along CT 154—the street nearest the river—watch for this roadside stand offering smoked shad, a seasonal and increasingly rare southern New England delicacy. Shad has been sold at this local landmark since 1930. American shad make their annual run up the Connecticut River in May (the season for legal shad fishing is April 15–July 1).

Sundial Herb Garden (860-345-4290), Brault Hill Road, off CT 81, Higganum; 3 miles south of CT 9, exit 9. By reservation only, tea is served Sunday afternoon 2–4:30 from May through October. A choice of 20 blends, accompanied by a light or full complement of traditional favorites—cucumber sandwiches, scones and lemon curd, fruit tarts, occasionally madeleines and other European specialties. Light tea menu $8.95; full tea, $14.95.

ENTERTAINMENT

MUSIC

Oakdale Music Theatre (203-265-1501), 95 South Turnpike Road, Wallingford. The Oakdale presents the stars of popular music, covering the styles and signature personalities of the '40s to the present. A veteran of the performing arts scene in Connecticut, the Oakdale started out in 1954 as a classic summer theater, striped circus-style tent and all; it has graduated into a year-round performance venue.

Wesleyan University Center for the Arts (860-347-9411, ext. 2867), Wesleyan University, Middletown. Taking its cue from the wide-ranging interests of this prestigious university, the Center for the Arts schedules dance programs, concerts, and theatrical productions representing the familiar and the exotic and mixing many genres and cultures.

THEATER

Goodspeed Opera House (860-873-8668), Goodspeed Landing, East Haddam. An architectural feast for the eye, the opera house was built in 1876 to entertain theater lovers who came by land and also by steamship from as far away as New York City. The dignified but whimsical white Victorian structure set on the banks of the Connecticut River has been compared to a wedding cake, and a sweet sight it is. Like their predecessors, today's audiences can walk out on the balcony at intermission and enjoy the play of light, the soothing ripple of the moving river, the spectacle of waterborne traffic coming and going. The Goodspeed, since its 1963 reincarnation—saved from demolition by local preservationists—is devoted to American musical theater. And fittingly, the Goodspeed delivers the true excitement of live performance: Audiences experience the songs, music, and speech directly, unmiked. Revivals are carefully staged, and new musicals are selected and launched, many to resounding and continuing acclaim. *Man of La Mancha, Shenandoah, Annie,* and *The Most Happy Fella* are among the Goodspeed's success stories.

Ivoryton Playhouse (860-767-8348), 103 Main Street, Ivoryton. A Connecticut classic, the playhouse—the nation's oldest professional, self-supporting theater—has helped launch many a showbiz career, Hartford native Katharine Hepburn's included. The River Rep players stage comedies, dramas, and musicals each summer; other productions are held throughout the year. Call for schedule.

National Theatre of the Deaf (860-526-4971 voice; 860-526-4974 TDD), Five West Main Street, PO Box 659, Chester 06412. This internationally recognized company is generally on the road, but if you telephone ahead, you'll be welcomed for a tour of the practice hall, and if you're lucky, you might be able to watch a run-through of a production. In June there's a storytelling hour Sunday afternoons. American Sign Language classes are offered (these are 6-week courses), and at holiday time a special course teaches carols, songs, and poems.

Norma Terris Theatre (860-873-8668), North Main Street, Chester. This offspring of the Goodspeed Opera House experiments with new musicals on a trial basis. Some go on to larger venues and audiences. Call for schedules, information.

Oddfellows Playhouse Youth Theater (860-347-6143), 128 Washington Street, Middletown. The state's most active year-round youth theater, started in the 1970s by a group of Wesleyan University students committed to involving children in the performing arts. Several productions are staged each year, including Shakespeare, original musicals, plays, even a children's circus. Call for schedule, information.

SELECTIVE SHOPPING

Barker Animation Gallery (860-272-CELS; 1-800-995–CELS), 1188 Highland Avenue (CT 10), Cheshire. Original drawings and production cels of cartoon characters—Mickey Mouse, Bugs Bunny, and so on—for sale. Also character toys, cartoon memorabilia. The outside stage area offers live plays and readings. Call for information.

ANTIQUES

Here, as elsewhere in the state, every road yields its share of antiques dealers, but on CT 154 between Old Saybrook and Chester you'll find them, singly and in group shops, at just about every turn in the road. In the list below we've included some; you'll find many more.

Black Whale Antiques (860-526-5073), Hadlyme Four Corners, Hadlyme. English, American, and French antiques.

Brush Factory Antiques (860-767-0845), 33 Deep River Road (CT 154), Centerbrook. Thirty dealers offering antiques, home decor, and collectibles.

Old Bank Antiques (860-267-0790), 66 Main Street (off CT 66), East Hampton. Furniture, jewerly, china, accessories.

One of a Kind, Inc. (860-526-9736), 21 Main Street, Chester. Fine antiques and silver; also appraising.

River Wind Antiques (860-526-3047), 68 Main Street (CT 154), Deep River. Three floors of furnishings, books, china, silver, jewelry, collectibles, quilts, linens.

Strempel's Clocks (860-526-5136), 91 Main Street (CT 154), Deep River. Antique and reproduction clocks; authentic Black Forest cuckoo clocks; sales and repairs. The Strempel family has been fixing clocks in town for 60 years.

T.F. Vanderbeck Antiques at the Business in the Barn (860-526-3770), 32 Town Street (CT 82), Hadlyme. Furnishings, decorative objects, lamps, chandeliers.

Valley Farm Antiques (860-767-8555), 134 Saybrook Road (CT 154), Essex. Furniture, clocks, guns, toys, and so on.

ARTISANS AND CRAFTSWORKERS

Connecticut River Artisans (860-526-5575), Four Water Street, Chester. Open Wednesday through Sunday 10–5; daily in summer. This nonprofit cooperative shows and sells works by local artisans: jewelry, paintings, pottery, hand-woven goods, hats, chalkware, block prints, and more. The shop features guests artists from the area and special theme displays. Staffed by artisans, the shop gives art lovers a chance to meet the artists.

Deep River Design (860-526-9270), 381 Main Street (CT 154), Deep River. Custom-design goldsmith; Russell and Lisa Cunningham have turned their 18th-century home into a showcase for gemstones, diamonds, estate jewelry, and arts and crafts by local designers.

Gallery 53 (203-235-5347), 53 Colony Street, Meriden. Changing exhibits of work by area painters, photographers, and artisans. Ask about poetry slams and other special events.

Nilsson Spring Street Studio & Gallery (860-526- 2077), One Spring Street, Chester. In their studio-gallery, artists Leif and Katherine Nilsson, who specialize in Connecticut impressionist landscapes in oil and watercolor, show works in progress and others for sale.

Wesleyan Potters (860-347-5925; 860-344-0039), 350 South Main Street, Middletown. Changing exhibits and a variety of crafts for sale. Wesleyan Potters took its name not so much from the local university as from the fact that many of the original crafters were wives of Wesleyan faculty members. Over the past 50 years, the reputation of Wesleyan Potters has grown, and the operation has increased in size without losing its original intensity. Tours of the pottery and weaving studios are available on request. Call for information on workshops and courses.

BOOKSTORES

Atticus Bookstore & Cafe (860-347-1194), 45 Broad Street, Middletown. Open weekdays 8–9; Saturday and Sunday 9–6. Because it also serves as the Wesleyan University bookstore (on the lower level), Atticus stocks an unusually wide range of works, making it exceptionally attractive to readers both academic and otherwise. College gear and gift items are also available. After book browsing, relax in the small but lively café with a cup of aromatic coffee, a sandwich, a bowl of soup, or a fresh pastry. Live acoustic blues and folk tunes some evenings; call for schedule.

The Buttonwood Tree (860-347-4957), 605 Main Street, Middletown. Open Monday through Saturday 11 AM–3 PM and 7:30–10:30 PM; closed Sunday. An eclectic, inviting bookstore, housed in a former storefront church. The adjoining art gallery and performance space is a popular venue for local talent, but also features artists and musicians from around the country.

Centerbridge Books (860-767-8943), 33D Deep River Road (CT 154), Centerbrook. Open Wednesday through Sunday 11–5. A comprehensive selection of old, collectible, and rare books. Specializes in art, children's literature, and New England titles. Many first editions.

Clipper Ship Bookshop (860-767-1666), 12 North Main Street, Essex. Open daily 10–5:30. Unpretentious, housed in a converted residence, the Clipper Ship carries an amazing variety of books, new rather than used, for mariners, children, travelers, cooks, collectors, even heavy thinkers. Clean, well organized, friendly—a lovely place to browse.

Naturally, Books and Coffee (860-526-3212), 16 Main Street, Chester. Open Tuesday through Sunday 10:30–8, closed Monday; call about off-season hours. Children's books, cookbooks, works on horticulture, health care, and animals, all tied to an earth-friendly environmentalist theme. Other goods in this tiny shop include clothing made of natural cotton with organic dyes, herb supplements, soaps, candles, and greeting cards. Coffee, tea, and cookies are available (see *Where to Eat—Snacks*).

FACTORY OUTLETS

Great American Trading Company (860-526-4335), 39 Main Street, Deep River. Open daily 10–5; Thursday until 8. A fun browsing experience for young and young-at-heart shoppers. Specializes in wooden games, toys, marbles (by the pound), and wooden boxes of all shapes and sizes. Some describe it as grandparents' heaven, and certainly if you have or know a youngster, you'll have a hard time walking away.

Napier Factory Store (203-238-3087), 74 Cambridge Street, Meriden. Open Tuesday through Saturday 10–6; closed Sunday and Monday. Discounts on what some consider the greatest line of costume jewelry. Necklaces, bracelets, earrings, and pins in 14- and 18-karat gold and silver, some plain, some studded with colorful stones. Faux pearls, of course, novelties, and some quite elegant pieces. Napier is the nation's oldest manufacturer of fashion jewelry, starting in 1875 by producing men's watch chains and novelty giftware.

Thompson Candy (203-235-2541), 80 South Vine Street, Meriden. Open Monday through Saturday 9–5. A universal favorite among residents, Thompson is a longtime local maker of chocolate novelty candies. Holidays like Easter, Christmas, and Mother's Day bring out the creativity in the candy designers. Irresistible temptations.

FARMS AND GARDENS

Lyman Orchards (860-349-1793), junction of CT 147 and CT 157, Middlefield. A Lyman family operation for more than 250 years, Lyman Orchards is an area institution. More than 1,000 acres, with 25,000 fruit trees that you can tour in spring to smell the blossoms or in late summer to pick the fruit. The Lyman Farm Store has, besides fresh produce, pies, cookies, tea, cheese, cider, gift items, and an offer to ship your gift direct. Enjoy your goodies on a sprawling deck overlooking the fruit orchards. Two golf courses are part of the complex (see *To Do—Golf*).

Sundial Herb Garden (860-345-4290), Brault Hill Road, off CT 81, Higganum; 3 miles south of CT 9, exit 9. Open Saturday and Sunday 10–5 most of the year. A little off the beaten track, but well worth the trip; the gardens are formal but inviting. In the main garden, geometric walkways radiate from a sundial; you can stroll through a 17th-century knot garden, or another garden featuring topiary. The plantings evoke tastes in landscapes over three centuries. Herbs grown on the premises are available in the shop, along with 20 varieties of tea. Formal Sunday teas are offered, by reservation, May through October. Seminars on historic gardening, tea, baking English scones, and other topics are held during the winter months; call for information. (See *Where to Eat—Snacks*.)

SPECIAL EVENTS

For details, contact **The Connecticut River Valley and Shoreline Visitors Council** (1-800-486-3346), 393 Main Street, Middletown 06457-3309.

April: **Daffodil Festival** (203-630-4259), West Main Street, Meriden. Plantings at Hubbard Park (some 549,621 daffodils, we're told) inspire an annual welcome to spring featuring arts, crafts, music, and the crowning of Miss Daffodil.

June (usually): **Greater Hartford Open,** (CT 99), Cromwell. Major PGA stop at the Tournament Players Club.

July: **Ancient Fife and Drum Corps Muster & Parade,** Deep River. An annual event since 1953; the oldest and largest of the musters; a rousing parade.

August: **The Great Connecticut Traditional Jazz Festival,** Moodus—a weekend devoted to the original old-time jazz; features jazz musicians from around the world. **Chester Fair,** at the Fairgrounds, CT 154, Chester—classed as a major fair; Friday, Saturday, and Sunday, late August. **Westbrook Muster,** Friday and Saturday events centered on a grand parade of the region's best fifers and drummers. **Connecticut River Raft Race** (860-458-6025), from Hurd State Park, East Hampton, to Haddam Meadows State Park, Haddam. Homemade rafts, a big splash of creativity, costumes, and good-natured fun. **Connecticut River Valley Bluegrass Festival** (860-347-5007), CT 151, Moodus. Features about a dozen bluegrass bands from around the country.

September: **Haddam Neck Fair,** Quarry Hill Road (east side of the Connecticut River)—a major country fair, Saturday, Sunday, Monday of Labor Day weekend. **Durham Fair,** CT 17, Fairgrounds—Connecticut's largest agricultural fair, last weekend of the month. **American Rare Breed Association Dog Show,** Haddam Meadows State Park, CT 154, Haddam. See foo dogs, Plott hounds, Nova Scotia duck tolling retrievers, Norrbottenspetses, and other dogs not recognized by the American Kennel Club.

October: **The Head of Connecticut Regatta,** Middletown—a Columbus Day weekend event. Internationally recognized rowing competition—singles, doubles, fours, eights.

November into December: **Wesleyan Potters Exhibit and Sale,** 350 South Main Street, Middletown. Through early December. **Victorian Christmas at Gillette Castle,** East Haddam, weekends only—the castle is open with period decorations and musical entertainment in the afternoon; through mid-December. **Festival of Lights** (203-630-4259), in Hubbard Park, West Main Street, Meriden. More than 300,000 lights on display with winter figures around the park.

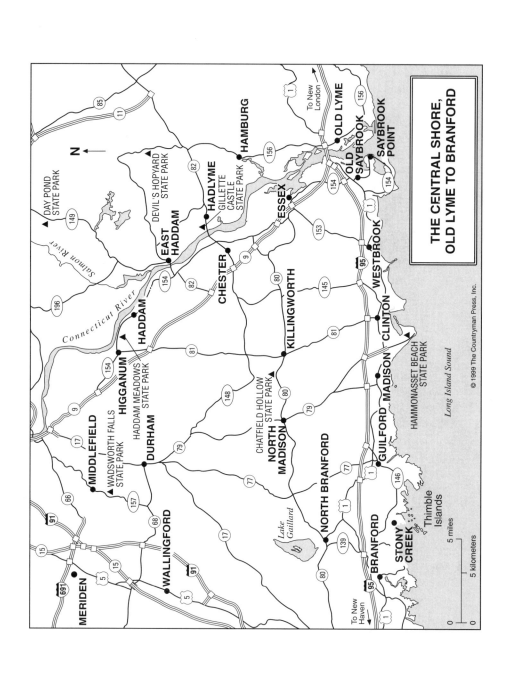

THE CENTRAL SHORE,
OLD LYME TO BRANFORD

© 1999 The Countryman Press, Inc.

The Central Shoreline, Old Lyme to Branford

With Long Island as a buffer against the Atlantic's nastier moods, the Connecticut shoreline is visited by water somewhat warmer and often calmer than the open sea. The absence of deep harbors brings water traffic in the form of pleasure boats more often than heavy shipping, and the nearly uninterrupted line of cottages hugging the coast from the mouth of the Connecticut River west to Branford is filled year after year by summertime vacationers. As a result, the Boston Post Road is rife with purveyors of fried clams, soft-serve ice cream, minigolf, and other family attractions that cater to the annual tourist tide. But tucked slightly inland, centuries-old village greens and picture-postcard scenes have been preserved in pristine splendor. Furthermore, these colonial-era shoreline towns may be lined up cheek by jowl, but each maintains its own particular flavor, making them ideal for exploring.

Old Lyme sits on the east side of the river as it enters the sound. This maritime village has a certain cachet in the art world, thanks to Miss Florence Griswold, who turned her father's splendid late-Georgian mansion on the Lieutenant River into a boardinghouse for summering artists, and effectively turned her town into a major hub of American Impressionism. Today the Griswold home is one of the foremost small art museums in the country.

On the west bank of the river's estuary, pleasure boats and fishing vessels ply to and from the marinas that dot Old Saybrook's shoreline. Meanwhile, the lovingly restored homes and immaculate churches on Main Street are a testament to the town's colonial past.

Continuing west along the coastline, US 1, the Boston Post Road, will lead you to Madison, named for the nation's fourth president, which centers on a dignified green set about with the grand homes of former sea captains and shipbuilders. Its waterfront boasts a magnificent 2-mile stretch of sandy beaches and dunes, the state's largest shoreline park. Next is Guilford, a community founded by a band of Puritans in 1639. Here you'll find New England's oldest stone house, and a stately tree-shaded green modeled after a 17th-century English common, flanked on all sides by steepled churches, classic New England clapboard mansions, bistros, and galleries. In Branford, the timeless fishing cove of Stony Creek harbors a string of offshore jewels—the Thimble Islands, home to celebrities and other solitude seekers, as well as the legendary stamping grounds (according to local lore) of Captain Kidd and his treasure-toting contemporaries.

AREA CODES
860 and **203**

GUIDANCE
Connecticut River Valley and Shoreline Visitors Council (860-347-0028; 1-800-486-3346; Web site: www.cttourism.org), 393 Main Street, Middletown 06457-3309. The council, which represents most of the towns covered in this chapter, publishes comprehensive brochures and guides listing lodgings, attractions, restaurants, theaters, galleries, charter boats, marinas, and golf courses. It also supplies literature from individual establishments, giving excellent one-stop service that includes referrals to specific local sources.

A state welcome center on **I-95** at Westbrook offers Connecticut vacation guides and maps, as well as respite from the interstate blues. The center is staffed during summer months by information specialists who provide assistance and answer questions.

Several towns maintain their own information centers, which operate during the summer months. One is on the town green in **Old Saybrook;** another is on the **Clinton** green, where information is available at the re-created 1630 House.

GETTING THERE
By car: I-95 is the north–south corridor through the region, although it runs east–west in Connecticut—something that happens in a state where the Atlantic Ocean is, in a sense, to the south. CT 9 is a north–south route along the Connecticut River, joining I-95 in Old Saybrook, and I-91 comes from northern New England to New Haven at the western end of this region.

By air: **Bradley International Airport** in Windsor Locks is the state's principal airport, with more than a dozen airlines scheduling flights in and out. USAir Express serves **Tweed New Haven Airport** (203-946-8285) and **Groton/New London Airport** (203-445-8549). Rental cars are available at all three airports.

By rail: **AMTRAK** (1-800-872-7245) runs from New York along the Connecticut coast with stops at New Haven and Old Saybrook.

MEDICAL EMERGENCY
The statewide emergency number is **911.**

Hospital of St. Raphael (203-789-3000), 1450 Chapel Street, New Haven. The emergency number is 203-789-3464.

Middlesex Hospital (860-344-6000), 28 Crescent Street, Middletown. The emergency number is 860-344-6686.

Yale–New Haven Hospital (203-688-4242), 20 York Street, New Haven. The emergency number is 203-688-2222.

TO SEE

Guilford Handcrafts Center (203-453-5947), 411 Church Street (CT 77), Guilford. Open year-round, welcoming visitors and browsers; Monday through Saturday 10–5, Sunday noon–4; closed major holidays. Free admission. Mill Gallery hosts 10 shows a year; classes are held covering a variety of skills and media. The center sponsors a prestigious outdoor show in July that draws thousands of visitors to the town green (see *Special Events*).

MUSEUMS

Company of Military Historians Museum (860-399-0460), Westbrook Place, North Main Street, Westbrook. Open year-round, Tuesday through Friday 8–2:30, and by appointment. Free admission. There's also a research and video library available year-round Tuesday through Friday (call for appointment for other times). The museum features the country's largest collection of American military uniforms. Completely restored and operable military vehicles representing World War II and subsequent conflicts are a further call to arms for military buffs.

Florence Griswold Museum (860-434-5542), 96 Lyme Street, Old Lyme. Open year-round: June through December, Tuesday through Saturday 10–5, Sunday 1–5; January through May, Wednesday through Sunday 1–5. Adults $3; children under 12 free. A gem in the state's collection of art museums. Around the turn of the century, Miss Florence opened her home as a salon for artists summering in the community. They were so inspired by the accommodations and the setting that they formed what came to be America's best-known Impressionist art colony and founded a local school for artists that still flourishes. Some paid the rent in original works on doors, mantels, and paneling. Meanwhile, the house—a late-Georgian mansion of considerable elegance—has become a National Historic Landmark, combining history and art, with original paintings by American Impressionists Henry Ward Ranger, Childe Hassam, and Wilson Irvine, among others. On the grounds, the Chadwick Studio has been renovated and opened to both visiting artists and museum visitors during the summer. Changing exhibits year-round.

Fort Saybrook Monument Park (860-395-3123), Saybrook Point, CT 156, Old Saybrook. Open year-round; free admission. Eighteen acres, with boardwalks, trails, great views of the mouth of the Connecticut River, and a permanent display on the origins and controversial early history of Saybrook Colony—founded in 1635 by John Winthrop Jr., scion of the Massachusetts Winthrops.

Lyme Academy of Fine Arts (860-434-5232), 84 Lyme Street, Old Lyme. Open Tuesday through Saturday 10–4, Sunday 1–4; closed Monday.

KIMBERLY GRANT

The Florence Griswold Museum contains many examples of paintings by the American Impressionist painters who flocked to Miss Florence's summer salons.

Donation. Changing exhibits year-round in the gallery; the school perpetuates the town's tradition of nurturing the arts.

Lyme Art Association (860-434-7802), 90 Lyme Street, Old Lyme, across from Old Lyme Inn (see *Lodging*). Open year-round; six major shows during the year. Admission $4. Call for schedule, information. Artists—including some of the Impressionists who summered at the Griswold mansion—have been exhibiting their work here for more than 100 years.

Nut Museum (860-434-7636), 303 Ferry Road, Old Lyme. Open May through October, Wednesday, Saturday, and Sunday 1–5; other times by appointment. Adults $3, children $2. Elizabeth Tashjian singlehandedly elevated the nut from snack food to art form when she opened the ground floor of her Victorian home as a shrine to all things nutty in 1972. Exhibits highlight nut jewelry, masks, sculpture, and paintings. Of course there are the nuts themselves, from the common cashew and pistachio to the exotic coco-de-mer, a 35-pound specimen from the Seychelles Islands.

WINERY

Chamard Vineyard (860-664-0299; 1-800-371-1609), 115 Cow Hill Road, Clinton. Open year-round, Wednesday through Saturday 11–4; you're advised to call ahead to confirm the schedule. One of the state's newer wineries to take advantage of the rich, stony soil of the coastal slope and temperatures moderated by the waters of Long Island Sound. Visitors tour the inviting winery, completed in 1988, which incorporates stonework and antique beams in typical New England style. Chamard's winemaking process combines modern technology with traditional methods, and tasting rooms afford a chance to judge for yourself the prizewinning chardonnay, Chamard's best-known and most popular wine.

HISTORIC HOMES AND MUSEUMS

Allis-Bushnell House and Museum (203-245-4567), 853 Boston Post Road (US 1), PO Box 17, Madison. Open May through September, Wednesday, Friday, and Saturday 1–4, and by appointment. Free admission. A handsome 1785 home with unusual corner fireplaces and original paneling featuring displays of ship models, toys, china, clothing, kitchenware. This is said to have been the home of Cornelius Scranton Bushnell, Civil War–era shipbuilder, president of the Union Pacific railroad, and chief sponsor of the USS *Monitor*.

Deacon John Grave House (203-245-4798), 581 Boston Post Road (US 1), Madison. Open summertime, Wednesday through Friday noon–3, Saturday 10–4:30, and Sunday noon–4:30. In fall it's open through Columbus Day, weekends noon–3; in winter, by appointment. Adults $2, children $1. For more than 300 years, descendants of local magistrate John Grave occupied this center-chimney survivor, which served variously as school, inn, tavern, courtroom, and wartime infirmary and weapons depot. The house, built in 1675, retains the framed overhang, clapboard siding, and small-paned windows typical of the era.

General William Hart House (860-388-2622), 350 Main Street, Old Saybrook. Open Memorial Day weekend to mid-September, Friday through Sunday 1–4. Donation $2. In 1767, Hart built this high-ceilinged, center-hall Georgian "mansion" to impress upon his associates the extent of his success in life. Transfer-print tiles, eight corner fireplaces, splendid period paneling indoors, and a restored garden outside memorialize the general, who was actually a major in the Revolutionary War. In true entrepreneurial fashion, he also dabbled in real estate, shipping, trade, even politics. A model of perseverance, he ran for governor five times, and lost five times.

Harrison House (203-488-4828), 124 Main Street, Branford. Open June through October, Thursday through Saturday 2–5, and by appointment. Free admission. Built in 1724, this dark red, well-kept traditional saltbox has the characteristic steep roof slope, as well as the center chimney and clapboard siding typical of Colonial homes. A bonus is the herb garden, and in the barn is a display of antique farm implements.

Henry Whitfield State Museum (203-453-2457; 860-566-3005), Old Whitfield Street, Guilford. Open February through December 14, 10–4:30; December 15 through January by appointment. Adults $3; children and seniors $1.50. Here's a rare gem: Connecticut's oldest house—1639—and reputedly the oldest stone building in New England. Though much of the structure is restored and re-created, this house is indeed a relic of early New England. Designed to serve as a pastor's home and fortress, it has two enormous fireplaces in the main chamber, thick walls, and small windows. Furnishings reflect three centuries of its residents. If you're

The Henry Whitfield State Museum is reputedly the oldest stone building in New England.

interested in restorations, this house has seen more than one: Frederick Kelly, the controversial authority on early Connecticut architecture, directed a 1930s restoration here. The gift shop carries appropriate crafts, books, and souvenirs.

Stanton House (860-669-2132), 63 East Main Street, Clinton. Open June through September, Tuesday through Sunday 2–5. Free admission. Eighteenth- and 19th-century furnishings enhance the interior of this big, solid 1790 manse. One of the exhibits is a collection of Staffordshire, and there's a re-created general store with period merchandise. Guides will show you the room where Yale's first classes met. The peripatetic college, founded in Saybrook, had a way-stop in Clinton before it finally settled in New Haven.

Thomas Griswold House (203-453-3176), 171 Boston Street, PO Box 363, Guilford. Open June through September, Tuesday through Sunday 11–4. Adults $2; students and seniors $1. A carefully restored 1774 saltbox featuring costumes, furniture, and a historic herb garden from the period of 1810, when George and Nancy Griswold lived here. (The Griswold family occupied the house until 1958.) A special feature is the blacksmith shop, anvil at the ready.

SCENIC DRIVES

A 12-mile stretch of **CT 146,** as it wanders south of the interstate through Branford to the junction with US 1 in Guilford, has been designated one of the state's scenic roads. And rightly so; this route travels through the true New England coastal plain—windswept trees, low vegetation, shorebirds, salt marsh, and an occasional glimpse of cottages and grand summer homes. This is also the road to Stony Creek, a cozy harbor village where you catch the sight-seeing cruises around the tiny Thimble Islands. It's well worth a detour to drink in the sights, sounds, and smells of coastal Connecticut.

Guilford is the starting point for another official state scenic road, **CT 77,** which intersects with CT 146 at the town green. From there it runs north to the Durham town line, a distance of just under 12 miles. Rural landscapes and rising hills in this sparsely settled section provide a peaceful interlude and tempt you to long for the times we like to think were simpler.

TO DO

BOATING

Old Lyme has two boat-launching areas—the Great Island boat launch on Smith Neck Road and the Four Mile River boat launch on Oak Ridge Drive. In **Clinton,** the Town Dock boat launch is on Commerce Street; in **Madison** you can launch a boat at Hammonasset State Park. **Guilford** has three launching spots: at Jacob Beach on Seaside Avenue, at the Town Marina on Whitfield Street, and on the East River at Neck Road. In **Branford** you can put in on the Branford River at Goodsell Point Road.

BOAT EXCURSIONS

Captain Bob Milne (203-488-9978; 203-481-3345), Stony Creek, Branford. A minicruise on the *Volsunga III* among the Thimble Islands is as delightful as the name suggests. Although the tiny islands are not open to casual visitors, the 45-minute tour allows glimpses of the lifestyles of those who seriously want to get away from it all. Captain Bob spins fact and lore about pirates and celebrities who have found the Thimbles inviting. Trips run mid-May through mid-October.

A minicruise among the Thimble Islands affords the visitor a look at how to seriously get away from it all.

Connecticut Sea Ventures (203-397-3921), Stony Creek, Branford. Mid-May through mid-October. A narrated tour of the islands, with the history of the area and a look at coastal wildlife.

Sea Mist **Island Cruise** (203-488-8905), 34 Sachem Road, Stony Creek Dock, Branford. Call for schedule and rates. Your choice of 45-minute daytime or moonlight trips among the 100 to 365 (depending on whom you ask) Thimble Islands, off Stony Creek. Some barely large enough to hold a single house, others sizable enough for a dozen cottages, the islands have an appeal that has encouraged residents to go to great lengths to build and vacation here. Capt. Mike Infantino provides background on engineering feats, pirate tales, and the lives of the local rich and famous.

Sunbeam Express (860-443-7259), Saybrook Point, Old Saybrook. Offers trips to see bald eagles nesting along the river February through mid-March, Sundays only 9–noon. Capt. John Wadsworth, 15 First Street, Waterford, runs the Old Saybrook excursions, which are designed to provide the best observation possible without disturbing the birds. His other trips sail from Waterford. (See also *Boat Excursions* in "New London, Norwich, and West of the Thames.")

FISHING

Fishing is permitted in **Chatfield Hollow State Park,** Killingworth, and in **Hammonasset Beach State Park,** Madison. This being the "insurance state," streams are stocked by the Department of Environmental Protection.

Charter boats are for hire, for half- or full-day trips on Long Island Sound and beyond. Captains are licensed by the US Coast Guard and registered by the State of Connecticut. In this area are the following:

Catch 'Em (860-223-1876; 860-399-5853), Pilot's Point Marina, North Yard, Westbrook, Capt. Richard J. Siedzik; the *Gypsy VI* (860-388-2664; 860-399-9968), Pilot's Point Marina, North Yard, Westbrook, Capt. Jack Miserocchi; the *Sea Sprite* (860-669-9613), Saybrook Point, Old Saybrook, Capt. Peter Wheeler; **Eden Charters** (860-388-5897), Ferry Point Marina, Old Saybrook, Capt. Paul Retano.

HIKING

State parks and forests offer good hiking trails along with other recreational activities. You'll find trail maps on-site at **Chatfield Hollow State Park,** Killingworth, and **Hammonasset Beach State Park,** Madison (see their descriptions under *Green Space*). Three local land preserves offer hiking trails and, in some cases, other sports. Please write ahead for information and maps.

Branford Land Trust (203-483-0465), PO Box 254, Branford 06405. Trails for walking and cross-country skiing and a pond for ice skating.

Madison Land Trust, PO Box 561, Madison 06443, has blazed trails for hiking and cross-country skiing.

Westwoods Trails, PO Box 200, Guilford 06437, offers an illustrated guide to its 40 miles of hiking trails.

KAYAKING

Stony Creek Kayak (203-481-6401), Stony Creek, Branford. Mid-May through mid-November; call for rates. Paddle the Thimble Islands in a sea kayak for an up-close glimpse at the area's coastal marshlands and wildlife sanctuaries. Owner Christopher Hauge offers instruction in basic paddle strokes and skills, as well as tours any time of day you like— sunrise, sunset, even under a full moon.

MOUNTAIN BIKING

Hammonasset Beach State Park, Madison, has an easy 2-mile trail through the dunes with water views at every turn. Park at any of the lots near the trail. Miles of wooded fire roads are waiting for off-road cyclists at **Chatfield Hollow State Park,** Killingworth (see *Green Space*). **Cycles of Madison** (203-245-8735), 698 Boston Post Road (US 1), Madison, rents bicycles. Phil Parkes and his friendly, resourceful staff can help you plan a ride, or at least tell you where to find the trailheads.

GREEN SPACE

Chatfield Hollow State Park (860-424-3200, Connecticut parks), CT 80, 1.5 miles west of Killingworth Center, Killingworth. More than 350 acres of wooded land; true to its name, Chatfield Hollow is rife with natural caves and rocky ledges, along with Native American stories. Minerals in the soil produce an unusual orange tint in the clear waters of the constructed pond. There are changing facilities, flush toilets, a telephone, a picnic shelter, and marked hiking trails that extend into adjacent **Cockaponset State Forest.** Ice skating in winter. Charge for admission.

If you're an off-season beach walker, solitude can be found at Hammonasset Beach State Park in Madison.

Hammonasset Beach State Park (203-245-2785), exit 62 off I-95, PO Box 271, Madison 06443. A sanctuary on Connecticut's otherwise heavily developed coastline. With a 2-mile stretch of beach as its focal point, this 923-acre park adds a number of other inducements. **Meigs Point Nature Center,** open during summer, offers exhibits and interpretive programs, including guided walks. Programs are geared to illuminate the abundance of birds, fishes, crustaceans, and other life-forms that thrive in the salt marshes and along the beach. Camping, picnicking, saltwater fishing, scuba diving, hiking, boating, swimming, and food concessions are available. Bathhouse and flush toilets for public use. The park is open year-round, meaning that if you're an off-season beach walker, solitude can be found here. Charge for admission.

LODGING

RESORT
Water's Edge (860-399-5901; 1-800-222-5901), 1525 Boston Post Road, PO Box 688, Westbrook 06498. A beautiful shoreline setting, once an estate, later a well-known resort, is now an inn-resort complex with health spa and fitness center. The imposing central building, set on a bluff, overlooks the sound. Thirty-three large rooms in the inn, all with private bath, and 68 oceanfront villas; private beach, tennis, outdoor and indoor pools, whirlpool, sauna, steam room, award-winning restaurant.

INNS

  Bee and Thistle Inn (860-434-1667; 1-800-622-4946), 100 Lyme Street, Old Lyme 06371. A 1756 mustard yellow clapboard house on the banks of the Lieutenant River. A well-tended garden and handsome old trees grace the 5-acre property. Porches and windows have been added, not to mention private baths; the 11 lovely guest rooms are comfortably fitted out with many antiques, and some have four-poster beds and fireplaces. A separate cottage offers more privacy. The inn is one of the shoreline's top romantic retreats. The restaurant serves three meals (see *Dining Out*), English teatime refreshment, and brunch on Sunday. Rates in the inn $75–155; for the cottage, $210.

  Lafayette Restaurant & Inn (203-245-7773), 725 Boston Post Road (US 1), Madison 06443. In the heart of Madison's "downtown," behind two-story fluted columns supporting a lofty portico, this carefully restored church meetinghouse is as gracious outside as it is inside. The furnishings reflect the inn's quiet elegance—intricate hand-woven rugs and painted armoires, first-edition books and antique writing tables have been chosen with care and taste. The five guest rooms are appointed with marble baths (one with a Jacuzzi), telephone, and color TV. Continental breakfast is served in the former steeple. Lunch and dinner are available Tuesday through Sunday (see *Dining Out*). Rooms from $100; suites from $175.

  Old Lyme Inn (860-434-2600; 1-800-434-5352), 85 Lyme Street, Old Lyme 06371. Across the street from the Florence Griswold house (see *To See—Museums*), where a group of American Impressionists also known as Old Lyme artists spent their summers. Some of their works adorn the walls of this gracious, rambling 1850 home. It has had a varied career, but is now rather an upscale version of a country inn. There are four guest rooms in the central building and eight suites in the north wing. Each room has a private bath, air-conditioning, telephone, and TV. The furnishings evoke Empire and Victorian styles. The restaurant serves continental breakfast to guests, and is open for lunch and dinner (see *Dining Out*). Room rates, double occupancy, $99–150.

  Saybrook Point Inn (860-395-2000; 1-800-243-0212), Two Bridge Street, Old Saybrook 06475. A European-style inn with marina and spa—a luxury accommodation. The inn is at the "point" where the Connecticut River enters Long Island Sound, and views, from either the grounds or inside the inn, are remarkable. The inn has set out to offer guests every comfort—working fireplaces, sitting areas, Italian tile in the bathrooms, data ports for the business guest, sauna, steam, or whirlpool, swimming pools outside and indoors, upscale dining. Master suites feature dining areas, wet bars, whirlpool baths, and terry robes. The service-oriented spa provides massage, facials, makeovers, and other forms of pampering, as well as exercise programs, spa menus, and weeklong programs. For those who arrive by water, there's a 120-slip marina. There are 62 rooms and five suites, with one or two bedrooms. Rates vary: In high season (summer) the range is from $180 for the least expensive room to $449 for a two-bedroom suite; in winter, $130–425.

BED & BREAKFASTS

In addition to the listings below, a number of bed & breakfast reservation services offer access to rooms in establishments throughout the state. For a list, see *What's Where—Bed & Breakfasts.*

Binder's Farm (860-399-6407), 593 Essex Road (CT 153), Westbrook 06498. Three generations of the Binder family have lived in this 1820 farmhouse, originally the home of a sea captain. It offers three air-conditioned guest rooms—all with private bath—and comfortable common spaces for guests. Full breakfasts feature farm-fresh eggs and homemade jams and jellies. The Binders' charm lies in the warmth of their welcome, the cozy arrangement of the rooms, and the baked goods served at breakfast. Rates $95–100.

Captain Dibbell House (860-669-1646), 21 Commerce Street, Clinton 06413. A century-old footbridge leads you to the entrance of this handsome 1866 Victorian home with generous windows and high ceilings, set in a well-tended garden. There are four guest rooms, each with its own distinct look—a bay window, hand-stenciled walls and original wood flooring, a sitting area with views of the garden. All offer private bath, fresh flowers, bathrobes, lots of books, and air-conditioning when needed. You're close to the shore—this was a captain's house, after all—so there's nearby swimming, with towels provided. Other amenities include pickup from the local airport, train, or marina, and bicycles for jaunts to the beach. Home-baked goodies are available at breakfast, and in the afternoon as well. Hosts Ellis and Helen Adams possess a storehouse of knowledge, which they share freely with their guests. Closed January through March. $85–105; senior discounts and off-season rates.

Captain Stannard House (860-399-4634), 138 South Main Street, Westbrook 06498. The 19th-century ship's captains who did well built homes that announced their success. Captain Stannard's four-square Colonial home is enhanced with ornate brackets under the deep eaves, double doors under a fanlight window, a cupola—from which supposedly the womenfolk might watch for his sails on the horizon—and several additions, one a distinctly Victorian tower. The attractive whole has been transformed into a commodious lodging, with six guest rooms, each with private bath and each nicely done with New England antiques. $105; $90 in winter.

Deacon Timothy Pratt Bed & Breakfast (860-395-1229), 325 Main Street, Old Saybrook 06475. This 1746 National Historic Register home features three exceptional period-style guest rooms with working fireplaces, four-poster beds, and private baths. Innkeeper Shelley Nobile has painstakingly restored her grand center-chimney Colonial: From the wide-board floors and original hand-forged door latches, to the beehive oven and cooking fireplace in the kitchen, no detail has been over-looked. Folk art and antiques fill the inviting common rooms, where guests can read, mingle, or relax before a roaring fire. Breakfast is a grand occasion here—the table is set with silver and china, and Nobile serves up heart-shaped pancakes, Belgian waffles, eggs Benedict, fresh fruit, and muffins. Rates $105–130.

Guilford Corners (203-453-4129), 133 State Street, Guilford 06437. A grand Georgian-style home built in 1732, splendidly transformed into a B&B by innkeepers Gary Parrington and Suzie Balestracci. Common areas are replete with random-width plank floors, 10-foot ceilings, working fire-places, Oriental rugs, and antiques. Four cozy guest rooms—one with a working fireplace—have private bath, four-poster beds, phone, TV, and other amenities. Guests can borrow a bike, relax on the porch swing, read or play games in the parlor before the fireplace, or soak in the outdoor hot tub. If arriving in Guilford by train, your hosts will happily come get you. Rates $110–170 in summer; $100–160 in winter.

Honeysuckle Hill (203-245-4574), 116 Yankee Peddler Path, Madison 06443. Located on a quiet street a short walk from Madison's downtown and beaches, this 20th-century home welcomes you to a generous-size room with queen-size bed, couches, TV, fireplace, full bath, and a smaller twin bedroom with its own bath. Full breakfast for guests. Open year-round. The suite is $100 on weekends; the twin room is $75; slightly less during the week.

Talcott House (860-399-5020), 161 Seaside Avenue, PO Box 1016, Westbrook 06498. On the beach, facing the water, this 100-year-old former summer home is designed to bring the outdoors inside. Each of the four guest rooms has a view of the sound and a private bath. Guests in the first-floor room have a private, brick-floored porch with immedi-ate access to sun and ocean breeze. A fireplace in the living room pro-vides cozy warmth in winter. A full breakfast is served at individual tables in the large common room. Rates $125–150; in winter, $90–110.

Tidewater Inn (203-245-8457), 949 Boston Post Road (US 1), Madison 06443. This handsome bed & breakfast was a stagecoach stop in the 1890s; today it offers nine antiques-filled guest rooms, all with private bath, TV, air-conditioning, and telephone. Some rooms have working fireplaces, as does the beamed sitting room, where guests enjoy a hearty breakfast. A couple of minutes' walk from the center of Madison. Rates $100–160; in winter, $90–140.

Welcome Inn Bed & Breakfast (860-399-2500), 433 Essex Road (CT 153), Westbrook 06498. The innkeepers are, respectively, a graphic artist and a cabinetmaker, builder, and restorer of furniture, so this 1897 farmhouse has received loving care and skillful restoration. A fireplace in the sitting room guarantees instant relaxation, and the three guest rooms are fur-nished with family heirlooms and fine reproductions. Full breakfast. The rates, depending on the season and private or shared bath, are $75–125.

COTTAGES

&⌀**Maples Motel** (860-399-9345), 1935 Boston Post Road, Westbrook 06498. Heated pool, efficiency cottages during the summer season; a 5-minute walk to a private beach on the sound. Run by the Crawford family since 1948, the Maples has 18 rooms, 10 efficiencies, and one suite. Rates in summer $55–70; in winter, $36–50.

HOTELS

& **The Castle at Cornfield Point** (860-388-4681), Hartland Drive, Cornfield Point, Old Saybrook 06475. On a low bluff, dominating its view of the Sound, sits a mansionlike fieldstone castle with wings, gables, towers, many windows, a porte cochere, and a distinctive red-tile roof. In the cool, quiet lobby, dark wood, a massive chandelier, and a mammoth fireplace (each stone was gathered from Cornfield Point) set a regal tone. There are 13 guest rooms, each with private bath, all recently refurnished and redecorated. Wall-to-wall carpeting on the stairs and in the rooms, generous bathrooms, and plenty of closet space mark this as a 20th-century edifice—it was built in 1906. Guests are served a continental breakfast, and dinner is available daily; brunch is served on Sunday. Rates $95–125.

& **Madison Beach Hotel** (203-245-1404), 94 West Wharf Road, PO Box 546, Madison 06443. Facing Long Island Sound, directly on the beach, this three-story, porch-wrapped delight has a history stretching back to the whaling era, when it opened in 1800 as a boardinghouse for shipbuilders. Open March through December, it has 35 airy suites and rooms, all with private bath, TV, and either queen-size or twin beds. An ideal base for strolls on the beach, swimming, basking, fishing. Continental breakfast is served to guests; **the Wharf** restaurant serves lunch and dinner. Rooms, with seasonal variations, are $75–130; suites $150–225.

CAMPGROUNDS

& **Hammonasset Beach State Park** (860-424-3200 for state parks information), exit 22 off I-95, Madison (write to the Connecticut State Bureau of Parks and Forests, Department of Environmental Protection, 79 Elm Street, Hartford 06106). The only state park campground in this area, Hammonasset Beach is on the sound and has 558 sites. Amenities include a dump station, flush toilets, showers, a concession, swimming, boating, fishing, and handicapped access. No individual connections to electricity and no firewood. Reservations are required; call the number above for procedure. Rates begin at $12 per site per day for four; additional individuals $2 each.

& **Riverdale Farms Campsites** (860-669-5388), 111 River Road, Clinton 06413. Member of the Connecticut Campground Owner's Association. Open April through October, 250 sites, with swimming, boating, fishing, hiking, canoeing, tennis, a recreation hall, store, swimming pool, and planned activities. Along with standard amenities, the area provides sewer hookups. Senior discounts.

WHERE TO EAT

DINING OUT

Bee and Thistle Inn (860-434-1667), 100 Lyme Street, Old Lyme. Set in a colonial inn and offering a sophisticated menu of eclectic choices, it's no wonder the Bee and Thistle is often cited as a romantic spot. Cocktails are served in the parlor, and although the menu changes, you can be assured of delectable appetizers and entrées such as lamb, duck, and Idaho trout—prepared and sauced with real flair. Desserts are splendidly tempting: The specialty is the pecan diamond, a shortbread base studded with nuts and basking in caramel sauce. Full bar. Reservations are recommended. Entrées $19–29.

  ♿ **Cafe Lafayette** (203-245-7773), 725 Boston Post Road (US 1), Madison. Open daily for lunch and dinner; on Sunday, Harvest Brunch and dinner. The inn that houses the café declares its elegance with a noble Greek Revival facade. The interior is even more striking; the walls of the four dining rooms are done in pale salmon, underfoot are Wilton rugs, tables are set with Limoges. The many windows invite the sun. The cuisine, with both regional and Continental overtones, does not disappoint. Your dinner might start with curried brochettes of chicken or confit of duckling with a dried cherry vinaigrette. Entrées are expertly prepared; try the seared salmon fillet in a horseradish broth, or the braised lamb shank—a ragout of flageolet beans makes a fine accompaniment. Full bar and wine list. Appetizers $6–11; entrées $16–24.

  ♿ **The Castle at Cornfield Point** (860-388-4681), Hartland Drive, Cornfield Point, Old Saybrook. This venerable hostelry on the sound has been rejuvenated, and is now open for both dinner and overnight accommodations. Of course you have a view of the water from the dining room, and between the wood paneling and the careful service you'll feel a privileged guest. The cuisine, described as American and Italian, sticks to basics, and does them well. There are fettuccine, linguine, and tortellini dishes, as well as seafood, chicken, veal, and beef as you like them. There are always specials as well, and a list of mouthwatering desserts you'll be challenged to save room for. Entrées average about $15, with the top price $24. Desserts are $4–5.

  ♿ **Le Petit Cafe** (203-483-9791), 225 Montowese Street, Branford. Serving prix fixe dinner at two seatings, Wednesday through Sunday. A charming, yet somewhat cramped, bistro with lace curtains, mustard yellow sponged walls, and a view of the village green setting a romantic tone. Chef Raymond Ip presents a changing menu of classic country French dishes with an international accent. Seaweed and cold noodle salad topped with sesame seeds, roasted chicken sauced with red curry on a bed of lentils, and steak *au poivre* are meticulously prepared and artfully presented. Desserts are sublime—warm chocolate soufflé and poached pear in burgundy wine stuffed with prunes are among the offerings. Reservations are recommended. Four-course prix fixe dinner $21.50.

& **Old Lyme Inn** (860-434-5352), 85 Lyme Street, Old Lyme. Serving lunch and dinner daily; brunch on Sunday. Continental cuisine and white linen service in either the Empire or the Champlain Room. Appetizers feature seafood: escargots, pesto, and pasta; New England crabcakes; Irish smoked salmon. Lobster bisque may be on the menu, and for entrées, a wealth of choices: crab-and-vegetable lasagna, herb-crusted rack of lamb, osso buco Provençal, grilled brace of quail. You can finish off with assorted fresh pastries. Reservations are recommended on weekends. Appetizers are $5.95–11.50; entrées, $20–28. There's also a **Grill Room** for less-formal dining.

& **Quattro's** (203-453-6575), 1300 Boston Post Road (US 1), Guilford. Open for lunch and dinner daily. This delightful Italian trattoria is named for its four owners, and is highly rated for its creative daily specials, which might include grilled prosciutto-wrapped Gulf shrimp stuffed with fresh mozzarella, or filet mignon topped with spinach and shrimp and sauced with cognac. Well-prepared, traditional Italian fare can be found on the regular menu, but the specials shine here. The service is warm and attentive. Appetizers $4.50–7.95; entrées $10–19.

& **Stone House Restaurant** (203-458-2526), 506 Whitfield Street, Guilford. Open year-round for dinner. A waterfront dining landmark since the 1940s, the Stone House is deservedly well known for its traditional seafood, steak, and pasta dishes, as well as impeccable service. Most entrées around $12.

& **Water's Edge Inn and Resort** (860-399-5901; 1-800-222-5901), 1525 Boston Post Road, Westbrook. A splendid glass wall gives patrons a view of the sound. In summer, you can dine outside the wall, on the deck, where a grill provides suitable fare. In the dining room, the atmosphere is more formal: white linen and an elaborate menu featuring seafood, four or five pasta dishes, prime rib, duck, and lamb. A huge fireplace makes the restaurant equally inviting in winter. Live music is provided on weekends. Breakfast, lunch, and dinner served daily, with a popular brunch on Sunday. $12–24.

EATING OUT
Bistro on the Green (203-458-9059), 25 Whitfield Street, Guilford. Open for lunch and dinner Monday through Saturday; on Sunday, brunch and dinner. Bistro on the Green is not only located on Guilford's lovely green, but it's also not far from the historic 1639 Whitfield House (see *Historic Homes and Museums*). High ceilings, black-and-white checkerboard floor, and original art on the walls. The softly lit dining room is intimate; service is warm and attentive. At your table adorned with white linen and fresh flowers, you can savor French-influenced lamb, veal, and seafood dishes. Entrées $12–20.

   ᕷ   **Cuckoo's Nest** (860-399-9060), 1712 Post Road, Old Saybrook. Open daily, serving lunch and dinner; brunch on Sunday. A popular shoreline cantina among locals and summer visitors for 20 years. Traditional and exotic Mexican specialties, with Creole and Cajun creations as well. Colorful surroundings in a comfortably weathered barn, with south-of-the-border textiles and crafts. Specialties include Cajun prime rib, fresh seafood, and, of course, fajitas, empanadas, and enchiladas. For gringos, the menu includes a glossary defining terms from "burrito" to "sopaipilla" to "tostada." Mexican combination plates $8–12; entrées $9–20.

   ᕷ   **Dock 'N Dine** (860-388-4665), at the end of Main Street on the dock, Old Saybrook. Open daily for lunch and dinner; closed Monday and Tuesday in winter. A friendly bar and lounge, entertainment on weekends, and water views from every table in the dining room. Seafood is a specialty, but the menu is extensive, with a wide choice of American favorites and a salad bar with dinner. After your meal, stroll the docks along the Connecticut River and watch the procession of waterborne traffic ply its way to and from the sound. Reservations suggested; entrées $10–17.

ᕷ✐**Dolley Madison Inn** (203-245-7377), 73 West Wharf Road, Madison. Lunch and dinner daily, Sunday breakfast; full bar. Just a block from the shore, the Dolley Madison has retained its popularity with locals and visitors as a dependable dining spot. American-style cuisine—chicken, prime rib, pasta variations, and seafood. Entrées are generally under $20. The inn has 12 rooms for guests.

✐ᕷ**Friends & Company** (203-245-0462), 11 Post Road (US 1), Madison (on the Madison-Guilford line). A friendly sort of place with an amazing variety of choices, serving lunch Wednesday through Saturday and dinner daily. Bistro offerings include burgers, quesadillas, and a chicken teriyaki sandwich. There's a children's menu, a wine list, and a choice of meals for the health-conscious diner, light on the meat, salt, and oils. Calories, protein, carbs, cholesterol, sodium, and fat contents are listed on the menu. For devil-may-care appetites, choose from sirloin, scrod marinated in sherry, Portuguese seafood stew, veal, and pastas. Lunch around $7; dinner entrées $10.50–18.

ᕷ✐☞**Pat's Kountry Kitchen** (860-388-4784), 70 Mill Rock Road East (CT 154), Old Saybrook. Large but cozy, open daily from 7 AM, Pat's has a statewide reputation as a fun place for good food. Homemade soups and pies; seafood specials like shrimp with clam stuffing and flounder stuffed with fresh veggies. Famous for her clam hash, Pat also offers chicken and meat dishes, but dieters take heart: There are egg-white omelets, sugar-free desserts, and entrées as free of fat as is humanly possible. No reservations; full bar; children's menu. The top price here is $12.

ᕷ✐**Saybrook Fish House** (860-388-4836), 99 Essex Road (CT 154), Old Saybrook. Open daily for lunch and dinner; on Sunday, dinner only, 1–9. This is a brown-paper-for-tablecloth fish house, winner of numerous awards, and known for fresh, correctly cooked seafood (there are three other Saybrook Fish Houses, in Hamden, Canton, and Rocky Hill). Children are accommodated with pizza, macaroni and cheese, and pigs in blankets; for entertainment, there's an ongoing drawing contest. An extremely popular shoreline eatery; be prepared to wait for a table in summer. Early-bird specials, full bar. Dinner entrées $12–20.

   Su Casa (203-481-5001), 400 East Main Street (US 1), Branford. Open for lunch and dinner daily. Muted adobe-colored walls sport tapestries, pottery, masks, and murals in this locally acclaimed restaurant serving up traditional Mexican fare. Two fireplaces and live guitar music add to the festive ambience. Entrées $8–16.

SNACKS

Along US 1 (the Boston Post Road) you'll find, in summer, a succession of hot dog, clam roll, fried shrimp, and ice cream stands. Nobody drives hungry through Connecticut's shoreline towns.

Bishop's Orchard Farm Market (203-458-PICK), US 1 at I-95 exit 57, Guilford. Open daily until 6. Five generations of the Bishop family have been providing shoreline customers with farm products since 1871. Pick-your-own fruits in season, and farm-fresh produce year-round. For a tasty snack, try a perfect apple or peach, fresh-baked bread, a wedge of cheese—and maybe a packet of fudge. (They also make pies, including the sugar-free variety.)

Great Harvest Bread Co. (203-458-1819), 80 Whitfield Street, Guilford. Open Tuesday through Sunday; closed Monday. The raison d'être here is, simply yet exquisitely, bread—onion-dill rye, sunflower, rosemary garlic, spinach feta, and pumpkin nut, to name a delicious few.

James Gallery (860-395-1406), Two Pennywise Lane, Old Saybrook. Open daily Memorial Day through Columbus Day; weekends only in winter. Something new: a gallery devoted to marine art and Connecticut River scenes, with the added attraction of an authentic old-fashioned Vermont marble soda fountain, dispensing genuine old-fashioned ice cream treats. Gourmet coffee, pastries, and sandwiches also available. Also see *Selective Shopping—Artisans and Crafts Shops.*

Madison Gourmet Beanery (203-245-1323), 712 Boston Post Road (US 1), Madison. Open daily. This cozy, aromatic café features seven daily coffee flavors, a light breakfast menu, muffins, scones, and other tasty goodies. The quiet, casual surroundings are adorned with paintings and photographs by local artists. Breakfast sandwiches around $3.

   Stony Creek Market (203-488-0145), 178 Thimble Islands Road, Stony Creek, Branford. The handwritten menu posted on the wall in this pleasant, unpretentious eatery/store changes daily, featuring terrific soups, sandwiches, and pizzas. Eat on the deck in view of the Thimble Islands.

Sweet and Savoury (203-245-7101), 749 Boston Post Road (US 1), Madison. Open Monday through Saturday for breakfast and lunch, as well as unlimited snacks, to eat in or take out; closed Sunday. (Dinners available for takeout only.) A bright, cheerful storefront eatery at the heart of downtown Madison. Place your order at the counter and seat yourself at a tiny café table. The changing menu features eclectic vegetarian dishes—wild rice and lentil salad with sweet celery vinaigrette, Indian curried chickpeas over basmati rice, and quiche with spinach, portobello mushrooms, and shallots are examples. There are giant cookies, pastries, scones, muffins, and more. Breakfast dishes are under $3; lunch around $6.

&. **Tastebuds of Guilford, Inc.** (203-453-1937), 51 Whitfield Street, Guilford. Tempt your taste buds with the unusual soups and sandwiches this little café is notorious for. On one visit, pumpkin butternut bisque was on the specials board, as well as a strawberry and Brie melt on French bread with honey mustard. Grab a white chocolate brownie or a slice of cheesecake, and you have the makings for a picnic on the nearby village green.

ENTERTAINMENT

MUSIC
Branford Folk Music Society (203-488-7715), PO Box 441, Branford 06405. At Trinity Church on the Branford green, vocal and instrumental tradition-based performers from the United States and abroad are presented in monthly concerts, September through May.

Chestnut Hill Concerts (203-245-5736), at the first Congregational Church on the green, Madison. A long-standing shoreline summer series featuring classical chamber music with world-acclaimed musicians. Concerts the first four Fridays of August, 8 PM. Each is followed by a cookies-and-punch reception, an opportunity to meet the musicians. Preconcert picnics on the church grounds are encouraged; box suppers are available by reservation. Discounts for students and seniors. Call for schedule and information.

THEATER
Puppet House Theatre (203-488-5752; 203-931-6326), 128 Thimble Island Road, Stony Creek, Branford. Operating year-round, this nationally acclaimed company presents both plays and concerts as well as workshops and classes by professional puppeteers. A collection of life-size Sicilian puppets is on display inside the theater. Call for schedules, information.

SELECTIVE SHOPPING

ANTIQUES SHOPS
On CT 154 between Old Saybrook and Chester, you'll find antiques dealers, alone and in group shops, at just about every turn in the road. Many specialize in New England antiques. We single out these to get you started:

Essex-Saybrook Antiques Village (203-388-0689), 345 Middlesex Turnpike (CT 154), Old Saybrook. A three-story post-and-beam barn, home to the largest consortium of antiques dealers on the shoreline. Inside 135 dealers offer virtually everything from furniture to knicknacks—Staffordshire, porcelain, pottery, prints, miniatures, ephemera, jade, jewelry, flow blue. Refreshments are available.

John Street Antiques (860-669-2439), 23-A West Main Street (US 1), Clinton. Both small and large items: jewelry, toys, furniture, architectural items, and advertising memorabilia.

Madison Trust Antiques—Consignments (203-245-3976), 891 Boston Post Road (US 1), Madison. Quality paintings, prints, silver, rugs, furniture, crystal, china, and lamps.

Old Saybrook Antiques Center (860-388-1600), 756 Middlesex Turnpike (CT 154), Old Saybrook. A trim, brown, barn-shaped building houses more than 125 dealers in fine glass, porcelain, jewelry, American and European silver, 18th- and 19th-century furniture, and an unusually large selection of original artworks. High-quality goods. Open daily.

Trolley Square Antiques & Collectibles (860-399-9249), 1921 Boston Post Road (US 1), Westbrook. A general line of furniture, accessories, and unique items.

ARTISANS AND CRAFTS SHOPS

Branford Craft Village at Bittersweet Farm (203-488-4689), 779 East Main Street, Branford. Open year-round Tuesday through Saturday 11–5, Sunday noon–5; closed Monday and holidays. Some 20 artisans—potters, glassblowers, and leatherworkers among them—maintain studios and shops in a villagelike area, offering, on an informal basis, a chance to watch works in progress. There is a restaurant serving lunch here and, on Sunday, brunch.

Gallery 12 (203-458-1196), 29 Whitfield Street (on the green), Guilford. Selected works of contemporary craftsworkers.

Guilford Handcrafts (203-453-5947), 411 Church Street (CT 77), Guilford. Open year-round, Monday through Saturday 10–5, Sunday noon–4; closed major holidays. A prestigious crafts center; visitors may observe classes and artisans at work. Gallery shows, scheduled at intervals throughout the year, display fine arts and crafts by members. The gift shop, open year-round, features work of American artists: pottery, quilts, textile and fiber creations, woodenware, glass, toys, jewelry.

James Gallery (860-395-1406), Two Pennywise Lane, Old Saybrook. Open daily in summer, weekends in winter; call for hours. In the gallery, you'll find marine art and Connecticut River scenes, along with an old-fashioned soda fountain. According to lore, General Lafayette visited in 1824 when he was touring the new United States. The French hero of the American Revolution apparently spent a night in town and came to what was then a general store to buy supplies (historians can't agree on Lafayette's purchase—wool stockings and saddle soap are two ideas bandied about). In this century, that general store became a pharmacy and soda fountain. It was eventually owned by Anna James—Connecticut's first female, African American pharmacist—who ran the James Pharmacy for some 50 years.

BOOKSTORES

Breakwater Books (203-453-4141), 81 Whitfield Street (on the green), Guilford. Complete bookstore.

R.J. Julia Booksellers, Ltd. (203-245-3959), 768 Boston Post Road, Madison. Attractive and comprehensive, one of the state's finest bookstores. Exceptional authors, signings. Coffee, soups, sandwiches, and pastries available in a tiny café at the rear of the store; look for the hanging teacup.

FACTORY OUTLETS

Westbrook Factory Stores (203-399-8656), Flat Rock Road (I-95, exit 65), Westbrook. Sixty-five outlets—clothing, housewares, specialties—also a food court and 12-screen movie theater. Reebok, Rockport, Corning-Revere, Oneida, Pfaltzgraff, Leather Loft, Boston Traders, Dockers, Carter's Children, Oshkosh, L'eggs-Hanes-Bali, J. Crew, and more.

Clinton Crossing Premium Outlets (860-664-0700), CT 81 (I-95, exit 63), Clinton. The shoreline's newest mecca of upscale bargain shopping. Seventy stores—Mikasa, Donna Karan, Liz Claiborne, Saks Fifth Avenue, Crate & Barrel, to name a few. Food court to nourish hungry shoppers.

SPECIAL EVENTS

For details, contact the **Connecticut River Valley and Shoreline Visitors Council** (1-800-486-3346), 393 Main Street, Middletown 06457-3309.

April: **Civil War Living History Encampment and Battles** (860-526-4993), Hammonasset Beach State Park, Madison. Hundreds of "soldiers" from across New England reenact the 1863 Battle of Chancellorsville.

July: **Guilford Handcrafts Expo,** on the green, Guilford.

August: **Annual Westbrook Muster,** Ted Lane field—midmonth; up to 50 fife and drum corps participate; parade at 11 AM, followed by muster in the park with units playing and demonstrating fancy formations and drills; flea market. **Bluefish Festival,** Clinton Town Dock—celebration of the catch of the season, with lots of seafood and fishing lore.

✍ **Hamburg Fair** (860-444-2206), Lyme Grange, CT 156, Lyme. Agricultural exhibits, farm animals, children's games, animal pulls, entertainment.

September: **Guilford Fair,** Lover's Lane, Guilford. Midmonth, Friday, Saturday, Sunday event; one of the state's major country fairs.

November into December: **Holiday Festival of Crafts,** Guilford Handcrafts

Center, 411 Church Street, Guilford. Juried exhibit and sale; through Christmas Eve.

December: **Old Saybrook Torchlight Parade of Fife & Drum Corps,** Main Street. Fife and drum corps, their uniforms enhanced by seasonal decorations, strut down Main Street, sometimes amid falling snow. Spectators bring candles or flashlights to provide illumination. Caroling at the end of the parade on the town green. A local holiday tradition; bring your flashlight.

Index

ABOUT THE AUTHORS

Barnett D. Laschever was born and raised in Connecticut. He was the director of tourism for the state for 17 years, and for more than 30 years has been a travel editor and writer for such newspapers as the *Hartford Times* and the late *New York Herald Tribune.* For three years he worked as managing editor and contributing writer for Fodor's Modern Guides.

Andi Marie Fusco, a lifelong resident of Connecticut, is a journalist and elementary school teacher. She is a graduate of the school of journalism at Boston University, and has written for several newspapers.

Books from The Countryman Press

EXPLORER'S GUIDES

Explorer's Guides focus on independently owned inns, B&Bs, and restaurants, and on family and cultural activities reflecting the character and unique qualities of the area.

Cape Cod, Martha's Vineyard and Nantucket: An Explorer's Guide Third Edition
Maine: An Explorer's Guide Ninth Edition
Massachusetts: An Explorer's Guide Second Edition
New Hampshire: An Explorer's Guide Fourth Edition
Vermont: An Explorer's Guide Eighth Edition
Rhode Island: An Explorer's Guide Second Edition
The Best of the Hudson Valley and Catskill Mountains: An Explorer's Guide Third Edition

A SELECTION OF OUR OTHER GUIDES AND BOOKS ABOUT NEW ENGLAND

The Architecture of the Shakers
Living with Herbs
Blue Ribbons & Burlesque: A Book of Country Fairs
Reading the Forested Landscape: A Natural History of New England
Covered Bridges of Vermont

Backcountry Guides
50 Hikes in Connecticut
50 Hikes in Massachusetts
50 Hikes in Vermont
25 Bicycle Tours in Vermont
25 Mountain Bike Tours in Massachusetts
25 Bicycle Tours in Maine
Walks and Rambles in the Western Hudson Valley
Walks and Rambles in Westchester and Fairfield Counties
Walks and Rambles in Dutchess and Putnam Counties

We offer many more books on hiking, fly-fishing, travel, nature, and other subjects. Our books are available at bookstores and outdoor stores everywhere. For more information or a free catalog, please call 1-800-245-4151 or write to us at The Countryman Press, PO Box 748, Woodstock, Vermont 05091. You can find us on the Internet at www.countrymanpress.com.